Empire of Sand

Empire of Sand

How Britain Made the Middle East

WALTER REID

BIRLINN

First published in 2011 by
Birlinn Limited
West Newington House
10 Newington Road
Edinburgh
EH9 1QS

www.birlinn.co.uk

ISBN: 978 1 84341 053 9
eBook ISBN: 978 0 85790 080 7

British Library Cataloguing-in-Publication Data
A catalogue record for this book is available from the British Library

Typeset by Hewer Text (UK) Ltd, Edinburgh
Printed and bound in the UK by MPG

For Dan, David, Frances, John and Judith, all regarded as members of my family – which some of them are.

CONTENTS

ACKNOWLEDGEMENTS

When I was an undergraduate at Jesus College, Oxford, I lived for a year in what had been T.E. Lawrence's rooms. They contained a portrait which his mother had given to the College. For that year the first face I saw every morning, after my own in the shaving mirror, was his. I can't say that the experience left me with a burning interest either in him or in the Middle East, but in the course of my years at Jesus I did make some friendships that have lasted almost half a century – and none has been more special than that with John and Frances Walsh, who are among those to whom this book is dedicated.

Dr Patricia Clavin, one of John's successors as History Fellow at Jesus, was kind enough to read the book in draft, as did Avi Shlaim, Professor of International Relations at Oxford. I am very grateful indeed to both of them for the time they took and for the comments and suggestions they made. The book is very much the better for them. I have also to thank Professor Niall Ferguson for finding time to help in the midst of all his activities on both sides of the Atlantic.

I am indebted to Professor Susan Pedersen of Columbia University for her assistance, which included making available to me a copy of her essay, 'The Meaning of the Mandate System: An Argument'. Similarly, I am very grateful to Dr Penny Sinanoglou of Harvard University for supplying me with a copy of a fascinating paper, 'Half a Loaf? Re-evaluating the Peel Commission's Enquiry and Partition Proposal, 1936–1938'. I must record my gratitude to Dr Simon Anglim of the University of Reading for his help in connection with Wingate, particularly his kindness in allowing me to read in draft the chapter on Wingate in Palestine from his now published book, *Orde Wingate and the British Army, 1922–1944*.

My interest in the subject-matter of this book was kindled in the course of long, passionate and hugely enjoyable discussions with Zara and Luway Dhiya and they accordingly have much to answer for. My thanks to them for their friendship. Thanks also Marc Accensi for alerting me to the textual significance of *Tintin and the Land of Black Gold*, originally *Tintin au Pays de l'Or Noir*, and to Peter Martin for suggesting that a bulge in the frontiers of Transjordan

('Winston's hiccup') was caused by a post-prandial incident at the Cairo Conference.

I'm glad have the opportunity to acknowledge the help of Mteer Salem Albluyee, Christopher Khalaf, Sharif Masooh, Omar Namruga, Hasan Al Sabateen and Uri Simcha. The staff of the National Library of Scotland, particularly Elaine Simpson, were very helpful, as were the staff of Glasgow University Library. Thanks, once again, to Liz Bowers at the Imperial War Museum and also the team at its Photograph Archive.

Doris Nisbet came to work with me for two weeks in 1976 and stayed for 35 years. I'd like to think that her stay was due to my relaxed and easy-going style, but the general view seems to be that it has more to do with her patience and forbearance. Thanks, anyway, for secretarial back-up and friendship over these years.

I was fortunate that at Birlinn Hugh Andrew has a special interest in the subject of this book, and was able to suggest important lines of enquiry. As always, it was fun to be working with Andrew Simmons, and Dr Lawrence Osborn is so much more than a superb copy-editor.

My family's interest in the book has been a support and stimulus. My daughter, Bryony, read the book in draft, and her input in terms of the structure of the argument and in other respects was invaluable. Janet read the draft more often, I imagine, than she would have wanted. But her comments, from a background of journalism, were essential. While the book was being written we celebrated our fortieth wedding anniversary. Neither writing the book nor anything else I have done in the course of these last forty years would have remotely been as much fun if it hadn't been based on a very special partnership.

Beauly, Bridge of Weir, August 2011

LIST OF ILLUSTRATIONS

A British Army convoy ambushed in Palestine in 1936 during the Arab Revolt of 1936–1939.

British soldiers searching Arabs during the Revolt.

The Peel Commission at Victoria station on the way to Palestine.

Ernest Bevin is widely regarded as having been one of the greatest British Foreign Secretaries of the twentieth century. At the time, however, his policies did not enjoy the unqualified support of his Party.

Jewish refugees arrive at Haifa Harbour on 1 July 1946, packed tight on the *Josiah Wedgwood*.

The King David Hotel, Jerusalem, blown up on 22 July 1946.

A Jewish boy is sprayed with DDT before being taken to a British troopship in August 1946.

The End. Women and children forming part of the first wave of British civilians to leave Palestine.

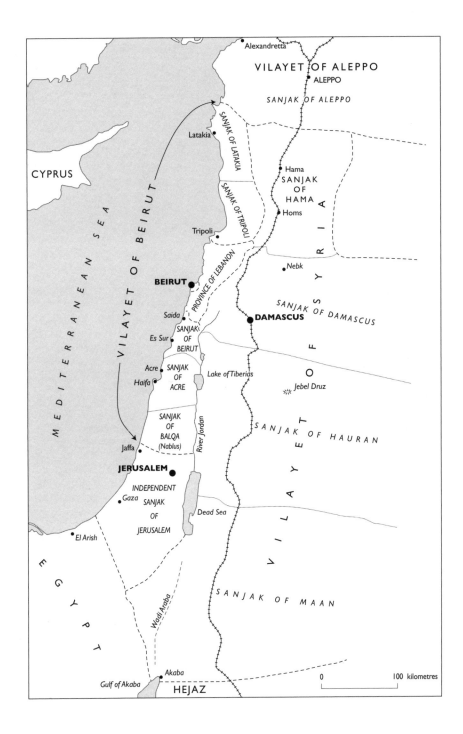

1. The Ottoman Middle East and its administrative units.

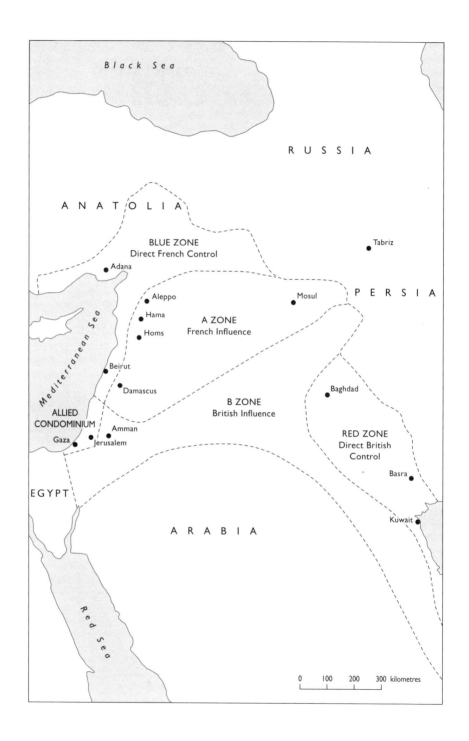

2. The Sykes – Picot Proposal.

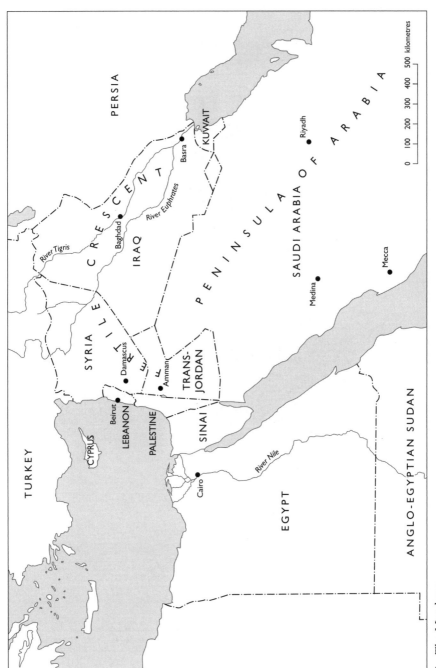

3. The Mandates.

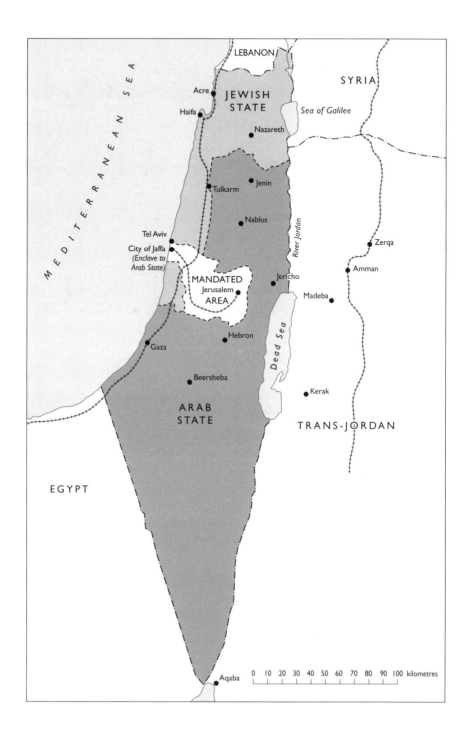

LEBANON

SYRIA

MEDITERRANEAN SEA

Acre

JEWISH
STATE

Sea of Galilee

Haifa

Nazareth

Jenin

Tulkarm

Nablus

River Jordan

Zerqa

Tel Aviv

Amman

City of Jaffa
(Enclave to
Arab State)

MANDATED
AREA

Jerusalem

Jericho

Madeba

Dead Sea

Hebron

Gaza

Beersheba

Kerak

ARAB
STATE

TRANS-JORDAN

EGYPT

0 10 20 30 40 50 60 70 80 90 100 kilometres

Aqaba

4. The Peel Commission Partition Plan A, 1937.

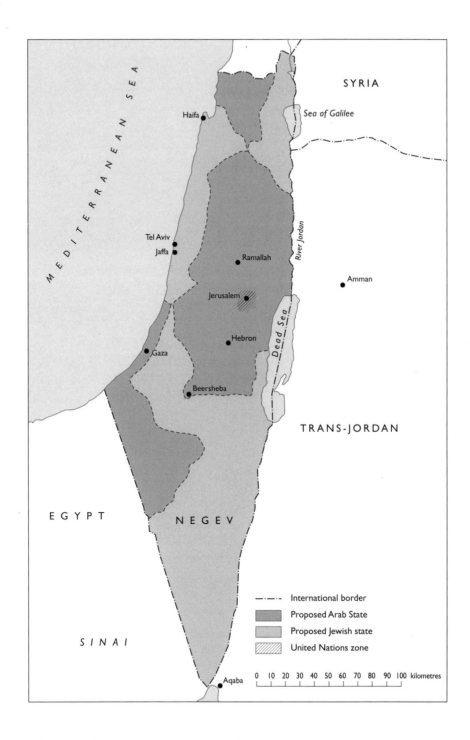

SYRIA

MEDITERRANEAN SEA

Haifa

Sea of Galilee

Tel Aviv

Jaffa

Ramallah

River Jordan

Amman

Jerusalem

Hebron

Dead Sea

Gaza

Beersheba

TRANS-JORDAN

EGYPT

NEGEV

SINAI

International border

Proposed Arab State

Proposed Jewish state

United Nations zone

0 10 20 30 40 50 60 70 80 90 100 kilometres

Aqaba

5. The United Nations Partition Plan, 1947.

I

BACKGROUND

I

INTRODUCTORY

Surveying the extent of the British Empire in 1883, Sir John Seeley, the Regius Professor of Modern History at Cambridge, said, 'We seem, as it were, to have conquered and peopled half the world in a fit of absence of mind.'[1] The lecture in which he made the remark was published and remained in print until 1956, the year of the Suez expedition. His line has been remembered, but is often misunderstood. He was not being whimsical, nor did he admire the amateurish spirit in which the globe had been painted red. He was deprecating the lack of serious planning behind an enterprise that had so much potential.

The Empire he was looking at was the Second British Empire, the empire that Britain built up after the loss of the American colonies. Contemporary documentary evidence shows clearly that Seeley's epigram was unfounded on fact. Even before Yorktown a great deal of detailed thought was being given to extending Britain's overseas territories for strategic and mercantile reasons. A fit of absence of mind is not an appropriate expression in relation to that carefully planned exercise.

It is a much more appropriate description of the way in which the Third British Empire, the Empire in the Middle East, was acquired. The repercussions of that acquisition still reverberate. The reasons for it, largely unexplained, are fascinating.

The scale of this forgotten Empire was enormous. Between 1914 and 1919 the superficial area of the Empire expanded by roughly 9 per cent and in the 21 years from 1901 its population increased by some 14.5 per cent. By 1922 the Empire comprised 58 countries covering 14 million square miles, with a population of 458 million people. The extent of the Empire was seven times that of the Roman Empire at its greatest span. George V ruled over a quarter of the land surface of the planet, and his navies controlled effectively all its water surface. No wonder he collected postage stamps. His empire contained a quarter of the population of the earth.

At the end of the Great War, the British statesman Lord Curzon, a Foreign Secretary and for two terms Viceroy for India, by then the pre-eminent if unofficial architect of the Empire, surveyed what had been added to it and declared: 'The British flag has never flown over a more powerful and united Empire . . . Never did our voice count for more in the Councils of Nations; or in determining the future destinies of mankind.'[2]

And it was in the Middle East that the enlargement of the Empire primarily took place. What was gained there was a huge extension from Egypt through Palestine and into Persia. Iraq alone brought 3 million inhabitants within the imperial nexus. The Royal Navy controlled the Black Sea and the Caspian. Britain had acquired some 200,000 square miles of additional territory. Before the outbreak of the First World War, Britain held sway in Iran and power in Egypt, important but contested by France; but nothing else. In 1925 British influence in the Middle East was enormous: Britain controlled Egypt and Iran and ran what are now Israel, Iraq and Jordan. France, the only other Western power with authority in the region, had to make do with Syria and Lebanon, much less desirable pickings.

It was a significant transformation in the scale and shape of the Empire, a transformation which Britain had not sought when she entered the war and which she did not entirely want when the war finished. How did all this happen? Above all, how did it happen 20 years after Kipling had written 'Recessional', at a time when many politicians, thinkers and political economists in Britain had concluded that the days of the Empire were over?

By the early twentieth century, partly because of post-Darwinian notions of decadence, there was a view that the days of the British Empire as a great power were ending. It was a matter of concern that it had proved difficult to raise enough healthy recruits for the South African war, and this fact stimulated belief in ideas about 'racial decline and degeneration. The advancing front of the empire was threatened from the very centre.' Gibbon's description of the decay and decline of the Roman Empire seemed unpleasantly relevant.[3]

The jingoism of mid nineteenth-century imperialism had been replaced by a much less confident approach; at its climax the Empire was attended by anxieties. 'After the mid-Victorian years the British found it increasingly difficult to think of themselves as invariably progressive; they began worrying instead about the degeneration of their institutions, their culture, their "racial stock" . . . [T]he imperial gothic themes of regression, invasion and the waning of adventure [in the stories of Conan Doyle and Rider Haggard, for example] express the narrowing vistas of the British Empire at the time of its greatest extent, in the moment before its fall.'[4] Even Churchill, not notably introspective, was more concerned with reducing the size of the imperial commitments because of their cost, than with extending or even maintaining them.

It was precisely this concern about national degeneracy and a little England outlook, the lack of a sense of what Empire could do for Britain, that prompted Seeley to criticise the absent-minded approach and to advocate a positive, forward Imperial policy. He was not alone. Joseph Chamberlain, for example, felt that the Empire could provide a guarantee of continued greatness, and Leo Amery, whom we shall meet again, was one of those who were seized by this idea. In the particular circumstances of British involvement in the Levant during the First World War the neo-imperialists exercised a disproportionate degree of leverage, but they were far from typical of policymakers.

Most politicians and officials were against expansion, or at the very least not in favour of it. After all, in 1914 Britain entered the First World War declaring that she had no territorial ambitions. How then did she emerge with so many possessions? Did she act in bad faith? Did she deceive and manipulate her allies? That is what this book is about.

British foreign policy in the Middle East in the war was topsy-turvy. She acquired her new possessions from the Ottoman Empire, a state Britain had ardently wanted as her ally but which in the event was her enemy. Her allies, on the other hand, were those countries which had been her traditional rivals.

Confusion and wartime expedients were powerful motors for the extension of the Empire in the Middle East. But while formal governmental policy was not behind much of what happened, there were some elements of planning and design. I have tried to give due weight to the role, which seems to me crucial, of individuals and groups who operated at fairly low political levels or in the capacity of administrators and who shaped events in the Middle East in the war and post-war years. Some of them had no significant status at all. The desperate conditions of a war of a sort for which no one had planned propelled ambitious enthusiasts into positions of great importance. Colonial administrators and Oxford archaeologists found themselves constructing new polities.

A cast of privileged individuals fills the pages of this history. Many of them knew each other from childhood. If not, they met as their careers crossed. They shared an élite background of influence and of wealth which freed them from the need for gainful employment. Despite their fortune, they threw themselves into their project with verve and engagement, and it is difficult not to like most of them. Characters such as Aubrey Herbert, Captain William Shakespear, Mark Sykes, Lord Kitchener, Arnold Wilson, Percy Cox, Gertrude Bell, Charles Tegart, T.E. Lawrence, Orde Wingate, Leo Amery, St John Philby, will come on and off the stage regularly.

I have deliberately sought to highlight such people because I believe that they were the true decision-makers so far as concerns Britain in the Middle East in this period. Much recent history of the area has been written 'from below'. It looks, for instance, at the history of Iraq under the British mandate from the perspective of the governed. Such partisan approaches shed little light on the *intention* of the quasi-colonial power. It is very often asserted that Britain entered the Middle East for purely selfish reasons such as gaining access to oil reserves. My aim is to examine motives, to explore the subject subjectively and to seek to identify the intentions of those who made the decisions and implemented them.

Britain's territorial gains were effected through the new system of mandates, the licence which the recently created League of Nations gave to certain of the victor nations in the Great War to administer former enemy territories (here former parts of the Ottoman Empire) for the benefit of the inhabitants and to prepare them for self-government. The first question this book addresses is whether Britain by the standards of the time, which did permit some legitimate self-interest, and by her own lights, addressed the acquisition and the administration of the mandates in a different way from that in which other territories, such as Egypt, were handled, or, say, from that in which France acquired and handled her mandate, Syria. The earlier parts of the book deal with the acquisition of the mandates, and in the later parts I have focused, after a brief look at alternative systems (France's version of mandate in Syria and Lebanon, and British influence in Egypt and Iran), on Britain's mandates in Jordan, Iraq and Palestine.

Secondly, how well did the British mandates operate? They were intended to move the mandated territories towards self-government. How did they do so? Could anything better have been done? Did Britain selfishly cobble together incoherent and disparate communities purely to serve her own interests?

In the course of the First World War, Britain made a series of assurances that related to the Middle East. An important undertaking was given to France. Several were given to different groupings of Arabs. The Balfour Declaration made commitments to the Jews. Some – particularly Arab commentators – say that Britain broke commitments which she gave in bad faith and never intended to honour. The third task for this book is to try to assess whether, and if so how far, this is the case.

Finally, the most lasting legacy of British policy in the period with which we are concerned here is the establishment of a Jewish national home in an area, Palestine, in which the Arabs were a majority. This has led to the existence of the State of Israel, and the polarisation of the Middle East and much of the rest of the world into its supporters and its enemies. Was Britain party, as some allege, to an Anglo-Zionist plot? Jews and Arabs before 1917 lived together tolerably well. Now their antagonism for each other is terrible and tragic. How far is Britain responsible for this?

Readers must find their own answers to these critical questions in the course of the narrative which follows. My own views are not disguised, and my conclusions are summarised in the final chapter. Some of the criticism of Britain's role in the passage of history with which the book deals is merited. Many silly things and some bad things were done. But overall I believe that Britain did not do badly in the very difficult circumstances in which policy was being made.

Much of the criticism stems from the circumstances of the times, which are notoriously difficult to analyse. There is also a danger associated with hindsight. Oil, for instance, was not as great a factor in policy as is often assumed. The hostility between Jews and Arabs, and the polarising effect of that hostility was not inevitable. Equally, subsequent events were not entirely dictated by Britain. All the parties involved must take responsibility for their own actions. Thus, in relation to Palestine, it will be seen that neither the Arabs nor the Jews ever made any serious effort to make the experiment work. The Arabs stood aside, not participating, trying to sabotage. The Jews purported to cooperate but worked all the time to move things to their advantage and marginalise the Arabs.

The structure of the book is broadly chronological, but with the chronology focused on a series of themes. This compromise necessarily involves occasional references to events that have already been mentioned. I hope this will assist those who are not familiar with the history of the region.

My original research is in the Cabinet records and other state papers. But this is also a work of synthesis. I have tried to bring together recent writing and specialist publications to make the history of the British role in the making of modern Middle East more comprehensible.

If I may be permitted a more elevated aspiration, it is to contribute to a process in which sufficient illumination is cumulatively directed on to the events of those years to dispel the penumbra of myths, suspicion and mistrust that have generated so much enmity in a horribly troubled region. Darkness is the breeding ground of the phantasm of conspiracy.

2

THE OTTOMAN EMPIRE

1. The Rise and the Long Decline

On 29 May 1453, at the age of 21, the Ottoman Emperor, Mehmet the Conqueror, captured Constantinople, entering the city on a white horse. He brought the Byzantine Empire to an end and thereby shattered the security of Christendom. The assumptions of continuity that had persisted after the fall of Rome vanished. The end of Byzantium was a dramatic blow to the notion that the classical empires of Rome and Greece had never come to an end. The establishment of the Ottoman Empire was one of the great geopolitical events in European history.

Moreover the new Empire endured. It was already more than 150 years old when Mehmet entered Constantinople, and it did not end until 24 July 1923, as a result of the forces which this book describes. It lasted longer than the Roman Empire and almost as long as the Holy Roman Empire, much longer than the British Empire lasted or the American Empire can be expected to last. At its height, under Suleiman the Magnificent (1520–1566), it took in not only what Byzantium had held, but also the Balkans and Hungary, its expansion only halted outside Vienna.

There were many diamonds in the Ottoman crown: a powerful army, sophisticated administration, a state education system and outstanding universities, as well as artistic achievements that remain among the most brilliant of civilisation's jewels.

But the Ottoman Empire never enjoyed the respect accorded to other empires. Occasional travellers were captivated by it, and its exoticism commended it to some composers and artists, but on the whole it was regarded as decadent and corrupt. Shakespeare has nothing very good to say about it. Lear uses the Turk as a synonym for a lecher, and Othello's great final speech ends with the fatal story of what happened in Aleppo, when 'a malignant and a turban'd Turk/ Beat a Venetian and traduced the state': 'I took by the throat the circumcised dog,/ And smote him, thus.' In the nineteenth century, Carlyle was briefer: 'The unspeakable Turk'. By then contempt for Islam was the confluence of a number of streams. To a caricature of what was exotic, myth and prejudice were added. Muslims were blamed for the Indian Mutiny. Atrocities against Christian communities were well documented, and, politically, Turkish hostility to movements for independence, in the Aegean, for instance, served to represent the Ottomans as the enemies of progress and enlightenment. Gladstone referred to the Koran as 'that accursed book'.

Decadence was the crux of the matter, not just in the sense of moral degeneracy, but decay in the system of the Empire itself. The Empire's decline fascinated Western observers and absorbed statesmen's attention for several hundred years. It was Tsar Nicholas I who first used the term 'the Sick Man' (though not 'of Europe') to refer to the Empire. He did so in 1853, but the debate about what would replace the authority of the Ottomans had become a live issue as long before as 1699 and the Peace of Karlowitz.

That peace treaty involved the Ottoman surrender of substantial European territory, including Hungary. It was assumed that the total collapse of the Empire was imminent. The assumption was reinforced by the subsequent Russo-Turkish Wars and a proposed partition by Catherine the Great and the Emperor Joseph II.

A powerful symbol of Ottoman weakness was the concessions they were required to make to foreign powers: 'Capitulations', humiliating derogations from the normal status of sovereignty. The Capitulations were in theory bilateral agreements between the Ottoman Empire and European powers. They were contractual and ostensibly conveyed advantages to both contracting parties. In reality, they were distinctly one-sided and conceded benefits to the European power in question – usually France. Originally the word 'capitulate' meant simply to place items under headings, and the pejorative sense derives from the history of the Ottomans. The Capitulations existed until 1923, when they were abolished by Article 28 of the Treaty of Lausanne.

The Sick Man of Europe was, however, a long time a'dying. Land was lost year by year and repeated humiliations were imposed by the great powers, but the Empire was still in existence in 1914. Competition among those who eyed the spoils worked to the Empire's advantage. It would have survived the war if it had joined the Ententes and not the Central Powers, as it might well have done. The Middle East might have had a happier history if it had. Talk of 'The Eastern Question' began after 1821, when the Greeks claimed independence. But the Question, like the interest in the Sick Man's Health, was founded on flawed premises. The Answers were sound, but the Question was not. More than a century after the Eastern Question was enunciated, Turkey, at the western end of the empire, was recovering, regaining confidence, and preparing to emerge as a strong modern lay state, which would withstand the turbulence of the twentieth century.

2. France and the Ottomans

On 1 July 1798 Napoleon landed at Alexandria. His mission was to annexe Egypt. He proclaimed himself the Liberator of the Ottoman Subjects. Exactly one month later, Nelson engaged the French fleet at the Battle of the Nile. Using inspired and unorthodox tactics he inserted part of his command between the shore and the French vessels and destroyed virtually every one of them. On land, Napoleon's army enjoyed some successes, but without his fleet and facing strong resistance, his mission was doomed.

His reaction was to turn defeat into a personal success. His subordinate, Kléber, was left in Egypt to extricate a defeated and demoralised army, but Napoleon himself hastened back to France to report a triumph, not a disaster, and to create a legend. There were few to question his account, and his speech before the Battle of the Pyramids, just three weeks after his arrival at Alexandria, was the stuff of epic adventure: 'Soldiers, forty centuries are looking down on you!' Despite its failure, Napoleon's Egyptian campaign continued a tradition and reinforced French ambition. There were echoes of the achievements of the French crusading knights who had been dominant in the Levant, and France's interest in the area was refreshed and reinvigorated.

The Commercial Capitulations granted by Suleiman the Magnificent in 1536 had marked the beginning of France's eminence in the Middle East, a domination achieved in part by support for the Ottomans. Only from 1840, when the British intervened to save Egypt from Turkey, did Britain begin to challenge France in the area. In 1856 and 1877 Britain became further involved, supporting Turkey against Russia. British influence consolidated as a result of her involvement in the Suez Canal.

Increasingly, Britain's power base in the region lay in Egypt. France's political influence there came to an end when the system of Dual Control finished in 1883. Dual Control was a humiliating arrangement which meant that French and British officers ran the Egyptian economy – only one of a series of embarrassing devices that brought Egypt under the supervision of foreign governments during the rule of Ismail, whose descriptive title, 'the Magnificent', had more to do with his ambitions than his achievements. By the end of the nineteenth century, at a political level, Britain had supplanted France as the dominant power to the extent that in 1903 the Persian Gulf was being referred to as 'the Curzon Lake'. But France's ambitions in the area were certainly not at an end.

Her cultural and financial influence continued to be very important. By 1913 she had no fewer than 402 educational establishments in the Middle East with 112,000 students.[1] French was almost the official language of the Ottoman Empire.

From Britain's perspective, the importance of the area was that it controlled the approach to her most valuable overseas possession, India. Britain's interests in India were vulnerable. For most of the nineteenth century, the threats to the Indian connection were from Russia and France. These threats coalesced with the Franco-Russian Alliance of 1894, and to them was added a new threat from Germany, whose naval power was beginning to challenge Britain's, and who had obtained a concession for the Baghdad railway in 1903.

At times, Britain's fears of German ambitions regarding India seem slightly paranoid, the Great Game here a little remote from reality. But as relations between the Entente and the Central Powers deteriorated, Germany did develop certain definite policies. The Kaiser was personally involved and went out of his way to woo the sultan, Abdul Hamid. Following the sultan's repression of an Armenian uprising in August 1896, the Kaiser sent him a signed photograph to mark the sultan's birthday, just as the latter was being denounced by other European leaders as Abdul the Damned. The Kaiser had been emotionally captivated by a tour of the Middle East, from which he emerged in the guise of *Hajji Wilhelm*, a defender of the Muslim peoples offering his protection, via the sultan, 'to 300 million Moslems' the world over. At another level, there was the practical strategy of stripping Britain of her Indian Empire. In the moods of despair and elation which alternated in the days running up to the declaration of war he could see 'the famous encirclement of Germany . . . has now finally become an accepted fact'. But 'if we are to be bled to death, at least England shall lose India'.[2]

To address the new situation, Britain entered into two important agreements, the Ententes, the first with France, and then the second, with Russia. We shall look at them after considering what India meant to Britain.

3. The Indian Dimension

In 1807 Napoleon and Tsar Alexander I of Russia were at war. Napoleon had just defeated the Russian armies at the Battle of Friedland. On 7 July the Emperor and the Tsar met on a barge on the River Niemen at Tilsit, now the Russian city of Sovetsk, to talk about ending their war. The Fourth Coalition, the alliance against Napoleon of which Britain was a member, was at an end.

As France and Russia made their peace they agreed to combine to take India from Britain. The plan came to nothing, but the threat was taken seriously. On their own account six years earlier the Russians had indeed assembled an invasion force to threaten India. From this time until almost the eve of the First World War, British foreign policy was preoccupied by nothing more than the threat to India that was posed by France and Russia, either separately or, in the worst nightmare, together.

France was Britain's traditional enemy, well known for her expansionist visions. The Russian Empire was equally and inescapably expansionist. For some hundreds of years it had been expanding its size by around 20,000 square miles a year. At the beginning of the nineteenth century, Britain and Russia were 2,000 miles apart in Asia; by the end of the century, they were only some hundreds of miles apart, sometimes less.[3]

India, a vital component in Britain's mercantile model, 'an English barrack in the Oriental Seas',[4] was set in waters ruled by the Royal Navy and defended by a standing army paid for by the subcontinent and not by the metropolitan power: almost a quarter of a million men, as many as made up the legions with which Marcus Aurelius defended the Roman Empire.[5] In addition, about half the *British* Army was stationed in India in the run-up to the First World War. India's own army was far larger than the British force. The Indian Army was not used only for policing the subcontinent. It was used widely outside India itself.

Gladstone, sounding like an early Automobile Association scout, talked of the link to India as being like the Great North Road. The link was partly by sea, but partly by land. The land approaches ran through the Levant, and whoever controlled these approaches controlled India. That simple sentence explains British policy in the area from 1798 until 1948. The importance of India from a strategic point of view and from the point of view of its significance in the thinking of the time was critical. It was not just *part* of the British Empire. It was an Empire in its own right. At the beginning of the twentieth century 80 per cent of the inhabitants of the Empire lived in India, 20 per cent of British trade was with India and 20 per cent of British investment was in India. When the Committee of Imperial Defence was set up in 1904, its analysis of Britain's strength placed the Indian interest at its centre: 'The British Empire is pre-eminently a great Naval, Indian and Colonial Power'.[6]

To understand the British role in the Middle East in the years of this narrative, it is important to remember that the government of India operated independently of London. Until the days of modern communications, it was inevitable that this should be so, and by the time communications became speedier, the viceroy and his administration had established powers which they had no intention of releasing.

India had its own foreign policy. To protect itself, it established a network of alliances and spheres of influence throughout south Asia and the Middle East. Aden was annexed as early as 1839. It was from India, and not London, that relations with lower Mesopotamia and Afghanistan were handled. Persia was split in two, with India dealing with one part, and London the other. Indian officials reported to Delhi, and Foreign Office officials reported to London. The two did not talk to each other. There were two policies and two spheres of influence. This must be kept in mind.

The Suez Canal was opened in 1869. Until then there were three routes to India, one by sea, one by land from Alexandria to Suez and then by the Red Sea, and one by land over the North Syrian Desert and down the Euphrates to the Persian Gulf. The vulnerability of the land routes was evident when Mehmet Ali installed himself as Viceroy of Egypt and then seized Syria in 1834. Mehmet Ali was thought to be pro-French, and he controlled the land routes to India. Britain preferred the sea route, for reasons of economy and security. For this reason, Palmerston proposed digging the Canal. Now there were four routes to India.

As late as 1940, the security of India dominated British strategy. While Britain was still at imminent risk of invasion, Churchill had to take the courageous decision to move substantial numbers of troops from the defence of Great Britain to Egypt. The acquisition of certain parts of Africa in the nineteenth century derived not from the value of the territories in themselves, but from their role in defending access to India, the eastern of the two axes on which British international power rested.

Palmerston declared that 'Turkey is as good a guardian of the route to India as any Arab would be' and so it was worth remaining on good terms with the Ottomans. Moreover, the Muslim population of India, in all its immensity, meant that Britain had to be very sensitive in how she dealt with the Ottomans. The Indian Muslims saw the Ottoman sultan as their spiritual leader. In the aftermath of the First World War, Gandhi threw the support of the predominantly Hindu Congress Party behind the Muslim League and their support for the caliphate.* There was a response throughout India which included a General Strike and the events in which the Amritsar massacre took place. The Muslim factor greatly influenced Britain's Middle Eastern policy.

4. The Ententes

The first Entente, the Entente Cordiale of 1904, was an agreement between Britain and France which was intended to reconcile the differences that had come close in recent years to bringing the countries to war over colonial rivalries. France accepted the British position in Egypt, and Britain accepted the

---

* 'The caliphate' originally meant those lands where Islam held sway – essentially the Ottoman Empire – but could come to refer to a potential republic replacing existing states and founded on the teachings of Islam, a disruptive notion that threatened the status quo.

French position in Morocco. Additionally, France waived its right to the international supervision of traffic through the Suez Canal, which was prescribed by
the International Suez Canal Convention of 1888. The Entente gave Britain
naval safety in the Mediterranean and security for Egypt. Concern about Turkish
disintegration in the Balkans was consequently reduced.

The main problem that remained was to do with Russia, the Straits, the Persian
Gulf and Afghanistan. Abdul Hamid II, Abdul Hamid the Damned, succeeded to
the Ottoman throne in 1876, just in time for the Congress of Berlin in 1878, when
further partial dismemberment of the Empire followed defeat by Russia. The
Empire lost two-fifths of its territory and a fifth of its population. Britain could not
risk seeing Russia dominate the Bosphorus. One approach was to be kind to Abdul
Hamid, an Anglophile who loved the Sherlock Holmes stories, which he had translated into Turkish and read when he was not working in his carpentry room on
marquetry.[7] Another was to bring Russia into the nebulous Entente system, and the
Triple Entente of 1907 did this. Russia and Britain agreed to live together in Persia,
with a sphere of influence for Russia in the north, a sphere of influence for Britain
in the south, and a no-man's-land in the middle.

The Russian Entente was never as cordiale as the French one, but it was an important *rapprochement*, and after 1907 the main threat in these critical areas came not from
France or Russia, but from Germany and Austria–Hungary. It was consequently of
concern that after the Young Turks' Revolution in July 1908, Austria–Hungary
annexed Bosnia and Herzegovina in the Bosnian crisis of 1908 to 1909.

The reason, then, that the Ottoman Empire survived the nineteenth century
was not that it was not weak, but that none of the great powers dared topple it
in case another reaped the benefit. During that century, indeed, although the
Ottomans lost European possessions and Christian territories, things were
fairly quiet in the eastern part of the Empire. In the west, the Ottomans benefited from British rivalry with Russia, as in the Crimean War.

With the creation of the Ententes, the motive for Britain's traditional policy
in the Middle East was removed. The events with which this book deals represent the
attempt to come to terms with that fact. The paradox was that in the First World War
not only did Turkey, the ally Britain desired, side against Britain and France, but
Russia, Britain's traditional rival in the East, sided with and not against Britain.

5. Britain and the Allure of the East

In the case of France, the romantic appeal of the Middle East was based on the
notion of a historic national association with the region. Britain's links were not
of an institutional nature. They were much more haphazard, resting on individual, eccentric travellers who were captivated by the exotic appeal of the

desert, and often came to believe that they had an intuitive insight into its ways. As we shall see, this belief persisted into the administration of the new Empire, sometimes with unfortunate results. The peculiar reaction of many of these visitors to Arabia, as opposed to those who travelled to India, say, or Africa, was to feel that they somehow *belonged*, that they truly empathised with those who lived there, understood them, were of their society.

From medieval times the East exercised a romantic pull on men from northern Europe, and there was a steady stream of English travellers. Not only men: Arabia seems to have attracted a high proportion of intrepid female visitors, at a time when women scarcely travelled anywhere on their own, let alone far beyond the reaches of Europe. Lady Hester Stanhope, 'Star of the Morning', was one of the earliest. She had looked after her uncle, the younger Pitt, and after his death she travelled through the wildest parts of the Middle East wearing male Arab dress and riding astride her horse, taking serial lovers, fêted wherever she went and often greeted with clouds of rose petals.

Around the middle of the nineteenth century larger numbers of travellers from Britain started arriving in the Middle East. Lady Lucie Duff Gordon is just one example of the remarkable people who settled there. They were fascinated by what they found, and the public at home was intrigued by their adventures. The travellers certainly saw their travels as adventures. Charles Montagu Doughty travelled dangerously as a Christian and an Englishman. Many of the others wore Arab dress. It was probably safer for them to do so, but there is little doubt that they enjoyed the garb. They continued to wear Arab robes and headdresses long after it was necessary – to the irritation of the other members of the British delegation, T.E. Lawrence even wore his headdress at the Paris Peace Conference – and they affected native dress and adopted native customs in a way that was not done elsewhere in the Empire.

Richard Francis Burton is a good example of the eccentric English Arabian. At Oxford he fought a duel with another undergraduate who laughed at his moustache. Later he was sent down for attending a steeplechase. He already conceived of himself as a wandering outsider. His motto was, 'Do what thy manhood bids thee do; from none but self expect applause'. He joined the army of the East India Company, but was separated from his fellows by his interest in native customs and by keeping a large number of monkeys so that he could learn their language. He lived dangerously, frequently engaging in single, hand-to-hand combat, and under the name of Mirza Abdullah donned disguises to obtain intelligence. He went to the length of having himself circumcised, a painful concession to authenticity. On one occasion he made the mistake of standing up and parting his robes to urinate, instead of squatting as an Arab would, and was only just able to convince his companions that he was not an impostor. In the Middle East he travelled extensively and participated in the *hajj*, a dangerous venture for a non-believer. He had a voracious appetite for information about and probably experience of unusual sexual practices, and published the *Kama Sutra* in Britain. He also translated and published 16 volumes of the *Arabian Nights*, which excited great interest as had done Doughty's *Arabia Deserta*. He and his wife are buried in the London suburb of Mortlake in a mausoleum in the shape of an Arab tent.

These were unofficial visitors. At the level of government, information was obtained in the usual way, through the institutions of the Foreign Office, rather than from the insights of oddball travellers. That does not mean that the information was particularly reliable. The cultural changes in the Ottoman Empire in the years leading up to the war were largely unrecognised by Britain. The British ambassador in Constantinople was Sir Gerard Lowther, an urbane diplomat who earlier in his career, as Secretary of Legation in Tokyo, had found himself in charge of the Legation. He was out of his depth and performed badly in the east. He married an American heiress, was much liked in America and was thought to be a candidate for the Washington Embassy. His posting to Constantinople was a surprise. Gerard Fitzmaurice, his First Dragoman and adviser on oriental affairs, described him as stout, placid and rather indolent, and wondered in a letter to George Lloyd whether the Foreign Office would 'put enough pitch under his tail to keep him going for a decade in this capital'.[8]

In the event, Fitzmaurice and Lowther harnessed together comfortably and shared outlooks. They had a very jaundiced opinion of the modernising force in Turkish politics, the Committee of Union and Progress, the CUP. In particular, they believed that the party was part of a Jewish Freemason conspiracy. Lowther referred to the CUP as 'the Jew Committee of Union & Progress'. London tended to accept these views uncritically. John Buchan, Director of Information for the British government during the war, described the CUP leaders as 'a collection of Jews and gypsies'. The Ottoman government was the instrument of world Jewry. Enver Pasha he confused with another officer with a similar name, and he became 'a Polish adventurer'. If Enver was an adventurer, he was certainly not Polish.[9]

Lowther gave covert support to a counter-revolution against the CUP. The initiative failed, allowing the Germans, whose hands were clean, to retrieve a pre-eminency they had lost when the CUP came to power. By now the government in London and in particular Edward Grey, Foreign Secretary for 11 years to the day from 10 December 1915, was beginning to recognise that the CUP was the way forward. Lowther was recalled, but it was too late. War was imminent, and the damage was done.

6. *Turkey's Health on the Eve of War*

In the Ottoman Empire the immediate period running up to the outbreak of the First World War was one broadly of reform and recovery in which a tradition of religious tolerance for non-Muslims continued. The Young Ottoman organisation was founded in 1865, and their successors, the Young Turks, seized power in 1908. There was counter-revolution within two months, but modernisation continued. Although amorphous and lacking cohesion, the CUP, which assimilated the Young Turks, became increasingly influential.

In 1909 Abdul Hamid II was deposed and Mehmet V was installed as a figurehead replacement sultan. By 1913 the struggle between the Young Turks and their opponents had resulted in the emergence of a CUP triumvirate of Enver Pasha, Talat Pasha and Djemal Pasha.

It was significant that the reinvigoration of Turkey under the Young Turks and the CUP was not directed eastwards, but westwards, towards Europe. The Young Turks were Turkish Nationalists, not Ottomans. They emphasised the Turkish, rather than Ottoman, character of the regime. When war broke out in 1914, the Ottoman Empire had been very substantially reduced in size but in the west at least it was modernised and strengthening. Even in the east it was less ramshackle than before.

The effect of this increasing emphasis on Turkish culture and nationality was to alienate the Arab élite in the Empire. In the eastern Empire a number of distinctly Arab organisations were established in the run-up to the war. The largest of these was the Party of Ottoman Administrative Decentralisation, founded in Cairo in 1913 with branches in Syria.

The nature of Arab nationalism – what it was and whether indeed it even existed in these years – is a key question when considering what Britain meant by the promises she gave to Arabs and Jews during the war, and what was understood by these promises. The Arab interpretation of these years sees the Arab Conference in Paris in 1913 as the start of Arab nationalism. That is to misunderstand what the Arabs were trying to do. There was no true spirit of nationalism among the Arabs. They did not have serious reasons to be unhappy about life in the Ottoman Empire. Ottoman rule was flexible, enforced differently in different places. Arab notables ran their own areas. Local customs and freedoms were respected. There was a resulting sense of grass-roots identity which did not exist in the artificial constructs which Britain and France were to establish. A desire for decentralisation was not a call for independence.

II

THE WAR

3

Turkey and the War

1. A Delicate Neutrality

What was the Ottoman Empire going to do in the war? From the 1880s onwards there was a strong German influence within the army; later a corresponding British influence affected the navy. Of the two, the German was the stronger, represented by a powerful cadre of officers and instructors. Lowther's mismanagement tended to promote German influence.

Opinions were, however, fairly closely balanced in Constantinople, and how Turkey would jump was far from a foregone conclusion. As frenetic diplomatic and much more discreet clandestine negotiations took place, the more powerful argument appeared, however, to be for siding with Germany – or at any rate not siding openly with Britain and France. The argument was based not so much on affection for Germany and Austria–Hungary, or a dislike for Britain or France, as on the traditional rivalry with Russia, the ally of Britain and France.

In the course of the war, Winston Churchill was successively First Lord of the Admiralty, Minister for Munitions and War Minister. Immediately after it he was Colonial Secretary and had responsibility for the Royal Air Force, which was charged with much of the defence of British interests in the Middle East. It his hardly surprising that his career repeatedly criss-crosses the history of the area. At the outbreak of war, as First Lord he had to decide what to do with two dreadnoughts which Britain was building for Turkey. The inevitable decision had to be to impound the ships. This decision, together with the botched Royal Naval action that followed, has often been thought to have manoeuvred Turkey into the arms of the Germans.

The acquisition of these two great ships by a largely navy-less Turkey was a matter of huge importance for national self-regard, a symbol of the process of modernisation. The money to build them, the equivalent of what was then £6 million, had been collected by public subscription on the streets of Constantinople. But the moral significance of the ships outweighed even their material cost. Churchill was aware of that. He wrote to Enver Pasha, 'I know the patriotism with which the money had been raised all over Turkey.' Women had sold their hair to raise money for the ships. The story of what happened to them is more complicated than it seems.

2. Seizing the Reshadieh and the Sultan Osman I

Churchill could not risk handing these weapons of mass destruction to a country that might at any moment become Germany's ally. He claimed that he did no more than was explicitly provided for in the contracts with Turkey. In accordance with the contract terms, Turkey was offered £1,000 a day as compensation for the duration of the war, provided she remained neutral. But, as he often did, Churchill left a slightly sanitised account of his actions for history. He said that in seizing the Turkish ships, he simply followed standing orders relating to *all* foreign ships in British yards. In reality, in a memorandum he sent to the First Sea Lord on 28 July 1914, he singled out the Turkish ships for special treatment. He was advised that from a strictly legal point of view there were doubts about seizing the ships, but that there was no time for niceties. The Turks were aware of what he was thinking. The Foreign Office warned the Admiralty that the *Sultan Osman I* was taking on fuel and preparing to depart even though work on the ship was not complete.

British officials were told to make sure that the Ottoman flag was not raised – that would have turned the ships into Ottoman territory – so the ships were impounded without delay. *Sultan Osman I* and *Reshadieh* became HMS *Agincourt* and HMS *Erin* and entered Royal Naval service, where their squat lavatories (*'à la Turque'*) were unpopular with British sailors.

The Turks were quite as savvy and statesman-like as Churchill. While London was eyeing up the ships, Enver was negotiating with the German ambassador at Constantinople, Hans von Wangenheim. Von Wangenheim had been authorised to offer an alliance to the Ottomans – but only if they could show that they could materially contribute to victory. On 1 August 1914, therefore, Enver offered the *Sultan Osman I* to Germany. On the face of it, it was inconceivable that Turkey would voluntarily surrender her national icon in such a way, but Enver knew that it was no longer within his power to deliver the *Osman*. Von Wangenheim took the bait and agreed to an alliance. A week earlier he had not thought that Turkey's contribution to the Central Powers' war effort would be significant.[1] Enver's disingenuous offer did the trick.

Turkey was now Germany's ally. She was still not in the war, but in the matter of battleships Britain contrasted badly with Germany. While Britain had denied Turkey her own precious ships, Germany now made her a present of two German warships, the *Goeben* and the *Breslau*. But first they had to get them to Turkey. The Admiralty knew where the ships were, and that they must not reach Constantinople, but in one of the most pathetic British naval episodes of the war the battlecruisers were pursued ineffectively round the Mediterranean. In the course of the pursuit HMS *Gloucester* engaged the *Goeben* and *Breslau* in the first naval clash of the war, on 7 August 1914. At the age of six Barbara Tuchman, who wrote *The Guns of August*, that gripping account of the outbreak of the First World War, was an observer. She was the granddaughter of the United States ambassador at Constantinople, Henry Morgenthau, and was on a passenger steamer en route from Venice to Constantinople to visit her grandfather. She saw all three ships fire, but no one hit anyone else. The young Barbara was invited to tell her tale to Hans von Wangenheim, who subjected her to 'a most minute but very polite cross-examination'.[2]

The Admiralty's orders were ambiguous, and senior officers made judgements that were reasonable but wrong. Margot Asquith told Churchill, 'It was all the Admiral's fault. Who but an Admiral would *not* have put a battle-cruiser at both ends of the Messina Straits, instead of putting two at one end and none at the other?'[3]

The German ships managed to penetrate the Bosphorus on 11 August. The traditional story was that the Turks received them with delight. In fact, they did not welcome them with open arms. The Grand Vizier's initial reaction was only to allow them sanctuary on very stringent conditions, and finally Turkey took possession of them in the face of German protests. Germany made the best it could of the situation and said that the Kaiser had taken an initiative to replace the two warships seized by the British. The 'gift' was largely symbolic: for practical purposes the ships continued under a German crew, albeit wearing the Turkish fez with the ships renamed *Yavuz Sultan Selim* and *Midilli*, and flying the Turkish flag.

But the gesture did do something to restore Turkey's self-confidence, and the incident strengthened the position of those Young Turks who wanted the Ottomans to ally with Germany. Churchill, thinking of the Dardanelles, said later that the escape of the German ships from the pursuing Royal Navy caused 'more slaughter, more misery and more ruin than has ever before been borne within the compass of a ship'. Turkey was still not in the war. It was very much open to Britain to put an end to Turkey's flirtation with Germany. But ignorance of Ottoman politics in London was too dense. The Foreign Secretary, Edward Grey, got it very wrong: 'Nothing but the assassination of Enver would keep Turkey from joining the Germans'.[4] There was no awareness of the deep fissures among the Young Turks. London did not know that Turkey was playing off her two suitors. It was assumed that there was straightforward collusion between Constantinople and Berlin. In reality the outcome was still open.

On 8 September, the Empire unilaterally abrogated the Capitulations of *all* the powers, German and Austrian as well as French and British. The German ambassador was so angry that he threatened to leave for home at once with his military mission. There then followed an extraordinary alliance between the warring powers, a sort of diplomatic armistice, in which the Central Powers and the Ententes came together to present a joint protest to the Porte, as the Ottoman Foreign Ministry was now known. It was ineffective. Two months after taking over the ships, Turkey asked Germany for a loan of 5 million Turkish lire. Germany did provide an immediate loan of 2 million lire but said they would not get more unless war were declared. On 11 October, Germany was told that the Turkish navy, under its German Admiral, Souchon, would indeed attack the Russian Black Sea fleet. On the following day, some Cabinet members had cold feet, and wanted to remain neutral until the spring and then test the waters again. It was too late. Events were moving too fast.

Enver allowed Admiral Souchon to take the *Goeben* and *Breslau* out under their new names to attack Russian vessels in the Black Sea. Souchon was supposed to represent his action as a defensive one as a result of an attack on his warships, but he disobeyed and opened fire, not on an attacking vessel, but on the Russian coast. He frankly said later that his aim was 'to force the Turks, even against their will, to spread the war'. Enver tried to repair things and prepared to apologise to the Russians, but on 2 November Russia declared war on Turkey.

London issued an ultimatum, requiring the expulsion of the German military mission from Constantinople and the removal of German officers and men from the two battleships. The Turks did not comply, and without even referring the matter back to Cabinet, Churchill told the Mediterranean Fleet to begin hostilities against Turkey. On 4 November, Asquith said that Britain was now in fact at war with Turkey, and on the following day the necessary legal formalities were completed.

On 11 November, the sultan declared war and called for *jihad*. The sultan, the supreme spiritual leader of the Sunni Muslims, was the Khalif of the Faithful. It was to him that, for instance, the bulk of the Muslims in India owed their spiritual allegiance. The separation of the millions of British Muslims from their leader which had been the subject of nightmare for generations had taken place, and no one knew just how serious the consequences would be, whether indeed the Raj would survive.

Like the declarations of war in August 1914, the declarations of November were made reluctantly by all sides, inevitable products of the network of alliances and commitments that had been allowed to build up. It would have been possible, but difficult, for Turkey to remain neutral. If she had to side with one bloc or another, it was probably inevitable that she would side against Russia. And of course things nearly worked out very well. In Russia, Turkey had chosen the right enemy. By the end of the war, the Russian Empire was destroyed and the Russian threat had gone. Turkey's contribution to the Central Powers' war effort was much more substantial than anyone might have expected. Her misfortune was that Russia's allies won the war and their victory destroyed the Ottoman Empire for ever.

At the time it was a major diplomatic failure for Britain that Turkey did not remain neutral. In the long run, it was well for Britain that Turkey fought on the side of the Central Powers. If she had not done so, many things would have been different. Britain would not have created the Middle East, and this book would not have been written. Britain would have been in a much weaker position in the Second World War. We shall never know, but the Middle East would probably have been far happier and more stable than it is.

Churchill was particularly touchy about the idea that he was to blame for bringing Turkey into the war. Gallipoli was bad enough. Churchill and Lloyd George met on 24 January 1921 and talked about the consequences of seizing the Turkish ships. Lloyd George infuriated Churchill by the simplistic assertion that he had turned Turkey into Britain's enemy by precipitately commandeering the vessels. Churchill was stung into responding the following day:

> Some of your statements to me yesterday morning were so staggering that if only to safeguard you from repeating them in the future I must place you in possession of the true facts.
>
> You accuse me of having driven Turkey into the war by seizing the Turkish ships and later bombarding the Dardanelles forts. It is, of course, true that the Turkish ships were taken over, as our margin of superiority was so small that we could not afford to do without them. Still less could we afford to see them transferred to a potentially hostile power . . .
>
> Any other course therefore than that which I took (of course with the assent of the Cabinet) would have jeopardised the very existence of the country. No less diametrically opposed to the actual facts was your statement that I bombarded the Dardanelles forts in order to force Turkey into actual hostility. The alliance between Turkey and Germany had, as we now know, been signed on 4 August. The following telegram now in our possession, sent by the German Admiralty to the *Goeben* at Messina on 4 August [was] as follows:- 'An alliance has been signed with Turkey. Proceed at once to Constantinople' . . .
>
> On 27 October the *Goeben* and *Breslau*, together with several ships of the Turkish Navy, were sent by the Germans with the connivance of Enver Pasha

into the Black Sea to bombard various Russian ports (Novorossisk and Sebastopol) and thus forced Turkey into a state of active hostility. In consequence of this, diplomatic relations with Turkey were broken off on October 30. It was not until the morning of 3 November that the first shots were fired by the British ships in the preliminary bombardment of the Dardanelles forts. It is impossible to over emphasise these simple facts.[5]

4

INDIA IN THE WAR

Britain's war in the Middle East was distinct from her war alongside her allies. It was a private war run by India to keep the Germans out of Persia and to protect the oilfields. As early as 2 October 1914 the Cabinet ordered forces to the Gulf. 'Force D', as it was called, arrived off Bahrain on 23 October.

Force D never disembarked at Bahrain. On 3 November it arrived in the Shatt al-Arab, the confluence of the Tigris and Euphrates rivers, at the top of the Persian Gulf. There it met three British ships already on station. On 6 November the combined force cleared the fortifications at the mouth of the river, and on 22 November the Ottoman territory of Basra was occupied by the Indian Expeditionary Force, commanded by Brigadier-General Delamain, whose instructions were to protect the oil facilities and to assure the local inhabitants of Britain's support.

Oil had been produced in south-west Persia since 1908, and in the year to March 1914 the pipeline to Abadan carried 275,000 tons of crude oil.[1] The significance of the oil factor will be considered later. In addition to the importance of securing the oil supply, officials at the India office stressed broader reasons for maintaining a strong presence in the Gulf. One was the negative effect on British prestige which a withdrawal from the Gulf would have had. The other was positive: with the encouragement of some vigorous British activity, Arabs would rise to throw off the shackles of the Ottomans.

Some local potentates were already well disposed to Britain. Others, such as Ibn Saud, in Saudi Arabia, were less committed. As early as 2 October 1914, the Cabinet approved an India office proposal that Captain W.H.I. Shakespear should present himself to Ibn Saud and try to win his support.

This venture was essentially an Indian one. The viceroy, Lord Hardinge, initially cautious, threw himself behind it. In London, the Assistant Under-Secretary at the Foreign Office, Sir Eyre Crowe, confirmed that 'the administration (temporary or permanent) must be undertaken by the G[overment] of I[ndia] . . . Presumably there can be no question of H.M.G. sharing the cost & (eventual) profit. Nothing will ever be done if the Treasury are imported into the administration.'[2]

Choosing the right Arab partner opened up divisions between officials in London and the men on the spot in India. The Indian government had a high opinion of Ibn Saud. London much preferred the sophisticated Hussein, the Sharif of Mecca. Ibn Saud was not only exotic, but much less powerful, and dependent on the extreme Wahhabis, as the conservative Sunni sect that follows the teachings of an eighteenth-century scholar are derogatively called.

Ibn Saud was a larger than life character, almost too good to be true as a caricature of the Desert Chieftain. He was an impressive figure, 6 feet, 3 inches tall, and of massive build, wrapped in white robes and wearing a chequered *kafeeyah*. He had 65 wives and a black pointed beard. When he joined the allies, he came with a dramatic background of escape from Kuwait, the seizing of Riyadh and his defeat of the Turks in 1914.

William Shakespear was not an outstanding diplomat, but he was a brave man and a shrewd judge of character. He was particularly effective in drawing Middle East intelligence-gathering together. He had been consul and political agent at Kuwait. It was on consuls that much of Britain's intelligence work devolved. The chargé d'affaires in Constantinople wrote, 'I often wish we had no Vice Consul at Mosul, [for he] has nothing to do and so gets into scrapes'. Consuls, unlike military officers travelling in Mesopotamia, could sketch Turkish fortresses under the guise of gentlemanly scholarship.[3] Shakespear was also a distinguished explorer. In 1907 he bought an 8 horsepower, single-cylinder Rover in which he drove from Bushehr, on the Persian Gulf, to England, through Persia, Turkey, Greece, Macedonia, Montenegro, Croatia and Italy. There were no paved roads between Persia and Italy. He explored the Arabian interior, navigating by sextant.

Earlier in 1914, in the course of his longest journey, 1,800 miles in 111 days, he stayed with Ibn Saud at Riyadh. This was not his first meeting with Ibn Saud. He had met him in February 1910 at Kuwait, when he took the first known photograph of him. The men were reciprocally impressed. Shakespear was already convinced that Ottoman power was on the wane in Arabia, and he came to the view that Ibn Saud could fill the vacuum. He was, however, realistic, and in 1913 and again in 1914 warned Ibn Saud that he could not expect much of Britain. On the latter occasion, he had to warn him that Britain would not recognise him as the ruler of the al-Hasa region, from which he had just expelled the Turks. In May 1914, Ibn Saud had therefore to accept his title (of Wali of Najd) from the Ottomans.

Shakespear continued to argue the Emir's case with both London and Delhi. He had no success until the Ottomans entered the war and changed everything. Now, for the second time in 1914, on 31 December, Shakespear went to meet Ibn Saud, this time in the desert, 200 miles north of Riyadh, where the emir was campaigning against allies of the Turks. Shakespear drafted a treaty between Ibn Saud and Britain. The treaty was signed a year later, but in the meantime, still with Ibn Saud, Shakespear was hit by a stray bullet and killed. Ibn Saud wrote to Sir Percy Cox: 'Our beloved friend Captain Shakespear was hit from a distance by one of the enemy's shots and died . . . We pressed him to leave us before the battle, but he refused to do so and was insistent on being with us.[4] Ibn Saud's recruitment by the India Office, which cost Shakespear his life, did not substantially assist Britain's war effort and created lasting difficulties with London's protégé, Hussein.

Decisions had to be made about what to do with the Arab territories that Force D was to acquire. According to the Secretary of State for India, it was not to be assumed that any areas that were taken over should be run on the model of an Indian district. In the event, the matter of how the areas that Britain gained from the Ottomans were to be dealt with was a bitter source of dissension between Delhi on the one hand and London and its Egyptian outstation on the other. In practice, the Indianisation of Mesopotamia was to begin very speedily indeed. Within a week of the occupation of Basra, civilian police on the Indian model were introduced along with the Indian currency and judicial system.

At a military level, as well as a political one, the venture was Indian. The occupation of Basra was carried out in accordance with plans originally formulated in India in 1912. The plans were implemented by the Indian Army, and not the British army. Although Kitchener, Secretary of State for War in London, initially sent telegrams to the Indian commander-in-chief, Sir Beauchamp Duff, Lord Crewe, the Secretary of State for India, ruled that on constitutional grounds this was not acceptable.[5]

5

MAKING POLICY IN THE WAR

1. Sunset of Empire?

As the war went on, and particularly after 1917, a real gap opened up between imperialism on the one hand, and acceptance of the new notions of self-determination and nationalism on the other. Even among the imperialists there was a division between those who argued for a forward policy – such as Leo Amery, of whom more later – and the less focused.

Sir Arnold Wilson, the soldier, diplomat and administrator who will appear frequently in the course of this story, wrote in 1930, 'Before the Great War my generation served men who believed in the righteousness of the vocation to which they were called, and we shared their belief. They were the priests and we were the acolytes of a cult – *pax Britannica* – for which we worked happily and, if need be, died gladly. Curzon, at his best, was our spokesman and Kipling, at his noblest, our inspiration'[1].

That was one view. It was not the only one. Here is one very important Arabist, actively involved in the wartime expansionist policy, writing to another and no less famous architect of the new British Middle East. We shall get to know both of them well. In April 1920, David Hogarth wrote to Gertrude Bell: 'The Empire has reached its maximum and begun its descent. There is no more expansion in this . . . and that being so we shall make but a poor Best of the Arab countries'.[2] This was written not in the sunset of Empire but at the very moment that Britain was consolidating her hold on her new territories.

2. What to do with the Ottoman Empire?

So what can be said of Britain's policy in respect to the Ottoman Empire in the run-up to the war and during it? Did she have a policy at all, rather than a series of desperate improvisations? The answers to these questions will be suggested in the chronicle of Britain's approach to the different component parts of the Empire, but some broad observations are appropriate at this stage.

The first is that, as has been seen, plans for grabbing any parts of the Empire only arose as a result of failure in the cardinal aim of not going to war with Turkey at all. For 50 years it had been fundamental policy to remain friendly with Turkey in order not to jeopardise access to the Straits. Since 1907 the Triple Entente had more or less removed the Russian threat. But now the Russian threat was replaced with another. Turkey had been allowed to fall into the hands of Germany and Austro-Hungary, and Britain's naval security was seriously compromised.

Since Britain had not intended to go to war with Turkey, since indeed she had wanted Turkey's friendship in the war, it followed that she had no preconceived war aims for Ottoman possessions. But an interest in the Middle East was prompted by early events during the war. By the end of 1914 Britain's policymakers were looking at an area near Alexandretta, concerned by French claims on Syria and Russian moves southward. The Ententes were not as cordial as all that. Conflicting claims to Syria were to disturb relations with France throughout the war and afterwards. Edward Grey, the Foreign Secretary, was anxious above all to avoid precipitating a break with France, but Ronald Storrs, Oriental Secretary at the British Agency in Cairo, was in favour of a Near Eastern Vice-Royalty from Sudan to Alexandretta precisely because he did not expect the Entente to last.

An Admiralty Paper of 17 March 1915 recorded that 'The War is teaching us that the Mediterranean is still, as it always was, the centre of world politics, and it is there we must establish the gate of our new acquisition as a counterpoise to the new weight that Russian is acquiring in the dominant area'.[3] In 1917 the Bolshevik Revolution took Russia out of the equation, but the effect of that was only to enhance the status of France as a Mediterranean rival.

Kitchener was a strong proponent of this forward policy. Establishment of 'the gate of our new acquisition' was to be through an Arab Khalifate. This idea may have influenced the correspondence carried out on his behalf by Sir Henry McMahon, the British High Commissioner in Cairo, with King Hussein, starting in the summer of 1914, which will be looked at in detail later.

There was no cohesion in policy: all was fluid. Grey thought that Britain was already burdened by enough possessions. The prime minister, Asquith, on the other hand, said that Britain would not be doing her duty if 'we were to leave the other nations to scrabble for Turkey'.[4] Lloyd George, who succeeded Asquith as prime minister in 1916, was already looking to Palestine rather than Alexandretta. From the point of view of the Middle East, and its inhabitants, the continued existence of a modernised Ottoman Empire might well have been best, but that was never going to happen. No fewer than five secret agreements dealt with the carve-up of the Empire, despite the fact that it continued to look reasonably robust throughout the war. The vultures that circled over the body were Britain, France, Russia and Italy. In the event, Russia disappeared from the conspiracy, relinquishing her claims after the Revolution. Italy played only a minor role in the share-out of prizes.

The various agreements, some secret, some not, included the Constantinople Agreement (1915), the Treaty of London (1915), the Hussein-McMahon correspondence (1915–16), the Sykes–Picot Agreement (1916), the Agreement of St Jean de Maurienne (1917), the Balfour Declaration (1917), the Hogarth Message (1918), the Declaration to the Seven (1918) and the Anglo-French Declaration (1918). To these can be added Wilson's Fourteen Points, Four Principles, Four Ends and Five Particulars.[5]

It is always important to remember, and often overlooked, that although Britain and France were required to operate as allies throughout the war, there was incessant friction both at diplomatic and military levels. Further, although the major sources of Anglo-French rivalry in North Africa had been settled by the Entente, that was far from an end to their conflicting claims in the Middle East, which continued during the war at a muted level and after the war at a level that was certainly not muted. The tensions in the Middle East between the two countries persisted throughout the interwar years and were the cause of very difficult passages with de Gaulle during the Second World War and even afterwards. When we look at the Sykes–Picot Agreement later, it in particular should be seen in the context of these rivalries and suspicions.

In the absence of any self-defining war aims for the Middle East, in 1915 Asquith set up an interdepartmental committee, the 'de Bunsen Committee', under Sir Maurice de Bunsen, Assistant Under-Secretary at the Foreign Office from 1915 to 1918, to try to think up what the government should be looking for. The committee was appointed on 8 April 1915 and reported on 30 June of the same year. Sir Mark Sykes sat on the committee as Kitchener's personal representative, and he established a domination over Middle Eastern policy which persisted for the rest of the war.

The larger than life men (and at least one woman) who come on stage in the theatre of the Middle East will be introduced as they make their major entrances, and it is time to meet Sykes.

3. Sir Mark Sykes

Sykes was a sport of nature. He had little formal education, a couple of spells at public school and just two years at Cambridge, mostly involved in dramatic societies – he was not rigorously educated. He left Cambridge without taking a degree. He was inclined to adopt extreme positions thoughtlessly, but inconsistently. He had written off urban Arabs as cowardly, insolent and as 'vicious as their feeble bodies will admit'. The Bedouins were no better: 'rapacious animals'. When he became a convert to the Arab cause and Arab independence, he changed his opinion radically. He had a morbid and obsessive fear of Jews.

He was an amateur of practical jokes. T.E. Lawrence said 'He saw the odd in everything, and missed the even. He would sketch out in a few dashes a new world, all out of scale'.[6] His mother was drunk and promiscuous. His father was withdrawn and cold. Sykes died of Spanish influenza at the Peace Conference. Because he was buried in a lead casket, permission was given in 2007 for his body to be exhumed, in the hope that lessons could be learned from one pandemic which might avert another. He represents a rare example of public service: even in death he continued to work for his country.

Harold Nicolson described his reaction to the news of that death in his diary for 17 February 1919:

Mark Sykes died last night at Hotel Lotti. I mind dreadfully. He is a real loss. It was due to his endless push and perseverance, to his enthusiasm and faith, that Arab nationalism and Zionism became two of the most successful of our war causes. To secure recognition of these, his beliefs, he had to fight ignorance at the F.O., suspicion at the I[ndia] O[ffice], pass the money at the Treasury, obstruction at the W.O., and idiocy at the Admlty yet he conquered all this by sheer dynamic force. He made mistakes, of course, such as the Sykes–Picot Treaty, but he kept to his ideas with a fervour of genius. I shall miss him – boisterous, witty, untidy, fat, kindly, excitable – with a joy in his own jokes and little pictures (that brown fountain pen scribbling pictures and Mark giggling as he did so). I feel glum and saddened.[7]

Despite his lack of formal training, and his largely undefined public position, he came to play an important and extensive if unofficial role in the formulation of British policy in the Middle East. He was enormously committed to his causes. T.E. Lawrence called him 'the imaginative advocate of unconvincing world-movements' – a typically mean and shallow assessment. He was an example of the sort of gifted amateur who enjoyed huge influence in the formulation of policy in the First World War. These clubbable chaps, often eccentric and always with a high opinion of their own abilities, were allowed into the inner circles of power to a remarkable extent, a phenomenon that scarcely existed in the Second War. John Buchan's novels are full of such men in fiction, and in real life many were his friends. We meet some of them in the course of this narrative.

Empire of Sand

Sykes's relationship with Kitchener was intriguing. He was appointed as Kitchener's personal representative although he scarcely knew him and never got the opportunity to know him better, despite several attempts. He reported daily to Colonel FitzGerald, Kitchener's former military secretary, and FitzGerald relayed his master's instructions. Sykes, however, enjoyed the advantage of being assumed to be close to Kitchener, his mouthpiece. He was able to use that role to relay his own very strong opinions, opinions which carried weight because of his personal experience of the Ottoman Empire and that of his chief, experience that no other member of the committee had.

The de Bunsen Committee completed its deliberations and submitted its report with great expedition. The report, *British War Aims in Ottoman Asia*, contemplated the partition of the Ottoman Empire between the Allies: Britain's position in the Persian Gulf would be secured by the annexation of the vilayets of Basra, Baghdad and most of Mosul, together with the creation of a port on the Mediterranean. It will emerge that although Britain wanted several vilayets, she had no idea what a vilayet was. Sykes was sent to discuss the proposals with the men on the spot.

4. Sykes's Journey

Sykes's journey took six months, and he visited Egypt, the Persian Gulf, Mesopotamia and India, before returning to Egypt. In India, he found the de Bunsen proposals under a sustained attack, led by the viceroy, Lord Hardinge.

Hardinge was an out-and-out India man. His grandfather had been Governor General before the Mutiny. He was carrying great responsibilities and had suffered heavy blows. He faced great difficulties as viceroy, and was under attack both in India and from home, where Curzon was a particularly violent critic. In 1912 he had been very badly wounded by a needle-bomb thrown into his howdah. He suffered a huge gash to his neck and back that exposed his shoulder blade beneath the lacerated muscle.

He managed to hand his bloodstained speech to an aide with the instructions that planned ceremonies were to continue. He was then carried off for surgery. His determination brought him back to work within two months. In 1914 his wife, to whom he was devoted, died suddenly, and shortly afterwards his eldest son was killed in a war in which seven of his aides were to die. He was badly affected by his wife's death and was not consoled even by the vivacity of his daughter, Diamond, who took her place as hostess and enlivened life in the viceregal lodge – she made a floury apple-pie bed for the Maharajah of Gwalior.

When war broke out Hardinge and Force D's commander, General Sir John Nixon, were over-optimistic about the Force's prospects and urged on the

Cabinet the advance up the Tigris to Baghdad that was to lead to a victory at Ctesiphon that was only a little better than a defeat and then to the disastrous siege at Kut, which will be described in course.

Hardinge was intolerant of any suggestion other than an Indian annexation of Mesopotamia. The de Bunsen proposals for control from Cairo were 'absolutely fantastic'. This view was symptomatic of the compartmentalised outlook that held that the interests of each compartment were more important than the interests of the whole. He was on firmer ground when he dismissed the concept of Arab independence as absurd: 'Sykes does not seem to be able to grasp the fact that there are parts of Turkey unfit for representative institutions'.[8]

Sykes may not have been the most practical of men, but he could see that the dispersal of British energy through different agencies in Cairo and Delhi was inefficient. It might have been acceptable in the past, when each agency dealt with different problems; but not now, when each was dealing with the same enemy. He identified no fewer than 18 subordinate agencies that had to be consulted before a decision could be agreed, as well as five principal authorities, Delhi, Cairo, the Foreign Office, the War Office and the Admiralty.

In addition to these bodies, always operating simultaneously and without coordination, the Eastern Committee of the Cabinet was responsible for the evolution of war aims for the region. Its chairman was the able and immensely ambitious Lord Curzon, distinguished for his services to the Empire at the highest levels, including the viceroyalty of India, but currently frustrated by the limited attention paid to him and by his lack of power. He complained about being asked to do 'odd jobs' for the government – although he had used precisely that phrase when offering his services. The Marquess of Crewe, now president of the Board of Education, but a former Secretary of State for India, said that Curzon was 'a Rolls-Royce car, with a highly competent driver, kept to take an occasional parcel to the station.'[9]

From 1917, Curzon worked increasingly with the young politician Leo Amery. The removal of Russia as an ally meant that Curzon and Amery were able to promote forward policies in the Middle East – a reaction to Germany's *Drang nach Osten*. As chairman of the Eastern Committee, Curzon was able to promote the policy with vigour.

Leo Amery and Mark Sykes were Assistant Secretaries of the War Cabinet. They had both a practical concern and a dream. The practical concern was that the remnants of the Ottoman Empire might find their way into German hands, even after a British victory. Amery argued that if Germany were to control Palestine, the safety of the Eastern Empire would be at risk. He supported an old friend, Lieutenant Colonel John Paterson, and his plan for a Jewish Legion. Paterson was an Irish Protestant, and a keen student of the Bible. As well as being a professional army officer, he was an amateur lion-hunter. He had commanded a Jewish corps at Gallipoli and now, at the instigation of the Russian Jewish journalist Vladimir Jabotinsky, was anxious to set up a Jewish unit. Jabotinsky was keen on the idea partly so that the British would see that the Russian Jews in Britain were not shirking military service simply because they were not United Kingdom citizens. He was also seized of the idea that a Jewish corps might liberate Palestine and establish Zionism there. By no means everyone was receptive to the idea, but Lloyd George was: 'The Jews might be able to render us more assistance than the Arabs' in Palestine.

It took three years, but eventually in 1917 the government agreed to allow an explicitly Jewish unit to fight – and to fight against the Turks in Mesopotamia. The association between Crusading Christianity and the war in Palestine is frequently explored, but the role of militant Judaism much less so.

5. Militant Zionism

There was eye-catching significance in a Jewish unit fighting Muslims in what was to be Palestine. It was only the second time since the destruction of the Temple in Jerusalem that an independent Jewish army unit had existed. The force was technically the 38th, 39th, 40th, 41st and 42nd battalions of the Royal Fusiliers, collectively known as the Jewish Legion. There were a number of nicknames, some facetious, others, like that devised by the *Manchester Guardian*, seriously appreciative: 'The New Maccabeans'. The *Jewish World* of 6 February 1918 described the 38th Battalion's march through Whitechapel and the city on 4 February 1918, which was followed by a lunch at The Mansion House. There was no doubt that they were on their way to liberate the Holy Land from occupation by the Turks: 'Never before has London beheld the proud sight presented to it on Monday last, when some hundreds of the Judeans, as the regiment of Jewish soldiers has come to be fondly known, marched through the City prior to taking their departure from England . . . And every worthy emotion that can stir Jews must have been aroused when these brave lads, with swinging gait, marched to their station to their journey, to the Land of Jewish Hope . . .'[10]

An editorial in the *Jewish Chronicle* emphasised a link with Zionism: 'The Judeans are a living refutation of many a silly legend that has clung to the name of Jew, and the cheers of the London populace . . . testified that the whole edifice of calumny and ignorance – the work of centuries – had toppled to the dust . . . [What would become of the] equally inveterate fables that the Jew can never become an agriculturist, can never build a State, can never govern his own land?' When Lieutenant General Sir Francis Lloyd inspected the battalion

in Great Alie Street, he said that he felt sure that 'you will prove worthy followers of the ancient Jewish warriors . . . for the glory of the Jewish nation'.

After their lunch, when the battalion, accompanied by the band of the
Coldstream Guards, marched off to entrain at Waterloo for Southampton, they
were presented with a Torah scroll, which was carried at the head of the proces-
sion. Rabbi Lipson presented it, saying, 'I give in to your keeping this Book of
the Law, to be in all circumstances and at all times your never-failing
guide . . . [In] the remote past, the law went forth from Zion; happy are you
that take it *unto* Zion, to establish the Sacred Land'.

The nature of the mission was thus very explicit. Jabotinsky had achieved
exactly what he wanted. He was made an honorary officer in the 38th Battalion
(known to the soldiers as 'Captain Jug O'Whisky'). Jacob Epstein was also in
the 38th. The 40th, which was composed mainly of Palestinian refugees,
included David Ben-Gurion and Levi Eshkol, the first and third prime ministers of Israel.

Jabotinsky himself spoke of 'Those boys! Those tailors! Shoulder to shoulder, their bayonets dead level, each step like a single clap of thunder, clean,
proud, drunk with the National Anthem, with the noise of the crowds and all
the sense of a holy mission . . . [L]ong life to you, my tailors of Whitechapel,
Soho, Leeds and Manchester . . .'

Most newspapers were sympathetic. The *Daily Mail* said 'London's
Ghetto, refuge of generations of oppressed Jews . . . rocked with martial
pride . . . and the homage of the people from among whom the bulk of the
[battalion] were recruited.' The *Daily Sketch* pointed out that some of the
men had already seen active service and wore stripes on their sleeves. But
some newspapers could be condescending or downright offensive in a way
that is difficult to understand today. The *East London Observer* of 9 February
said that 'the men bore themselves bravely and had in large measure assimilated some of the best traditions of Thomas Atkins Esq.'. It went on to say
that the men were going 'to meet the Infidel Turk who has been so long the
tyrant of Jerusalem'. The *Pall Mall Gazette* described the Jewish soldiers:
'The heavy, high-cheek-boned countenance of the Russian predominated,
though there were a few stubby round-headed figures which looked as
though they had got into khaki by mistake . . . their speech however
betrayed the men more than their appearance. It is a curious fact that in
spite of their marked linguistic ability, Jewish people may live in England
almost all their lives without losing that tell-tale accent.' No mention of
the stunted men in the plucky British bantam battalions. There were hints
of the idea that the Jewish race was unsoldierly and allegations that some of
the men had deserted in the course of the march. The allegations were

untrue. In the course of its short existence the 38th Battalion suffered 32 officers and men killed, four wounded. Its men were awarded a DSO, five MCs (three with bars), one DCM and six Military Medals. Eight were Mentioned in Despatches.

6

MAKING POLICY: THE ARAB DIMENSION

The caliphs were originally the successors of Muhammad. Subsequently there was dispute about who the true caliphs were, and no clarity about their role. Eventually the title was asserted by the Ottoman leaders, who came to claim that their authority extended to Muslims outside the boundaries of the Empire. The claim was not disputed by the powers, and Muslims in British India looked to the caliph for protection. Thus, paradoxically, the caliphs' influence extended as their boundaries shrank.

When Turkey declared war on Britain and Russia, and the sultan, also the caliph, proclaimed *jihad* in November 1914, there was a good deal of noise in Constantinople and a good deal of propaganda in Berlin. Nothing else happened, but Britain could not know that the breach between the caliph and her Muslim subjects might not have the disastrous consequences that had been the nightmare of Indian officials for so long. It was widely felt that the reason a holy war had not turned into a shooting war was simply that Turkey did not – yet – control Mecca and Medina, the holy places of the Hejaz, the land on the edge of the Red Sea in the west of what is now Saudi Arabia.

The consequences of a Muslim rising would have been potentially enormous, involving, notably, the Muslim subjects of the British Empire in India and elsewhere. They would also affect France and Russia. Britain had to declare her hand. In November, Kitchener said, 'Till now we have defended and befriended Islam in the person of the Turks. Henceforward it shall be that of the noble Arab.'[1]

For London, though not Delhi, the critical faction was the Hashemite dynasty, the descendants of Muhammad's daughter, Fatima, of whom the current head was Hussein, the Sharif of Mecca. The Hashemites not only had political aspirations to supplant the Ottomans; they were also well qualified as members of the Prophet's own clan, and custodians of the holy places of Mecca and Medina. The title 'Sharif' which Hussein carried can be used only by those who are descendants of the Prophet.

Hussein and Britain had already been tiptoeing round the question of coming together. In 1914, before the outbreak of war brought him into the Cabinet, Kitchener was the British Agent in Egypt. His Oriental Secretary was Ronald, later Sir Ronald, Storrs, an important moulder of British policy.

Abdullah, one of Hussein's sons, called on Kitchener in February 1914. Abdullah had a fairly cosmopolitan upbringing. He had been educated in Constantinople as well as in the Hejaz, and he had also stayed in the city for some time while his father was a prisoner there. He obtained some polish and became involved in politics. In the two years before the war, when he sat in the Ottoman Parliament as Deputy for Mecca, he absorbed the idea of Arab nationalism and applied its gloss to his father's simpler wish for an independent Hejaz. It was on his way back to Mecca from Istanbul that he met Kitchener in 1914. The idea of British assistance in the conflict with the Turks began to germinate, and he took the idea with him to Mecca, where he became his father's foreign minister and political adviser.

At his meeting with Kitchener he indicated that relations between Turkey and his father were strained and that indeed it was feared that Turkey intended to depose the Sharif. Without saying anything explicit, he left the impression of having enquired what Britain's position would be if there were to be conflict between the Arabs and the Turks.

Kitchener said little – he was good at that – but he arranged for a meeting between Abdullah and Storrs. Storrs and Abdullah built up a friendship, and they shared an interest in chess. But this was an insufficient basis for giving Abdullah the machine guns he wanted, and little more happened until war broke out.

By then Kitchener was back on leave in England. He became Secretary of State for War, and a great recruiting poster, and never returned to Egypt. But that did not mean that he played no part in devising policy for the Middle East. He directed events as closely from London as he had done in Egypt, where he had left behind a band of devoted followers, who continued to look to him as their chief.

In *Greenmantle*, in which plucky British amateurs defeat a German plot to win the war by destabilising the Middle East, John Buchan, who fancied he knew a thing or two about geopolitical threats, wrote, 'There is a dry wind blowing through the East, and the parched grasses wait the spark. And the wind is blowing towards the Indian border'. Kitchener was concerned by this threat. It had to be addressed in some temporary way for the moment; he planned to dispose of the risk forever after the war by ensuring that the caliph was Britain's nominee and an Arab. One of the flaws in his plan was that he took no account of the divisions between the different elements in Islam, of the spiritual dimensions as well as the political ones. More perspicacious observers, such as Arthur Hirtzel, secretary to the Political Department of the India Office, and Lord Crewe, Secretary of State for India, were aware of the spiritual importance of the hints in Kitchener's messages to Hussein of an Arab caliphate.

Indian opposition to Kitchener went further than that. Whereas he was attracted by the idea of a new Raj in Arabia, Indian officials preferred 'not a United Arabia: but a weak and disunited Arabia, split up into little principalities so far as possible under our Suzerainty, but incapable of co-ordinated action against us, forming a buffer against the Powers in the West'.[2] That view was predicated on the idea that policy should be devoted to safeguarding the Indian interest. Kitchener, on the other hand, had a wider vision: he was looking forward to a renewed expansion of the British Empire after the war. As far as the prosecution of the war itself was concerned, he was a firm believer in the Western Front. In that sense, but only in that sense, he was not an Easterner.

As soon as the war broke out, and even before he was appointed Secretary of State, recognising that the Arabs were more important in August than they had been in February, he authorised Storrs to find out from Abdullah what the Arabs would be likely to do if Turkey came into the war.

Hussein's sons were divided on the advice they gave to their father, but Abdullah and the Sharif thought they had more to gain from the Allies than from relying on Turkish gratitude. In October 1914 Abdullah wrote a guarded letter to Storrs. He might be prepared to favour Britain, but could not, as a Muslim, be anything other than neutral unless Turkey precipitated a crisis. He could speak only for the Hejaz, and he could do nothing unless effective support were provided by Britain.[3]

Kitchener was carefully non-committal. Britain had by no means determined on a hostile policy against the Ottomans, and nothing was to be done which might upset the Turks. In any event, even at the meeting with Storrs, Abdullah was delicately vague about what his aspirations amounted to. The balance was very nice: while the Turks were not to be alienated, Hussein's ambitions were strongly founded on his critical role as guardian of the holy places, the goal for pilgrims to the Hejaz, hugely significant for the Muslim world.

On 16 October 1914, Sir John Maxwell, commanding the British forces in Egypt and an old friend of Kitchener, wrote to him: 'I do not know what the policy of the Foreign Office is, but I think the Arabs about Mecca and the Yaman [*sic*] ought to be approached and set against the Turks'.[4]

Once Turkey was actually in the war Kitchener moved. He sent a message from Cairo for onward transmission to Abdullah. It advised him that if he sided with Britain he would be guaranteed the retention of the status of Grand Sharif. There was an indication of support for the Arabs in a struggle for independence if they allied themselves with Britain. Some eight months later these early communications were followed by the first of the letters from Hussein to Sir Henry McMahon which were to make up the McMahon Correspondence.

These tentative and fairly non-committal exchanges in the summer of 1914, hesitant and haphazard as they were, and reflecting no great policy decision on the part of the British government, were the basis of much that followed – the McMahon Correspondence, Lawrence, the Arab Revolt and the creation of new states and new dynasties. The result in the middle term was to secure the approach to India. In the short term the outcome of the First World War was scarcely affected.

7

THE MCMAHON–HUSSEIN CORRESPONDENCE

1. Background

The exchange of letters between the British government and Hussein, the Sharif of Mecca, between 14 July 1915 and 30 January 1916, known as the McMahon–Hussein Correspondence, created the prism through which the Arab world for decades to come viewed British, indeed Western, policy, policy which appeared to be informed by treachery and bad faith.

The correspondence originated from the contact between Kitchener and the Emir Hussein which has been mentioned. '[T]he great service which Hussein rendered to the Allied cause in relation to the Holy War was one which no one else was in a position to render. And Kitchener's move in securing his goodwill before it was too late was nothing less than a master-stroke of acumen and foresight.'[1] That claim, by George Antonius, rests on the basis of Hussein's prestige in the Muslim world as a descendant of the Prophet and Custodian of the Holy Places, whose failure to endorse the call to *jihad* could be considered as critical.

Antonius was a Greek Orthodox Christian. Part of his education was at Cambridge, and he worked for the British government within the mandate system until he resigned in protest against British policies and the way in which he felt he had been treated. His subsequent work was informed by scholarship, by considerable knowledge of the facts and by contact with some principal personalities of the Arab Bureau in Cairo, but was underscored by a commitment to demonstrate British bad faith and to show that the use of the mandates frustrated Arab nationalism.

Whether Hussein's role *was* critical is doubtful in view of subsequent events. In a secret memorandum of 1 July 1916 the War Office said that Hussein had 'always represented himself, in his correspondence with the High Commissioner [McMahon], as being the spokesman of the Arab Nation, but so far as is known, he is not supported by any organisation of Arabs nearly general enough to secure . . . automatic acceptance of the terms agreed to by him'.[2] All the same, in the long term the perception of broken promises and hostility to Arab nationalism left Britain resented and distrusted in the Arab world.

Hussein's approach to Britain was made on his initiative and not on Kitchener's: Kitchener had been far from ready to grab at the feelers that Hussein and Abdullah had put out. In 1914 there was no solidity to the relationship between Hussein and Britain. In the early months of 1915, Hussein did receive moderate encouragement from Sir Reginald Wingate, the Governor General of the Sudan. That encouragement was still infinitely delicate and insubstantial, but a change was under way. The context was of course the growing realisation that the war Britain was fighting was not going to be the very short and glorious one that so many in London had expected. The reality was proving to be a new kind of industrial conflict which might last indefinitely and in which victory was far from certain, and it would not be fought on one front.

It is interesting that Kitchener was one of the few who realised from the outset that the war would be a long one, and his men in Cairo buckled to. It is important to know who these men were. By early 1915, the key players in Cairo were Sir Henry McMahon, who was appointed High Commissioner for Egypt and the Sudan in January 1915, Ronald Storrs, the Oriental Secretary, and G.F. Clayton, the Director of Military Intelligence.

Ronald Storrs was known as 'Oriental Storrs', a play on the name of an unreliable shop in Cairo. He had a silky, auburn moustache which contained 'a hint of dilettantism in the way it curled up slightly at the ends'.[3] He thought that he and his colleagues worked hard, although their day finished at noon, after which they moved to the Turf Club or the Gezira Sporting Club.

Storrs's experience as Oriental Secretary in Cairo meant that Kitchener came to value his advice. When Kitchener became War Minister, he asked Storrs to stay in London with him. Civil Service rules did not allow this, but Storrs continued to work closely with Kitchener even at a distance, regarding Kitchener, rather than the new High Commissioner, Sir Henry McMahon, as his chief. Storrs was receptive to Hussein's ambitions, which fitted in with his plan for a new, British, Middle East, replacing the Ottoman one and based on an Egyptian Empire that would include Syria. Kitchener and Mark Sykes were captivated by his vision, but it was a flawed one. Intelligence in Cairo was poor, and lacked coordination. The resistance of Muslims to rule by others was not understood. Storrs himself, though cultivated and sophisticated in his tastes, spoke much poorer Arabic than he was prepared to admit.

This affected the correspondence with Abdullah and Hussein. Storrs, and an assistant whose Arabic was even poorer, were not qualified to translate accurately the messages that came from the Sharif via a shadowy intermediary, Muhammad al-Faruqi. Storrs was frequently absent, and others had to translate. Some oral messages were never recorded.

Storrs admired T.E. Lawrence and was principal pall-bearer at his funeral. Lawrence was typically ambivalent and opaque about Storrs:

> His shadow would have covered our work and British policy in the East like
> a cloak, had he been able to deny himself the world, and to prepare his mind
> and body with the sternness of an athlete for a great fight.[4]

Gilbert Clayton, who worked with Storrs in Cairo, was commissioned in the Royal Artillery in 1895 and served under Kitchener in the Sudan campaign. From 1908 to 1913 he was private secretary to Sir Reginald Wingate, Governor General and Sirdar of the Sudan, 1899–1916. From 1913 onwards he served as Sudan Agent in Cairo, the official representative of the Sudan government in Egypt. Simultaneously he was Director of Intelligence of the Egyptian Army. On 31 October 1914 he became head of all intelligence services, in charge of Civil Intelligence, British Army Intelligence and Egyptian Army Intelligence. For once, things were simplified: there was now one source of intelligence data and not three. By the end of the war Clayton was a general. He was not a martinet: he had a warm and avuncular relationship with the varied bunch of archaeologists and Orientalists who served under him. He has been described as 'perhaps the ultimate "Cairene"', or supporter of the Arab cause from Cairo.[5] In 1929 he was appointed High Commissioner and commander-in-chief in Iraq, but almost immediately died of a heart attack in the course of a game of polo. He was just 54.

The intelligence operation over which he presided was not very impressive. Lloyd George considered that the British authorities in Cairo knew nothing of what was going on within the Ottoman Empire. He blamed this lack of information for the fact that Britain was not able to 'crumple up' the Turks and defeat Germany through the Balkans. Certainly the Egyptian government was riddled with spies until 1916 when Wyndham Deedes, a remarkable, saintly man and an effective intelligence officer, discovered the extent to which the Egyptian police forces had been infiltrated by the Turks. As early as 1914, even before the Ottomans were in the war, the British Army commander, General Maxwell, complained to Kitchener that he could get no information about conditions within the Ottoman Empire, whereas he was well aware that the Germans knew all about what was going on in the British sphere.[6]

Storrs and Clayton worked closely with Sir Reginald Wingate in Khartoum. Wingate's address – The Palace, Khartoum – was remote, socially as well as geographically, from his birthplace, the shipbuilding town of Port Glasgow at the mouth of the Clyde where he had lived frugally after the early death of his father, a textile merchant. After his spell as Governor General and Sirdar, or military commander, in the Sudan, Wingate went to Egypt as High Commissioner.

Storrs and Clayton were uncritical of information that came their way and took material from a single source without question. This dangerously subjective approach was applauded instead of being deprecated. George W. Steevens, the journalist who created the Kitchener myth, credited Wingate with the ability to assess a native's credibility with uncanny intuition. The science of Intelligence was in its infancy in the Great War, and respect for this intuitive appraisal as opposed to rigorous analysis was dangerous. In *Greenmantle*, John Buchan, Director of Information in London, said that 'The truth is that we are the only race on earth that can produce men capable of getting inside the skin of remote peoples. Perhaps the Scots are better than the English, but we are all a thousand per cent better than anyone else'. An unrealistic conceit.

The odd thing is that in other regions, British Intelligence of these days was quite different. It has been described as 'dogged empiricism'. In the Middle East, by contrast, the approach was peculiarly intuitive. It was not that Britain was the only power that spied in the Middle East before the First World War. In 1909 Vernon Kell, the founder of what was to be MI5, urged that Britain should be at least as deceitful as Germany, France and Russia. He was pressing on an open door and Britain was to send more agents into Arabia than any other country. What was peculiar was that Britain's fascination with the culture and sheer unfamiliarity of the Middle East prompted a departure from the scientific and disciplined approach that was practised in other geographical areas of intelligence.[7] Other countries were not distracted by exoticism. As Edward Said put it, 'there were no French Lawrences or Sykeses or Bells'.[8]

Cairo was inclined to overestimate Arab potential as a result of the defection from the Turks of Mohammed al-Faruqi, who had been ADC to the commander of the Ottoman 12th Army Corps. He claimed that there was a substantial nationalist organisation which was prepared to ally itself with either Britain or the Ottomans. That was almost certainly not the case, but Gilbert Clayton and General Sir John Maxwell, the commander of the British Forces in Egypt, believed Faruqi.[9]

Storrs and Clayton sought to develop the earlier exchanges between Kitchener and Abdullah. Wingate came to the conclusion that the Arabs would not be won over without substantial commitments from the British. Kitchener agreed and McMahon, who will make a proper appearance shortly, was authorised to make a public declaration. There was no great precipitation. A declaration was not published until early June.

2. Kitchener and the Middle East

Kitchener was an ambitious and conscientious officer: a bachelor, wedded to his career. He started out as an engineer, but saw that the route to eminence lay through the cavalry. In 1882 he made a second critical career move and arranged to be seconded to the Egyptian Army. Within ten years he was its commander-in-chief, the Sirdar. He was tall, lean, and with legs that seemed too long for his body. His chest was narrow and his shoulders bottle-shaped. The sun of Egypt bleached his moustache almost white, in contrast to his bronzed face. His thick shock of fair hair refused to go grey. His greatest problem as Sirdar was his fear that without grey hair he would not be taken seriously.

An unknown sapper without money, connections or remarkable intellect, by a combination of judicious silence and careful self-advertisement, sustained by perfect health and intermittent hard work, he rose to become a military figure of huge stature in Egypt and throughout the Empire. No one who knew him thought him to be particularly bright, but very few people did know him. He always stood a little apart from a world with which he did not wholly engage. The distinct cast in one eye made people feel that he was looking right through them and he deployed this characteristic to intimidate and to contribute the impression that the popular press promoted – that of a stern, silent leader.

In Cairo at this stage in his career he used the press to build the image. Later he could afford to dismiss journalists as 'a drunken rabble', but for the moment they were very helpful. Steevens of *The Daily Mail* was particularly important, and his book, *With Kitchener to Khartoum,* created the image of Kitchener as 'the Sudan Machine', the 'Man of Destiny'.

He mastered colloquial Arabic and fostered the idea that he was skilled in the intricacies of local politics. Stories spread about travels in the desert in Arab disguise. By the time he left Egypt and was able to jettison the press, his career was unstoppable. As Sirdar, commander-in-chief, in Egypt, he was the victor of Omdurman and subdued the Sudan. He went to the South African War as chief of staff and then to India as commander-in-chief, before returning to Egypt as Agent and Consul General.

After the Sudan he developed bizarre acquisitive habits. He was often offered a gift in recognition of his achievements. He always asked for gold plate. When he stayed with friends he asked them for any of their possessions that took his fancy. Like Queen Mary, he sometimes took them without asking. By the time he died, he had built up an extensive collection of pottery and porcelain. He never married, although there were flirtations, a possible engagement and a

wooing of Helen, Lord Londonderry's daughter. In his old age he was friendly
with Catherine Walters, 'Skittles', the celebrated serial mistress and, when she
lived in France, *grande cocotte*, just one rank away from *grande horizontale*.

Kitchener tended always to operate as an independent force, and his reputation was such, particularly so far as the east was concerned, that no one could
stop him from doing so. By the outbreak of the First World War he was
regarded by the public with a combination of awe and affection. It is some
measure of the peculiar hold he had on their imagination that when he went
down with the *Hampshire* in 1916 a neo-Arthurian myth should so speedily
have developed: he was resting on some remote island, from which he would
return to save the country. The public found him much more congenial than
political leaders, for whom indeed he had little time. When he was photographed with some eminent Cabinet colleagues he was described as looking
like an officer who found himself among a group of strolling players, trying
hard to make it look as if he did not know them. When he joined the Cabinet
at the outbreak of the war, he regarded his political colleagues with contempt
and declined to give them any military information, on the grounds that they
would simply pass it on to their wives – except in the case of Lloyd George, who
would pass it on to other people's wives.

It was only by chance that he was in London when war broke out. He was
there for the ceremony surrounding his elevation to the peerage. He told the
king that he wanted to go to India as viceroy, but in the meantime his intention
was to head back for Egypt. He attempted to do so as late as 3 August, despite
the deteriorating European situation. He was told to stay, but he continued to
feel that the East was where he should be, and he rented a house in London for
what he regarded as no more than a temporary stay.

It is important to remember that Egypt, unlike India, was a fairly recent
acquisition. It had only been occupied by Britain in 1882, and then ostensibly
on a short-term basis. Kitchener and his Egyptian officials did not sit well with
the organisations established for control in the area: the Foreign Office in
London for the west of the Arabian areas and the India Office for the east.
Additionally, although Cairo dealt with an Arab-speaking country, it was a
very different country from the Arab-speaking parts of the Ottoman Empire.
But the extension of the Egyptian sphere as a result of the Sudan campaign
meant that Kitchener and his aides took themselves very seriously indeed. They
began to carve out their own policy, independent of both London and Delhi.
This policy was to be one of extension of the Arabian possession as a counter-
weight to India, ruled not directly as in India, but through the agency of a local
monarch. Ronald Storrs put it rather well: 'We deprecated the Imperative,
preferring the Subjunctive, even the wistful, Optative mood'.[10]

Kitchener knew a great deal about the Middle East, whereas London knew very little indeed. He had, for instance, completed a secret survey and mapping exercise in 1913–14. There were very few other maps of the area. At Gallipoli Britain had just one map, and a faulty one at that. Sykes was one of the few MPs who knew anything of the East, and he complained that there was not one proper history of the Ottoman Empire in English. What did exist was based on a German work that only brought matters down to 1744.

3. Competing Views

Wingate opposed the views that came from the India Office.[11] Similarly, Kitchener's plans for an Arabian Raj were completely unacceptable to the India Office. There, Hirtzel, for instance, saw the Mesopotamian provinces as no more than an adjunct to India which could provide irrigation and labour for India.[12] There was direct competition for the territories.

After Cairo and the India Office, the third line of thinking within the government was that of Asquith and Grey, prime minister and Foreign Secretary, who did not think Britain, either from Cairo or from Delhi, should take any new territory at all. Asquith had wavered but concluded that he and Grey

> both think that in the real interest of our own future, the best thing would be if, at the end of the War, we could say that . . . we have taken & gained nothing. And that not from a merely moral and sentimental point of view . . . but from purely material considerations. Taking on Mesopotamia, for instance – with or without Alexandretta – . . . means spending millions in irrigation & development with no immediate or early return; keeping up quite a large army white & coloured in an unfamiliar country; tackling every kind of tangled administrative question, worse than we have ever had in India with a hornet's nest of Arab tribes.

The fastidious prime minister told his Cabinet that when they discussed the opportunities that lay in the Ottoman Empire their 'discussions had resembled that of a gang of buccaneers'.[13]

There was then no unanimity among the British policymakers. Curzon wrote to Cromer on 22 April 1915, deprecating the idea of making promises to the Arabs and doubting whether they were capable of administering the substantial state that was being promised to them. He was not alone. The Committee on Asiatic Turkey (Sir Maurice de Bunsen's Committee) regarded partition as substantially undesirable. Curzon's views were informed by his time as viceroy; many of those who took the opposite view were conditioned by their time in the Sudan to be critical of Indians in contrast to Arabs, for whom they had an almost sentimental affection.

The way in which Wingate's staff at Khartoum subsequently spread throughout the area, forming a network of significant and influential senior officials committed to a specific Arab policy has been analysed. 'The literary Arabophiles, Colonel Lawrence and Miss Bell, cannot sustain comparison with such weighty and durable influence: they supplied the myth and the *panache* but little would have been accomplished had the officials themselves not been the convinced and confident upholders of the policy.'[14]

The Arabists conceived of an Empire for themselves which would rival anything that the India Office had: Storrs wrote to Kitchener's military secretary in March 1915: 'A North African or near eastern vice-royalty including Egypt under Sudan and across the way from Aden to Alexandretta would surely compare in interest and complexity, if not in actual size, with India itself'.[15]

McMahon was not seized of such an ambitious vision. Later he tried to explain what he had been trying to do:

> It was the most unfortunate date in my life when I was left in charge of this Arab movement and I think a few words are necessary to explain that it is nothing to do with me: it is a purely military business: it began at the urgent request of Sir Ian Hamilton at Gallipoli. I was begged by the Foreign Office to take immediate action and draw the Arabs out of the war. At the moment a large portion of the [Turkish] force at Gallipoli and nearly the whole of the force in Mesopotamia were Arabs, and the Germans were then spending a large amount of money in detaching the rest of the Arabs, so the situation was that the Arabs were between the two. Could we give them some guarantee of assistance in the future to justify their splitting with the Turks? I was told to do that at once and in that way I started the Arab movement.[16]

While McMahon was entrusted with 'this Arab business', the India Office was proceeding more speedily in its overtures to Ibn Saud. Cairo knew very little about Ibn Saud. It is symptomatic of the poor intelligence on which Kitchener relied that he and his staff knew nothing of the revival of Wahhabism. Wahhabism strengthened from 1912 onwards with a movement known as the Ikhwan. Ibn Saud placed himself at the head of the movement, which now concentrated itself behind him.

Sykes was not much better. At a War Cabinet committee meeting on 16 December Kitchener asked Sykes, 'Wahabism [*sic*], does that still exist?' Sykes replied, 'I think it is a dying fire'. Even two years later, Clayton was only beginning to report to Sykes on 'indications of a revivalist movement on Wahhabi lines'.[17]

McMahon felt himself under pressure from Wingate to make specific commitments to Hussein but he refrained from doing so. Clayton confirmed that McMahon had been careful to make no significant commitments at all. No one was sure what Wingate wanted. He said that McMahon and Hardinge, the viceroy, were wrong in thinking that he was in favour of 'a consolidated Arab Kingdom under the Sharif – Of course any such notion is altogether remote from my real views, but it has suited me, as I believe it has suited all of us, to give the leaders of the Arab Movement this impression and we are quite sufficiently covered by the correspondence which has taken place to show that we are acting in good faith with the Arabs as far as we have gone'.[18] What he was really saying was that the correspondence did not quite mean what Hussein thought it meant.

It is wrong then to think that wild promises were made in the course of the correspondence, which Britain subsequently chose casually to abrogate. Those involved at the time were very clear about what they were doing and what they were not doing. The Foreign Office did not consider that any obligation arose on Britain's part unless the Arab part of the Ottoman Empire united in rising against the Turks. They were confident that this would never happen. Grey said of the correspondence that 'the whole thing was a castle in the air which would never materialise'.[19]

The emptiness of the correspondence can be seen in relation to India. Hardinge's *amour propre* was wounded because there was nothing in the correspondence for the subcontinent. McMahon told him that 'I had necessarily to be vague as on the one hand HMG disliked being committed to definite future action, and on the other hand any detailed definition of our demands would have frightened off the Arab'. The correspondence would neither 'establish our rights . . . or bind our hands'.[20]

4. McMahon

Henry McMahon was an Indian civil servant. In 1914 he retired from the office of political secretary to the government of India. He arrived in Egypt in December to replace Kitchener as High Commissioner – really to hold the fort for him. Amery said that he was 'not very impressive, [and] has a very small head, but evidently [has] a lot of sense in it'.[21]

In accounts of the Middle East, McMahon is always treated rather dismissively, as a personage of little consequence. In fact, in India his service had been very impressive. He is routinely referred to as 'elderly', and was indeed at about retirement age for the subcontinent. But he was only 52 in 1914, and Storrs said he was a young-looking 52. He did come with scarcely any Arabic and without any experience of Egypt and its indirect mode of government. In India the supreme authority was that of the viceroy. In Egypt – notionally – the supreme authority lay with the Khedive, the native figurehead, and his ministers, even if in reality the Khedive and those ministers were the puppets of the British.

McMahon was sympathetic towards Arabs. That was not to be assumed: although he was now Foreign Office, his background was in the Indian Political Service. Indian Civil Servants generally did not like Arabs as much as Foreign Office men did.

Hardinge, the viceroy, knew and liked McMahon, but thought him rather reactionary and slow-minded. All the same, he described him as 'a very straight little man'. Another colleague, Sir Ronald Graham, said, 'we can none of us understand your little McMahon – he is pleasant and shrewd, but it is impossible to make him take a decision of any kind.'[22]

McMahon's mission statement was, 'What we have to arrive at now is to tempt the Arab people on the right path, detach them from the enemy, and bring them on to our side. This, on our side, is at present largely a matter of words, and to succeed we must use persuasive terms and abstain from haggling over conditions.'[23] That prescription describes exactly his approach to the Correspondence.

5. Why Did McMahon Write to Hussein?

Just six months after he arrived in Egypt, McMahon started to woo Hussein. Why did he do so? In the first place, because Kitchener told him to, and in any event, there was an approach from Hussein which had to be responded to. But in Cairo it made sense to deal with him and his family, the Hashemites, rather than with Ibn Saud. Britain was worried about *jihad* and one of the reasons for establishing links with Hussein was to counter the risk. The Hashemites had the necessary spiritual authority.

Hussein, 'a small, neat, old gentleman of great dignity and, when he liked, great charm', whose phone number was MECCA 1,[24] was fiercely proud of his clan's history and fired by ambition for its future. He came with the added credibility of having been a prisoner of the Turks in Constantinople. He also had the polish and urbanity of a Hashemite. He was rather more Western than the other Arabs.

As emir of Mecca, Hussein occupied, as we have seen, a critically prestigious position in the Ottoman Empire. He was hostile to the CUP and to Turkey generally, and from the outset of his time as emir he sought to build up his strength and establish his independence from the CUP. With the outbreak of war the CUP government urged him to support the caliph's *jihad*. In pursuance of his policy of independence, he did not respond to the caliph's call. He saw his future in the consolidation of the position of emir as a hereditary office for his family. It was for this reason that he made overtures to Turkey's enemies.

The famous correspondence between McMahon and Hussein consisted of eight letters written between July 1915 and January 1916. The British kept the French in the dark about the negotiations and the correspondence: the French did not know about the promises that were being made or not being made to Hussein. They did not know about the extent of the Arab ambitions. They did not know about the nature of Britain's ambitions in the area. Their Foreign Minister, Pichon, complained about all this at the Peace Conference in March 1919. These matters rankled.

Sykes, on the other hand, was charged with a separate set of secret negotiations, arrangements with France which conflicted with some of the terms of McMahon's missives. He was aware of the exchange of correspondence, although he may not have been aware of its detailed content. The Sykes–Picot Agreement will be considered later.

6. The Correspondence

As usual, policy was implemented sloppily. On Kitchener's instructions, Hussein received correspondence in duplicate, one strand coming from McMahon in Cairo and the other from Wingate in Khartoum. Less damage was done than might have been expected. For once, each kept in touch with the other and both with the Foreign Office. McMahon brought to the correspondence his knowledge of India. Wingate had a wider knowledge of Arab affairs, as Governor General of the Sudan and Sirdar of the Egyptian Army. Wingate's relationship with McMahon was not a close one, but he did keep in touch with others at Cairo, including Clayton, the Director of Civil and Military Intelligence. Keeping in touch was not something that the imperial authorities were generally very good at.

So there was conflict between the McMahon correspondence and the Ibn Saud agreement, the treaty of independence drafted by Shakespear and signed in early December 1915 between Ibn Saud and Sir Percy Cox, who was with the army at Basra. Equally, Cox knew nothing of the Sykes–Picot Agreement, which was communicated to Cairo, but not Basra. Sykes later apologised to Cox: 'I was assured that you had a copy of it as far back as ten months ago'.[25] Similarly, while Cox was negotiating with Ibn Saud he was not in touch with what McMahon was doing from Egypt.

In these dark days of 1915–16, the war in France was being fought on the

static Western Front. Kitchener's New Armies were only just becoming available for service. The only ally that really mattered for Britain was the ally that
was providing most of the men who were dying on the Front: France. Even so,
while Britain went through the forms of respecting the interests of that crucial
ally, she did not consider it necessary to share much of the information about
eastern entanglements with her. If the Foreign Office failed to talk to the India
Office, which had promised part of the territories offered to Hussein to Ibn
Saud, it is hardly surprising that they failed to talk to the Quai d'Orsay. At the
Peace Conference, and afterwards, Britain's failure to consult her allies, both
the French and others, attracted a good deal of criticism at home as well as
abroad. A British government memorandum of January 1922 brushed off such
criticism: the arrangements were a 'war measure forced upon the Allied Powers,
by the exigencies of the Great War'.

The first element of the correspondence was a note from Hussein to
McMahon. It was undated and, in accordance with custom, unsigned. It was
sent about the middle of July 1915 and did not reach Cairo until some time in
August. In a covering letter, Abdullah suggested that there was now no need
for any more aerial distribution of propaganda leaflets: some cash would be
more effective propaganda.

The Hashemites were prepared to cooperate militarily with Britain in
exchange for recognition of Arab independence. The territory they sought
would be bounded on the north by Mersina and Adana and then the 37th
degree of latitude. The eastern boundary was the Persian frontier as far as the
Gulf of Basra; on the south, the Indian Ocean, excluding Aden; on the west, the
Red Sea and the Mediterranean back to Mersina.

McMahon's reply on 30 August 1915 was in very general terms and altogether was remarkably unresponsive. It does not do much more than say that
Britain was in favour of Arab independence and an Arab caliphate. 'We declare
once more that His Majesty's Government will welcome the resumption of the
Caliphate by an Arab of true race. With regard to the questions of limits, frontiers and boundaries, it would appear to be premature to consume our time by
discussing such details in the heat of war . . .'[26] But Hussein pressed on. He
highlighted an issue which was later to cause problems between France and
Britain. Hussein said that the occupation by France of 'the thoroughly Arabian
districts of Aleppo, Hama, Homs and Damascus would be opposed by force of
arms by the Arabs'.[27]

McMahon's responses tended to be evasive and necessarily appear weak.
Some general assurances were given, but he argued that a detailed discussion of
what the assurances meant or of the area of Arab independence was inappropriate at the present time, under the stresses of war. Antonius: his 'note makes

foolish reading, not only on account of its palpable insincerity but also because it tried to reconcile two irreconcilables: to win the Sharif over to an effective alliance and at the same time deny him the only means by which he could make that alliance effective.'[28] McMahon's note, written in English but translated, was decorated with 'a medley of Turko-Persian toadyisms . . ., flummery [which] served only to annoy Hussein, who showed his irritation in his reply'.

Hussein did indeed become very irritated by the guarded nature of McMahon's undertakings. In his letter of 9 September 1915, he told McMahon fairly peremptorily to cut out 'the highly-decorated phrases and titles and start being specific'. In a sentence which started warmly but ended very coldly he pointed to McMahon's lack of enthusiasm: 'With great cheerfulness and delight I received your letter, dated 19 Shawal, 1333 (30 August 1915), and have given it great consideration and regard, in spite of the impression I receive from it of ambiguity and its tone of coldness and hesitation with regard to our essential point.'[29]

After consultation with London, McMahon sent the pivotal letter of the whole correspondence to Hussein on 24 October 1915. He said that Mersina and Alexandretta and 'the parts of Syria lying to the west of the Vilayets of Damascus, Homs, Hama and Aleppo could not be looked upon as merely Arabian'. They were excluded from the territory under discussion. This exclusion was later to emerge as being critical, partly for its own sake, and partly because the word 'vilayet' was ambiguous, meaning both 'district' and 'province'. As will be seen, the distinction was of importance.

McMahon always insisted on the exclusion of this area to the west of the line Aleppo, Hama, Homs, ostensibly because the inhabitants were not truly Arab, but in reality because of France's interest in this part of Syria. Hussein never accepted the exclusion. The question was never resolved, any more than the question of whether Palestine was included.

As regards the vilayets of Baghdad and Basra: 'The Arabs will recognise that the established position and interests of Great Britain necessitate special measures of administrative control in order to secure these territories from foreign aggression, to promote the welfare of the local populations and to safeguard our mutual economic interests'.[30]

Britain also qualified the agreement by saying that it was made 'without prejudice to our existing treaties with the Arab Chiefs'. And Britain could only commit herself to the remaining territories in which she had 'a free hand, as far as she does not injure the interests of her ally, France'. But with these important reservations and modifications Britain was 'willing to recognise and support Arabian independence within the territories included in the limits and frontiers proposed by the Sharif of Mecca'.[31]

That was pretty much it. Hussein continued to claim the excluded territories, other than Mersina and Adana, but eventually said that he did not want to upset Britain's relationship with France and would leave it till after the war to renew his request for what France now occupied in Beirut and on the coast '(what we avert our eyes from today)'.

The exchange concluded with McMahon's note of 30 January 1916. The eight notes making up the McMahon Correspondence, spread over a period of many months, are vague and woolly.[32] The terms were so lacking in specification, the import so vague and the significance so debatable that in September 1919 Hussein had to ask to see a copy of the correspondence, which was duly sent to him by Curzon.[33]

The Political Intelligence Department of the Foreign Office later tried to clarify Britain's position by drafting a Memorandum on British Commitments to King Hussein to record exactly what had been promised. The team which produced the draft was a strange one. It consisted of Sir Reginald Wingate, Arnold Wilson and also the French Colonel Edouard Brémond. Brémond had been appointed head of the French Military Mission to the Hejaz in August 1916, created to stem any dilution of Sykes–Picot which might follow from the Arab Revolt. The purpose of the Mission was pretty overtly anti-British, and the British did not like Brémond. Lawrence was against him and by May 1917, Bertie, the British ambassador in Paris, was pressing for recall of his mission. Indeed, a month earlier even Picot was pressing for its recall: it had 'aroused all sorts of sensitivity' in the British, and he did not think much of Brémond.[34] It was odd to have a Frenchman involved in drafting such a sensitive document; having this particular one was a major attempt at solidarity. The final text of the Memorandum is not to be found in the Cabinet Office and the draft which exists is marked by heavy official annotations to indicate mistakes in fact and ambiguity in technical terms. The description of Lebanon as a vilayet has been amended to sanjak. The Memorandum emphasised that any commitments to Hussein were not embodied in a formal treaty, unlike commitments of sovereign states and even other independent Arab rulers such as Ibn Saud.

As well as the looseness of any commitments, the Memorandum stresses Britain's intention to do nothing to injure her relationship with France both during and after the war. It is stressed that Hussein had told Lawrence on 29 July 1917 that Beirut and Lebanon must in no circumstances be given to the French. 'They are Arab countries, but I will neither take them myself nor permit anyone else to take them. They have deserved independence and it is my duty to see they get it.' In the context of an analysis of the relationship of the commitments to 'British *Desiderata*' the unknown Foreign Office annotator decided to add in reference to Sir Mark Sykes the words 'never truthful!'

Hussein, while affecting to disdain personal ambition, purported to have no option but to speak for the Arabs: 'Had it not been for the determination which I see in the Arabs for the attainment of their objects, I would have preferred to seclude myself on one of the heights of a mountain – but they, the Arabs, have insisted that I should guide the movement to this end.' Later, Hogarth reports to Wingate that 'It is obvious that the King regards Arab unity as synonymous with his own kingship, and as a vain phrase unless so regarded . . .'

There was some back-pedalling on the question of a promise of the caliphate to Abdullah. On 31 October 1914, Kitchener had written to Abdullah, 'It may be that an Arab of true race will assume the Khalifate [*sic*] at Mecca or Medina, and so good may come by the help of God out of all the evil that is now occurring'. What the Memorandum refers to as 'any possible ambiguity' in Kitchener's message was, it was argued, clarified by the Foreign Office Telegram No. 173 of 14 April 1915, sent not to Abdullah, but to McMahon: 'His Majesty's Government consider that the question of Khalifate is one which must be decided by Mohammedans themselves without interference of non-Mohammedan powers. Should the former decide for an Arab Khalifate, that decision would therefore naturally be respected by His Majesty's Government, but the decision is one for Mohammedans to make.' It is not clear whether McMahon passed on the contents of that telegram to Abdullah and it is interesting that the Foreign Office considered that Kitchener's letter could have been construed as an undertaking. The Memorandum as a whole is an unsatisfactory *a posteriori* attempt to impose coherence on what it started by describing as vague and incoherent.[35]

Hussein had written his side of the Correspondence himself in a convoluted idiom which he had acquired in his time in Constantinople, 'when it was often safer for a man, if he had to speak his mind, to speak it unintelligently . . . [T]he result', said Antonius, 'was a mode of expression in which his native directness was enveloped in a tight network of parenthesis, incidentals, allusions, saws and apophthegms, woven together by a process of literary orchestration into a summary rigmarole'.[36]

On his side, McMahon was allowed a remarkably free hand by Grey, the Foreign Secretary. The contrast between the importance which the promises to Hussein later had and the inconsequential way in which they were made at the time is surprising and very important to remember. McMahon wrote a great deal of his letters without specific approval by London. Although drafts went back and forward to some extent, he was left a good deal of discretion. But it was clear that McMahon would take the blame if London did not like the way in which his discretion was exercised. He was pretty courageous in sending the letter of 24 October without final approval. What he had done was immediately criticised. Hardinge, the viceroy, thought that he had sold out. Giving up Baghdad, subject to a special administrative status, for instance, was unacceptable. Britain was abandoning far too much of her Mesopotamian victories and storing up problems for herself.

Hirtzel and Austen Chamberlain, Secretary of State for India, were at least equally unhappy. They thought that India had been sold short. In Chamberlain's view, Hussein was 'a nonentity without power to carry out his proposals'.[37]

Even Clayton emphasised the minor role which Hussein played in Mesopotamia.[38] Sir Arthur Nicholson, Permanent Under-Secretary at the Foreign Office, 'said from the first that an independent Arab State was an absurdity and was an impracticable proposal'. Later he said that he did not believe that the negotiations would 'ever fructify into anything really definite'.[39] Hirtzel minuted in 1916 that 'a strong Arab State might be more dangerous to Christendom than a strong Ottoman State, and Lord Kitchener's policy of destroying one Islamic State merely for the purpose of creating another has always seemed to me disastrous from the point of view no less of expediency than of civilisation. The justification of the policy of H.M.G. lies mainly in the fact that the Arabs have shown themselves incapable of creating or maintaining such a state . . .'[40]

7. What Did the Correspondence Achieve?

The Correspondence prompted, or at least encouraged, the Arab Revolt against the Ottomans. The revolt's military importance is questionable and will be considered later. It was at least useful from a propaganda point of view and avoided the alienation of Muslim opinion in India.

What had Britain paid for this propaganda? In particular, what had Hussein been promised? That question was to inject asperity into relations with the Arabs for generations. Harold Nicolson:

> These communications were shrouded in the ambiguity inseparable from all oriental correspondence, yet the impression left on the mind of King Hussein was that Great Britain had assured him support in the foundation of a united Arab empire with its capital at Damascus. It is true that in the course of correspondence the British government (who were bound by an understanding with France dating from 1912 to 'disinterest themselves' in Syria) had made some vague reservation about Damascus. This reservation, however, had not been studiously precise, and it is significant that the subsequent Sykes-Picot Agreement was not communicated by us to the Arabs, even as our pledges to King Hussein were not, until March of 1919, disclosed to the French.[41]

The official but confidential summary of the correspondence which was circulated at a senior level in Britain said that the British government had indicated that it was ready to promote independence in Arabic-speaking Asia, but had not committed itself to forms of government or precise boundaries.[42] McMahon had been carefully vague, for the precise reason that while Hussein had to be conciliated, France also had to be considered. Moreover, as Wyndham Deedes pointed out in 1916, there were three groups of Arabs all with irreconcilable wishes, and while one of those groups, led by Hussein, wanted an Arab kingdom, many other Arabs wanted no such thing.[43]

But the real importance of the Correspondence was in its later significance. During the war, many Arabs viewed it as a treaty which bound Britain to secure their independence. When Britain made no effort after the war to work for that independence, when indeed it was revealed that at the same time as making promises to Hussein, Britain was entering into undertakings with the Jews and with the French which were quite at odds with what these promises seemed to mean, Arab opinion concluded that Britain acted throughout in bad faith. The lesson that the Arab world took – and still takes – supports the view that the West is not to be trusted and foments the notions of conspiracy – Zionist or otherwise – that bedevil attempts to find rational common ground in the Middle East. The damage that the McMahon–Hussein Correspondence did is difficult to exaggerate, while the benefits it brought Britain are nebulous.

8. What About Palestine?

One of the problems about the Correspondence was that it contained no specific mention of Palestine. McMahon accepted, subject to reservations, frontiers proposed by Hussein. For the Arabs, since Palestine was not mentioned, it followed that Palestine must have been included. For Britain, that was not the case, and that was why Britain considered herself entirely at liberty to promise Palestine to Zionist Jews, as was done in the Balfour Declaration of 1917, a historic document of immense significance which will be separately dealt with later.

Palestine consisted of the Sanjak of Jerusalem, with part of the Vilayet of Beirut. McMahon did not mention the Sanjak of Jerusalem, but Britain argued that Palestine was clearly excluded by implication, because McMahon told Hussein that 'portions of Syria lying to the west of the districts of Damascus, Homs, Hama and Aleppo' were excluded from the independent area. In 1922, Churchill adopted this argument, saying that the word 'districts' in the phrase meant vilayets and that since the Vilayet of Damascus included the part of Syria to the east of the River Jordan which became Transjordan, it followed that the

part of Syria to the west of the Jordan which became Palestine was similarly one
of the territories reserved by McMahon.

In an attempt to clarify the issues, Commander David Hogarth, the head of
the Arab Bureau, delivered a letter from Sykes to Hussein in January 1918. The
Hogarth Message, as it became known, made a commitment, but scarcely a
full-blooded one, to work for Arab independence: 'The Entente Powers are
determined that the Arab race shall be given full opportunity of once again
forming a nation in the world. This can only be achieved by the Arabs themselves uniting, and Great Britain and her Allies will pursue a policy with this
ultimate unity in view'.[44] Whether the Hogarth Message modified McMahon–
Hussein or the Balfour Declaration is far from clear, but it looks like a warning
to Hussein that he should not read too much into the Correspondence, as the
Arabs were always inclined to do.[45]

The trouble is that although a lot of care was taken over the wording of
McMahon's notes, they were not a formal legal document. They were not
intended, as the Arabs subsequently tended to believe, as a treaty. They were a
fairly broad indication of policy, given in good faith. When they were later
subjected to detailed analysis, they could be read in different ways. For instance,
Curzon, as chairman of the Eastern, formerly Middle Eastern, Committee of the
Cabinet, said on 5 December 1918:

> The Palestine position is this. If we deal with our commitments, there is first
> the general pledge to Hussein in October 1915, under which Palestine was
> included in the areas as to which Great Britain pledged itself that they should
> be Arab and independent in the future . . . Great Britain and France – Italy
> subsequently agreeing – committed themselves to an international adminis-
> tration of Palestine in consultation with Russia, who was an ally at that
> time . . . A new feature was brought into the case in November 1917 when
> Mr Balfour, with the authority of the War Cabinet, issued his famous decla-
> ration to the Zionists that Palestine 'should be the national home of the
> Jewish people, but that nothing should be done' – and this of course was a
> most important proviso – 'to prejudice the civil and religious rights of the
> existing non-Jewish communities in Palestine'. Those, as far as I know, are
> the only actual engagements into which we entered with regard to Palestine.[46]

The Arabs argued that since Palestine was not excluded explicitly from the
boundaries of what Hussein was to get, and since international law construes
treaty obligations strictly, it must have been included. But the Correspondence
was never meant to be construed as a treaty. Secondly, they argued, Palestine lay
to the south of the line Damascus/Homs/Hama/Aleppo, and therefore was not

excluded. Palestine does, however, lie to the west of a line through these districts and projected southwards (there being no more towns for the line to go through). They also argued that there was no Vilayet, in the sense of province, of Damascus; that the Sanjak, or district, of Damascus comprehended just the city; and that Palestine actually lay in the Vilayet of Syria A-Sham, which was not excluded.[47]

Britain has always fairly frankly said that it was difficult to reconcile all the differing statements that were made during and after the war. Grey, who had been Foreign Secretary when McMahon wrote his Notes, said so in the House of Lords on 27 March 1923 and argued for publishing the lot. A Parliamentary committee in 1939 said much the same: all the various texts had to be studied.

Though it was questioned by Grey, who had had at least nominal responsibility for what McMahon pledged on his behalf, the British position is set out definitively in the *locus classicus*, Churchill's White Paper of 1922:

[I]t is not the case, as has been represented by the Arab Delegation, that during the war His Majesty's Government gave an undertaking that an independent [Arab] national government should at once be established in Palestine. This representation mainly rests upon a letter dated the 24th October, 1915, from Sir Henry McMahon, then His Majesty's High Commissioner in Egypt, to the Sharif of Mecca, now King Hussein of the Kingdom of the Hejaz. That letter is quoted as conveying the promise to the Sharif of Mecca to recognise and support the independence of the Arabs within the territories proposed by him. But this promise was given subject to a reservation made in the same letter, which excluded from its scope, among other territories, the portions of Syria lying to the west of the District of Damascus. This reservation has always been regarded by His Majesty's Government as covering the vilayet of Beirut and the independent sanjak of Jerusalem. The whole of Palestine west of the Jordan was thus excluded from Sir Henry McMahon's pledge.[48]

Britain consistently argued, right from the time the Correspondence was concluded, that Palestine was intended to be part of the excluded area. That was Britain's position before the Balfour Declaration. It was not adopted as a result of the declaration. In 1922 McMahon wrote,

It was my intention to exclude Palestine from independent Arabia, and I hoped that I had so worded the letter as to make this sufficiently clear for all practical purposes. My reasons for restricting myself to specific mention of

Damascus, Hama, Homs and Aleppo in that connection in my letter were:
(1) that these were places to which the Arabs attached vital importance and
(2) that there was no place I could think of at the time of sufficient importance for purposes of definition further south of the above. It was as fully my
intention to exclude Palestine as it was to exclude all the more northern
coastal tracts of Syria.[49]

That statement seems to me very clear and convincing. The Arab response is
simply to say that what McMahon thought is not important; what he said
is what matters.

In negotiations with the Arabs regarding Palestine, the British were repeatedly referred to the promises that had been made to Hussein. As late as 1939,
the government was still having to try to explain what had been meant and
why the Balfour Declaration was not a breach of faith.

A conference was held in London in that year to consider an important
White Paper on Palestine which we shall look at later. At the sixth meeting of
the Arab and UK delegations to the conference on 15 February 1939 it was
agreed to set up a committee of Arab and British dignitaries. Its remit was 'to
consider certain Correspondence between Sir Henry McMahon and the Sharif of
Mecca in 1915 and 1916'. It reported on 16 March 1939. It will come as no
surprise that the committee did not identify a scintilla of agreement. Its report
does, however, set out the respective positions helpfully and succinctly.

The Arab case in 1939 was that Palestine had not been reserved from the
areas allocated to Hussein. On the contrary, it was quite intentionally included,
in order that the French claim to Palestine could be denied.

The British response was, first, that the exclusion of Palestine was very much
in contemplation because of its special position for the three religions. Secondly,
the phrase 'portions of Syria lying to the west of the districts of Damascus,
Homs, Hama and Aleppo' included part of southern Syria that consisted of
portions of the former Vilayet of Beirut and the former Sanjak of Jerusalem,
now Palestine. Thirdly, in any event, the reservation applied to all territory that
France claimed, and France of course claimed Palestine. Additionally, although
it was recognised that this was not a factor in a legal construction of the correspondence, it was pointed out that McMahon, and Clayton who had also been
involved in drafting the letters, had subsequently specifically confirmed that it
had been the intention that Palestine be excluded. In 1937 McMahon wrote, 'I
feel it my duty to state, and I do so definitely and emphatically, that it was not
intended by me in giving the pledge to King Hussein to include Palestine in
the area in which Arab independence was promised.' Sir Gilbert Clayton said,
'I was in touch daily with Sir H. McMahon throughout the negotiations with

King Hussein, and made the preliminary drafts of all the letters. I can bear out the statement that it was never the intention that Palestine should be included in the general pledge given to the Sharif; the introductory words of Sir Henry's letter were thought at that time – perhaps erroneously – clearly to cover the point. It was, I think, obvious that the peculiar interests involved in Palestine precluded any definite pledges in regard to its future at so early a stage'.[50]

9. The Immediate Reaction

From an Arab perspective the criticisms are entirely understandable. Within Britain, objections inevitably came principally from those with a particular interest, who were not required to keep the larger picture in mind. But British statesmen who had experience of the wartime period were never greatly embarrassed by what had happened. Bonar Law said in the House of Commons, 'It is true that, in October 1915, the British government declared that they were prepared to recognise and support the independence of the Arabs within those portions of the territories claimed by the Emir Faisal [Hussein's son] in which Great Britain was free to act, but it was added, "without detriment to the interests of her ally, France . . ."'[51]

The proviso that Britain could only give assurances where she could 'act without detriment to the interests of her ally, France' lacked specificity. That is not surprising. McMahon confessed to Grey on 26 October 1915 that he had been trying to provide for commitments to France which he did not know about.[52]

Hogarth certainly thought that nothing very specific had been said. He thought that few believed that Hussein was 'the spokesman of one united Arab nation about to rise from the ashes of the war. . . . [N]either to him or to any other Arab did we ever explicitly guarantee or even promise anything but liberation from the Turk. We are guiltless, therefore of any betrayal of King Hussein. The sole condition of his action – that he be freed from his Ottoman overlords and recognised as an independent sovereign – has been fulfilled'.[53]

Similarly, Churchill told the House of Commons that no promises had been broken by the retention of Palestine from the Arab territories: 'No pledges were made to the Palestine Arabs in 1915 . . . It was stipulated that the undertaking applied only to those portions of the territories concerned in which Great Britain was free to act without detriment to the interests of her Allies. His Majesty's Governments have always regarded and continue to regard Palestine as excluded by these provisos from the scope of their undertaking'.[54]

Equally, in a brief immediately post-war period, some French statesmen took a realistic view about the desperate and *ad hoc* measure of a nation fighting with its back to the wall. A generous and realistic response was not, however, typical of the general view in France.

Lawrence's perspective was purely Arabian: 'The Arab Revolt had begun on false pretences. To gain the Sharif's help our Cabinet had offered, through Sir Henry MacMahon [*sic*], to support the establishment of native governments in parts of Syria and Mesopotamia, "saving the interests of our ally, France". The last modest clause concealed a treaty (kept secret, till too late, from MacMahon, and therefore from the Sharif) by which France, England and Russia agreed to annex some of these promised areas and to establish their respective spheres of influence over all the rest'.[55]

Lawrence's position is interesting. In *Seven Pillars of Wisdom*, he claimed that he had not known much about the McMahon correspondence or Sykes–Picot; but 'not being a perfect fool I could see that if we won the war the promises to the Arabs were dead paper'.[56] He squared his conscience by resolving to 'make the Arab Revolt the engine of its own success, as well as hand-maid to our Egyptian campaign; and vowed to lead it so madly in the final victory that expediency should counsel to the Powers a fair settlement of the Arabs' moral claims'.

10. Reality

The first revelation of the details of the Correspondence to the public at large was in an appendix to Antonius's *The Arab Awakening* in 1938. He announced that in the Correspondence Britain had promised Hussein an independent state consisting of all of Arabia, including even Palestine. He argued that on the basis of this promise Hussein embarked on the Arab rising and, secondly, that the rising itself was of crucial importance to Britain's war effort in the Middle East.

The official British narrative was also challenged by Elie Kedourie, the distinguished British historian of the Middle East. Kedourie resisted the British downplaying of the Correspondence's significance. He alleges that Storrs told Abdullah that he had been working for a decade on a way of enhancing the British role in Arabia. Kedourie maintains that Storrs promised more than Kitchener had authorised him to do. By April 1915 the Arabs were promised that 'the Arabian Peninsula and its Mahommedan Holy Places should remain independent. We shall not annex one foot of land on it, nor suffer any power to do so'.[57]

It is scarcely surprising that when she contemplated defeat in the field and starvation at home, Britain's primary interest was not in a beautiful intellectual consistency in her foreign policy. It is perfectly true that just as Britain was saying different things to Hussein and to the French, she was saying different things to Hussein and Ibn Saud.

In later days of peace, the inconsistencies and conflicts needed some explaining, and the Memorandum of the Political Intelligence Department of the Foreign Office, referred to above, was an attempt to do so in January 1922. The document has been described as 'an official explanation, decidedly apologetic in tone.'[58] There had been an unbridgeable gap between the ideal and the practicable. 'To reach a settlement acceptable to all the Allied States and peoples concerned, and which should yet attain ideal solutions or even any large measure of such solutions, was beyond the possibility of attainment'.

What had been agreed, in spite of grave and inevitable defects, did keep the Allies together. The incompatibilities were depicted as perfidious and cynical manoeuvres. It is really truer to regard them as extemporised and desperate throws founded on muddle and confusion. Practical requirements separated the ideal from the possible, settlements acceptable to all the Allies were unobtainable, what had been done 'in despite of grave and inevitable defects carried the Allies over a difficult period'.[59]

McMahon–Hussein was all about the Arab Revolt. What was the Arab Revolt? How much did it matter?

8

The Arab Revolt

1. ARBUR

The prospect of an Arab revolt excited the enthusiasts who composed ARBUR, the Arab Bureau: the revolt was indeed their brainchild. In story and in David Lean's magnificent film *Lawrence of Arabia*, the idea of stirring up the Arabs, particularly the Bedouins, to revolt against the Turks was Lawrence's. That was not the case. There were others who were even keener on the idea. The less stable members of ARBUR got very excited about the prospect.

A number of highly individual characters are separately credited with establishing the Bureau. The truth is that these people, widely disparate in many ways, spontaneously coalesced, drawn together by the one thing they shared: a romantic obsession with Arabia. Sykes had an important role. Meeting such a lack of coherence among official views in the different agencies which he encountered in the course of his six months in the east after the de Bunsen Committee had reported, he came to favour the establishment of a single office with specific responsibility for Arab affairs. Clayton was enthusiastic. He started to assemble the nucleus of an office and encouraged Sykes to urge the project on London. Hardinge, on the other hand, was very much against the idea of any office that would interfere with his Indian jurisdiction, and if Sykes were involved in it then it was particularly unwelcome.

India did not like Sykes, and Sykes did not like the way India was trying to run the Middle East. In evidence which he gave to the War Cabinet in July 1916 he said that India was not working wholeheartedly with Cairo and was insensitive in her handling of the Arabs. He was also concerned that Arab loyalties were divided by the fact that there were two policymakers operating in the region. He argued that Sir Percy Cox, at this time chief political officer with the Indian Expeditionary Force, should be under the direct control of the Foreign Office and not of the India Office.

Cox, of whom more anon, was not in fact committed to applying Indian methods and installing the machinery of government that worked in India (and could be justified because it worked well there). He and, for instance, Gertrude Bell could see that a less paternalistic approach was required in the Arab world. Lawrence approved.

An interdepartmental conference was set up in January 1916 to consider an Islamic Bureau, which the Secretary of State for India, Austen Chamberlain, wanted. The conference agreed on an Arab Bureau – but not as a separate body, simply a section of the Cairo Intelligence Department. The Foreign Office and the War Office did not want to lose any degree of control. Sykes gained only the form of what he wanted; policy continued to be dispersed.

McMahon was in favour of the idea. The vagueness of his correspondence with Hussein had not mattered a great deal until the Arab Revolt was in discussion. Now he and others came to the conclusion that there had to be more formality in the elaboration of policy otherwise conflicts would arise through the operations of freelance individualists. He promoted the idea of the Bureau, probably run by Sykes, despite India's opposition to the idea and to the man. Eventually Hardinge was reassured: Sykes would *not* be in charge, and India would be represented by a senior officer.

ARBUR was established in 1916. Gilbert Clayton, as Director of Intelligence, was nominally in charge. In practice, it was run by David Hogarth. Hogarth was a brilliant scholar, author, traveller and archaeologist, a former Director of the British School in Athens and Keeper of the Ashmolean Museum in Oxford. Since the outbreak of the war he had been in the Geographical Division of Naval Intelligence (he was given the rank of lieutenant commander) under Clayton. Now 'Blinker' Hall, the Director of the Intelligence Division in London, renowned for his ill-fitting false teeth, as well as the bushy eyebrows through which he blinked, decided to develop intelligence operations through ARBUR, at the same time as Arab affairs were gently moved to Cairo from the India Office, which was felt not to have distinguished itself over the defeat at Kut, which will be described at its proper place in the narrative.

Once established, ARBUR speedily assumed an independent *persona*. Hogarth could say 'Well – in a sense I *am* the Arab Bureau'. And this at a point when he had no official standing at the Bureau. In 1918 the Treasury found that the Bureau, with a budget of £3,000 a year, had been spending £14,000. It was pretty well autonomous. 'Unlike any other intelligence staff, the Bureau members devised their own campaign plan, chose their own chiefs, established and pursued their own objectives, and shaped policy at Whitehall'.[1]

Hogarth made his way to Cairo via Athens, where he met Compton Mackenzie in that den of spies. In Cairo he found among others Lawrence and a great friend of his sister, Janet: Gertrude Bell. She had been personally briefed in London by Blinker Hall. The Bureau operated from three rooms in the Savoy

Hotel in Cairo at a cost of £4,000 per annum. In a touch typical of the times, Hogarth personally paid for its important Middle Eastern library. The team stayed next door to the Savoy, in the Grand Continental.

The Bureau's responsibility was for developing British-Egyptian (as opposed to British-Indian) policies for Arabia, and to this end it produced a number of influential reports. Hogarth worked closely with Clayton and shared the views of Wingate: he was in favour of an Arabia controlled by Egypt and not from India. He differed on occasions from Sykes: when Sykes and Picot went to meet Hussein in May 1917, Hogarth travelled to London to urge that the revolt should not be sabotaged by concessions to France which would undermine Arab ambitions. The revolt was indeed his baby: in June 1916, Hogarth went on HMS *Dufferin* along with Storrs and Kinahan Cornwallis, an Egyptian civil servant who joined Clayton's staff and who succeeded Hogarth as Director of ARBUR, to deliver £10,000 of gold bullion to Hussein. Delivery of the money detonated the revolt.

Hogarth was, then, the *de facto* director of the Bureau. Among those involved with ARBUR were Aubrey Herbert MP and T.E. Lawrence, who came to be quite out of sympathy with British military methods in Mesopotamia. Cox retained the responsibility for central Arabia and the Gulf. He and Lawrence could not understand each other and had to clarify their meaning through telegrams.

Relations between the Bureau and Delhi remained difficult. Lord Chelmsford replaced Hardinge as viceroy in the spring of 1916 and complained that the Bureau was making policy rather than leaving final decisions to London. Worse, Hardinge had now become Permanent Under-Secretary in the Foreign Office (the position he had held before he became viceroy) and thus India had powerful spokesmen both in Delhi and in London.

The Bureau published a newsletter known initially as *Arab Bureau Summaries* and then as *The Arab Bulletin*, which appeared sporadically from June 1916 until the end of 1918. The first editor was Lawrence. Hogarth then took over for three months, and subsequently the editor was Kinahan Cornwallis.

The Bureau became the haven for a strange mixture of career administrators and irregulars. Kinahan Cornwallis came from the Sudan government. G.S. Symes had been Wingate's secretary in the Sudan. Lawrence came aboard along with Aubrey Herbert MP and George Lloyd MP, two of a triumvirate completed by Sykes. Wyndham Deedes came in as Depute Head of the Egyptian Intelligence with a useful Turkish background in the Ottoman Gendarmerie.

Aubrey Herbert is said to have been the model for John Buchan's Greenmantle. He was also asked by the Albanians to be their king after the war. The Albanians went about finding a king in the same way as the elephants chose Babar. He was not the only man who is thought to have been the model for Greenmantle, and he is not the only man that the Albanians asked to be their king. He is, however, the only man who achieved the double distinction. He was cultured and intelligent. He spoke French, Italian, German, Turkish, Arabic, Greek and Albanian, the last an important qualification for potential kings of Albania. When he was appointed to a job in Naval Intelligence in 1916, the Admiralty comment was that only a very immoral man would know so many languages.[2]

He joined the Irish Guards at the outbreak of war. He was almost blind and would not have passed a medical examination, so he simply bought a second lieutenant's uniform and fell in as the Guards embarked for France. After the war he returned to Oxford (where, despite his blindness, he had been an intrepid roof-climber as an undergraduate) for a Gaudy, a feast at his old College, Balliol. There he accepted the advice of his old tutor, A.D. Lindsay, now Master, that he should have all his teeth taken out, as this was the cure for blindness. He developed blood poisoning and died at the age of 43. Academic philosophers should not give medical advice.

ARBUR's nominal director, Colonel Clayton, was balanced and thoughtful. Not all the others were. Aubrey Herbert, for example, was picaresque and unconstrained in his enthusiasms. Before the war he had advocated the annexation of the whole Gulf by Britain. So when Herbert came out to Egypt in 1915, he was welcomed by Sykes who was already seized with enthusiasm for the plans which Kitchener and FitzGerald had formulated for setting the desert alight.

Sykes greeted Herbert in a very interesting letter, which foreshadowed Lawrence's exploits: 'Now the important people whom we should get over on our side are the Beni Sadir – they are desert Badawin [*sic*] and hate the Turks in their souls . . . [W]e should establish a base at Akaba and an intelligence officer there with large powers . . . then try and establish relations with the Druses of the Hauran. Get some of their people down to Akaba . . . [I]f possible keep the whole of the Hejaz railway in a ferment and destroy bridges'.[3]

Sykes and Aubrey Herbert were always close. They were both always linked, too, to George Lloyd, a convinced imperialist later to play an important part in colonial administration and in the debate about Empire: they were collectively nicknamed 'The Three Musketeers'. All three were at the British Embassy in Constantinople in 1906, where they were honorary attachés. They all became Conservative Members of Parliament. They were all at the Arab Bureau in Cairo during the war, although their Dumas identity was acquired despite the fact that they were not truly all for one and one for all. Lloyd was stiff and pompous. Sykes and Herbert were certainly not. When Sykes wrote to Aubrey, addressing him as 'Dear Pompey' and ending 'love, Caesar', he made a point of referring to Lloyd as 'Crassus'.[4]

The links among these young Arabists were close. Very soon after receiving that letter, Herbert met Lawrence. That first meeting was not propitious. Herbert noted in his diary: 'Lawrence, an odd gnome, half cad – with a touch of genius'. Lawrence wrote home, 'Then there is Aubrey Herbert, who is a joke, but a very nice one: he is too shortsighted to read or recognise anyone'.[5] They got over these initial reactions. Lawrence and Herbert, enthusiasts for Arab liberty, came to reject the *realpolitik* which dictated that Sykes would accept France's interest in Syria. Later in the war, when Herbert heard about Sykes's agreement with the French in the Sykes–Picot Agreement, which will shortly be examined, he wrote, 'I am afraid that swine Monsieur P[icot] has let M[ark] S[ykes] badly down . . . it is an awful pity both for the thing itself, and for M. and also because it is one up to the old early Victorians who are in a position to say, "We told you so. This is what comes of disregarding the ABC of Diplomacy, and letting Amateurs have a shy at delicate and important negotiations".'[6]

As usual there was not only a lack of consistency among the British policy-makers, but a degree of hostility among them. London and Cairo felt that the India Office people were unhelpful about what they and Hussein were trying to do. Equally, the India Office was alarmed by the degree of independence allowed to the free spirits in Cairo – Hogarth, Storrs and Clayton and Lawrence, all individualists, and drawn together from different backgrounds. The Arabs noticed the confusion. When 'The British Government' was mentioned to Hussein, he replied, 'I see five governments'. Ibn Saud, unhappy about the favoured treatment Hussein was receiving, told Cox that 'although you yourself probably appreciate my fears', he was afraid that the British Government did not understand his concerns.[7]

Not truly within ARBUR, but closely associated with its members, is Gertrude Bell: in some ways the most attractive and fascinating of all the Arabists of the period.

2. Gertrude Bell

Gertrude Bell, 'The Diana of the Desert', is one of the great English personalities who were captivated and captured by the Middle East. She was as tough as she could be romantic. She moulded many lasting institutions in modern Iraq, and she could bend formidable figures to her will. She was very intelligent indeed, and she had a fierce temper. She was of the élite, but she was endearing. She was an emotional woman. In that lay her charm, but it was a weakness as well, and it led to frequent flaws in her judgement.

Aubrey Herbert met Gertrude Bell in Japan in 1903. They took to each other. 'Aubrey Herbert came to tea with us – he is a delightful creature' she said. Herbert told his mother, 'She is really a rather wonderful person, gives you information quicker than you can digest'.[8]

Hardinge, the Indian viceroy, was one of her many influential friends. He recommended her to Percy Cox, whom she came to idolise, with unintentional condescension: 'She is a remarkably clever woman with the brains of a man'.[9] Cox was the most important administrator of British Iraq. We shall meet him again.

She first met Cox in India early in 1903. She had come to India shortly after a celebrated display of courage and endurance on the mountains of Switzerland. It was not her first climbing expedition: she had climbed the Engelhorn in a previous year. On this occasion she was involved in a dramatic and difficult technical climb in appalling conditions, in the course of which her eyesight was affected by lightning. She and the guides found themselves marooned on an isolated arête from four o'clock one morning until eight in the evening. The following night was spent on a glacier, and an expedition that began at 1 a.m. on 31 July 1902 did not end till she hobbled into her hotel at 10 a.m. on 3 August, frostbitten and with swollen toes. Her guide later said that without her courage and determination the whole climb would have died. He said that he had known no amateur climber, man or woman, who equalled her 'coolness, bravery and judgement'.[10]

These mountaineering expeditions were complemented by six long, arduous treks through the desert, which left her with a knowledge of geography and topography of the Middle East which few Westerners could match. She saw her role as a critical one. She was well aware of the fact that little was known in London about Mesopotamia and those who lived there: 'frankly, who knows if I don't?' She attempted to list every one of the Euphrates tribes with details of their characteristics and their achievements. She produced much detailed research, including a collection of essays, *The Arab of Mesopotamia*, 'as good a plea as I can make for the Arab race'. Her intention was that governance should be based on knowledge. It was 'the making of a new world . . . I want people to listen'.[11]

In appearance she was striking, red-haired, green-eyed, very straight. She had a full mouth, and in photographs her lips are often parted, giving her a slightly breathless appearance. She was an early woman student at Oxford and the first woman to gain a First in Modern History, a special sort of double First.

Her amateur travelling and exploring gradually mutated into government employment. In 1915 she was sent to Cairo Military Intelligence (soon to be the Arab Bureau) as a staff officer, and she operated as a spy behind enemy lines during the war. In Cairo she found herself part of a collegiate team, among them many whom she had met in her travels. Her relationship with other members of the team, with one or two exceptions, was remarkably good considering the fact that her sex put her in a tiny minority. Although she was undoubtedly attractive, what tended to impress those whom she met, whether among her Western colleagues or Bedouin chieftains, was her force of personality and intelligence. She neither downplayed nor exaggerated her femininity. She was always well and memorably dressed in long skirts and flowery hats. An interviewer in the *New York Times* referred to her 'Paris frock, Mayfair manners'.[12]

She took a great interest in the clothes that she had sent out from England. 'I had a vision of some nice trailing muslin gowns with floating sleeves' she wrote from Baghdad in May 1917.[13] In June 1924 she asked her stepmother to send a new bathing costume: 'The kind I like is in two pieces, drawers and jumper, and I like it black with a coloured border of some sort round all the edges. I prefer silk tricotine to silk and I like best a square or v-shaped opening at the neck . . . Bathing clothes are so exiguous that I think it might be sent by letter post . . .'[14]

She was no sun-dried administrator. If she had a fault it was that her enthusiasms could lead her to extravagances in her views. She died in her sleep on 12 July 1926, aged just 57, probably as a result of an overdose of sleeping pills, possibly intentionally administered. When the High Commissioner for Iraq announced her death, the official notification ended with these two sentences: 'Her bones rest where she had wanted them to rest, in the soil of Iraq. Her friends are left desolate.'[15] Even today Iraqis who are far too young ever to have known her, still speak with awe of 'Miss Bell'.

There are rumours of affairs with Arabs, but they are probably unfounded. She had an early fiancé, who did not have the means to marry her. While he was trying to acquire these means, he fell in a river and died of pneumonia. Later she had an unconsummated affair with a married man, Dick Doughty-Wylie. Doughty-Wylie had been a military vice consul in Turkey. In the tradition of Arabian intersections, he was a nephew of Charles Doughty, the author of *Arabia Deserta*. He was a brave and vigorous soldier-diplomat who died of a bullet in the head at Gallipoli. He was awarded a posthumous VC. Such was the intensity of the affair that it is difficult to think that it would not have changed the direction of Bell's life if he had survived. Her villa beside the Tigris was known as 'Chastity Chase'.

Given her later support for Arab nationalism, and for the mixture that became Iraq, it is interesting that in 1907 she wrote, 'of what value are the Pan-Arab associations and inflammatory leaflets that they issue from foreign presses? The answer is easy: they are worth nothing at all. There is no nation of

Arabs; the Syrian merchant is separated by a wider gulf from the Bedouin than he is from the Osmanli, the Syrian country is inhabited by Arabic speaking races all eager to be at each other's throats, and only prevented from fulfilling their national desires by the ragged half-fed soldier who draws at rare intervals the Sultan's pay.' Eight years later she said more simply, 'The Arabs can't govern themselves' and in 1918 of Iraq, 'They can't conceive an independent Arab government. Nor, I confess, can I. There is no one here who could run it'.

3. The Revolt

British policy towards the Arabs had two objectives. The first was negative, to detach the Arabs from the Turks in order to reduce the risk of a liaison between the Muslims of the British Empire and the Muslims of the Ottoman Empire. The second objective was positive, to enlist Arab military support against Britain's enemies.[16]

The first objective was secured. How important it was is very doubtful indeed. Despite the sultan's declaration of *jihad*, there never was the Muslim unrest in the Empire that had been the subject of so much pre-war anxiety, nor did anyone make any very strenuous efforts to stir it up.

The second objective came to nothing. There was an Arab Revolt, but it was of no military consequence, and the best that can be said for it is that since some Arabs, largely Bedouin, participated in it, there was at least no great Arab resentment about British operations in Mesopotamia.

The revolt began on 10 June 1916, with a proclamation from Hussein which portrayed the CUP as betrayers of Islam and the caliph as their prisoner. Hussein's ambitions were personal, and not Arab, and the rising was not a truly Arab rising. It was largely supported by the Hashemites themselves and not widely by other Arabs.

'[T]he Arab Revolt was in essence an Anglo-Hashemite plot'.[17] That much is certain: whether it was an Arab Nationalist movement or an Islamic one is more obscure, and the sparse support that Hussein's proclamation received justifies doubts about whether it can be called a revolt at all. Only the Bedouins of the Hejaz took to the field in any numbers. They captured Mecca, Taif and Jeddah, but thereafter the forces of three of Hussein's four sons were tied down in investing Medina, and only Faisal's contingent took part in the British advance in Palestine and Syria. While Hussein grandiloquently styled himself 'King of the Arab Countries', Britain only recognised him as king of the Hejaz – and even that only after some delay.

Hussein was 55 by the time he became Sharif of Mecca in 1908. He was conservative by disposition, and there is no suggestion that he had any interest in the idea of Arab nationalism before the First World War.[18] His second son, Abdullah, was more interested in fomenting the revolt in the desert than his third son, Faisal, even though Faisal was physically more involved with the war against the Turks and is more associated with it in popular memory.

At home, the nebulous idea of a rising had very little support. Even when it was underway, the government had its doubts. When Sykes left London to go to the Middle East as Head of the Political Mission to the commander-in-chief of the Egyptian Expeditionary Force on 3 April 1917, he had a meeting at 10 Downing Street with Lloyd George, Curzon and Hankey. Sykes suggested that he should try to stir up tribal unrest when he was in the Middle East, but it is interesting that the overwhelming advice he was given was to do nothing that could jeopardise relations with France or prejudice a British-inspired Zionist movement. The conference notes recorded that 'The Prime Minister laid stress on the importance, if possible, of securing the addition of Palestine to the British area in the post-war Middle East'. Sykes was not to make pledges to the Arabs 'and particularly none in regard to Palestine'.[19]

Despite this discouragement, Sykes believed that an Arab rising could be fomented. But even he did not expect much of Hussein unless he received substantial British aid. Further, Cairo needed the support of the viceroy if the Arab Revolt were to go ahead. It would be India that would provide troops and money. Hardinge was known to be lukewarm. Gertrude Bell happened to be in India at the same time. She had known Hardinge since she was little more than a girl and her chief in Cairo, Gilbert Clayton, encouraged her to call on the viceroy and do what she could to win his support.

Hardinge did not immediately veto the proposal, but very soon afterwards he declared his opposition. It was a 'displeasing surprise'. The Muslims in India would see it as interference with the Islamic religion.[20] When news of the revolt reached India there was a reaction, and Hardinge's misgivings are very understandable. There were no fewer than 70 million Indian Muslims, which made the whole issue of Britain's hostile relations with Turkey immensely delicate. For example, although Indians fighting for Britain secured the fall of Baghdad, the news of the fall was downplayed hugely in the subcontinent, in case Muslim susceptibilities were disturbed. Local celebrations of the victory were permitted, but only after consultation with Delhi.

There continued to be significant censorship in handling the news of the revolt. Muslims were concerned about the holy places, and on 26 June 1916 the Council of the All-Indian Muslim League recorded its 'abhorrence' of what the Muslim rebels were doing. A.H. Grant of the Indian Foreign Department was aware of the significance of the revolt from the point of view of government policy, but could not help hoping all the same that it might 'quietly fizzle out'.[21]

At a military level, when the revolt appeared to deliver disappointing results, the Indian government, and indeed even the Arab Bureau, was very reluctant to reinforce it. The main supporters of reinforcement were Wingate and Chamberlain, and the main source of reinforcements were Arab prisoners held in India. Sykes was of course enthusiastic. He envisaged an Arab League of 10,000 men and sought to inspire them with a telegram: 'Oh Arabs, be wise, be disciplined, be calm, be steadfast . . . [L]ook neither to the right nor the left, beware of speculations and intrigues, beware of suspicions . . . [T]hese words I send you from a distance; would that I could speak them in your ears'.[22] Sykes's Ten Thousand never played a substantial part in the revolt.

Hussein benefited greatly from British naval control of the coastline, but despite it he made little progress. Sir Archibald Murray, in command of the British Army in Egypt, could not spare any troops beyond the Arab prisoners of war from the Mesopotamian Front. It was France, when she saw the revolt threatening to collapse, which sent a small mission of 42 officers and 983 men. This embarrassed Britain into responding with some further officers.

Even then the revolt made no real progress. A British Expeditionary Force from Egypt arrived on the scene in 1917. The spur was Lloyd George. He was all for reducing the concessions to France which Sykes–Picot had made, and conquests by Britain in the east would provide a justification for that. 'Once we are in military possession it will make a great difference'.[23]

But at any rate the Arabs were now part of the British campaign. In Mesopotamia, Allenby used Arab forces on his right wing. Their performance was variable. At their best they were impressive, though not so impressive as allied air power. The Handley Page bombers and their escorts of fighters prefigured the way in which Britain was going to police the Middle East between the wars. Allenby's British, Dominion and Indian troops, particularly the cavalry units, were also effective. General Liman von Sanders, the defender of Gallipoli, had to flee from Nazareth in his pyjamas after virtually the whole Ottoman army was destroyed at the battle of Megiddo. The Anzacs, who had suffered so much at the hands of the Turks at Gallipoli, enjoyed a bloody revenge on the Turks and their Arab supporters. Allenby's Arabs also resorted to war crimes as they avenged themselves against the Ottomans.

4. How Much Did the Revolt Matter?

What was the significance of the Arab Revolt? The Arab view is that it tied up large numbers of Turkish troops and greatly assisted Allenby's success in Palestine.[24] Antonius claims that the revolt caused losses with which Turkey could not cope, with 4,800 killed, 1,600 wounded and 8,000 captured in

Turko-Arab engagements by the end of March 1919, desertions to the Arab cause adding to these figures. Taking into account garrisoning, he estimates the total Turks, killed captured or contained at 35,000.[25] The more objective truth is that the Arabs achieved very little, taking Jeddah and Mecca, but not Medina, fighting mainly for loot. Without the myth of Lawrence and the *Seven Pillars of Wisdom*, perhaps not a lot of attention would have been paid to the Arab Revolt. The Arabs contributed little to the success of the British operations.

Afterwards the British Agency in Jeddah drafted a pretty miserable appreciation of Hussein's rising. By then it was realised that the figures that had been given as his supporters had been hugely exaggerated. The 1919 appreciation estimated 1,000 regulars, 2,500 irregulars and a few thousand more Bedouin tribesmen. Fighting qualities were considered 'poor'. Even the less objective Arab Bureau reported in 1918 that 'It must be said that 90% of the Sharif's troops are nothing more than robbers'. Allenby's intelligence officer, Colonel Meinertzhagen, said that 'It is safe to say that Lawrence's desert campaign had not the slightest effect on the main theatre west of Jordan'.[26] Some accounts take a more positive view of the Arab contribution, but it should certainly not be overrated.

5. *The Arab Awakening*

British history celebrates the Arab Revolt because of the Lawrence legend and because Arab polemicists subsequently made much of it in the context of Arab nationalism and what is known as the Arab Awakening. The phrase 'The Arab Awakening' already existed before George Antonius used it as the title of the hugely important book in which he set out a powerful criticism of British policy towards the Arabs. It has been described as 'the most eloquent, able and influential exposition of Arab Nationalist claims that has so far been written'.[27]

But whether there ever *was* an Arab awakening is debatable; and nationalism, in the context of the time when there is said to have been an Arab awakening, is certainly nothing to do with the sort of nationalism which was to develop a generation later. The views that are represented as being expressive of nationalism often reflected no more than the desire of local notables to improve their position within the Ottoman Empire, not to seek independence from it. If there was an Arab awakening, it did not find expression in the Arab Revolt, but rather was stimulated by it.[28]

And yet, even if retrospective claims ignore the lack of coherence, tribal loyalties, splits between Ibn Saud and the Sharif of Mecca, and the multiplicity of minorities, Druze, Christian and Kurd, together also with the division between urban communities and the Bedouin, it certainly remains a widespread Arab view that there was a powerful spirit of Arab Nationalism which was frustrated by Sykes–Picot and other secret deals between Britain and France. The Arab sense of betrayal by the West which dates from the promises and campaigns in the First World War have been said to find expression and statement by Osama bin Laden.[29] In 1998 bin Laden reached back to 1918 when he referred in a statement to 'the suffering of the past 80 years'.[30]

9

KUT AND BEYOND

The British military campaign in Mesopotamia started badly. Its most humiliating moment was the defeat of the troops besieged at Kut in 1916.

Gertrude Bell was in Mesopotamia, waiting for news of developments at Kut when Lawrence arrived. On 9 April 1916, she wrote, 'This week has been greatly enlivened by the appearance of Mr. L, sent out as Liaison Officer from Egypt. We have had great talks and make vast schemes for the improvement of the universe'.[1] She and Lawrence got on well. She was one of the few women whose Christian name alone Lawrence used in his diary.

On 27 April 1916 she wrote from Basra to her father regarding the 'Mesop. [sic] campaign':

> Politically . . . we rushed into the business with our usual disregard for a comprehensive political scheme. We treated Mesop. as if it were an isolated unit, instead of which it is part of Arabia, its politics indissolubly connected with the great and far reaching [sic] Arab question, which presents indeed different facets as you regard it from different aspects, and is yet always and always [sic] one and the same indivisible block. The co-ordinating of Arabian politics and the creation of an Arabian policy should have been done at home [and not in India and the Middle East] – it could only have been done successfully at home . . . [W]hen people talk of our muddling through it throws me into a passion. Muddle through! why yes, so we do – wading through blood and tears that need never have been shed.[2]

On paper, the British commander at Kut, Sir Charles Townshend, was a good man for a siege. He had become famous in 1895, when he commanded British troops under siege in Chitral so successfully that he received the thanks of the government, was given a brevet majority and awarded the CB, all at the age of 34. His early success may have gone to his head. He was unpopular with other officers, arrogant and high-handed, and in 1916 he was suffering from the after-effects of a fever he had contracted the year before. He seemed emotionally unbalanced. Although Townshend had a very real interest in the science of his profession – something that was pretty rare even among senior officers – and was familiar with the works of writers like Clausewitz and Hamley, he had an equal interest in Parisian café society. His wife was French. As viceroy, Curzon was bemused to be entertained by Townshend. The walls of his mud house were decorated with 'daring' illustrations from *La Vie Parisienne,* and 'he regaled us through a long evening with French songs to the accompaniment of a banjo'.[3] He was 'Charlie' to his troops, but 'Alphonse' to his officers.

His campaign had begun well in the previous year, when he was given the command of the 6th Indian Division, one of two under the command of Sir John Nixon, an aggressive, pushing commander. He chased the Turks northward 90 miles up the Tigris from Kurna to Amara, making use of 'Townshend's Regatta', a fleet of barges supported by three sloops and various other craft. At Amara the main body of the Turkish troops was defeated, and Townshend caught the fever that was to dog him the following year. He was sent to India to recover.

By the time he returned to duty in September 1915 the Turks had regrouped and were in a much stronger condition. But Nixon ordered him, despite increasing supply problems, to advance a further 150 miles to Kut. He took Kut with some skill on 29 September. The Turks fell back further to Ctesiphon to defend Baghdad. Townshend's advance came to a halt 60 miles beyond Kut. His troops were exhausted, and the river was too shallow for further advance by water. But despite his strongly expressed objections, he was obliged by Nixon to continue. His victory at Ctesiphon was Pyrrhic, and marked the end of his advance. Thereafter Townshend faced onslaughts from very effective Ottoman forces. He effected a skilful retreat and returned to Kut. Many wounded went with him. There were no stretchers and deaths en route were high.

At Kut, Townshend's army was surrounded by Ottoman forces and a siege began, the longest the British Army has ever endured. It lasted 146 days, thus beating the record of Ladysmith (121) and of Plevna (143) in the Russo-Turkish war of 1877. It was a grim ordeal, reminiscent of the worst moments of the Indian Mutiny. A relief force did not arrive for a long time. When it did, it too was defeated by the Turks. Supplies that were parachuted to the defenders were blown off course. River-boats went aground or were stopped by chains that the Turks had strung out across the river.

A last, plaintive message was sent out by the radio operator at Kut on 29 April 1916, and a humiliating surrender followed. Townshend and other senior officers were conveyed in some comfort to Constantinople, but for most of the survivors of the siege there was a long march across the desert under conditions in which many died. Townshend was accommodated on the island of Prinkipio, from which he was released early to plead the Turkish cause at the Armistice. His subsequent career never recovered from the impression that he had been uninterested in the fate of his men.

These men were treated very differently. More than 13,000 British and Indian troops were taken prisoner, and many of them died in captivity. They were separated from their officers. Their water bottles and boots were taken from them. They were driven through the desert at bayonet-point, stragglers raped or murdered. The Kurds who guarded the troops on the death-march were particularly brutal. Those men who reached Baghdad were subjected to public ridicule. The American consul was killed when he tried to come to their aid. They were then pushed on to Anatolia, subject to what one of them called 'an extended massacre'.[4]

In Anatolia they worked in appalling conditions in chain gangs on the railway. Of 2,592 Britons taken at Kut, only 837 survived the war. The Indian prisoners were better treated: 7,423 out of 10,486 survived.[5]

Almost as shameful as the surrender was what preceded it. In desperation Townshend suggested to London that he offer the Turkish Army commander £1 million to go away. Lawrence was to be the intermediary. Cox, the political officer, was horrified. He refused to instruct Lawrence, saying that his own position as a political officer of the government of India would be untenable if the intrigue became known, as it was bound to be. Nonetheless, Lawrence, without instructions from Cox, proceeded to Kut along with Aubrey Herbert.

By the time Lawrence and Aubrey reached Kut, 23,000 British soldiers had already been killed. Townshend now proposed negotiations with the Turkish General Khalil, but the Turks simply refused to parley. Surrender could not be bought off, and the failed attempt at bribery simply exacerbated Britain's military disgrace. Lawrence's mission now moved into black comedy. He, Herbert and a Colonel Beach were unaware of the surrender. They climbed out of their trench and advanced under a white flag, when they were met, blindfolded and taken to General Khalil to learn that it was too late to be offering bribes. They tried to salvage something by suggesting an exchange of prisoners, but an agreement had already been made. They were given a meal and sent away, and the disaster of the surrender of Kut, together with the publicised attempt at bribery compounded Britain's humiliation. Kut was the worst British military disaster since the surrender at Yorktown and the loss of the American colonies. Townshend said so at the time; so did Kitchener.

Kut brought the Cairo–Delhi conflict to a head. An enquiry was ordered, and a Mesopotamian Commission was set up. It revealed Indian incompetence on a large scale. The Secretary of State, Austen Chamberlain, felt obliged to resign – it was on this occasion that F.E. Smith made his famous remark about Austen always playing the game and always losing it.

Before the commission's report was debated, some of the shame of Kut had been redressed. The army had pushed forward under General Maude and captured Baghdad. His intelligence chief, General Money, did not think much of it: 'not much of a place to look at . . ., a filthy, dirty place'.[6] There were no signal victories in the second Mesopotamian campaign. Liddell Hart said that 'a sledge-hammer was used to crush a flea and the flea escaped being crushed'.

But in the end Britain made substantial gains. In 1917, Britain launched her third attack on Ottoman possessions. This went much better than Gallipoli and Kut. There was an assault from Egypt under Allenby and a second thrust in Mesopotamia, which is where the Arab Revolt fitted in. These campaigns were eminently successful. By the end of 1917 Allenby had taken the whole of Palestine, and by November 1918 much of the Syrian coastal region was in British hands. Damascus fell.[7]

There was now a huge crisis in British policy-making. The Indian government and the London government differed on what should happen to these acquisitions. Delhi was strongly against any promises of independence, and in London there was a chasm between the Foreign Office on one hand and Lloyd George and his advisers on the other. The prime minister's circle was simply in favour of taking what was on offer. The Foreign Office was much more punctilious about honouring undertakings to the French. These divergences were compounded by the conflicting promises to Ibn Saud and the Emir Faisal. All of these doubts and conflicts coalesced to form the vacuum of policy in which Mesopotamia – Iraq – was to languish for a decade.

One of the casualties of indecision was the relationship between Britain and France. The traditional enemies had of necessity become close allies during the war. Within five years of the war's end, diplomatic relations between them were almost ruptured. France believed – and it was indeed easy for her to believe – that Britain had shamelessly broken solemn promises about the Middle East. It is time to look at what these promises were, how they came to be made and what they meant. They were contained in the document which keeps the name of Mark Sykes alive, the Sykes–Picot Agreement.

SYKES–PICOT

1. The Agreement

The Sykes–Picot Agreement, concluded by France and Britain during the dark days of 1916, competes with the Balfour Declaration for the distinction of being the policy document that has done most damage to goodwill towards Britain in the Arab world. The Balfour Declaration, which we shall look at in the next three chapters, created and continues to create a tragic gulf between the Arabs on the one hand and the Jews and their Western supporters on the other. Sykes–Picot was not a waypoint of the same size, but it established a tradition of distrust and perceived betrayal between the Arabs and the West, and a sense of bad faith between the French and the British that brought the two former allies close to hostility. Not bad for a document that was the work of a junior official on each side.

France stood back from the Middle East in the early years of the war. She took the view that the conflict would be short and that there was no need to make a political commitment about the division of the Ottoman spoils. Constantinople would fall, and then the prizes would be shared out.

All the same, France held it to be central to her rights that she would receive rewards in the east of the Mediterranean commensurate with her influence in the West. Georges Leygues, a future French prime minister and minister of marine, said in the Chamber of Deputies on 10 May 1915, 'The axis of French policy is the Mediterranean. One of its poles is in the west, through Algeria, Tunisia and Morocco. It is necessary that the other pole be in the east, with Syria, the Lebanon and Palestine'.[1]

It was inevitable that France had been offended when Britain made Egypt a protectorate in 1914. It was a slap in the face for a power that had regarded itself as having had an Egyptian interest since Napoleonic times. To recompense her, to bind together a wartime alliance that had become stressed by the divergence in the scale of the military contributions of the partners and to allay her concerns about Britain's ambitions in the Levant, secret negotiations took place which resulted in the agreement that bears the names of the negotiators, Sykes for Britain and Picot for France.

Antonius enunciated the classical Arab condemnation of the agreement: 'The Sykes–Picot Agreement is a shocking document. It is not only the product of greed at its worst, that is to say, of greed allied to suspicion and so leading to stupidity: it also stands out as a startling piece of double-dealing.'[2] The argument is that the agreement cut up 'the Arab Rectangle in such a manner as to place artificial obstacles in the way of unity' – possibly intentionally.[3] Additionally, the areas to be ruled by foreign administrations were much more mature politically than the areas which were to be independent countries.

2. Sykes and Picot

We have met Sykes already. As the war went on he became increasingly prominent as a government adviser, and by 1917 was an important part of the War Cabinet Secretariat. Like Gertrude Bell, he was an intrepid traveller. In 1905 Gertrude Bell met Mark and Eva Sykes in Jerusalem, and she discovered that, like her, Sykes was planning an expedition to meet the Druze. They got on well, but just a few weeks later Sykes was writing to his wife complaining that Bell had deliberately misled him and was taking the route he had planned, having said she was going somewhere else. He wrote to his wife in remarkable and intemperate terms, complaining that it was Bell's fault that the Turks were not letting him go to the Druze. Bell was a 'silly chattering windbag of conceited, gushing, flat-chested, man-woman, globe-trotting, rump-wagging, blethering *ass*!'[4]

It would be wrong to imagine that Sykes was too frivolous to be committed to his work. He did not complete the agreement with Picot without an immense process of adjustment, clarification and examination of British and French interests in the course of which he chose to ignore the McMahon correspondence, of which he was aware.[5] He had strong views on the nature of nationalist identity, which informed his views on the future of the Middle East.

He was not pro-French: far from it. He was very critical of the French, not least because they would not behave like the English upper classes. He was against France getting Syria. But he was a moderate. He opposed the partition of the Ottoman Empire in the de Bunsen Committee, rejecting the views of those in favour of partition, like Hirtzel.[6]

His commitment to his work is clear from a note he wrote for Balfour on 20 July 1917:

Now for two years I have given the best where I could to these middle Eastern
affairs. I have only had one object in view and that has been the better prosecution of the war, I have refused office and decorations, I have backed up
whatever government there was and I have done my best to keep the Entente
together in trumpery questions and I have endeavoured to work up every
available political asset on the Entente side . . . I have tried to work on war
lines and not on pre-war lines viz: Nationalism, Co-operation and Alliance,
instead of Imperialism, isolated action and special individual war aims.
Hitherto the work has been fairly successful, but I have had to contend as you
know with many difficulties, the prejudices of the past, both British and
French, the mutual suspicions and susceptibilities of out-of-date minds, the
anti-British policy of Brémond, the anti-French attitude of Lawrence and
Newcomb, and the Fashoda memories of the functionaries in Cairo. The
immense difficulties of dealing with the Indian government you will also
remember . . .

[I]n spite of all this Picot and I managed to pull things along, Picot
having the same difficulties in Paris and Egypt as I have had in London and
Egypt. Picot is accused in Paris of having given everything to England, just
as Curzon never ceases twitting me with having given everything to France.[7]

His opposite number, François Georges Picot, came from a family with a colonialist background and was a leading spokesman for a colonialist policy. In early
1915 Picot had been behind a parliamentary campaign attacking the French
ministers who were prepared to defer to Britain in the Middle East. He had been
Consul General in Beirut and was the Quai d'Orsay specialist on the Middle East.
He arrived in London to begin negotiations on 23 November 1915. Sykes met
him at the French Embassy every day until 3 January, reporting each night to
FitzGerald and thus to the inaccessible and reclusive Kitchener. Kitchener and
FitzGerald kept no record of the transactions, and Sykes said later, 'I could never
make myself understood; I could never understand what [Kitchener] thought,
and he could never understand what I thought'.[8]

3. What They Agreed

By the beginning of January 1916, Sykes and Picot could see the fundamental
points which their agreement had to reflect. France wanted recognition of her
claim to Syria, together with compensation for the loss of financial and other
concessions within the Ottoman Empire. On Britain's side, the essential was
that her traditional interests in the Gulf and the approach to India had to be
secured, along with her more recent interests in Mesopotamia.

The agreement that was reached has been described as 'the last responsible attempt on the part of Europe to cope with the dissolution of the Ottoman Empire, and to prevent the dissolution from bringing disaster'.[9] But that was not all that it was about. The agreement was not a solid piece of long-term statesmanship, but a temporary expedient. It was of course incompatible with the McMahon–Hussein correspondence, and it was illustrative of the lack of cohesive policy in an area in which the different departments of state, together with Cairo, which operated with a degree of independence from the Foreign Office, all played their separate parts. 'The outcome was a classic case of continuous administrative confusion in which Cairo commonly played the active role and the various London departments had to react.'[10]

The agreement was approved by the British and French Cabinets at the beginning of February 1916: the British reaction was generally that too much had been given away. Sykes–Picot was formally embodied in the Grey–Cambon exchange of 9–16 May 1916. There was a definition of French and British shares of Asiatic Turkey. France would receive Cilicia, part of central Anatolia, the Lebanon and the Syrian coastal strip but not various excepted parts of Syria. Britain was to receive Baghdad and Basra, with the ports of Haifa and Acre on the Syrian coast. Beyond that, there were two zones of influence. Britain had the area between Palestine and Mesopotamia. The French zone comprised Damascus, Aleppo, Homs, Hama and Mosul. The inclusion of the last of these was to cause friction with Britain.

4. *Sykes–Picot, Russia and Palestine*

Sykes had a strange role in the House of Commons, as both an outspoken backbencher and a government adviser. He could be very critical of the administration and of Asquith's relaxed way of waging war. The prime minister was always glad to get Sykes out of the way: he was sent off to Petrograd to join Picot in helping to buy the Russians into their agreement. In Russia, Sykes's latent anti-Semitism was reinforced, and he was easily persuaded that Jewish influence was everywhere and threatened the Allied cause.

The Russian dimension was important. Russia had always been part of the tension implicit in the Turkish Question. The Russian Entente had relieved that tension, but the Entente had been strained by Russia's concern about the Straits. On 4 March 1915, the Russian Foreign Ministry told Paris and London that they required Constantinople and the Straits. In return for that, Russia would be sympathetic to Britain and France in respect of their claims to other parts of the Ottoman Empire. This sort of arrangement was in line with the thinking of the Liberal Party and presented no great difficulty to the government.

At its outset Sykes–Picot, then, involved Britain, France and Russia; but after the Revolution Russia abjured her claims to the Ottoman Empire. Sykes–Picot was no longer triangular. That was a bonus. The downside was that Lenin went public and revealed not only the existence of the agreement but also its terms. That immediately started the damage that the agreement has done to Western relations with the Arabs, damage that has lasted to the present day.

But the bonus was a big one. In 1914 it was unthinkable that the war could end with both Germany *and* Russia knocked out. But that is what happened. It was a remarkable outcome. Both Britain's major pre-war rivals, one her enemy in the war and one her ally, were eliminated. Britain ended the war having had the double benefit of having had Russia fighting hard for her, and not being around to share in the prizes.

So far as Palestine was concerned, Sykes and Picot had settled for saying that the country should be placed under an international regime. That was good enough for Picot, but not for his masters, and on 25 March 1916, Aristide Briand, the French prime minister, agreed with Russia that an international regime was impractical and that a French one would be much better. Russia agreed to work with France in support of her claim.

When Russia withdrew from the scene in 1917 after the Revolution, France was left to debate the issue with the British on her own. The situation certainly was not free from doubt. The British zone of influence covered the area between Palestine and Mesopotamia. What about Palestine itself? That question remained live, as will be seen, at least until the San Remo Conference and Churchill's White Paper of 1922. In the course of that time Britain's position hardened. Initially Palestine was indeed not seen as a British administrative area, like the Mesopotamian territories: it was to be administered internationally. That did not remain the plan.

5. The Arab Dimension

The agreement envisaged an Arab state. On the other hand, it had nothing whatsoever to do with the sort of notions of Arab independence that Hussein thought Britain was recognising. Arab rights were to be severely circumscribed except in the Hejaz. Even the Arabs in the Hejaz were not made aware of the agreement.

Picot probably knew nothing about McMahon–Hussein. Sykes was aware of the discussions in general terms, but he was not in close touch with the Cairo Office and involved in its correspondence with Hussein. He was not aware in any detail of what had been promised to the Arabs. From a British perspective, Sykes–Picot was intended to reconcile Britain's relations with France *and* her promises to the Arabs. Sadly but not surprisingly, the Arabs would think they had been betrayed; it is equally unsurprising that the French too thought that they had been tricked. What was intended to be an exercise in reconciliation proved to be an enduring source of conflict.

Possibly the most damaging aspect of the Sykes–Picot Agreement from the Arab point of view was that, just as the McMahon–Hussein correspondence was never disclosed to the French, so the Sykes–Picot Agreement was never disclosed to the Arabs. Sykes – and indeed Picot – met Hussein in May 1917, but made no mention of their agreement. Hussein later complained that he only learned of it from the Turks, when they relayed what the new Bolshevik regime had announced and disavowed. The Turks, under Djemal Pasha, lost no time in publicising the agreement and putting out peace feelers.

The Arab view, by Antonius:

[T]he British . . ., needing tools and catspaws to serve their own ends, encouraged certain Arabs to rebel by giving them mendacious promises and hoodwinking them with false hopes . . .

Eventually, the unfortunate Sharif Hussein fell into the trap made for him by the British, allowed himself to be ensnared by their cajoleries, and committed his offence against the unity and the majesty of Islam. The British, having received his assurance that he would revolt, then decided to secure the defence of the Suez Canal by advancing in the Sinai Peninsula. In fact, it was only after they had made certain of the Sharif's defection that they crossed the Canal. That they are outside the gates of Jerusalem today is the direct outcome of the Sharif's revolt in Mecca.[11]

Fortunately for the Allies, Hussein summarily rejected the Turkish peace overture, but he did send the whole correspondence to Egypt, asking for an explanation about the secret agreement. The British response was misleading. It originated with Balfour himself:

Documents found by Bolsheviki in Petrograd Foreign Ministry do not constitute an actually concluded agreement, but consist of records of provisional exchanges in conversations between Great Britain, France and Russia, which were held in the early days of the War, and before the Arab Revolt, with a view to avoiding difficulties between the Powers in the prosecution of the war with Turkey . . .

Djemal Pasha . . . has . . . ignored the fact that the subsequent outbreak and the striking success of the Arab Revolt, as well as the withdrawal of Russia, had long ago created an altogether different situation.'[12]

6. Evolution of Sykes–Picot

As soon as it became known, the agreement was criticised. It was criticised at home as well as abroad. Arnold Wilson, at this time Cox's deputy chief political officer with the Indian Expeditionary Force, said it was 'counter to every sound principle', and Lloyd George described it as 'a fatuous arrangement judged from any and every point of view'.[13]

As early as April 1917, the Committee of the Imperial War Cabinet appointed to consider British Territorial *Desiderata* came to the conclusion that Palestine should not be internationally administered, as Sykes–Picot envisaged, but like Mesopotamia should for strategic reasons be under British control. In 1918 Sir Stewart Symes, Wingate's private secretary, recorded that 'private advices' from London revealed that Sykes–Picot was no longer in effect. There is evidence from a number of sources that by then Sykes–Picot was regarded as having been superseded by events.[14]

After the United States came into the war, they had to be told something about the secret treaties and agreements. Arthur Balfour, Grey's successor as Foreign Secretary, dealt with the matter by divulging the treaties to President Wilson as a secret, on a 'man to man' basis, whatever that meant. The president's adviser, Colonel House, thought they were thoroughly bad, and said so. President Wilson in a *lapsus* into wit said that Sykes–Picot sounded like a kind of tea. It was 'a fine example of the old diplomacy'.[15] Wilson's New Diplomacy emphasised open treaties, openly entered into.

In 1918 Sykes–Picot received two tweaks. In September the agreement was modified by a new understanding to which Sykes and Picot were again parties, along with Cecil of the Foreign Office and Crewe of the India Office. Occupied Enemy Territory Administration (OETA) West was given to Picot as a French High Commissioner. OETA East, which included most of Syria, was under the military control of Allenby. Later Faisal became OETA East's military governor in Damascus.

The second tweak was more than a tweak. An Anglo-French Declaration, in a sense a rider to Sykes–Picot, but a very important historical document in its own right, was published on 7 November 1918 and released in Baghdad on 8 November. It promised 'the complete and definitive liberation of the peoples so long oppressed by the Turks' with their own national governments and administrations based on the 'initiative and free choice of indigenous populations'. To that end, France and Britain undertook to assist in the establishment of regimes in Syria and Mesopotamia, already liberated, and also in the countries that were still to be liberated. The latter would be recognised as soon as they were effectively established. No particular institution would be imposed anywhere: governments would be adopted by the free rule of the populations.

The Declaration was an odd idea. It was made after the war with Turkey was over. It was not needed to win that war. It was not like the earlier commitments to the Arabs. On the other hand, it certainly stirred up aspirations. Gertrude Bell said that it did 'an enormous amount of harm'. It stirred up 'a great number of windy theories'.[16] At the time, Cox said of the declaration that 'it bids fair to involve us in difficulties as great as Sir Henry McMahon's early assurances to the Sharif of Mecca'. Later it was simply 'a disastrous error'.[17]

On 28 October, Lawrence saw the text of the Anglo-French Declaration. While he thought it was satisfactory, he pointed out that it was contrary to Sykes–Picot, but that Sykes–Picot was not explicitly disavowed. In London, India and in the Mesopotamian administration, however, there was a degree of assumption that Sykes–Picot *had* been disavowed. Of course, Arab opinion welcomed the declaration and was all the more disappointed when it later appeared to have been ignored. But all the declaration really said was that overt annexation would not take place: Arab opinion took it to be more or less positive.

From the start then, Britain tended to feel that Sykes–Picot was altogether too generous to France; and concessions to the French seemed much less important after Russia dropped out of the war. Sykes now began to think of giving the French nothing in Arabia other than the Lebanon. Their consolation prizes would be elsewhere.[18] Britain's increasingly less generous interpretation of Sykes–Picot was also prompted by the fact that in the last phase of the war the victories over the Ottomans were pretty much entirely British ones. If the Mesopotamian theatre were viewed in isolation it seemed unnecessary and unreasonable to reward the French, who had not borne the burden of the fighting there.

So there came to be a fairly pervasive feeling in British political circles that not only was Sykes–Picot extravagant, but that the commitments to the French need not be taken too seriously. It is interesting that whenever there was talk of abrogating promises to Hussein, there was an immediate chorus of criticism about letting the Arabs down. When promises to Picot were to be abrogated, nobody was particularly worried about letting the French down.

On 3 October 1918 the Minutes of the War Cabinet recorded that:

The Prime Minister said he had been refreshing his memory about the Sykes–Picot Agreement and had come to the conclusion that it was quite inapplicable to the present circumstances and was altogether a most undesirable agreement from a British point of view. Having been concluded more than two

years ago, it entirely overlooked the fact that our position in Turkey had been
won by very large British forces, whereas our Allies had contributed but little
to the result.[19]

Balfour, supported by Bonar Law, pointed out that 'the original idea had
been that any territories that the allies might acquire should be pooled and
should not be regarded as the property of the nation which had won them. The
theory had been that the fighting in one theatre of war, where there was little
gain, might be just as important a contribution to the cause of the allies as
much easier fighting in other theatres where great successes were achieved.'[20]
Lloyd George did not accept that argument; on the contrary, he responded by
suggesting that Britain and Turkey conclude a peace agreement immediately,
rather than simply an armistice. In this way Britain might get a favourable
settlement, which Balfour and Bonar Law seemed anxious to avoid.
Unfortunately, the Allied heads of government, whom Lloyd George shortly
met in Paris, vetoed an immediate peace treaty. They did, however, accept that
an armistice should be negotiated by whichever power Turkey approached.

By this time, Turkey was putting out peace feelers. Britain was torn between
not wanting to make concessions and desiring to separate Turkey from Germany.
In the meantime, Allenby was urged to capture as much ground as possible,
particularly Mosul and Aleppo. Temporising to avoid imminent defeat had
been replaced by a mood of acquisitiveness.

In tune with this new mood, on 13 January 1919 Cox, now in Teheran,
wrote to Curzon congratulating him on the outcome in Mesopotamia – 'a grand
sphere' now. He could hardly believe that even Mosul had been acquired.[21]

Cox's reaction was that of a man of India. Amery took a wider view. He
complained that the United States was imperialistic in Central America and
that France was getting the valuable territory of Alsace-Lorraine and other
useful assets. Britain on the other hand was not getting enough, partly because
the Empire was seen as synonymous with Britain and not as a group of nations,
each of which was entitled to its own rewards. While Curzon was slightly side-
lined, because of imperial views which were thought to be really old-fashioned,
Amery and those who supported a British *Drang nach Osten* were powerfully
influential.

In the course of the war many *ad hoc* and tentative policy démarches were
executed and forgotten. Some, like Sykes–Picot and the McMahon–Hussein
correspondence were not forgotten and, because of subsequent developments,
remain crystallised as historic, signal events and often as shameful, reproachful
memorials. Some argue that Britain and Sykes were well aware of the problem
and conflicts inherent in their agreement, and planned to sort them out later;

but the truer appraisal is that at the time no one invested Sykes–Picot with the significance it was subsequently to assume. Grey, for instance, never thought the agreement would be implemented. The formulation of policies that were, *ex facie*, contradictory would have been morally reprehensible if they had been thought from the start to be cast in stone.

Sykes–Picot was a thoroughly old-fashioned piece of power politics, largely designed to reassure the French about British aspirations in an area which France regarded as particularly hers. It worked in that it kept France happy and in the war. It was a desperate remedy for desperate times. No one was trying to reconcile promises made to all and sundry in the heat of the moment, at a period when national survival was in question. It was the misfortune of Sykes–Picot that it came to be considered later in more open days, when Wilsonian doctrines had gained some acceptance. 'The Sykes-Picot Agreement has been widely denounced not only as a prime specimen of the so-called evils of secret diplomacy, but as a bad treaty from any point of view'.[22]

Lawrence, looking at Sykes–Picot as policy for Arabia when it was merely designed to secure the alliance with France, described it thus: 'Each party making the terms considered only what it could take, or rather what would be most difficult for her neighbours to take or refuse her, and the document is not the constitution of a new Asia, but a confession, almost an advertisement, of the greeds of the conquerors. No single clause of it will stand the test of three years' practice, and it will only be happier than the German treaty in that it will not be revised – it will be forgotten'.[23] It was not.

The Background to the Balfour Declaration

1. Introduction

There is a very short list of documents that have affected the course of modern history as radically as the Balfour Declaration. The *Ninety-five Theses* that Luther nailed to the door of the Church in Wittenberg is one. The Declaration of the Rights of Man and of the Citizen is another. But there are not many, and the executive clause of this one consists of just 66 words, in the course of an informal letter of only 116 words.

It has been described not only as a crucial document of state, but also as a remarkably ill-advised policy initiative. According to Elizabeth Monroe, although little interest was initially taken in the declaration at home – it was not even mentioned in *The Times* in the week it was published – it 'brought the British much ill-will, and complications that sapped their power. Measured by British interests alone, it was one of the greatest mistakes in our imperial history'.[1]

More recently, Avi Shlaim has said much the same thing: 'My own view is that the Balfour Declaration was one of the worst mistakes in British foreign policy in the first half of the twentieth century. It involved a monumental injustice to the Palestine Arabs and sowed the seeds of a never-ending conflict in the Middle East'.[2] Shlaim's judgement is sound, if narrow British interests are excluded. Monroe's is not, because she explicitly says that the declaration was a mistake measured by British interests alone. It can be argued, as I shall suggest at the end of this book, that the declaration served British interests tolerably well for 40 years. But that is not to say that the declaration may not have been a tragedy for the rest of the world.

But was it intended to be a document of state at all? The remarkable amount of study and revision that it received before it was issued indicates beyond all doubt that its importance was understood, but the different motives that animated the quite different groups who were responsible for its existence puts in doubt the idea that it represented an identifiable single strand of policy that can be said to be either right or wrong. To arrive at a judgement, one must understand why it was issued and what it really committed Britain to.

The document that is known as the Balfour Declaration was a letter from Balfour to Rothschild, which was signed on 2 November 1917. It is remarkably scruffy, looking as if Balfour had typed it himself, and the handwritten 'Yours' preceding the signature has blotted. It reads as follows:

Dear Lord Rothschild,

I have much pleasure in conveying to you, on behalf of His Majesty's government, the following declaration of sympathy with Jewish Zionist aspirations which have been submitted to, and approved by, the Cabinet.

'His Majesty's Government view with favour the establishment in Palestine of a national home for the Jewish people, and will use its best endeavours to facilitate the achievement of this object, it being clearly understood that nothing shall be done which may prejudice the civil and religious rights of existing non-Jewish communities in Palestine, or the rights and political status enjoyed by Jews in any other country.'

I should be grateful if you would bring this declaration to the knowledge of the Zionist Federation.

The declaration itself consisted of just the central paragraph of the letter to Lord Rothschild, indeed a single sentence. The substantive part of that paragraph amounts to no more than 'viewing with favour' and 'using best endeavours', the latter phrase one that lawyers particularly like because it sounds so good, but involves so little positive commitment. The second half of the sentence contains an enormous proviso that undermines much of what has gone before.

2. The Myth

The simplest and least accurate explanation of how the Balfour Declaration came into existence was given by Lloyd George.[3] In 1915 he was chairman of the Munitions War Committee and was concerned by the lack of acetone, a crucial element in the manufacture of cordite. By 1915 supplies from America were becoming limited and Germany was cornering the market. C.P. Scott, the editor of the *Manchester Guardian* and a pro-Zionist, introduced Lloyd George to the chemist Chaim Weizmann. Weizmann told him that he could devise a process for producing acetone in the laboratory, but was not sure how long it would take to produce on an adequate scale. Weizmann asked, 'How long can you give me?' Lloyd George replied, 'I cannot give you very long. It is press-ing.' Weizmann's response was, 'I will go at it night and day.' Within a few weeks acetone was being produced, not from the traditional wood pulp, but from potatoes and later maize and horse chestnuts. Lloyd George nationalised the factory and the production of cordite was assured. Weizmann's industrial process for making acetone has been described as making 'acetone from conkers'.[4]

Lloyd George's famous and romanticised account of what followed runs thus: 'When our difficulties were resolved through Dr. Weizmann's genius, I said to him: "You have rendered great service to the State, and I should like to ask the Prime Minister to recommend you to His Majesty for some honour". He said: "There is nothing I want for myself". "But is there nothing we can do as a recognition of your valuable assistance to the country?" I asked. He replied: "Yes, I would like you to do something for my people." He then explained his aspirations as to the repatriation of the Jews to the sacred land they had made famous. That was the fount and origin of the famous Declaration about the national home for Jews in Palestine.'[5]

Weizmann disposed of the fable early on: '[Lloyd George's] narrative makes it appear that the Balfour Declaration was a reward given me by the govern-ment when Lloyd George became Prime Minister, for my services to England. I almost wish that it had been as simple as that, and that I had never known the heartbreaks, the drudgery and the uncertainty which preceded the Declaration. But history does not deal in Aladdin's lamps.'[6]

Balfour's niece, Blanche Dugdale, is equally dismissive: 'Mr. Lloyd George is not quite accurate in describing British policy in Palestine as a kind of *quid pro quo* for the patriotic action of the Zionist leader. The Balfour Declaration was not part of a bargain, nor a reward for services rendered.'[7]

3. The Personalities

Weizmann

There is something improbable about the role of a Manchester chemist in inti-mate relation to what was, intentionally or not, perhaps the most important British document of state in hundreds of years. But it was an important role, if not as simple as Lloyd George suggested.

Chaim Weizmann, who was born in 1874 and lived until 1952, four years after the state of Israel was established, had been born in Russia, and educated at universities in Germany and Switzerland. He travelled in the Russian Pale, part of Western Russia, and came to Britain in 1904 to teach organic chemistry at Victoria University, Manchester. In Britain he was a pivotal and forceful advocate of Zionism and did more than anyone else to dispose the government to favour his cause.

In 1906 he had a crucial meeting with Arthur Balfour, then leader of the Conservative Party in opposition. Balfour had sympathised with the French Captain Dreyfus when he was victimised because he was Jewish. It is intriguing that it was a Mr Arthur Dreyfus, the Jewish chairman of Balfour's Constituency Association, who arranged the meeting because of an interest in the Zionist cause Balfour had already expressed. The meeting between Balfour and Weizmann was supposed to take just a quarter of an hour. It turned out to last an hour and a quarter. They did not meet again for eight years, but Balfour had been convinced that a Jewish national home could be established in Palestine. Very much later he told Blanche Dugdale that it was from the discussion of 1906 that he 'saw that the Jewish form of patriotism was unique'.[8]

When they met again, on 12 December 1914, Weizmann found that Balfour had remembered everything that they had talked about eight years earlier. Speaking then, some years before the declaration, Balfour told Weizmann that he might see faster developments in his project after the war. They met again in March 1915, and in September 1915 Weizmann became technical adviser to the Admiralty – in relation to acetone supplies – when Balfour was First Lord. There was a further long meeting in 1916, when Balfour asked Weizmann to see him to discuss technical questions in connection with high explosives.

He invited Weizmann to stay on for dinner. When Weizmann was leaving, Balfour offered to accompany him the 200 yards from 1 Carlton Gardens to the Duke of York's Column. In the course of their stroll they turned again to Zionism, as well as other matters. They were so engrossed that Balfour asked Weizmann to continue walking with him. They walked back and forward that 200 yards for two hours.[9] Weizmann asked if Britain would sponsor the idea of a Jewish national home in Palestine. Balfour said that the United States would be a better bet.[10]

Balfour

The signatory of the declaration, Arthur James Balfour, is one of the most fascinating figures to flit across the political stage in the late nineteenth and early twentieth centuries. He is all the more fascinating because although he was on that stage – indeed often dominated it – he was always apart from the rest of the cast.

Lloyd George was asked what history would make of A.J. Balfour. He said he would be like the scent on a silk handkerchief. That was a pretty casual dismissal of someone who had been leader of his party for many years and prime minister for three. Before then he had occupied high office, and was

– surprisingly – a notably tough Chief Secretary for Ireland. But leading his party in the tumult that followed Chamberlain's declaration for protectionism was an effort, and he was happy to resign the burden in 1911.

Thereafter, without appearing to want to do so, he continued at the top of politics. He was First Lord of the Admiralty after Churchill's fall, and he was Foreign Secretary until 1919. As a young man he had accompanied his uncle, Lord Salisbury, who was then Foreign Secretary, to the Congress of Berlin in 1878. As Foreign Secretary himself he attended the Paris Peace Conference in 1918. He was the only man to participate at both these great assemblies.

His role in shaping the history of the Middle East, which included pressing for the advance from Basra to Baghdad that resulted in the humiliation at Kut, his time as Foreign Secretary and, above all, his part in the formulation of the declaration which carries his name did not involve any detailed knowledge of the countries whose destinies he touched. He was no traveller, and his geographical boundaries were those of the country houses at which he golfed and played tennis and dallied, probably virginally, with so many Edwardian beauties. He contrasted with Curzon, the most travelled Cabinet Minister of his time, and not only a traveller: an expert on the countries he studied and wrote about. Curzon never thought that Zionism would work.

But, for all his worldly achievements, there is something evanescent about Balfour, something difficult to capture. Lloyd George was right in that sense. He was wrong, however, in suggesting that no one would wish to capture the essence of the man. In recent years some excellent biographies have appeared – more than have been prompted by Lloyd George and the question of his place in history. And in the context of the present narrative Balfour is crucially important not just because of the declaration, but also because of his contribution to the debates at Versailles and over the question of how Britain should handle its new Middle Eastern Empire.

The Romanes and Gifford Lecturer and author of *The Foundations of Belief, Being Notes introductory to the Study of Theology*, and *Questionings on Criticism and Beauty* among many other publications, Balfour was intellectually formidable. He was capable of penetrating thinking as well as off-the-cuff brilliance. The latter may have distracted attention from the former, and the effect was compounded by a languid and lethargic manner. Another description of him by Lloyd George was 'Not a Man but a Mannerism'. He was easily bored, and it took little to exhaust him. The office of prime minister or party leader meant little to him, and he passed these responsibilities on to others without any sense of loss. He loved the company of women but preferred to avoid the effort of committing himself to marriage. His smile was said to be like moonlight on a tombstone. Few men have stayed at the centre of politics for so long without trying.

The dilettante statesman, the philosopher who also loved his tennis and golf, used each of his personae to conceal another. His languor obscured his determination. He stayed in bed all morning, but only to get work done. Ultimately the languor was more significant than the effectiveness. He said that he could 'remember every argument, repeat all the pros and cons, and even make quite a good speech on the subject. But the conclusion, the decision, is a perfect blank in his mind'.[11] Observers frequently noticed his indecisiveness. Churchill said that if he wanted nothing done, 'A.J.B. was undoubtedly the best man for the task'.[12]

While it has been claimed that the declaration stands to a degree apart from the rest of Balfour's work, an argument can be made for the contrary case. Balfour emphasised his commitment to Zionism in later years; but even at the outset there was a degree of passion in his commitment. 'No man', he said, 'who is incapable of idealism is capable either of understanding the Zionist movement or effectually contributing to its consummation'.[13] The same passion and idealism brought tears to his eyes when he took Weizmann's hand in his and said, 'It is not a dream'. The Zionists certainly believed in his commitment. The first post-war Jewish settlement in Palestine was called Balfouria.[14]

Low Church identification with Israel was communicated through his mother, an Evangelical. But there is confusion in his approach to the declaration. He was for Dreyfus and against bans on Jewish membership of golf clubs. On the other hand, he was capable, like so many of his background, of tasteless, anti-Semitic jokes. He told Weizmann that he shared many of Cosima Wagner's anti-Semitic ideas.[15] He was concerned about the immigration of Russian Jews to Britain. His government brought in the Aliens Act of 1905, which excluded 'undesirable aliens'. He spoke of 'the undoubted evils' which had fallen on portions of the country from an alien immigration which was largely Jewish'.[16] He tried to explain that by saying that 'anti-Semitism was a great evil which had to be guarded against by preventing abuse of British hospitality'.[17] The argument seems specious, and his position reflects a conflict between general theory and practice.

It is not difficult to identify ambivalence towards the Jews even among such people as Balfour and Sykes. The paradox of a simultaneous upper-class anti-Semitism in the departments of state in Britain during the First and Second World Wars and in between, coupled nonetheless with benevolence towards a Zionist state, is sometimes explained by a distinction between the way in which 'assimilationist' Jews were seen, as opposed to 'proper' Jews in a Zionist State.[18]

Balfour read George Eliot's *Daniel Deronda* (1876), an early articulation for the general reader of the claims of the Zionist cause; and he claimed, as has been seen, that he had been convinced as early as 1906 by Weizmann that a Jewish home had to be in Palestine.[19] That is probably true, even if it is no less true that his views developed and became more cohesive after the declaration. His 1906 commitment pre-dated the practical arguments that arose during the war for a national commitment to Zionism, and even in the course of the war Weizmann found that Balfour simply did not see the advantage that would accrue to Britain in promoting Zionism. Indeed he rejected and resisted the idea of linking political or strategic considerations with a commitment to a home in Palestine.[20]

George Eliot is not an obvious geopolitical catalyst, but she did her bit for the creation of the state of Israel. Edward Said, in *Orientalism* and in an essay, 'Zionism from the Standpoint of its Victims', saw *Deronda* as a colonialist tract. It is not easy to agree with his view, but it influenced Weizmann and the influential Zionist writer, Theodor Herzl, as well as Balfour and 'hundreds of thousands of assimilated Jews [to whom] the story presented, for the first time, the possibility of a return to Zion'.[21] '*Daniel Deronda* must surely rank high among works of literature that (excluding the Bible and other religious texts) have had the greatest effect on the world.'[22]

Balfour was not a member of the Committee on Territorial *Desiderata* in the Terms of Peace and indeed was out of the country when the War Cabinet accepted the recommendation that Britain should seek exclusive control of Palestine, thus creating a continuous block of territory from the Mediterranean to the Persian Gulf. This policy opened the way to renegotiation of the Sykes–Picot Agreement with its now apparently unduly generous bias in favour of the French. He, for his part, was against any rowing away from Sykes–Picot or further acquisitions north of the Equator. In due course, he would argue for a US mandate, rather than a British one, in Palestine.[23] His position was thus very different from that of the neo-imperialists. To understand the position of the neo-imperialists it is helpful to look again at their epitome: Leo Amery.

4. A Neo-Imperialist: Leo Amery

From 1916 onwards, when he was appointed a political secretary to the Cabinet, Leo Amery, then only a backbench MP, had an increasingly important influence on the formulation of Middle East policy. He had that influence because he wanted it, and he wanted it because he had a clear vision of British interests in the world.

Amery's dream, his idea of the British Empire, is set out clearly in a good-natured letter which he wrote to Lloyd George when they were involved in the Supreme War Council together. Lloyd George had chaffingly suggested that Amery was a land-grabbing imperialist, a predatory Saxon as opposed to the prime minister, a sensitive Celt. Amery defended his position:

We have battled and will continue to battle our hardest for the common cause in Europe. But on behalf of that cause, as well as in the defence of our existence, we shall find ourselves compelled to complete the liberation of the Arabs, to make secure the independence of Persia, and if we can of Armenia, to protect tropical Africa from German economic and military exploitation. All these objects are justifiable in themselves and don't become less so because they increase the general sphere of British influence, and afford a strategical security which will enable that Southern British World which runs from Cape Town through Cairo, Baghdad and Calcutta to Sydney and Wellington to go about its peaceful business . . .[24]

The concept was of a world composed of a series of substantial and stable blocks. This reinforcement of the theory of balanced power which appeared to have discredited itself in 1914 'stood no chance against President Wilson's facile slogan of self-determination, pressed home to its limits by the victorious smaller nations, or against the specious sham of a world authority . . .'[25]

Amery is an important figure in the formulation of the new imperialism. He was Acting Secretary of State at the Colonial Office for four months in 1919 when Milner attempted to calm uprisings in Egypt, and he was himself Colonial Secretary from 1924 to 1929, when he was pleased to find that 'the Colonial Office is very much a domain of its own' where he could get on with things without any bother from Parliament or indeed the Cabinet.[26] When Amery completed his diary for the year 1917 and looked back at what he had achieved, he was able in all modesty to say that it was he who had done 'all the work on peace terms which gradually drive into [his colleagues'] heads the importance of East Africa, Palestine and Mesopotamia and the Imperial outlook generally'.[27]

After taking a First in Greats (classics, philosophy and ancient history) at Oxford in 1896, Amery was elected to a fellowship in history at All Souls. He studied the Austria-Hungarian and Turkish Empires, and had more knowledge of the Middle East than most of the other policymakers. He also had a working knowledge of 14 languages. He was not strictly one of Milner's Kindergarten, the group of young men who worked with Milner during the period of reconstruction in South Africa after the war there, but he was closely associated with it, and Milner regarded him with approval and promoted his career. For Amery, the Empire was 'the final object of the patriotic emotion and action'.[28] He particularly elaborated the concept of a 'frontier Empire' from the Middle East to the Indian frontier.

Amery, Milner's protégé and his disciple, took the view that Milner was the greatest statesman of the Empire, which he had defended during the Boer War and the First World War. Succeeding Milner, he, himself, 'became the theorist *par excellence* of British Imperialism'.[29] He used All Souls both as a resource for information and as a platform for the dissemination of his views. He was a Zionist by conviction, but also for a practical reason. 'Our ultimate end is clearly to make Palestine the centre of a Western influence, using the Jews, as we have used the Scots, to carry the English ideal through the Middle East and not merely to make an artificial oriental Hebrew enclave in an oriental country'.[30]

Amery's position was not initially an important one in the hierarchy, but he saw himself as a member of an influential élite, in a position to direct the thinking of the War Cabinet. One of the ways in which he was able to do this was in the preparatory work he carried out for the Imperial Conference of 1917. His idea was to enlarge the War Cabinet by bringing in some of the 'strongest men in the Empire'.[31] By that year the notion of Imperial Federation had given way towards the evolution of sovereign dominions within the Empire, but that was not a development which Amery regarded as inimical to the Empire's development. Amery's approach to the Arabs was severely practical. He was satisfied that 'the Arabs trust us and dislike the French'.[32] His Britain and the Arabs would together exclude potential enemies from the Middle East, notably the French, against whom, in his word, a series of Arab states could be 'buffers'. The geographical situation of Palestine made it the most important of these buffers. Accordingly, he strongly opposed the idea that Palestine should be given to 'the Americans with their vigorous but crude ways'.[33]

Despite Amery's views about the Americans' ways, well before the end of the war the War Cabinet was considering transferring Palestine to the United States. While Lloyd George had seen and was again to see Palestine as a useful asset for Britain in the post-war years, his approach was always mercurial and impulsive. Balfour continued to advocate United States' control well into 1919, and only desisted when it was clear that America had no intention of taking responsibility. By then some in Britain could see that the declaration had released a bigger genie than they had imagined. Early in 1919 Lloyd George said that 'If the Zionists claim that the Jews are to have domination in the Holy Land under a British protectorate, then they are certainly putting the claims too high'. By now there was no obvious British commitment to an overtly Zionist Palestine.[34] But there was no going back.

It has been said that if Amery had been half a head taller and his speeches half an hour shorter, he would have been prime minister. For a generation, and largely from the back benches, his influence was pretty powerful. It had a very direct bearing on Middle East policy when he was in the front benches, at the Admiralty in 1922 and as Colonial Secretary from 1924 to 1929. Even in 1916 he was not insignificant. He injected into the leaders' incoherent improvisations a degree of theoretical consistency. He favoured a military advance into Palestine and Syria. He was reinforced in this policy by the fact that he already had doubts about the permanence of the British presence in Egypt.

His imperial philosophy was informed by Joseph Chamberlain's idea of a united Empire and Milner's concept of an imperial economic and political system, a 'Southern British World, stretching from South Africa to Egypt, to the Middle East, to India and to Australia and New Zealand'. When Lloyd George became converted to radical imperialism, he was very close to Amery's position, and during the Second World War Amery contrasted the two wartime prime ministers. Amery and Churchill were close, but not very close, never quite seeing eye to eye. It is tempting to think that Amery remembered being thrown into the swimming pool at Harrow by Churchill. Churchill was his junior and had been misled by Amery's size. He tried to make up for a serious breach of school protocol by telling Amery that his own father was a great man, and also not tall. While Amery was far from dismissive of him, he regarded Churchill as essentially 'a retrospective Whig of the period 1750–1850, with very little capacity for looking forward'. Lloyd George on the other hand was a constructive Radical, who shared Amery's views and those of Joseph Chamberlain and Milner.[35]

There were two political secretaries to the Cabinet. The other one was Mark Sykes, who was appointed in 1916. Amery was initially unaware of the Zionist movement, but Sykes won him over and he came to see the existence in Palestine of 'a prosperous community bound to Britain by ties of gratitude and interest' as a means of consolidating the military positions in Palestine and Syria.[36]

Amery claimed that such was Sykes's enthusiasm that he was practically in charge of the negotiations which led to the declaration. Having made a purely practical assessment of the value of Zionism, Amery came to be seized, as so many others also were, by the idea of 'what Jewish energy in every field of thought and action might mean for the regeneration of that Middle Eastern region which was once the home of the world's most ancient civilisations'. Writing in 1953, as blood was being spilled in consequence of the declaration of the State of Israel, he still felt that, 'in spite of all that has happened [I am not] . . . prepared to believe that the young nation of Israel may not eventually be accepted by its neighbours as one of themselves'.[37]

Even if Amery exaggerated Sykes's role, there was a great deal of Zionist activity around him ahead of the declaration. The distinguished Zionist Nahum Sokolow got hold of Picot in London in early 1917. Picot was unhelpful, and would not even admit the existence of the agreement to which his name was attached. Sykes had already been contacted by Weizmann and other

Zionists in January and February 1917. They showed him perhaps the earliest draft of what would be the declaration. He told Picot that given the British military role in Palestine there was going to be a preponderant British presence in the region. Eventually and rather limply the Quai d'Orsay said that 'it would be a deed of justice and of reparation to assist, by the protection of the Allied Powers, in the renaissance of the Jewish nationality in that Land from which the people of Israel were exiled so many centuries ago'.[38] That did not go very far. It certainly did not go as far as recognising what would then have been called a British protectorate, and nothing was said that would later imply that France had agreed to the mandate.

5. The Evolution of Zionism

Modern Zionism, directed particularly towards Palestine, finds its source in Russia and the anti-Semitism of Alexander III and Nicholas II. The motor behind Zionism was the huge number of Jews in Russia, 12–13 million. They made up 80 per cent of the world's Jewish population. They were subject to pogroms and persecution. Whereas the condition of Jews in most of Europe improved through the nineteenth century, the reverse was the case in Russia. Jews were required to live within the Pale. They were not citizens and were subject to many forms of prejudicial treatment.

The pogroms began in 1881 and continued in the twentieth century. From the start of the pogroms, Jews began to move towards Palestine, where they sought to buy land. They were regarded as a threat, and hostility, expressed in outbreaks of violence, was developing towards them well before the outbreak of war.

An agency known as The Lovers of Zion established small agricultural settlements in Palestine in the last two decades of the nineteenth century. In 1882 Leon Pinsker published a booklet called *Auto-Emancipation* which argued that anti-Semitism could never be defeated and that Jews had to take matters in their own hands. The work was very influential and stimulated the appearance of a number of new Zionist bodies. Part of the outcome of this activity was the publication of Theodor Herzl's *The Jewish State* in 1896. That book had a huge impact and resulted in the establishment of the first Zionist Conference in 1897 at which over 200 delegates agreed to secure a Zionist home in Palestine. The World Zionist Organisation was established.

Herzl negotiated with the Ottomans for a Zionist Palestine. He became convinced that he would get nowhere with them and turned his attention to Britain and Joseph Chamberlain. Chamberlain was sympathetic, and their discussions led to the suggestion that a Jewish community should be established in Sinai. Herzl required a British lawyer to handle the matter. The firm that was chosen was Messrs Lloyd George, Roberts and Co., and the partner who dealt with the matter personally was David Lloyd George. The proposal eventually fell through, but an important political contact had been made.

The Foreign Office vetoed the Sinai idea, but Chamberlain found an alternative settlement within his own area of responsibility, in Uganda. Balfour, independently sympathetic to Zionism, was supportive of Chamberlain. Again it was Lloyd George, still in opposition and acting in his professional capacity as a solicitor, who dealt with the matter.

There was a significant sense of identity between Protestants and the Jews. This was particularly true in the case of Evangelicals or Nonconformists. Protestants generally, separated from and sometimes persecuted by the Roman Catholic Church, identified themselves with the wandering, isolated Israelites. The culture of Nonconformists was particularly informed by the legal discrimination to which they had been subjected and they saw themselves apart, the victims of prejudice. Lloyd George came from this tradition. The Church of Scotland had been violently harried and persecuted during the Covenanting period when some of its members were put to death, and the Church continued to see itself reflected in the sufferings and wanderings of the Jewish people. Balfour's mother came from this Low Church background, and Balfour himself, as a product of Scotland, was familiar with the culture of the Church of Scotland.

The Earl of Shaftesbury, in the mid nineteenth century, promoted an evangelical movement within the Church of England, aimed at bringing back the Jews to Palestine, in order to convert them and hasten the Second Coming. Palmerston was inspired by the movement, provided British consular protection to Jews in Palestine and urged the Ottomans to create a Jewish Palestine. This mid-century movement never died away, and tended to revive with the approach of the war. C.P. Scott, the editor of the *Manchester Guardian*, for example, was persuaded by Weizmann of the merits of Zionism, and the paper's military correspondent, Herbert Sidebotham, argued the military case for the peopling of Palestine with an intensely patriotic people.

12

Gestation of the Declaration

It is tempting to look for the first sighting of the declaration. At a Cabinet meeting as early as 9 November 1914, as soon as Turkey had joined the Central Powers, Lloyd George referred to 'the ultimate destiny of Palestine' and after the meeting Herbert Samuel, then Postmaster General, highly intelligent, effective and unpopular, sent a memorandum to Grey, advocating the establishment of a Jewish State there and stressing the desirability of Britain's being involved in view of the proximity of the Suez Canal.[1]

In January 1915 he followed it up with an approach to Asquith, who reacted to it with quiet amusement, as he always did to enthusiastic outpourings from those colleagues who were less restrained than he. In March of the same year the memorandum, polished up further, was submitted to the Cabinet, of which Samuel was by now a member.

Samuel's efforts were supplemented by an approach from the American Zionist Horace Kallen. Sokolow, the leader of the World Zionist Organisation in London, together with Chaim Weizmann, who was president of the English Zionist Federation, were appointed to liaise with the British government. Although those behind the drafting of the declaration took no account of Sykes–Picot, Sokolow was well aware of what Sykes and Picot were up to. There were, as we have seen, discussions with both Sykes and Picot; and Sykes in particular was very much in touch with the Zionist movement.

Others were also thinking about what should be done with Palestine. Oswald FitzGerald wrote on behalf of Kitchener to Storrs for his views, and Storrs replied that:

France would be a better neighbour than Russia, but we cannot count on the permanence of any Entente, however Cordiale, when the generation that is full of war memories passes away. A buffer state is most desirable, but can we get one up? There are no visible indigenous elements out of which a Muslim Kingdom of Palestine can be constructed. The Jewish State is in theory an attractive idea; but the Jews, although they constitute a majority in Jerusalem itself are very much in a minority in Palestine generally, and form indeed a bare sixth of the whole population.

Storrs signed off, 'Please remember me to the Chief [Kitchener]. Egyptians are hoping that he will continue to direct their fate from afar.'[2] As Beaverbrook wrote, 'The tall old soldier cast a long shadow over the future of the Middle East'.

Lloyd George had a radical's dislike of the ramshackle and reactionary Ottoman Empire. John Buchan had worked for Milner in South Africa, and on Milner's recommendation Lloyd George appointed Buchan Director of Information and instructed him to launch a propaganda campaign against the Turk. The slogan *'The Turk Must Go!'* went down well. Always doubtful about the Western Front, Lloyd George tended to look to the east as the place that the war could be won. Later he claimed that 'nothing and nobody could have saved the Turk from complete collapse in 1915 and 1916 except our General Staff'.[3]

There was an interesting but largely ignored episode in 1916, when Grey consulted the French and Russians about 'an arrangement in regard to Palestine . . . in such a way as to bring over to our side the Jewish forces in America, the East and elsewhere which are now largely, if not preponderantly, hostile to us'.[4]

Early in 1917 there was a significant meeting in Washington between Balfour and Louis Brandeis, the jurist and a Zionist. Balfour was impressed by Brandeis, and at the end of their discussion said simply 'I am a Zionist'.[5]

Lloyd George was particularly seized by the romantic appeal of Zionism; he admitted that he was more familiar with the geography of the Holy Land than with the Western Front. A late but enthusiastic convert to imperialism, he was also aware that Palestine would be a useful acquisition for Britain. And protection of the Zionist community in Palestine provided a way of excluding France. On 3 April 1917 he told Sykes to work for 'the addition of Palestine to the British area' of Sykes–Picot and spoke of 'the importance of not prejudicing the Zionist movement and the possibility of its development under British auspices'.[6]

Sykes was to do everything he could for a British Palestine, with no pledges to the Arabs and no prejudice to the Zionist movement. The government was increasingly focusing its attention on a pro-Zionist policy, not least because Weizmann was telling them that Germany was now courting the Zionist community. Curzon, by now a member of the War Cabinet, was present at the meeting with Sykes. He was less enthusiastic than the prime minister and said that Jewish claims to Palestine were based on historically weaker grounds than English claims to bits of France. Not everyone was in favour of Zionism. Curzon pointed to real objections, not least the identity of the present possessors of Palestine: 'They and their forefathers have occupied the country for the best part of two thousand years. They own the soil which belongs either to individual landowners or to village communities. They profess the Muhammadan faith.'[7] But if Curzon was not an uncritical Zionist, the Foreign Office Minister in the Commons, Lord Robert Cecil, described himself as 'a Zionist by passionate conviction' after meeting Weizmann in 1915.[8]

One of the innovations Lloyd George made on becoming prime minister was to concentrate the direction of the war in a small War Cabinet. Initially there were just five members, Lloyd George, Curzon, Bonar Law, Arthur Henderson and Milner. Milner's influence on Lloyd George was significant. Almost from the start of Lloyd George's premiership, and even before he became Minister for War in 1918, Milner had exerted huge influence on the evolution of policy. He and Lloyd George and the Cabinet Secretary, Hankey, met with the Chief of the Imperial General Staff at 11 a.m. every morning, an hour before the War Cabinet itself met.

Milner was at the centre of a group known as the Round Tablers, called after the magazine *Round Table* which advocated imperial union. The Round Table Movement was founded by Milner's assistants in South Africa, the 'Kindergarten'. There was an affinity between the Round Table Movement and a group influenced by Milner at All Souls, some of whom had worked for him to bring the fractured South Africa together. Lloyd George frequently attended their meetings and in 1917 Hankey, the Cabinet Secretary, identified the group as being among those agencies which exercised most influence on his chief.

Later Smuts and Carson joined the War Cabinet along with George Barnes, the ILP Member of Parliament who replaced Henderson. It seems remarkable that the Foreign Secretary, Balfour, and the Secretary for India, Montagu, were not members. The small size of the War Cabinet meant that decisions could be made quickly. Its Zionist disposition also meant that steps towards the declaration were easier to take than they would otherwise have been. This small governmental clique was animated by an idealistic, but relatively incoherent, range of views about Zionism which contrast with other arguments, founded on utility. The role of these other, practical reasons for the declaration should not be exaggerated. The War Cabinet echoed a fairly widespread view that prevailed in British politics until the Second World War, a benevolent disposition towards the Zionist cause.

Montagu, the only Jewish member of the Cabinet, was the Cabinet member who denounced Zionism most bitterly. He did so on the same grounds as many other Jews, who felt that their position in the societies in which they lived and had established themselves would be eroded if they were regarded as citizens of Palestine: 'Palestine will become the world's ghetto'.[9] As Secretary of State for

India he had to consider the Muslim reaction in the subcontinent, but his main concern, the down-grading of assimilated Jews, was one that had occurred to many Jews, particularly those in America. Zionism was not a deeply rooted tradition in Judaism, deriving essentially from the Russian experience and publicised by Eastern European thinkers such as Herzl.

There is dispute between those who maintain that the declaration was made for practical and propaganda reasons, and those who think it was based more on sentiment. The argument that the declaration was born of benevolent idealism rather than practical self-interest is supported by the fact that it made no mention of British control of Palestine. Although Balfour used the propaganda value argument to promote his views, he explicitly denied in February 1918 that he and the prime minister were bidding for Jewish support in the war.[10] They had wanted to 'give the Jews their rightful place in the world; a great nation without a home is not right'.

It is not easy to be convinced by the alternative view: 'the British wanted Palestine – and very much so – for their own interests, and . . . it was not the Zionists who drew them to the country . . . [N]either was it the Zionists who initiated the negotiations with the government . . . [T]he government opened up negotiations with them . . . [H]ad there been no Zionists in those days the British would have had to invent them'.[11] The dispute will be considered further in the course of the next chapter.

That is not to say that Britain did not come to want Palestine. Britain certainly had no wish to see France succeed in her claims to the land. The Curzon Committee on the Terms of the Peace recommended on 28 April 1917 that the Sykes–Picot Agreement be amended to give Britain exclusive control over Palestine, with the frontier of the British sphere of influence on the River Litani. But none of that shows that the government played the Zionist card essentially to help her get hold of Palestine.

So in Cabinet discussions when Balfour argued for a commitment to Zionism, Curzon was against it for a variety of convincing practical reasons: not only the antipathy between the Jews and the Arabs, but also the poor resources of Palestine. Curzon did not think that what Balfour was predicting would ever be achieved. The declaration would raise 'false expectations which could never be realised'. But ultimately, and with reservations, he admitted the propaganda value of the declaration.

From these discussions, the text of the declaration gradually evolved. It was drafted and redrafted by many hands. In view of the breadth of interpretations that can be put on it, it is easy to think it was knocked out without any great thought. Far from it: agonies of appraisal and adjustment were undergone. The successive drafts can be read to great advantage.[12]

President Wilson had no hand in the document. That is slightly surprising, as British policy consistently envisaged that America should be involved in the administration of Palestine. The declaration was cleared with him, and appears to have had his approval, though he gave it no concrete endorsement. He was a Presbyterian, and a minister's son, and he liked the arrangement. 'To think that I the son of the manse should be able to help restore the Holy Land to its people.'[13]

The British Cabinet played down what they were proposing and described it simply as an expression of sympathy for Zionism. Wilson's confidant, Colonel House, was sceptical. He said, 'the English naturally want the road to Egypt and India blocked and Lloyd George is not above using us to further this plan'.[14] All the same, the declaration went down well in the United States. At the beginning of the war, there were only 12,000 Jews in the United States Zionist Federation. By 1919 there were 175,000.

13

THE BIRTH OF THE DECLARATION

1. 'Dr Weizmann, It's a Boy!'

There was significant opposition to the declaration in the wider political world. Bonar Law and other politicians as well as some senior civil servants were hostile. It was not until 31 October 1917 that the War Cabinet finally agreed to publish a declaration. Sykes ran out of the Cabinet Room exclaiming, 'Dr Weizmann, it's a boy!'

By then every word in it had been weighed and was the outcome of innumerable changes in drafting. The reference to not prejudicing the rights and political status enjoyed by Jews in any other country was designed to deflect opposition to the declaration from those Jews who felt settled elsewhere in the world and whose sense of security was threatened by the idea that their national home, their *only* national home, would now be in Palestine.

But, for all the care in its drafting, there was a good deal of doubt about its meaning in the minds of even those most intimately involved in preparing it. Balfour himself in the years that followed put additional glosses on his interpretation of the declaration. He really had not fully thought through the document he had signed. As soon after the declaration as 18 November, Sykes suggested a second declaration clarifying the first, a proposal which was vetoed by Allenby, responsible for military operations in Palestine. But the difficulties to which the declaration gave rise after the war were more the result of post-war developments than of wartime pledges that had been made carelessly and opportunistically.

The neo-imperialists were practical builders. Balfour's position, on the other hand, was much more idealistic. In 1919 he told Brandeis that Palestine should be *the* Jewish homeland and that there should not just be *a* Jewish homeland in Palestine (the emphases are mine).[1] He made such statements more than once.

The officials who were involved in drafting the memorandum, such as Milner, Leo Amery and Balfour himself, were influenced by the nineteenth-century interest in anthropology and ethnology. In Amery's draft of the declaration, for example, he replaced the words 'Jewish people' with the words 'Jewish race'. 'Home' gave way to 'national home'.[2]

But what did Balfour himself really mean by a 'national home'? Initially probably simply some sort of protectorate; but within the year he was declaring that the Jewish land would not speedily develop into an independent country. As early as 31 October 1917, Balfour said that he understood that the words 'national home' meant

> some form of British, American, or other protectorate, under which full facilities would be given to the Jews to work out their own salvation and to build up, by means of education, agriculture and industry, a real of centre of national culture and focus of national life. It did not necessarily involve the early establishment of an independent Jewish State, which was a matter for gradual development in accordance with the laws of political evolution.[3]

But by 1921 Balfour, together with Lloyd George and Churchill told Weizmann that in the declaration they had 'always meant an eventual Jewish State'.[4]

By that time Balfour had to reconcile the declaration with the League of Nations and its Covenant. Balfour recognised that the declaration contravened the terms of the Covenant:

> The contradiction between the letter of the Covenant [of the League of Nations] and the policy of the Allies is even more flagrant in the case of the 'independent nation' of Palestine than in that of the 'independent nation' of Syria. For in Palestine we do not propose to even go through the form of consulting the wishes of the present inhabitants of the country though the American Commission is going through the form of asking what they are.
>
> The Four Great Powers [Britain, France, Italy and the United States] are committed to Zionism. And Zionism, be it right or wrong, good or bad, is rooted in age-long traditions, in present needs, and future hopes, of far profounder import than the desires and prejudices of the 700,000 Arabs who now inhabit that ancient land. In my opinion that is right.[5]

Although there were some 55,000 Jews and 700,000 Arabs in Palestine, he considered that 'Arab claims were infinitely weaker than those of the Jews'.[6] That was because he regarded the Jews of the Diaspora as part of the equation. Immigration was also central to the paradox implied by this remarkable statement. He was against the investigation on the ground by the League's US-dominated commission, the King–Crane Commission, and argued that if a plebiscite were to be held it should poll Jews throughout the world, and not simply the inhabitants of Palestine. The Jews were entitled to special treatment in Palestine, just as the Arabs were receiving special treatment of their own in the establishment of Arab kingdoms in place of Ottoman rule. But the crux of the matter was that the Arabs in Palestine were a tiny minority if Jews world-wide were taken into account.

In his last illness Balfour told Blanche Dugdale that his support of Zionism might prove of more value than anything else he had done.[7] It is notoriously difficult to know how deep Balfour's views were on any subject. There was certainly brilliance on the surface. Some thought that there was much more to it than that. Birkenhead, though pretty unreliable, described his as 'one of the greatest intellects ever to engage in British politics'.[8] Curzon on the other hand, said that 'he possessed the mind of a marshmallow'.[9] He certainly held views of his own, distinct from those of his advisers. Arnold-Foster, Secretary of State for War from 1903 to 1905, said that it was a waste of time briefing Balfour, because his mind would already be made up on the basis of his own knowledge and prejudices and 'mis-applied general propositions'.[10] Towards the end of his life he told Blanche Dugdale that he could not remember what his policy on protectionism had been at the time of Joe Chamberlain's campaign. 'Was I for it or against it?' 'That,' she replied, 'is what we all wanted to know.'

Much of what we know of Balfour, particularly of his views on Zionism, comes to us through the writings of his niece. It is important to remember that she herself was a fervid Zionist, and also that much of what she learned of her uncle's views was based on his tranquil recollections long after the event, when he may have fought to give his views greater consistency and a greater basis in theory than had been the case.

Part of the difficulty was that the momentum behind the issuing of the declaration had been quite independent of the other strands of Middle East policy. It was produced in isolation from Sykes–Picot, McMahon–Hussein and Hussein–Ibn Saud. It was not designed to dovetail with any of these initiatives. Equally, there was no attempt to see whether it conflicted with any of them. It seems clear that those who drafted the declaration did not even look at McMahon–Hussein, let alone consider whether Palestine was comprehended within the arrangements set out in that correspondence.

2. Idealism or Propaganda?

The traditional view of the Balfour Declaration was that it was the expression of an idealistic reaction to the claim of the Jews to their traditional land. In the last 40 years, it has been explained in more utilitarian terms as having been designed to secure a territorial advantage for Britain in the area between the

Suez Canal and India, and as a propaganda move, directed to appeal to opinion
in the United States and Russia. More recently still, it has been suggested that
the Jews were perceived, in a distinctly anti-Semitic way, as pro-German or
pacifists, and that the declaration was designed to win them over.[11] Jewish
Freemasons came under particular suspicion.

In official circles it was indeed widely believed that Jews in Russia were overwhelmingly in favour of Germany. In 1915, in *The Thirty-nine Steps*, John Buchan
said '[T]his is the return match for the pogroms. The Jew is everywhere . . . with
an eye like a rattlesnake . . . [H]e is the man who is ruling well just now, and he
has his knife in the Empire of the Tsar'. The British ambassador in Petrograd
reported in March 1915 that 'there cannot be the slightest doubt that a very large
number of Jews have been in German pay and have acted as spies during the
campaigns in Poland. Nearly every Russian Officer who returns from the Front
has stories to tell on the subject'.[12] The evidence shows that the stories were no
more than a myth, but they were uncritically accepted by the Foreign Office as
the truth, and they chimed in with the widespread belief – shared, for instance,
by Sir Cecil Spring-Rice, the British ambassador in Washington – of a worldwide
Jewish conspiracy in favour of Germany. Thus Sykes, so involved in the evolution
of the declaration, wrote to Sir Arthur Nicolson, Permanent Under Secretary at
the Foreign Office, on 18 March 1916: 'With "great" Jewry against us there is no
chance of getting the thing [a transfer of support to the allies] through – it means
optimism in Berlin, dumps in London, unease in Paris'.[13]

This anti-Semitic view, the feeling that there was a supranational conspiracy
to influence events in favour of some overriding Jewish interest, can now clearly
be seen to be without any foundation in fact, but there is no question that such
views did exist at the time. Robert Cecil, Parliamentary Under-Secretary for
Foreign Affairs, committed Zionist though he was, said that 'It is not easy to
exaggerate the international power of the Jews' and Lloyd George claimed in
1917 that 'influential Jews' wanted peace, for their own advantages, at a time
when it was premature for Britain.[14]

The truth was that Russian Jewry was not substantially against the war.
Indeed the revolutionaries in Russia who *were* against the war were hostile to
imperialism and annexation, and Jews in Russia did not welcome a British
dimension to Zionism. Kerensky, the socialist leader of Russia between the
February Revolution of 1917 and the Bolshevik October Revolution, looked at
the evidence and concluded that the Jews were not a German Fifth Column and
that '99% of the Russian Jews were against the Bolsheviks and in favour of the
Provisional Government'.[15]

The facts that Kerensky revealed were indeed so widely known at the time
that Barbara Tuchman concluded (wrongly, in my view) that it was impossible 'to

assume the British Government was either so naïve or so uninformed as to be ignorant of the anti-Zionism of the people they were supposedly attempting to influence'.[16] But in his *War Memoirs*, their accuracy admittedly always to be doubted, Lloyd George said that 'Russian Jews had become the chief agents of the German pacifist propaganda in Russia. By 1917, the Russian Jews had done much in preparing for the general disintegration of Russian society . . . it was believed that if Great Britain declared for the fulfilment of Zionist aims in Palestine . . . the effect would be to bring Russian Jewry to the cause of Entente'.[17]

There were then two strands of support for the declaration, the idealistic and the practical. The former can be subdivided into a religious sub-strand and a more general desire to do justice to a people who were felt to have suffered at the hands of Gentiles, and whose fate remained unfinished business. The latter strand subdivides into a propaganda function on the one hand and a geopolitical and military one on the other. The closer one comes to the inner circle of politicians, the more prominent is the first strand. At the level of the professional advisers, the second strand is more significant.

The declaration was put into commission almost immediately for propaganda purposes. C.F.G. (Charlie) Masterman, head of Wellington House, the government propaganda machine, from the outbreak of war until he was replaced by John Buchan in February 1917, minuted to the War Office that he, Sykes, Amery and others had been pressing for a statement to influence American and Russian feeling. A Jewish section of the Department of Information was now set up and the London Zionist Bureau established a propaganda committee within the Department of Information. Over a million pamphlets were printed and distributed. The terms of the pamphlet were not understated. The Balfour Declaration was represented as prefiguring the restoration of Jewish national sovereignty in the Holy Land. The cautious and guarded words used in the declaration itself had been replaced with something much more explicit. When Britain captured Jerusalem and southern Palestine at the end of 1917, credibility was lent to the notion of an early establishment of national sovereignty.

3. Crusades

The concurrence of the practical on the one hand and the idealistic and romantic on the other should not be overlooked. For many in Britain the capture of Jerusalem from the Turks was a noble Crusade. Allenby was the first Christian soldier to capture Jerusalem since the Crusades, and his entry into the city was celebrated by the first ringing of the bells of Westminster Cathedral to take place in the war.

When the General made his entry into Jerusalem, *Punch* published a drawing entitled 'The Last Crusade' showing Richard Coeur de Lion looking down towards Jerusalem and rejoicing: 'My Dream Comes True!'[18] The crusading theme was not confined to *Punch*; but it was deprecated in a D-notice issued by the Press Bureau for the Department of Information at 1.45 p.m. on 15 November 1917: 'The attention of the Press is again drawn to the undesirability of publishing any article, paragraph or picture suggesting that military operations against Turkey are in any sense a Holy War, a modern Crusade, or have anything whatever to do with religious questions. The British Empire is said to contain one hundred million Mohammedan subjects of the King and it is obviously mischievous to suggest that our quarrel with Turkey is one between Christianity and Islam.'[19]

However, while the sensitivities of the king's 'Mohammedan subjects' had to be respected, at a high level within the government the prospect of defeating Islam in Jerusalem had a vivid appeal. Lloyd George saw the Middle East as a more fruitful theatre of war, from a military point of view, than the entrenched Western Front. He had told Allenby in June 1917 that the War Cabinet 'expected "Jerusalem before Christmas"'.[20] He could see other attractions too. He could see the propaganda importance of 'the moral and political advantages to be expected from an advance in Palestine, and particularly from the occupation of Jerusalem, which . . . would be hailed with the utmost satisfaction in all parts of the country'.[21] It was after all he who had ordered John Buchan to organise the campaign *'The Turk must Go'*.

Almost immediately, Buchan found himself addressed by officials who were concerned about the impact of the propaganda on Muslim opinion. This was a real and practical factor. In December 1917, for instance, Allenby had to withdraw a Pathan company from the front line because they could not countenance fighting their Turkish co-religionists.

The two objectives were never reconciled, and confusion became more confused as, for instance, Stephen Gaselee developed an official publication explicitly called *The Holy Land: A New Crusade*. He recorded in a commissioning letter to Benson, the Master of Magdalene College, Cambridge, that 'It is particularly on the sentimental, romantic and religious side of the Palestine campaign that the Prime Minister and Buchan wish emphasis to be laid, especially in the ecclesiastical press, and if you will keep the crusading idea in mind as you write the article, I feel certain that the results will be what they want'.[22]

The crusading theme appealed to writers, readers and soldiers themselves — or at least officers and others brought up in the romantic tradition of British history and the novels of Sir Walter Scott. John Buchan had written a *Life of Scott*. Sykes turned a cross on his estate into a war monument on which those killed were commemorated as modern Crusaders. After his death, his own monument represented him as a Crusader, with Jerusalem in the background. T.E. Lawrence's undergraduate thesis was a study of the Crusades. The coffin of the Unknown Warrior, deposited in Westminster Abbey in 1920, contains a real Crusader sword, a personal gift from the king.

Against all this limb of policy, Curzon, always informed and always sensitive to eastern considerations, pressed that the news of the entry into Jerusalem should be handled carefully to avoid alienating Muslim opinion. He liaised with Sykes to ensure that a proclamation stressed that all religious institutions in the city, whether Christian, Jewish or Muslim, would be safeguarded. The Mosque of Omar and the tomb at Hebron were placed under exclusive Muslim control. Allenby was told to stress that the hereditary custodians of the *Waqf*, an inalienable religious site under Muslim jurisdiction, at the gate of the Church of the Holy Sepulchre had been asked to continue their traditional duties.

As in more recent Western incursions into Arab countries, the word 'crusade' can sometimes sound more significant than was intended. It was sometimes, though not usually, used without regard to its origins. Thus in the Second World War, with no anti-Muslim sentiments in mind, Eisenhower delivered this message over the PA systems on the craft carrying the D-Day troops: 'Soldiers, sailors and airmen of the Allied Expeditionary Force! You are about to embark on a Great Crusade, towards which we have striven these many months.'[23]

At the same time as British newspapers were celebrating the success of the new Crusade, soldiers and officials in the Middle East noted an Arab prophecy which said that the prophet from the west would enter Jerusalem through the Golden Gate and end Turkish rule when Nile water was brought into Palestine. The men on the spot were delighted to realise that Nile water was now being carried into Palestine through a British pipeline and that Allenby's name, when written in Arabic spells 'al Nebi', 'the prophet'.[24] Alas Allenby could not fulfil the prophecy. He found that if he entered through the Golden Gate he would violate the sanctity of a Muslim graveyard and the Mosque of Omar.

Lloyd George was personally involved in the management of the historic events, which were used in film, drawings and photographs. Personnel had been sent in advance to record what happened. It was easier to stage-manage events in Jerusalem than to control exuberance at home. There was no religious element to the entry, the fact that the Palestinian campaign had been pretty well exclusively British was concealed by the use of troops from all over the Empire and even French and Italian contingents, no flags were flown, and above all, Allenby was instructed to enter on foot. When, previously, the Kaiser had entered on horseback 'the saying went round "a better man than he walked". The advantage of contrast and conduct will be obvious.'[25] Indeed, when the

Kaiser entered the city in 1898 he did so wearing a Crusader's costume. Allenby did nothing so crass. The Director of Military Intelligence said that Allenby on foot was 'the sort of touch which appeal[s] to Eastern feeling'.[26]

After the entry, discretion began to fragment. Sykes felt that the coverage had been far too highbrow: 'What is wanted is popular reading for the English church and chapel folk; for New York Irish; Orthodox Balkan peasants and Mujiks; French and Italian Catholics; and Jews throughout the world; Indian and Algerian Muslims. Articles should give striking actualities, and description of scenes; picturesque details. Rivet the British on to Holy Land, Bible and New Testament . . .'[27]

A much more populist theme followed in coverage of events in Jerusalem. But ambivalence persisted, with the D-notice still occasionally enforced. Representations of the events frequently depicted the British in the role of Crusaders. However innocent such a reaction was, capital was made of it.[28]

The propaganda value of the declaration was vigorously exploited. But efforts were made to avoid alienating Muslim opinion. Apart from issuing the Balfour Declaration, the government took no steps during the war to further Zionism, and propaganda efforts were directed at Muslims as well as Jews. A central message in Allenby's proclamation was that 'every sacred building, monument, Holy spot, shrine, traditional site, endowment, pious bequest, or customary place of prayer, of whatsoever form of the three religions will be maintained and protected'.[29]

Indeed even later Allenby was at pains to emphasise that 'It was not a last crusade . . . There was no religious impulse in this campaign'.[30] In Britain, things were seen slightly differently. *The Times* pointed out that two of the British commanders were descended from knights who had fought in the Crusades. An edition of Lloyd George's War Speeches was entitled 'The Great Crusade'.

Attempts were made to reassure Arabs who were concerned by the declaration. An unofficial Zionist Commission was established partly to further the establishment of a new Jewish nation, but partly also to emphasise that there was no hostility towards the indigenous population. The attempts were disingenuous. Crusading, in the full sense of the word, was part of the mental approach of Britons in the First World War where Turkey and Islam were involved.

4. Reaction

News of the declaration caused consternation in the Arab world. As soon as Hussein heard about it, he urgently asked Britain what it meant. This was the reason for sending David Hogarth to Jeddah in January 1918 to clarify the position and to deliver the Hogarth Message.

We have seen that the Hogarth Message acknowledged that 'the Arab race shall be given full opportunity of once again forming a nation in the world' but did not go very far to offer practical assistance to that end. Self-help was the idea. Policy was more specific in relation to Jewish aspirations. 'Since the Jewish opinion of the world is in favour of a return of Jews to Palestine and in as much as this opinion must remain a constant factor, and further as His Majesty's Government view with favour the realisation of this aspiration, His Majesty's Government are determined that insofar as is compatible with the freedom of the existing population both economic and political, no obstacle should be put in the way of the realisation of this ideal'.[31] In addition to respecting the freedom of the existing population, [in relation to Palestine, Britain was] 'determined that no people shall subject to another'.

Subsequently Hussein felt that he had been betrayed: that Britain had promised Arab independence in Palestine and that Hogarth had confirmed that promise. In reality, what Hogarth had promised fell short of an independent Arab Palestine. Indeed, by saying that 'no people shall be subject to another', he had ruled it out. He did, however, go on to tell Hussein that Jewish settlement in Palestine would not be allowed to conflict with *the political and economic freedom of the Arab population*'. Hussein took the trouble to make a manuscript note of these words, which go further than those used in the declaration itself, *'the civil and religious rights of the Arab population'*.

Hussein was sympathetic to the idea of providing the Jews with a refuge from persecution, but there was to be no compromise over Arab sovereignty. But it really is not clear that, at the time, Hussein was all that bothered about Arab independence for Palestine, and Hogarth had said enough to satisfy him for the moment.

Other Arabs were more concerned. In the spring of 1918 the combined effect of the Balfour Declaration and Sykes–Picot was causing real alarm among Arabs about the true motives of the British. This concern manifested itself in many ways including the presentation of a Memorial to the British government by a distinguished group of seven Arabs in Cairo, in which the British government was asked to clarify its position, in particular in relation to the government to be set up after the War in Syria, Palestine and Iraq. The Foreign Office responded on 16 June 1918 with what was called the Declaration to the Seven.

The Declaration to the Seven was received with great enthusiasm in the Arab world. It went even further than McMahon–Hussein in confirming undertakings to the Arabs. It dealt with four categories of territory. The first two were territories that were free and independent before the War and territories liberated by the Arabs themselves. In these cases, the British government recognised 'the complete and sovereign independence of the Arabs inhabiting those territories'.

For the third category, territories liberated from the Ottoman Empire by the Allies (Mesopotamia from the Persian Gulf to a line north of Baghdad and Palestine from the Egyptian Frontier to a line north of Jerusalem and Jaffa), 'the future government of those territories should be based upon the principle of the consent of the governed'.

The fourth category consisted of Arab territories still under Turkish rule – most of Syria plus Mosul. In this category 'the oppressed peoples . . . should obtain their freedom and independence', and Britain would work for the achievement of that objective.

The essence of the Declaration to the Seven was that in relation to Syria, Palestine and Iraq Britain would work for freedom and independence and no regime would be set up that was not acceptable to the populations. The declaration was hugely reassuring and did much to dispel the disquiet that had been caused by the revelations about Sykes–Picot and the Balfour Declaration.[32]

On 3 January 1919, Faisal signed an agreement with Chaim Weizmann about the Jewish homeland in Palestine. Faisal thereafter sent a letter to Felix Frankfurter, the head of the American Zionist delegation. The letter is a poignant record of what might have been: 'We feel that the Arabs and Jews are cousins in race . . . [and] have suffered similar oppression at the hands of powers stronger than themselves . . . [W]e Arabs, especially the educated among us, look with the deepest sympathy on the Zionist movement . . . We will wish the Jews a hearty welcome here . . . People less informed and less responsible than our leaders and yours, ignoring the need for co-operation of the Arabs and Zionists, have been trying to exploit the local difficulties that must necessarily arise in Palestine in the early stages of our movements'.[33]

Some British 'Arabs' were not equally reassured. Gertrude Bell's reaction to the Balfour Declaration was characteristically extreme: 'I hate Mr. Balfour's Zionist pronouncement. It's my belief that it can't be carried out, the country is wholly unsuited to the ends the Jews have in view; it is a poor land, incapable of great development and with a solid two thirds of its population Mohammedan Arabs who look on Jews with contempt. To my mind it's a wholly artificial scheme divorced from all relation to facts and I wish it the ill success it deserves – and will get, I fancy'.[34]

Gertrude Bell has appeared and been introduced already, but it is time now to step aside briefly from the march of events to encounter the two administrators with whom she was most closely associated, Percy Cox and Arnold Wilson.

14

PERSONALITIES

1. Percy Cox

Aubrey Herbert was on his first visit to Persia when he met Percy Cox in 1906. Herbert was not impressed by Persia: 'An immoral people; dirty streets; liars'. He liked Cox, however, who invited him to stay at the consulate. Cox, a soldier-consul, like many of the men who feature in this chronicle, already had a substantial reputation. Herbert seems to have found him quieter than he had expected. The household itself cannot have been quiet. It included ten cats, a dog, a parrot and several monkeys.[1] Cox could speak many languages. He was known for 'his ability to keep silent in a dozen'.[2] The Arabs respected him, almost loved him: 'Kokkus'. His very silence, along with his height, lean frame and a nose broken in a football match, endeared him to them and engendered respect.

He had a brilliant career in the administration of India before the war. In 1914 he was made Secretary to the Government of India, but when war was declared he moved to the Gulf as chief political officer with the Indian Expeditionary Force. He was promoted honorary major general in the course of the war and fought under Townshend. Indeed he wanted to stay with Townshend at Kut till the end, and had to be ordered to leave. But his main role was political and administrative. In November 1918 he went from Mesopotamia to Persia. But his advice was still indispensable in relation to Iraq, and he returned there in June 1920 as High Commissioner, when the stability of the region was threatened by the Euphrates Revolt. Gertrude Bell was his devoted Oriental Secretary. His relationship with the new king, Faisal, was precarious. He concluded at one stage that Faisal was forgetting his limited role. He had 'unmistakeably displayed the cloven hoof . . . [H]e is without doubt both crooked and insincere'.[3] Cox had to remind him on occasions who really was the master. The king came to heel, and by the time Cox retired in 1923 the new state of Iraq was established well enough to survive despite all its cracks and flaws. That it did so was largely due to his efforts. Major General Sir Percy Cox, GCMG, GCIE, KCSI, died in 1937, aged 73. His one son died in the Great War and his one daughter died at birth.

2. Arnold Wilson

Arnold Wilson was also a big man, over six feet tall, but much broader than Cox. Like Cox he was an outstanding linguist. He spoke several Indian dialects and was familiar with Persian poetry. He was physically strong and displayed great courage, winning the DSO while he was with the Indian army in Mesopotamia, where he was Cox's deputy chief political officer. Before the war he had surveyed parts of Persia wearing native dress and only just escaping capture and death. At Basra, dressed in old-style Indian army tunic, buttoning up to the neck – instead of the now usual collar and tie – and with belt and parallel shoulder straps – instead of Sam Browne – he reminded some of a hero of the Indian Mutiny, and he was in some ways a throw-back to earlier times. His office was covered in Latin mottoes to encourage his tireless energy.[4]

In 1918, when Cox was sent to Teheran, Wilson took over in Iraq as acting Civil Commissioner and Political Resident in the Gulf. He had thus to cope with the insurrection of 1920. He was only 34. He had huge self-confidence and considerable abilities, but his career never fully recovered from what was seen, not only by Bell, as a heavy-handed reaction to events. He interfered too much, and declined to involve local potentates. He came to see that the installation of a local ruler, preferably Faisal, was necessary, but by then he had lost the confidence of the government, and the initiative was not recovered until Cox came back.

Whatever view one takes of his policies, he was a remarkable man. Gertrude Bell spoke of his 'brilliant abilities, a combined mental and physical power which is extremely rare'.[5] He had a prodigious memory, great energy and capacity for hard work. He was well read and must have bewildered his colleagues in London with his references in his despatches to Bacon, Shakespeare, Milton, Virgil and Socrates.

He had been stiff with Gertrude Bell, initially – amazingly – quite simply ignoring the woman in the mess and excluding her from his confidence. Later he accepted her as a colleague though suspecting her of intrigue. She respected him and, given any encouragement, acknowledged his abilities, though eventually their diverging views on the future of Iraq would separate them.

On 30 August 1918 Bell heard that Cox was going from Baghdad to Teheran. She would be left with Arnold Wilson. 'However, Capt. Wilson and I are excellent colleagues and best of friends . . .'[6] By the end of the year she was still recording a comradely relationship with Wilson: 'A.T. Wilson and I spend a considerable part of our time laying down acceptable frontiers – by request. It's an amusing game when you know the country intimately, as I do . . . Was ever anything more fortunate than that I should have criss-crossed it in very nearly every direction'.[7] A couple of years later, when Wilson received his knighthood, Gertrude felt no resentment. 'A.T. has been given a K.C.I.E. – I'm very, very glad. He well deserves it . . .'[8]

At times she was more outspoken. Their paths diverged over just how Arab Mesopotamia should be, and Wilson never matched up to Cox in Gertrude's opinion. What was initially only sporadic irritation on her part finally crystallized into permanent estrangement or something pretty like it.

A critical view of Wilson and a fuller record of the annoyance he could cause her is recorded in the unedited version of her letters, though even when he annoyed her most she was not blind to Wilson's good points. Her stepmother also edited the letters to conceal her disappointment about the lack of affection Bell thought she received from her.

Wilson could have had a much more productive relationship with her if he had unbent a little, taken her more into his confidence and been readier to recognise her abilities. Instead he always saw her as a junior who could not be relied on not to sabotage his work.

Wilson entered Parliament as a Conservative in 1933. He was on the left on domestic issues, but far to the right in foreign affairs. He was well disposed to the regimes of Mussolini and Franco and was impressed by Hitler. But he was no anti-Semite, and was revolted by the Nazi attitude to the Jews. When the war broke out, at the age of 55 he joined the RAF, first as a pilot officer, and then in the most dangerous of all roles, as a rear-gunner in a bomber squadron. Rear-gunner Sir Arnold Wilson, KCIE, CSI, CMG, DSO, MP, was recorded 'missing believed killed' over France in 1940.

III

THE STRESSES OF PEACE

15

THE ENTENTE UNDER PRESSURE

1. The Approach to Damascus

The enduring French connection with Syria went back to the Crusades and the French knights with their estates and their castles. France felt that she had a peculiar and proprietorial interest. The links with Christian communities in the area were reinforced by commercial connections. This long history of contact had unfortunately generated no love for France among the natives, a fact which meant that France had to work doubly hard to implement her acquisitive policy.

France – not unreasonably – believed that Syria had been promised to her by Sykes–Picot. But as time passed, Britain, as has been seen, tended to regard Sykes–Picot as capable of modification. France was well aware of that, and the awareness reinforced her belief in habitual British bad faith. The increasingly poor relations between the wartime Allies informed the interwar history of the Middle East.

It is worth making a light-hearted digression. A charming insight into the tensions between Britain and France over Middle Eastern oil emerges from a study of *Tintin and the Land of Black Gold, Tintin au Pays de l'Or Noir* in its original French version, the fifteenth of the books about the youthful reporter, Tintin, and his little dog, Snowy, written and illustrated by the Belgian Hergé. It was written in the late 1930s. Part only was published in 1939 and 1940. The story turns on tampering with fuel, which is causing cars to explode all over the place. National economies are threatened as war approaches. Tintin and Snowy go off to investigate.

The action takes place in Palestine under the British mandate. The British presence is much in evidence. British warplanes drop leaflets. A sailor, O'Connor, who tries to bump off Snowy, claims to be from British Intelligence. Tintin himself is arrested by the British, who are far from the goodies in the story. There are other political elements, reflecting the conflict in Palestine. At various points, Tintin is taken prisoner by Zionist terrorists and by Arab gunmen.

After Belgium fell to the Germans, Hergé worked on a collaborationist newspaper. He stopped publication of the story, but it appeared in occupied France during the war, edited to avoid upsetting Pétainist sensibilities. The textual history of the book is interesting. It was published in France again in 1945, then by Hergé in 1948 in *Tintin Magazine*, and in 1972 in the version that is available today. Some appalling Belgian puns are constants (for example, Yussuf Ben Mulfrid is a reference to the Belgian staple, *moules frites*, and Bir Kegg does not require much explanation). But the political elements vary according to the place and date of publication. Happily for British fans of the little reporter with his quiff, by 1972 the anti-British sentiments have disappeared. Indeed the Brits have no role in the story, which is now set in a fictitious Arab state, and not Palestine.

At the Peace Conference in Paris, Lloyd George tried to secure an independent Syria, an Arab Syria, for Faisal, Britain's favourite Arab. Britain thought she could argue for Faisal without appearing to be breaking with the French. The policy was to assert as a fact that Faisal's supporters, the Sharifians, had seized Damascus by themselves before the end of the war. As will be seen, this was disingenuous: Britain had deliberately stood back and encouraged the Arabs to go first.[1] Even then, they did not quite get in first.

Hussein's troops advanced towards Damascus under a banner that Sykes had designed specially for him, the black, white, green and red echoing the glories of the Ottoman past and associating Hussein with them; Hussein slightly changed the tint of the red. The Foreign Office ordered that this flag should be the one flown over Damascus when it was captured. And it was important that it should be captured by Faisal, so that there was no question of a Christian occupation of a Muslim city. As Faisal was three days away when this decision was made on 29 September 1918, Anzac cavalry was instructed to pursue the Turks by riding *round* Damascus, and not through it.

T.E. Lawrence played an interesting role in this incident. He was a complicated man. No one has been able fully to understand him, and it is clear that he did not fully understand himself. It is worth at least trying to do so.

2. Lawrence and Links

Gertrude Bell met Lawrence for the first time on 19 May 1911 at Carchemish, on the borders of Syria and Turkey, where Lawrence and Campbell Thomson, Hogarth's assistant at the Ashmolean Museum in Oxford, were digging. Gertrude wore a long, divided skirt, linen jacket and a *kafeeyah* draped from the brim of a canvas hat. She was looking for 'a young man called Lawrence (an interesting boy, he is going to make a traveller) who had for some time been expecting that I would appear'. She found a short, strongly built man with yellow hair and blue eyes wearing a grey flannel blazer piped in pink, white flannel shorts, grey stockings and red Arab slippers. He wore a red tasselled Arab belt, the mark of bachelorhood, and the villagers assumed that Gertrude was coming out as his bride. When she rode out of camp at 5.30 a.m. the following morning she was surprised to be jeered by these villagers: Lawrence had told them that she was too plain for him to think of marrying her. Marriage was far from Lawrence's agenda, but he became fond of Bell and respected her. She had an equal affection for Lawrence. It rested on his enthusiasm for the Arab cause.

Lawrence had been turned down for military service because of his height. He was widely referred to as 'Little Lawrence'. He also looked about ten years younger than his real age. Unlike the gilded youths who filled the Arab Bureau, Lawrence came from a fairly ordinary background. He was illegitimate and had not gone to a public school. He had none of the glamour of his colleagues, many of whom had done dashing military service. He had worked for Hogarth at the Ashmolean Museum. Hogarth managed to wangle him into the geographical section of the War Office in the autumn of 1914 as a temporary second lieutenant-translator. He came out to the Middle East to prepare survey maps and managed to stay on. He impressed Hussein's son Abdullah and as a result met the Emir's other sons in the desert. There he was captivated by Faisal, 'an absolute ripper'. He pressed for Faisal's appointment as field commander of the revolt.

Despite or because of his lack of height, Lawrence did not lack panache. He was always ready to break rules and short-circuit chains of communication and command. He chose to report on his experience with Faisal direct to Wingate, the Governor General of the Sudan, who was about to replace McMahon as High Commissioner in Cairo. From Faisal in the Hejaz Lawrence returned not to Cairo but direct to Wingate. Wingate had always been in favour of using the Arab tribes to attack Turkey and indeed Wingate later claimed that it was he and not 'poor little Lawrence' who was behind the Arab Revolt.

Vyvyan Richards, who wrote a biography of Lawrence and contributed to *T.E. Lawrence by His Friends*, compared Lawrence with St Francis, Leonardo da Vinci, Odysseus, Shakespeare and Stonewall Jackson. The public appreciation of Lawrence may not have changed all that much since then, but he has a very different position in the view of those who have looked further at the facts. In 1938 Antonius argued in *The Arab Awakening* that Lawrence's role had not been what he claimed it to be, and Aldington's *Lawrence of Arabia: A Biographical Enquiry* in 1955 revealed false claims made on his behalf by his biographers piled on top of his own falsehoods. Antonius also revealed that the 1924 Lowell

Thomas book, *With Lawrence in Arabia*, so obviously bogus that Lawrence's supporters and even Lawrence himself disowned it, had been partly written with Lawrence's collaboration. In 1956, Kedourie in *England and the Middle East* effectively minimised the importance not only of Lawrence, but of the Arab Revolt itself. Lawrence himself admitted that he was unreliable, turning 'dull little incidents' into 'hair-breadth escapes', he was 'imprisoned in a lie'.[2]

Some of the revisionist biographies are almost as sensational and intemperate as the writings on which the myth rested. It is impossible to be certain about all details, but it is clear that many of the episodes in *Seven Pillars of Wisdom* never took place, such as the capture of Aqaba or the Battle of Tafilah. Lawrence was almost certainly not imprisoned and tortured because of the amorous ambitions of the governor of Deraa. The governor was extravagantly heterosexual, whereas Lawrence was a sexual masochist who craved attention from male assailants.

Lowell Thomas was a young showman from the United States who had never achieved very much until he managed to get to the Middle East with a cameraman, looking for a story to sell. In the autumn of 1918 John Buchan, in his role as Director of Intelligence at the Ministry of Information, attached him to Allenby's army as a war correspondent. He had a propaganda mission to fulfil, and he found it when he came face-to-face with the short (5 feet, 5 inches), blond and wholly un-Arabic Lawrence, whom Ronald Storrs improbably introduced to him as 'the uncrowned king of Arabia'.[3] Lawrence in his exotic robes was irresistible and the result was a show, a lecture with projected photographs, entitled, interestingly, *The Last Crusade*. It was only loosely based on reality, but was hugely entertaining. It played to enormous audiences in New York, moving to Madison Square Garden. It then came to London – Covent Garden and the Albert Hall. It ran for six months in London and about a million people saw it. Lawrence was one of them. He claimed to be embarrassed by the brash sensationalism, but he kept coming back from Oxford to see it. Thomas's wife saw him in the audience on at least five occasions. He blushed crimson and ran away. The show then went on round the world. 'It made young Lowell Thomas rich and famous and it converted "Lawrence of Arabia" into a world hero'.[4]

The inaccuracies are far too numerous to list in full. It exaggerated what the Arab rising had done. The Arab Army was said to consist of about 200,000 men instead of perhaps 7,000. And it vastly exaggerated Lawrence's role in the whole matter. From having been a minor official, largely working at a desk, Lawrence was transferred into the man who single-handedly masterminded and led the revolt.

When they met at the Peace Conference, Lawrence told Gertrude Bell that he planned to write a book in order to dispose of some of the myths that had been created by Lowell Thomas in the lecture shows and in Thomas's book

– though in the event he greatly embellished an elaborate narrative.[5] He claimed to be embarrassed by the ballyhoo, but he did nothing to put the record right. He adopted the myth and even developed it. Later he admitted that parts of *Seven Pillars of Wisdom* could not be relied on; but he never made any serious attempts to separate myth from reality. Thomas put it well. He said that Lawrence had 'a genius for backing into the limelight'.[6] He was hypocritical, or at least confused, in his attitude to the 'Lawrence of Arabia' myth, and certainly not as allergic to it as he claimed to be.

Amery on Lawrence: '[H]e was a strange, elusive creature, unsure of himself, alternating between extreme shyness and dislike of publicity, and a no less keen desire that his achievement should be known'.[7] Amery wrote that Lawrence had been sensible and balanced on Arab matters, but in the early 1920s he regarded him as 'a very strange creature, . . . mad'.[8]

Views of Lawrence always polarised. Fortunately for him, those who took him at his own estimation, like the romantic Churchill, were sometimes in powerful positions. There were others. Even the explorer and administrator St John Philby, of whom more later, not usually generous, was kind. When Lawrence worked with him in Jordan in 1921 Philby found him practical but unbusinesslike. Philby himself was neither. He described Lawrence going around the countryside, making snap decisions and leaving it to others to get on with administration.[9]

Antonius' judgement is fair:

Lawrence's understanding of the forces at work in the earlier history of the Arab National Movement is both incomplete and faulty. Not that there was anything so remote or so complex in the outward tendencies of the Movement as to elude his grasp; and his mind was sensitive and quick. But the barriers of language and temperament being what they were, sensitiveness and intelligence could not alone give him insight . . . Like all highly perceptive people, he was generally right, but he was apt to place too much reliance on his intuition . . . It is doubtful whether Lawrence was fully conscious of the extent of his limitations, though he frequently alluded to them in speech or in his writings. He was aware, for instance, that his knowledge of Arabic was far from perfect, yet he believed that he was sufficiently fluent in it to pass for an Arab in conversation with Arabs . . . [N]either his accent nor his use of words – to say nothing of his appearance, could have deceived anyone in Arabia for long.[10]

Now that most of the *personae* have been introduced, it is worth briefly returning to the theme of how closely linked they were. Among Aubrey

Herbert's closest friends were John Buchan, Rupert Brooke, the politicians Maurice Baring and Raymond Asquith and also Hilaire Belloc, who had tutored him at Oxford. Sykes received praise for his book *Dar-ul-Islam* from H.G. Wells, who referred to it frequently in his *Outline of History*. Rudyard Kipling also approved of the book: 'You ought to have been born in the east.' Sykes was a friend of Belloc and the politician George Wyndham. Shakespear's cousin was Olivia Shakespear, a close friend and lover of W.B. Yeats. Her daughter married Ezra Pound.

Richard Meinertzhagen, an intelligence agent before the war and Allenby's intelligence chief during it, was an extraordinary, improbable character. How much of what he claimed to have done truly took place is doubtful. He was known as 'the man who killed people with his bare hands'. His victims included his personal assistant in India, possibly his first wife in the course of routine shared revolver practice and according to Lawrence 'a cornered mob of Germans, . . . spattering [their] brains out one by one with his African knob-kerri'.[11] Meinertzhagen was involved from his youth in intellectual society through his mother's family the Potters. Beatrice Webb was his aunt. Herbert Spencer, Sir Francis Galton, Aldous Huxley, George Eliot, Bernard Shaw and Oscar Wilde were friends. Clement Atlee played with him when they were children, and he was at school with Winston Churchill. Joseph Chamberlain had unsuccessfully wooed his aunt.

Gertrude Bell had extensive connections. She could dedicate her book *Amurath to Amurath* to Lord Cromer. As Consul General and *de facto* ruler of Egypt for an enormous span, 1883–1907, Cromer had more influence in Egypt than any other Briton. Bell was related to Bertrand Russell and to Russell's confidante and mistress, Lady Ottoline Morrell. Bell's sisters were friends of Virginia Stephen, who married Leonard Woolf. These were not her only Bloomsbury friends. Harold Nicolson was related to her and, like his wife, Vita Sackville-West, was a close friend. Vita wrote the foreword to a biography of Gertrude. George Trevelyan, of the Cambridge intellectual dynasty, was her brother-in-law. He and Cecil Spring-Rice, the chargé d'affaires in St Petersburg who went on to be ambassador to the United States, also a relation, stayed with Gertrude Bell in summer of 1905.

David Hogarth was a close friend of Sir Wilfred Blunt, a well-known Arabist and famous poet. Again there are links here with Belloc, Ezra Pound and W.B. Yeats. Circles all intersected. Yeats and Blunt initially met at the home of Lady Gregory. Lady Gregory worked with Yeats, was Blunt's mistress for many years and although chiefly associated with Irish nationalism, had witnessed Egyptian nationalism during the revolt of Urabi Pasha in 1882. The Blunts were part of a circle that brought in Alfred Douglas, Arthur Balfour, G.K. Chesterton and

Churchill. This briefest of sketches only touches on the extent of a vast and interwoven network and the freemasonry which it engendered.[12]

3. *The Entry to Damascus*

Lawrence had urged Faisal to get to Damascus before Allenby and 'biff the French out of all hope of Syria'.[13] For Lawrence, Damascus, freighted with historical significance, was a jewel to be grasped by Arabs. He was horrified that the Australian Third Light Horse, told to bypass the city, had cut right through it. They were greeted by notables and received an official welcome, showered with confetti and rosewater. The inhabitants kissed the men's stirrups.

When Allenby's cavalry commander, General Sir Harry Chauvel, pushing far ahead of the infantry, reached Damascus on 10 October 1917, he found that Lawrence had slipped the lead and gone off into Damascus without permission. Chauvel headed after his liaison officer and found that Lawrence had driven into Damascus in an old Rolls-Royce armoured car and had proceeded to make appointments. He allowed Nuri al-Said, a Sharifian, a supporter of Faisal who was to be a key figure in Iraqi politics for a generation, to install an Arab governor. Lawrence was reduced to making weak excuses about having assumed that he was supposed to reconnoitre. Chauvel asked to see the governor and was surprised to be introduced to an Arab and not an Ottoman. Lawrence said that the Arab had been elected by the people after the Ottoman official had fled. Chauvel swallowed the story and confirmed the appointment.

It was some days before Allenby and Faisal arrived. When Lawrence asked permission for Faisal and his supporters to enter the city in triumph, Allenby was less than enthusiastic. 'Seeing that he, Faisal, had had very little to do with the double "conquest" of Damascus, the suggested triumphal entry did not appeal to me very much but I thought it would do no harm and gave permission accordingly.'[14]

Later that day Allenby summoned Faisal and Lawrence to the Hotel Victoria. Allenby had to sort out the politics of the situation. His original orders had been that the Turkish governor was to be retained for the moment, so that the French dimension would not have to be explored. Chauvel's confirmation of a Sharifian Arab had scuppered that. Allenby told Faisal that France was to be the protecting power and that Faisal, on behalf of Hussein, would administer Syria, but not Palestine or the Lebanon, under French guidance and with a French liaison officer, whom Lawrence would be expected to assist. Faisal wanted none of this. He said that he had not known anything about the French role and that he wanted the Lebanon, as a country without a port was no use to him. Allenby was astounded. He asked Lawrence if he had not explained to Faisal that the French were to have the protectorate.

> *Lawrence*: 'No Sir, I knew nothing about it.'
> *Allenby*: 'But you knew definitely that he, Faisal, was to have nothing to do with the Lebanon.'
> *Lawrence*: 'No Sir, I did not.'

Eventually Allenby reminded Faisal that he was a lieutenant general under British command and that he had to obey orders. Faisal accepted the situation and withdrew.

Faisal and Lawrence were of course not telling the truth. Lawrence subsequently claimed that Faisal meant that he had never been advised of the situation *officially*. What he himself had meant he did not explain. In *Seven Pillars of Wisdom*, he admits that he did know about the Sykes–Picot Agreement and indeed 'had earlier betrayed the Treaty's existence to Faisal'.[15]

But on the whole Sykes–Picot was a pretty well-kept secret. Cox only learned of it in April 1917. In 1916 when Hogarth learned about the pact, he had written to Blinker Hall, the Director of Intelligence, requesting an immediate cover-up: 'The conclusion of this Agreement is of no immediate service to our Arab policy as pursued here, and will only not be a grave disadvantage if, for some time to come, it is kept strictly secret'.[16]

Faisal went off, leaving Allenby with Lawrence. Lawrence told Allenby that he did not want to serve along with a French adviser and would like to take the leave to which he was entitled and go back to London. Allenby agreed, and indeed encouraged Lawrence to argue the case against France when he got home.

4. London

Lawrence appeared before the Eastern Committee of the Cabinet at the end of October. He started by misrepresenting the Declaration to the Seven, saying that it promised independence to the Arabs wherever they liberated themselves, rather than in the areas that had been liberated at the date of the declaration. He then claimed that Faisal and some 4,000 tribesmen had been the first to enter Damascus.

The Eastern Committee had no more sympathy than Allenby for the French position. A number of anonymous articles which Lawrence had written for *The Times* further exaggerated and embellished Faisal's achievement to the detriment of the French claim. Much of his story gained unofficial and even official acceptance, but Lawrence was well aware of what he was doing. When Robert Graves, writing a biography of Lawrence, said that he was going to base his account of the liberation of Damascus on what Lawrence had written in *Seven Pillars of Wisdom*, Lawrence warned him that 'I was on thin ice when I wrote the Damascus chapter and anyone who copies me will be through it if he is not careful. S[even] P[illars] is full of half-truth here'.[17]

Curzon and the Eastern Committee were all for abrogating the Sykes–Picot Agreement. It was, they said, out of date; but to Curzon's irritation the Foreign Office felt that the document had to be honoured. That was a surprising view: most British insiders did not regard Sykes–Picot as being the stuff of a treaty. Hogarth, head of the Arab Bureau, said that nobody took the agreement seriously or supported it, apart from Sykes. Curzon himself said the agreement was 'absolutely impracticable' as well as obsolete: 'When the Sykes–Picot Agreement was drawn up it was, no doubt, intended by its authors . . . as a sort of fancy sketch to suit a situation that had not then arisen, and which it was thought extremely unlikely would ever arise; that, I suppose, must be the principal explanation of the gross ignorance with which the boundary lines on that agreement were drawn'.[18]

A great deal of thought was given on how to get out of Sykes–Picot in regard to Syria without unduly upsetting France. Britain had already departed from the agreement in order to get Palestine. She did not want Syria for herself, but she did not want France to get it. Faisal and an independent Arab State would be much better.

Even Sykes himself had stopped believing in Sykes–Picot. On 5 October 1918 he discussed with Amery what should be done about it. His latest idea was that France should get nothing in Arabia apart from the Lebanon, but in compensation should get Kurdistan and Armenia. France did not welcome the proposal. In recognition of Faisal's argument that he needed a port, Sykes suggested transferring a French coastal port to the Arab portion of Syria. Picot seemed prepared to consider this, but ultimately the proposal was rejected. At the end of the day, Britain could not face the rupture with France (which, it turned out, was only two or three years away), and for the moment was more interested in British control of Palestine than Arab control of Syria.

Lloyd George did not view Syria in strategic terms. Many of the others, however, always looked at the area in the context of imperial planning. The General Staff said in a memorandum of 9 December 1918, 'It is difficult to see how any arrangement could be more objectionable from a military point of view than the Sykes–Picot Agreement of 1916, by which an enterprising and ambitious foreign power is placed on interior lines with reference to our position in the Middle East'.

It is important to remember that responsible officials could and did regard France as 'an enterprising and ambitious foreign power' in 1918. Curzon told the Eastern Committee, 'a good deal of my public life has been spent in connection with the political ambitions of France and almost every distant region where the French have sway. We have been brought, for reasons of national safety, into an alliance with the French, which I hope will last, but their political character is different from ours, and their political interest will collide with ours in many cases. I am seriously afraid that the great power from whom we have most to fear in future is France'. He told the Eastern Committee that it was imperative to exclude France from Syria.[19] Senior officials in Cairo thought that after the war there would be a return to the crises and confrontations of the Fashoda years, the colonial brushes that had brought France and Britain close to war before the Entente.

Lloyd George used the Lawrence/Faisal exaggeration of the Arab contribution to the capture of Damascus to bolster his arguments. In 1919 his office distributed a confidential background document to the press claiming that Faisal had 'materially assisted' Allenby and had entered 'the four great inland towns of Syria'. Further, the Sharifian forces were represented not as invaders from outside the area, which they were, but as native Arab troops. If on this view Syria itself had risen up against the Turks, it would be most un-Wilsonian to give the country to an outside power. Lloyd George knew very well that Faisal's troops amounted to just a few thousand men, but he happily adopted Faisal's claim that 100,000 had served with him or his father. That was the figure Lloyd George used in his negotiations with the French (although 'Eastern arithmetic is proverbially romantic' and he considered the Arab contribution to the conquest of Syria and Palestine to be 'almost insignificant').[20]

At the end of the day, he could not resist the French claim to Syria, but he was not impressed by it. At a meeting of the Big Four at the Paris Peace Conference on 20 March 1919, he said that it was 'England who had organised the whole of the Syrian campaign. There would have been no question of Syria but for England'. However, Arab help had been essential. He produced Allenby to his fellow-negotiators and asked him if that were not the case. Allenby said that Arab assistance had indeed been invaluable. Lloyd George went on to say that 'King Hussein had put all his resources into the field, which had helped us most materially to win the victory. France had for practical purposes accepted our undertaking to King Hussein in signing the 1916 (Sykes–Picot) Agreement . . . [I]f the British government now agree that Damascus, Homs, Hama and Aleppo should be included in this sphere of direct French influence, they would be breaking faith with the Arabs, and they could not face this . . .'[21] The argument was that British and Arab feats of arms had superseded any vague promises made to France in different circumstances.

The etymological significance of the words used to qualify the four towns was examined in depth. 'Districts' might mean vilayets, or provinces or, alternatively, *wilayahs*, or environs. A 'district' might also mean simply a town. In the edition of the *Encyclopaedia Britannica* then available, the four towns are shown as the *only* towns in inland Syria. Kedourie thought it strange to choose four towns which were inherently dissimilar, but they were the only points of reference that readily presented themselves to identify an eastern north–south boundary, the coast representing the western one. As we saw, Britain intended the line running through the four towns to be projected southwards, through an area without any geographical markers.

Britain felt tied to Faisal not just because of the wartime promises, but also because of genuine affection. There is a memorable description of him waited on by a British delegation as he passed through Palestine on his way to exile from Syria. Storrs described a British guard of honour meeting the train of exile. Faisal 'carried himself with dignity and the noble resignation of Islam . . . though the tears stood in his eyes and he was wounded to the soul . . . At Qantara Station he awaited his train sitting on his luggage'.[22]

5. *The Downing Street Meeting*

France did not properly get to grips with the British position until Clemenceau came to London in December 1918 to ask Lloyd George to confirm France's rights to Syria and Cilicia. The meeting was a crucial one. It confirmed Britain's pre-eminent position in relation to the oil of the Levant, in an exchange which was full of charm and goodwill at the time, and which later left France convinced that she had been cheated and dishonourably treated by her ally. In 1919 the Quai d'Orsay took the trouble to compile a dossier of British slights, deceptions and evidence of general bad faith as a sort of *aide-mémoire*, in case any should be overlooked.[23] Very soon afterwards relations between the two countries were as bad as they could have been short of a complete rupture, and their deterioration was rooted in what happened at Downing Street.

The problem was that Clemenceau, like very many statesmen of the time, did not understand the importance of oil. He said that if he wanted any, he went to his grocer. Lloyd George on the other hand was more aware what oil meant than most. He was particularly conscious of the significance of Mosul from that point of view. If the lack of importance attached to oil by most of the men of the time seems surprising, it must be remembered that while there were *hints* of the riches of the Middle East in these years, the bulk of the world's oil came from the United States and Mexico. The Anglo-Persian Oil Company did not start production until 1914, and as late as 1927 it was the only oil

undertaking in the Middle East that was producing oil. During and before the
First World War, 80 per cent of Britain's oil came from the United States. In
1913 the United States produced 140 times more oil than Persia.[24]

For all that, France and the United States were to attack Britain's interest in
the Iraq mandate on the basis that Britain was mainly interested in the potential mineral resources of Mesopotamia. The Americans in particular became
very interested in Middle Eastern oil as the war ended. France was slower to
realise the importance of the region's minerals, and that made the negotiations
at Downing Street all the easier for Lloyd George.

The other great difference between the two men was that France wanted to
acquire territory for its own sake, while there was very little popular interest in
Britain about the opportunities which Britain found herself with in the Middle
East. The days of simple jingoistic imperialism were over. In France, by contrast,
popular opinion supported claims to the Middle East. The Entente had
contained France's colonial rivalry with Britain but did not end it. France
had been disquieted by the extension of British rule in Egypt in 1914, and
Allenby's entry into Jerusalem reinforced concerns about Protestant Anglo-
Saxons displacing French Catholics. In 1918, as the British armies moved
forward, Picot told Sykes that his French countrymen were afraid of British
ambitions in the parts of Syria promised to France by Sykes–Picot.

Clemenceau was not a colonial expansionist. In the 1880s he had been
strongly against France's colonial ambitions. He was one of the most violent
debaters in the French Chamber and frequently demanded satisfaction on the
duelling field. Historians have found it difficult not to say that members of the
Chamber feared his sword, his pistol and his tongue. But he knew that, whatever his own preferences, his countrymen required him to come back from
London with some Arabian territory, and that was why he did not demur when
Lloyd George told him that he could indeed have Syria and Cilicia, provided
that Mosul was in 'the British sphere of influence' and with it Palestine.

Clemenceau and Foch arrived at Charing Cross Station in December 1918.
Foch was received with the protocol reserved for royalty, and Clemenceau with
shouts of 'Good Old Tiger!' They were driven to Downing Street through
crowds ten deep.

Lloyd George drove with Clemenceau, and later he described their conversation. 'When Clemenceau came to London after the War I drove with him to the
French Embassy . . . After we reached the Embassy he asked me what it was I
specifically wanted from the French. I instantly replied that I wanted Mosul
attached to Irak, and Palestine from Dan to Beersheba under British control.
Without any hesitation he agreed. Although the agreement was not reduced into
writing, he adhered to it honourably in subsequent negotiations.'[25] Clemenceau

honoured the agreement, but it was not only not reduced into writing, it was not even communicated orally to the Foreign Office. This fact put officials at a disadvantage in subsequent negotiations at Versailles. Lloyd George loved the biblical phrase 'From Dan to Beersheba' and often used it in Paris, but it was not until a year after the Armistice that Allenby was able to tell Lloyd George that they had found where Dan was. It was not where the prime minister had expected it to be, and Britain had to revise her boundary demands.

It is worth analysing the exchange (which took place in Downing Street, and not the French Embassy: Lloyd George's Memoirs are never very reliable). The concessions that Clemenceau made were enormous, and he later suffered for them politically. The only justification for them, from a French point of view, was that in return there would be something for France. That would be Syria. This was not set out at the time; the question is whether or not it was clearly implicit that something had to be given in return for what Britain received.

The minutes reveal that the dialogue went pretty much as Lloyd George recalled. It was not long-winded:

Clemenceau: What are we to discuss?
Lloyd George: Mesopotamia and Palestine.
Clemenceau: Tell me what you want?
Lloyd George: I want Mosul.
Clemenceau: You shall have it. Anything else?
Lloyd George: Yes, I want Jerusalem too.
Clemenceau: You shall have it . . .[26]

Balfour was present at the meeting, and later wrote an account of it, as if by Clemenceau, in order to point up France's generous position:

In Downing Street last December I tried to arrive at an understanding with England about Syria. I was deeply conscious of the need of friendly relations between the two countries, and was most anxious to prevent any collision of interests in the Middle East. I therefore asked the [British] Prime Minister what modification in the Sykes–Picot Agreement England desired. He replied, 'Mosul.' I said, 'You shall have it. Anything else?' He replied, 'Palestine'. Again I said, 'You shall have it.' I left London somewhat doubtful as to the reception this agreement would have in France, but well assured that to Great Britain at least it would prove satisfactory.[27]

The nub of the problem that arose from the Downing Street meeting was that Clemenceau expected that in return for transferring Mosul and its oil from the Sykes–Picot French zone ('A') to the British zone ('B') Britain would recognise and support France's claims to the remainder of the 'A' zone. Britain did not keep the agreement. They recognised that they could not themselves have it, but they used Faisal, whose expenses they met at the Peace Conference, to try to keep France out.

At the end of the little exchange Clemenceau mentioned that there would be difficulties about Mosul, and so there were. Apart from the importance that oil would come to have, there was a critical significance in France's perception of what Syria was composed of. For France, Syria was a country that included Mosul in the east and the Sinai in the south.

Indeed, France's vision went further than that. Fundamentally, France always tended to the view that Palestine was an essential part of Syria. There was consequently always disquiet about the claims for a British mandate. But there was never any real doubt that Palestine would be detached from Syria. Lloyd George had particularly strong views. Asquith recorded that Lloyd George thought it would be 'an outrage to let the Holy places pass into the possession or under the protection of "agnostic, atheistic French"'.[28] The rationale for a British Palestine, the congruity of Zionism and the defence of Egypt was overwhelming, and Sykes–Picot had to be amended. But the withdrawal of Palestine from the Sykes–Picot promise to France was implicit long before then.

The Anglo-French Declaration of 7 November 1918 that had promised complete and final liberation to the Arab countries had not been a symbol of Allied unity; rather it was based on different views about Arab nationalism. France did not believe that a collection of separate tribes could represent a nation. Britain took a different view and was confident that those independent nations would elect for Britain's protection. So Curzon would say, 'Play self-determination for all it is worth'. France saw through that. Faisal was 'British Imperialism with Arab headgear'.[29]

Self-determination and Wilsonism became inseparable, but President Wilson's own, original and preferred phrase was 'the consent of the governed'. It was Lloyd George, in a hugely important address to the Trades Union League at Caxton Hall on 5 January 1918, in which he sought the support of liberal neutral opinion across the world as well as that of the British left, who adopted the Bolshevik term 'self-determination', and associated it with the Wilsonian ideal: the postwar settlement had to respect 'the right of self-determination or the consent of the governed'. This speech marks the true birth of 'self-determination', and thereafter Wilson increasingly used the phrase. In his memoirs, Lloyd George later claimed without the slightest connection to truth that both he and Wilson intended it to refer only to the right of the inhabitants of the non-Turkish parts of the Ottoman Empire.

Clemenceau was later criticised for having been unduly relaxed about Britain's claims at the London meeting. He may have been *Le Tigre* during the war, but French opinion now regarded him as having been a pussycat in London – not nearly strong enough for France's interests. The reason for his acquiescence was never fully explained – no reference was made to a British–French memorandum of 15 February 1918 which in fact entitled Lloyd George to demand concessions – and the agreement was attacked in the Chamber in Paris in 1920 by Briand. Briand talked of Britain's policy in regard to the Ottoman Empire. 'People have spoken of their greediness. What do you expect? There is such a thing as a people's appetite just as there is an individual's appetite; where there is no appetite, there is no action, there is paralysis. The greatness of the English people is based on continued, incessant action, which is never satisfied. [Applause.]'[30]

16

The End of Turkey's War

1. The Armistice of Mudros

Turkey was very unlucky. She did not lose the war for the Central Powers: they did that by themselves. Her own war effort in Gallipoli and Mesopotamia was respectively impressive and not bad. But in other areas the war went badly for the Ottomans, and before they faced the consequences of the Peace bits of the Empire were falling away. Even the Turkish-speaking areas were threatened – to the extent that a 'Wilsonian Principle Society' was formed in Constantinople.[1]

A month before the Armistice with Germany, a caretaker Turkish government told Britain, her old friend, that peace was sought. Britain responded to the peace feelers fairly slowly. It was clear that the longer the war went on, the more would be gained from Turkey; at the same time there was a reluctance to impose terms so severe as to encourage the Turks to remain with the Central Powers, which still seemed capable of fighting on well into 1919. Eventually, Admiral Calthorpe, commanding the Mediterranean fleet at Malta, was ordered to Mudros, the outstanding natural harbour on Lemnos from which the Dardanelles campaign had been launched, to initiate negotiations. He was told to hold his hand until Britain had consolidated its position in Syria and Iraq.

France was well aware of what was happening. At the Allied Supreme War Council on 9 October 1918, Clemenceau argued that a French admiral should be in charge of the naval forces operating at Istanbul. He had logic to support him. The Supreme Naval Command of the Mediterranean was supposed to be in the hands of the French. Lloyd George had less logic, but did have British control over 75 per cent of the Allied fleet in the Aegean. It all got rather heated. He wrote to Clemenceau that Britain had taken 'by far the larger part of the burden of the war against Turkey in the Dardanelles and in Gallipoli, in Egypt, in Mesopotamia and in Palestine. . . . I do not see how I could possibly justify to the people of the British Empire that at the moment when the final attack upon Turkey was to be delivered, the command of Naval Forces which are overwhelmingly British, in a theatre of wars associated with some of the most desperate and heroic fighting by troops from nearly every part of the British Empire, should be handed over to a French Admiral . . .'[2]

Balfour pointed out that the French General Franchet d'Espèrey had negotiated the Bulgarian armistice without consulting Britain. Franchet d'Espèrey, 'Desperate Frankie' to the British troops, commanded the French armies when Bulgaria fell. On 8 February 1919 he entered Istanbul on a white horse, recalling Mehmet's entrance in 1453, unkindly underlining the fact that the Ottoman Empire was now ending as the Byzantine one had done.

Increasingly bitter correspondence went on, but in the meantime General Townshend, comfortably confined by the Turks since Kut and now released to plead their cause, arrived at Mudros. After discussions Admiral Calthorpe cabled London to say that 'the effect of a fleet under French command going up to Constantinople would be deplorable, nor could anything be more unpopular with the Greeks in Turkey'.[3] Calthorpe was told to get on with signing an armistice. This he did. Turkey was invited to Mudros to talk. The French protested, but the negotiations took place on Calthorpe's flagship, the *Agamemnon*. Calthorpe was inflexible, as he had been told to be, in excluding the French from the negotiations.

Hostilities ended at noon on 31 October. The Turkish representatives were delighted by their reception at Mudros. The terms of the armistice were pretty stringent: there was to be complete surrender, the Turkish ports were available to the Allies and the Allies were entitled to occupy any territory they wanted. But British public relations were magnificent, and for some reason the Turkish delegates were convinced that they were threatened by none of this. Later they were bitterly disappointed.

Calthorpe's government was pleased with him, and he moved on to be the British High Commissioner in Istanbul for nine months while still the British naval Mediterranean commander-in-chief. In extraordinarily difficult circumstances he acquitted himself well.

So, the agreement that was reached at Mudros was made between the Turks and Britain: the other allies, in particular France, were not involved. This struck a significant blow at Franco-British solidarity and some say permanently weakened French prestige in the Middle East. That may be an exaggeration, but the significance in having a British, rather than a French, admiral on the spot was critical: while the surrender was technically to the Entente, it was in reality to Britain, and the Straits were now in British hands.

The importance of the whole event in terms of its impact on Franco-British relations was lasting. It informed the increasingly heated competition between the two allies in their attempts to control the post-war Middle East. The exchanges between Lloyd George and Clemenceau had been acrimonious and intemperate. Lloyd George told Clemenceau that 'except for Great Britain no one had contributed anything more than a handful of black troops to the expedition in Palestine. I was really surprised at the lack of generosity on the part of the French government. The British had now some 500,000 men on Turkish soil. The British had captured three or four Turkish armies and had incurred hundreds of thousands of casualties in the war with Turkey . . . When, however, it came to signing an armistice, all this fuss was made'.[4]

The horrors of the Western Front and emphasis on the war there in the histories should not create the impression that the Mesopotamian war was an easy war against a soft enemy. That was very far indeed from the case. By the end of the war, Britain deployed over 400,000 men in Mesopotamia, and there were over 100,000 casualties including 30,000 dead, 'a gruesome story', in Lloyd George's words, 'of tragedy and suffering resulting from incompetence and slovenly carelessness on the part of the responsible military authorities'.[5] The sacrifices are all the more terrible in that they did nothing to shorten the war.

These sacrifices were far from forgotten in 1918 and 1919, and they should be remembered when considering Lloyd George's comments to the French in relation to Mudros and again at Versailles, when he argued very strongly that the British contribution to the war in the Middle East had altered the basis of the Sykes–Picot Agreement, concluded when France was the major contributor to the Allied war effort.

The Armistice of Mudros ended the war for the Turks. The Allies were to go to Paris and the Peace Conference ready, as they believed, to share out the Ottoman Empire among themselves. To see why the Allies had to modify their arrangements, it is necessary to consider what was happening in Turkey while the victors were at Versailles.

2. *Turkey after Mudros*

By the end of 1918 the Ottoman government was discredited by the reverses of the war. The CUP was identified with all that had happened, and the Three Pashas were sent into exile. The sultan, Mehmet VI, dismissed the old parliament. He planned to rule by decree, but he was the symbol of anachronism and the Allies proceeded to dismember his Empire. The treaties of Sèvres and Lausanne, which gave effect to the dismemberment, will be considered later in more detail. For the moment, it is enough to say that the Treaty of Sèvres in 1920 completed the humiliation of the Ottomans. Italy and France divided south-west Anatolia. An independent Armenian state was to be created. Greece was to receive territory in Thrace within 25 miles of Istanbul, together with the right to administer Smyrna and the country around it. The Straits were to be administered by an Allied Commission. The Capitulations were restored.

The response was the growth of an irresistible independence movement, out of which the dynamic and visionary Mustafa Kemal Atatürk would emerge to become president of the new Republic of Turkey that was established on 29 October 1923. In the process, a Grand National Assembly met in Ankara in the spring of 1920. A National Pact embodied a new constitution. The claims to the Arab provinces were dropped, but sovereignty was unequivocally asserted over all parts of the Empire inhabited by Turkish majorities. This extended to the parts of Anatolia given to the new Republic of Armenia at Sèvres.

A war of independence broke out, with campaigns on separate fronts against France, Greece and Armenia. In the autumn of 1920, Turkey and the new Soviet Union invaded Armenia and partitioned it between them. Greece was pushed back to the confines of Smyrna, and Atatürk threatened Istanbul, which was held by Allied garrisons. These successful campaigns restored territories lost in the final stages of the Great War. They were fought and largely ignored as the Allies discussed how they should distribute spoils that were at that very time being taken from them. The revival of Turkey's vigour and self-respect meant that the dispositions of Sèvres had to be revisited at Lausanne and afterwards.

The humiliation of the Turks which had begun with the Treaty of Mudros was at an end. The invasion of Armenia demonstrated that. In the course of the following year, France and the Soviet Union recognised the Ankara regime as the legitimate ruler of Turkey.

Turkey thus re-established itself as a world power only a few years after defeat alongside the Central Powers. At home the reforms of Atatürk, as Mustafa Kemal was to be known after 1935, were essentially a continuation of what had been happening before the First World War. In March 1924 the Caliph Abdul Nejid was deposed and the caliphate abolished. Sharia law was abolished in 1926 and the Koran translated into Turkish, an unimaginable breach with Sharia teaching.

Through the Second World War Inönü carefully kept Turkey out of hostilities until the outcome was clear beyond any shadow of doubt. He declared war on Germany only on 23 February 1945 – in time for Turkey to become a founder member of the United Nations. Turkey had learned from the First World War what a serious mistake it was to join the losing side.

IV

MAKING PEACE

17

VERSAILLES

1. The Last Great Peace Conference

The Paris Peace Conference of 1919 was one of the most remarkable gatherings of the twentieth century. It did not simply involve the victorious powers settling on the terms they would impose on the vanquished. The delegates who filled Paris arrived to carry out a much grander task. They were there to reshape Europe and indeed much of the rest of the world in accordance with a new order of things. Their ambition was far wider than that which informed the first meeting of the United Nations in San Francisco at the end of the next war.

The conference lasted from January 1919 into 1920. Most of the work was done by the main delegates by June 1919. In preparation for the conference, the British Foreign Office commissioned a book on the Congress of Vienna of 1815, which was the only template available. No one read the book and its account of the deliberations which had taken place 104 years earlier. Circumstances were very different. At Vienna, when the map of Europe was redrawn after the Napoleonic Wars, the British Foreign Secretary took 14 people with him. In 1919 there were 400, and Britain was only one of more than 30 countries. The matters to be settled at Versailles were worldwide, involving territories of the defeated powers all over the globe. Demands were made on the Big Three, the United States, France and Britain,* by countless delegations from unrepresented nations, in addition to those of the participating countries. Injustices were to be remedied, conflicting promises made in the heat of war reconciled. Everything was to be done very fast. There was chaos in the wake of the disappearing empires. New political dynamics were at work. The forces that had imposed some shape on the map were melting away.

---

* Originally there was a Council of Ten, two representatives for each of the five major powers, Britain, France, Italy, the USA and Japan. By March 1919 it was replaced by a more effective Council of Four, Britain, France, the USA and Italy. A month later, when Italy unwisely temporarily withdrew from the Peace Conference, the Big Three became the effective decision-making body in all major issues for the rest of the conference.

Much of the sense of expectation that gripped the delegates – and, perhaps even more, the ordinary people of Europe – was generated by the idealism of President Wilson and the philosophy behind his Fourteen Points.* After the tragedy of the fighting and the losses, he inspired a despairing continent with a sense of purpose. It is difficult now, after the betrayal of that optimism and the failure of the League of Nations, to share the mood of 1919, but a hint of what was felt at the time can be gleaned from photographs and newsreel footage of the crowds that waited for the president and mobbed him wherever he went. The countless streets and squares that are named after a man whose troops played only a small part in the war indicate something of the moral authority he wielded.

No one ever has received the sort of reception that Wilson did when the *George Washington* reached Brest on 13 December 1918, or in the months that followed. He was accorded that reception not because America had won the war, but because America was going to create a peace in which such a war would never happen again.

The French Poet and Nobel Laureate, Romain Rolland, addressed Wilson magnificently:

> Descendant of Washington, of Abraham Lincoln! Take in hand the cause, not of a party, of a people, but of all! Summon to the Congress of Humanity the representatives of the peoples! Preside over it with all the authority which your lofty moral conscience and the powerful future of the immense America assures to you! Speak! Speak to all![1]

The British economist John Maynard Keynes, no admirer of Wilson or Wilsonism, wrote that at the end of the war the president 'enjoyed a prestige and

---

* Wilson listed his Fourteen Points in a speech to a Joint Session of Congress on 8 January 1918. The Points emerged from work by the Inquiry, a team of 150 specialists working under Colonel House. They were intended to circumscribe the ambitions of the European powers in the peace negotiations, whenever they took place. Articles 2 and 3 were designed to facilitate capitalist competition by means of free trade and free navigation. Article 1 put an end to the old diplomacy: there would now be 'open covenants of peace, openly arrived at, after which there shall be no private international understandings of any kind, but diplomacy shall proceed always frankly and in the public view'. Peace would be secured by disarmament (Article 4) and the establishment of 'a general association of nations' (Article 14), which would emerge as the League of Nations. A number of Articles affected specific territories, among them Article 9: Italy's frontiers were to be re-established 'along clearly recognizable line of nationality'; and 12: 'The Turkish portion of the present Ottoman Empire should be assured a secure sovereignty, but the other nationalities which are now under Turkish rule should be assured an undoubted security of life and an absolutely unmolested opportunity of autonomous development . . .' Article 5 dealt a blow at old-fashioned appetites: 'A free, open-minded, and absolutely impartial adjustment of colonial claims, based upon a strict observance of the principle that in determining all such questions of sovereignty the interests of the populations concerned must have equal weight with the equitable claims of the government whose title is to be determined'.

a moral influence throughout the world unequalled in history'.[2] That is still an accurate statement. Kennedy's reception in Berlin, or even Churchill's throughout Europe in 1945, fell far short of the spirit in which Wilson, untarnished by responsibility for the war, was seen as the symbol of a system of regulating affairs that would ensure that there would never again be recourse to warfare.

America, under Wilson, had entered the war only reluctantly. In Wilson's second election campaign, as recently as 1916, he campaigned as 'the man who kept America out of the war'. When he decided that America must enter the war, he considered it essential that the basis on which she did so should be made clear. The war he fought was not to be an old-fashioned struggle for military victory: it was a campaign to purge the world of old ideas and replace them with new, liberal aspirations. America's entry into the war was accompanied by unprecedented propaganda efforts, made all the more effective by the use of the new technologies of telegraphy and telephony.[3]

H.G. Wells described in *The Shape of Things to Come* the phenomenon of Wilsonism, this strange process in which Europe, wearied and tarnished by war, felt that its guilt and shame could be removed and a new nobility replace it. There was an overwhelming desire to embrace something new, something hopeful and inspirational, something which was never properly articulated or understood.

> For a brief interval, Wilson stood alone for mankind. Or at least he seemed to stand for mankind. And in that brief interval there was a very extraordinary and significant wave of response to him throughout the earth. So eager was the situation that all humanity leapt to accept and glorify Wilson – for a phrase, for a gesture. It seized upon him as its symbol. He was transfigured in the eyes of men.

The moral chasm between the idealistic and very serious American president on the one hand and the representatives of the Old World, Lloyd George and Clemenceau, on the other, was immense, each side about as extreme an example of its kind as one can imagine. On 10 March 1919, Lloyd George had lunch with the Queen of Romania at Balfour's flat. She said she had bought a pink silk chemise and asked what she should talk to President Wilson about: 'The League of Nations or my pink chemise?' 'Begin with the League of Nations,' said Balfour, 'and finish up with the pink chemise. If you were talking to Mr. Lloyd George, you could begin with the pink chemise.'[4]

Clemenceau had no time for Wilson and his theories. Lloyd George was equally sceptical, but better at disguising the fact, and it was left to him to act as a catalyst in the negotiations. But even if they were tainted by cynicism, many – perhaps most – of the European statesmen shared Wilson's conviction that there should be a break with the past. Hankey, secretary of the War Cabinet and now also the secretary to the British delegation at Paris, carried a copy of the Fourteen Points with him all the time. The reality of the First World War was one of unimaginable horror, such as the world had never witnessed before. Clearly the old way of doing things had failed, and it was accordingly not only Wilson who believed that things must be done differently now. The problem for Wilson was partly that the major European leaders were always more concerned about their own interests than in a new world order, and partly that promises of self-determination had excited impossible and irreconcilable appetites among regions and countries that he had never heard of.

When Wilson briefly went back from Paris to report to the US Congress just a few months later, he admitted that when he had said that 'all nations had a right to self-determination' he had not been aware of the huge number of nationalities that would present themselves to him every day in Paris: 'When I gave utterance to those words [about self-determination], I said them without a knowledge that nationalities existed which are coming to us day after day . . . You do not know and cannot appreciate the anxieties that I have experienced as a result of many millions of people having their hopes raised by what I said.'[5] Some historians see Wilson, the notion of self-determination and the crucible of Versailles as the scientist, the catalyst and the laboratory that created twentieth-century anti-colonialism.[6]

By the time he came back again to Paris, things had changed for him. In his absence his close aide, Colonel House (the rank was purely honorific, conferred on him by Governor Hogg of Texas), had sold the pass on many issues, making concessions which Wilson deplored. House had been very influential as Wilson's foreign policy adviser in the approach to the conference and until now. But his importance reduced as a result of his decisions in Wilson's absence, because the president's second wife, Edith, did not like him much and because Wilson himself became increasingly difficult with his staff.

Political support at home was now moving away from Wilson. And his constitution was suffering under the strain of his work and the enormous burden of travelling he imposed on himself. His health in Paris became very poor and eventually, back in the States again, he suffered a serious stroke that left him so severely incapacitated that much of the function of government was discharged by his wife. At one stage in this decline Lloyd George was to say, 'The only faculty that remained unimpaired to the end . . . was his abnormal stubbornness'.

The exhaustion of the senior British delegates is mentioned by almost all observers. Only Lloyd George's vitality did not appear to have been sapped by the strain of the war. Indeed his vigour at Versailles contributed to the exhaustion of his colleagues. The principals spent much time in Paris, but they were still involved in running their departments at home and dealing with demobilisation, Ireland, housing and all the problems of peace. They were further distracted by the tensions within their own departments.

2. Balfour at Paris

The British Foreign Secretary, Balfour, now 71 years old, looked his age, or older. Before he left London he made a typical throw-away remark to Lord and Lady Wemyss: 'As I have always told you, it is not so much the war as the peace that I have always dreaded'.[7] When he reached the conference his exhaustion was widely remarked. His lack of vitality was not helped by the efforts of Ian Malcolm. Malcolm was married to Jeanne-Marie Langtry, the daughter of Lillie Langtry, 'the Jersey Lily'. Jeanne-Marie's father was ostensibly Prince Louis of Battenberg, but she was born before Lillie's three years as mistress of the Prince of Wales had come to an end, and she was the only one of Edward VII's illegitimate children whom he acknowledged as his.

Malcolm was appropriately known as 'the last of the Edwardians'. He was a close friend of Balfour – he had been on a cycling holiday with him in Germany – as well as his assistant. In the evenings he took Balfour to music halls and even a boxing match. How he could have imagined that to be a suitable entertainment for the aesthete known at school as 'Pretty Fanny' is difficult to imagine.

Balfour could be as amusing as ever. At a musical evening, the singer asked if anyone objected to German songs. Balfour replied, 'I don't; I will take them as part of the reparations that they owe us'.[8] He was still the man who had said that 'Nothing matters very much and most things don't matter at all' and some, like Clemenceau, who called him *'Cette vieille fille'*, 'the old maid', found him indecisive, others lethargic. Lord Selborne said 'I never could make out that he took any important part at all [in the conference]'.[9]

There was the usual divergence of views. Harold Nicolson said that when A.J.B. roused himself '[h]e launches off into a brilliant analysis of our guiding principles. It is crushing in its logic. When he *does* consent to intervene he is a whale among minnows.'[10] Nicolson also said that 'A.J.B. makes the whole of Paris seem vulgar'.[11]

Balfour was strangely disengaged from proceedings. While he may have been tired, he was not exhausted enough to stop playing tennis. He was inclined to deny any responsibility for the terms of the peace, so that Smuts had to remind him 'that he was Foreign Secretary'.[12] Nicolson again: 'A.J.B., in the intervals of dialectics on secondary points, relapses into somnolence'.[13] Clemenceau said that Balfour took his daily nap at the Supreme Council.[14]

3. Harold Nicolson at Paris

Harold Nicolson, who was attached to the British delegation to the Peace Conference, was taken by 'the infinite languor of Mr. Balfour slowly uncrossing his knees'. Other vignettes that remained in Nicolson's memory were 'the tired and contemptuous eyelids of Clemenceau, the black button boots of Woodrow Wilson [and] the rotund and jovial gestures of Mr. Lloyd George's hands'.[15]

Nicolson came to Versailles as a Foreign Office official, a student, and a young one, of traditional European diplomacy of the sort practised by the Foreign Office and the Quai d'Orsay. He found the new diplomacy practised at Versailles too open, too democratic, too amateur. 'The essential to good diplomacy is precision. The main enemy of good diplomacy is imprecision. It is for this reason that I have endeavoured in [his fascinating account of the conference, *Peacemaking, 1919,* to convey an impression of the horrors of vagueness. The old diplomacy may have possessed grave faults. Yet they were venal in comparison to the menaces which confront the new diplomacy... Amateurishness, in all such matters, leads to improvisation. Openness, in all such matters, leads to imprecision.[16]

Nicolson provides the *aperçu* that officials learned early on to look at the ceiling when they did not know the answer, and not at the floor. It was said that at Vienna the delegates danced for Europe; at Versailles they looked at the ceiling.

He was accurate in his contemporary evaluation of the proceedings, more accurate than subsequent observers who bring an *ex parte* bias to their analysis: 'I assume, and hope, that the future student of the Peace Conference will rid himself in advance of all emotional or ethical affects [*sic*] which the term "Secret Treaties" may induce. He will, I believe, be sensible enough to realise that in the heat of the belligerency statesmen are apt to grasp at any bargain such as may minister to the successful prosecution of war. They have done so in the past; they will continue to do so in the future ... In fact the objection to the Treaties concluded with our Allies during the course of the War is not that they were secret, but that they were unscientific and in many cases mutually contradictory. People who study the past under the conviction that they themselves would automatically behave better in the present are adopting a dangerous habit of mind. They are importing the ethical standards of tranquillity into the emotional atmosphere of danger.'[17]

4. Colonel House's Interpretation

The plenary session at which the treaty with the Germans was accepted by the Allies took place before the treaty had even been printed. Henry Wilson, the Chief of the Imperial General Staff, said, 'We are going to hand out terms to the Boches without reading them ourselves first. I don't think in all history this can be matched'. President Wilson later congratulated himself and his colleagues when he looked at the printed treaty: 'They have completed in the least time possible the greatest work that four men have ever done'. He added, without irony, 'I hope that during the rest of my life I will have enough time to read this whole volume.'[18] Very few delegates saw the treaty as a whole. When the American delegation did see it, about a dozen resigned.

The business had been truncated. What had been intended as a preparatory conference before the full Peace Conference had stumbled on into the full thing, so that the humiliated Germans now found that they were not, as they had expected, being invited to participate in a conference: when they were summoned to attend, the conference was already at an end.

History has not taken enough notice of Colonel House's 'Interpretation' of the Fourteen Points. On 29 October 1918, long before the Peace Conference opened, House, who possessed, according to Nicolson, 'the best diplomatic brain that America has yet produced',[19] cabled a 'commentary' on the Fourteen Points from Paris where he was at the time America's representative on the Supreme War Council.

The Interpretation was much more than it purported to be: it was a pretty thoroughgoing revision of the Fourteen Points, and if accepted as Wilson's real position goes some way to refute the notion that the final dispositions that the peace treaties effected were a complete betrayal of Wilsonism. 'Open Covenants', for example, was not to preclude confidential diplomatic negotiations. Free trade among the nations of the earth did not mean that home industries would not be protected. Italy would be entitled to the Brenner frontier, even though this would bring German populations under her control. So far as the Middle East was concerned, Constantinople and the Straits would be under international control. Central Asia Minor would remain Turkish. The Greeks might have a mandate over Smyrna. Armenia would be an independent state, protected by one of the powers. Critically, Britain was to have Palestine, Arabia and Iraq.

The problem about the Interpretation was that scarcely anyone knew about it. Churchill did, but not many others. Harold Nicolson, who was on the scene, looking at the ceiling when he did not know the answers, asks whether the Allies accepted the Fourteen Points, the Four Principles and the Five Particulars all on the basis of the Interpretation. He then makes the point that if they did, the defeated enemies should have been told. He concludes that Germany and Austria–Hungary accepted the Fourteen Points in their undiluted form, and that the Allies accepted them in the watered-down form which House has discussed with them and finally embodied in his telegram of 29 October.[20]

At any rate, interpreted or not, Germany was allowed to rely on the Fourteen Points when she surrendered, but Turkey was not. The Fourteen Points did not apply to the Ottoman settlement.

18

THE BALKANS AT PARIS

A persistent, minor theme of the Peace Conference was to be conflict between Greece and Italy. Events went badly from the start. As the Greek delegation's train made its way through Italy it ran into and killed two railway workers. There were only 19 members of their delegation, but they had reserved rooms for 80 at the Hôtel Mercedes. The Greek approach to the Peace Conference was ambitious.

The leader of the Greek delegation at the Peace Conference was the great patriot Eleutherios Venizelos. His reputation preceded him. His Christian name meant 'Liberator'. He was a Cretan, born when Crete and much of Greece itself was still ruled by the Turks. He took a prominent part in the war for independence in which three of his uncles died. His exploits, particularly at the Battle of Akrotiri, became the subject of poems and the stuff of legend. His persona and even his physical form were as substantial as his reputation, and he mesmerised the other delegates. Lloyd George described him exuberantly as 'the greatest statesman Greece had thrown up since the days of Pericles'.[1] Even Wilson, not usually impressed, described him as the biggest man he had met.

The hot-house politicians and diplomats at Paris could not fail to be captivated by this man, with his stories of guerrilla tactics in the Cretan mountains. Harold Nicolson described the impact of Venizelos in his diary for 28 January 1919:

Work all day. Otiose work. Dine with Venizelos. His sitting room overheated – mimosa and roses on the table – Venizelos very much the host. He is in great form. He tells us stories of King Constantine, his lies and equivocations. He tells us of the old days of the Cretan insurrection, when he escaped to the mountains and taught himself English by reading the 'Times' with a rifle across his knee. He talks of Greek culture, of modern Greek and its relation to the classical, and we induce him to recite Homer. An odd effect, rather moving . . . The whole gives us a strange melody of charm, brigandage, welt-politik, patriotism, courage, literature – and above all this large

muscular smiling man, with his eyes glinting through spectacles, and on his
head a square skull-cap of black silk.²

His delegation came to Versailles with the '*Megali Idea*', the great idea of
Greek irredentism. Venizelos wanted almost all European Turkey including
Constantinople, together with much other land in the Balkans. The basis for
these claims was the existence of Greek colonies throughout Turkey, some of
them founded centuries before. In Constantinople itself and in Smyrna there
was a strong Greek presence that stimulated nationalist demands. Quite apart
from those historical settlements, there had been much emigration from Greece
to Turkey in the years leading up to the war. The success of the Young Turks
and the growth of Turkish nationalism had reversed the tolerant cosmopolitan-
ism of the Ottomans and stimulated nationalism among minorities. There had
been talk of an exchange of Greek and Turkish populations before the war, but
by 1918 the respective strengths of Turkey and Greece had been reversed.
Venizelos was no longer a diffident petitioner.

Italy and Greece found themselves in competition for bits of the Balkans.
In their frustration the Italians temporarily withdrew from the Peace
Conference and unilaterally occupied bits of Asia Minor. The withdrawal was
a mistake, and the occupation irritated the Big Three. America threatened
military action, and Greece took it. The Big Three seemed to think that it
was acceptable, even desirable, for the Greeks to do what they criticised the
Italians for, and Venizelos was told to go ahead and occupy Smyrna and
protect its Greek community. It thereby obtained a valuable fertile province,
but, as General Metaxas foresaw, one which ultimately was not defensible.
The Greek soldiers had an easy entry into Smyrna. They were initially greeted
with enthusiasm, and the Turks were ready to capitulate quietly. But then
things went badly wrong. Sporadic shots were misunderstood, and a massacre
of the surrendering Turks followed.

But while Greece and Italy squabbled and the Big Three listened to their
claims for Turkey, Turkey itself was reviving and growing much stronger and
more confident than the West realised. Kemal had himself appointed as the
officer responsible for the whole of Anatolia.

He knew what he was doing. The Big Three did not. Their deliberations
degenerated into farce. Harold Nicolson noticed the reaction of the Italian
prime minister, Orlando, when someone said that mandates had to be made
with the consent of those concerned, 'Orlando's white cheeks wobble with
laughter and his puffy eyes fill up with tears of mirth'. Balfour was horrified by
what he saw: 'I have three all-powerful, all-ignorant men sitting there and
partitioning continents with only a child [Nicolson] to take notes for them'.

The deliberations proceeded on the premise that Turkey was finished and could be partitioned. Meanwhile Kemal's advance continued.

Armenia was sadly aware that Turkey was far from finished. Few deputations were received as sympathetically at Paris as the Armenians who came before the Supreme Council on 26 February 1919. From 1375 until 1918 the spirit of Armenian independence had lived, despite the heavy hand of occupying forces. The savagery the Armenians endured, the atrocities they suffered, were deeply rooted in the consciousness of the European powers and in America, where relief committees had flourished.

Turkish ill-treatment of her Armenian subjects had moved on to a new scale on 24 April 1914, when the first terrible campaign of genocide of the twentieth century began. Armenians were rounded up and taken on death marches of hundreds of miles without food or water, shadowed by rape and massacre. Those who survived were left in the desert of present-day Syria. It is thought that 1½ million died.

At the conference there was then unanimous agreement among the great powers – America, Britain, France, Italy – that the Armenians must receive their due. Orlando, the Italian prime minister, spoke for all (but not in English: he was at a disadvantage at Paris because, unlike his foreign minister, Sonnino, he had no English) when he said, 'Say to the Armenians that I make their cause my cause.'[3] But the aspirations of the conference were never disappointed so spectacularly as they were in the case of Armenia. Colonel House said that the United States would accept a mandate. Wilson disagreed. 'He could think of nothing the people of the United States would be less inclined to accept than military responsibility in Asia.'[4]

The massacres continued, and the Turks never faced any retribution for their massacre of hundreds of thousands of Armenian civilians. The world's indifference was noticed. Later, when Hitler was warned about the possible reaction to Nazi atrocities, his response was simply, 'Who remembers the Armenians?'

19

BRITAIN AND FRANCE AGAIN

In his first Paris draft of the prospectus for a League of Nations, Wilson said on 10 January 1919:

> In respect of the peoples of territories which formerly belonged to Austria, Hungary [sic], and to Turkey, and in respect of the colonies formerly under the dominion of the German Empire, the League of Nations shall be regarded as the residuary trustee with sovereign right of ultimate disposal or of continued administration in accordance with certain fundamental principles . . . and this reversion and control shall exclude all rights or privileges of annexation on the part of any Power.[1]

By 30 January 1919 it was agreed 'that Armenia, Syria, Mesopotamia and Kurdistan, Palestine and Arabia must be completely severed from the Turkish Empire'.[2] There would, however, be no further disposals.

Implementing the dismemberment of the Empire became increasingly difficult as the divergent interests of the British and French became clear. Curzon went to Paris with no affection for the Turks whom he equated with the Ottomans and associated with oppression and massacre. He went, however, with even more suspicion of the French. Lloyd George shared his mistrust of Turkey and France. He also regarded France as the bigger threat.

In a famous piece of thinking aloud overheard by Arnold Toynbee, one of the advisers to the British delegation, Lloyd George totted off in his head his shopping list of *desiderata* in the Middle East: Mesopotamia, oil, irrigation, Palestine, the Holy Land, Zionism, Palestine again; then 'Syria . . . h'm . . . what is there in Syria? Let the French have that'.[3] He changed his mind pretty quickly. For most of his life he had been very far from being an expansionist. He had been pretty close to being a pacifist in the early part of his career, almost against war in 1914; but he was excited by the opportunities that had accidentally been presented to Britain in the Middle East as a result of the hazards of war. He was, moreover, as keen to exclude the French from sharing in the new playthings as he was to consolidate the links from Suez to India and to establish loyal Arab dependencies along the Fertile Crescent.

Curzon's assumption that the Arab nations would choose British protection was optimistic, but it was at least certain that they would not want French protection. Curzon was well aware of Arab dislike of France. He understood it. As has been seen, there was a widespread feeling that Britain's wartime alliance with France had been an anomaly and that the two countries would now revert to rivalry if not downright hostility. This assumption had implicitly informed Middle Eastern policy throughout the war; now it was explicit. Further, many British, such as Lawrence and Lloyd George, thought they owed it to the Arabs to keep them out of the hands of France.

The doubts whether Britain would adhere to Sykes–Picot and let the French have Syria were real ones. The Foreign Office was prepared to do so, but the Eastern Committee under Curzon was not. Nor was the Army. The strength of ill-feeling between Britain and France over the Middle East is easy to underestimate, and the relationship deteriorated much more as other issues, such as the Rhineland, came along to disturb it. In France too resentments that had been subdued during the war, and resentments caused by the war, exacerbated intermittent tensions.

Part of the reason for these disagreements, but only part, was of course oil. There was surprisingly little hard information on whether, let alone just how much, oil was to be found in Mesopotamia, and it does not do to allow hindsight to inform our assumptions. Present-day observers tend to assume that Britain's interest in, for example, Iraq, had everything to do with oil. That was not the case. The value of oil was not set anything like as high then as it would later be, and there was in any case no certainty that the Middle East had significant oil reserves. All the same, as Margaret MacMillan says, 'When black sludge seeped out of the ground and lay in pools around Baghdad, or gas fires flared off swamps in Mosul, it was easy to guess. By 1919 the British Navy was arguing, without awaiting further evidence, that the Mesopotamian oil fields were the largest in the world.'[4] Gradually the significance and strategic importance of oil came to weigh with the British negotiators, particularly those with a responsibility for interests in the Middle East.

The Downing Street meeting between Lloyd George and Clemenceau might have helped, but it was informal and personal. A more enduring settlement was attempted in the Long–Bérenger Agreement of April 1919, which gave France a quarter share of the Turkish Petroleum Company in return for abandoning her claim to Mosul. The Americans were to be kept out. But the agreement achieved little, and indeed there was great confusion about what was being agreed, with Lloyd George and the Foreign Office acting independently of and without the knowledge of each other.

Lloyd George had come to Paris very much against the idea of giving away Syria, with its extended frontiers, to France. The stresses of working with his ally through the war had not endeared the French to him. He also genuinely did not want to break his promise to the Arabs. President Wilson was advised by Dr Howard Bliss that the Syrians, for their part, were very much against the idea of being mandated to France. Unfortunately for them, French public opinion, stimulated by the press and by political utterances, was in a phase of jingoism of the sort that had been expressed in Britain 40 years before. Britain and France did not finally resolve their differences over Syria until September 1919. Only then did Britain withdraw her troops from Syria, and even then, the frontier between Syria and Palestine was not agreed. It was not settled until 1922.

In the meantime, Britain and France did what they could. On 13 May 1919 Nicolson was called to Lloyd George's flat in the Rue Nitot.

20

THE MEETING AT THE RUE NITOT

When Nicolson reached Lloyd George's flat he was asked to spread his map out on the dinner table, and Lloyd George explained to those present – Balfour, Milner, Henry Wilson, the British official Louis Mallet and Nicolson – that the Italians, Prime Minister Orlando and Foreign Minister Sonnino, were coming round 'in a few minutes and he wants to know what he can offer them'.

Critical and far-reaching policies were being made on the hoof. Nicolson, nominally a Greek expert, suggested the Adalia Zone (in Turkey), with the rest of Asia Minor going to France. Milner, Mallet and Wilson opposed him and Balfour, of course, was neutral. 'We are still discussing when the flabby Orlando and the sturdy Sonnino are shown into the dining room. They all sit round the map. The appearance of a pie about to be distributed is thus enhanced.'

At one stage the Italians asked for Scala Nova. Lloyd George told them they could not have it because it was full of Greeks, and he then went over lots of other parts of the map, pointing out more and more Greeks. Nicolson had to point out to him that he had mistaken a relief map for an ethnological one, and thought that green meant Greeks and brown meant Turks instead of valleys and mountains respectively. Later Orlando and Sonnino asked for the Turkish coal mines at Eregli. Lloyd George, correctly this time, pointed out that it was 'rotten coal and not much of it'. Orlando's response was, *'Si, si, ma, l'effetto morale, sa!'*[1] Thus the negotiation of the Adriatic Treaty proceeded.

On the following day, Lloyd George on a whim took Nicolson along with him to a meeting with President Wilson. 'So I went in. There were Wilson and LL.G. and Clemenceau with their armchairs drawn close over my map on the hearth-rug. I was there about half an hour – talking and objecting. The President was extremely nice and so was LL.G. Clemenceau was cantankerous. The *"Mais voyons, jeune homme"* ["Now, look here, young man"] style. It is appalling that these ignorant and irresponsible men should be cutting Asia Minor to bits as if they were dividing a cake. And with no one there except me, who incidentally have nothing whatsoever to do with Asia Minor. Isn't it terrible, the happiness of millions being decided in that way, while for the last two months we were praying and begging the Council to give us time to work out a scheme?'[2]

Wilson, for idealistic reasons, and Lloyd George, for practical ones, were offended by the claims that Italy made for other people's territory in Europe and the Middle East. Indeed Wilson tried to appeal to public opinion in Italy over Orlando's head. That was why, on 24 April 1919, the Italian delegation turned their back on the Peace Conference and went back to Italy to nourish domestic support. The former allies consolidated against Italy in her absence. 'What a beginning,' said Clemenceau, 'for the League of Nations!'

When the Italians returned, President Wilson accused them of imperialism, while Lloyd George tried to win them over with a speech of such eloquence that Orlando broke down in tears. As he tried to compose himself at the window, he was observed by neighbours: 'What have they been doing to the poor old gentleman?'

Two days later, Nicolson was with Balfour. Sir Eyre Crowe, Assistant Under-Secretary of State for Foreign Affairs and head of the Political Section of the British delegation at Paris, Nicolson's hero, read the minutes of the meeting of the Council of Three, which had taken place two days earlier around Nicolson's map on the hearth rug. Crowe was very critical: 'These three ignorant men, with a child [Nicolson] to lead them'.[3] It is interesting that Balfour and Crowe, on separate occasions, chose to describe the cherubic Nicolson as a child.

All this time the relationship between Britain and France was steadily deteriorating. Eventually an attempt was made to resolve the situation. An important meeting took place at 3 p.m. on Thursday, 20 March 1919, again in Lloyd George's flat at 23 rue Nitot. The Council of Four – Lloyd George, Clemenceau, Orlando and Wilson – were present and so were Balfour and Pichon, the French foreign minister.

The meeting addressed the differences between the British and French positions on the Middle East, France founding on Sykes–Picot, and Britain on what had happened since. Britain's position also reflected her commitment to the Arabs, and indicates something of what that commitment was thought to mean.

Pichon sought to shame Britain into coming to heel by producing all the secret treaties. He met Lloyd George's argument that it was Britain alone which had won the war in Mesopotamia by pointing out that the reason that there were fewer French than British troops in the Middle East was there were more French than British troops on the Western Front. Clemenceau had done his best for the Alliance by his generosity in London in 1918. France was indeed still prepared to stand aside from Palestine, although they would have preferred to see that territory administered by an international condominium. But there were limits to France's open-hearted generosity towards her partner: she must have an entire Syria under her mandate.

Lloyd George responded in conciliatory style, but pointed out that at the very time that British armies were sweeping through the Ottoman possessions it was also Britain which was dominating the efforts on the Western Front in the great British-led offensive of the Hundred Days, the last three months of the war. And in Mesopotamia and the Caucasus Britain had also provided almost all the troops – between 900,000 and 1,000,000 British and Indian soldiers.

He argued that the French could not have Damascus, Homs, Hama and Aleppo without a breach of faith with the Arabs. He was supported by Allenby, who told the French that if they attempted to take on an unwilling Syria there would be immense trouble. Allenby had been well primed. Before the meeting, he had lunched with Lloyd George, who urged him to make it clear to the French that they would not be tolerated in Syria.[4]

Pichon countered that France had no treaty with the Arabs, and Britain had kept France in the dark about any treaty that *she* might have. The British argument in response was that Sykes–Picot had built on pre-existent promises to Hussein and that therefore France was implicated in these promises. In any event, Damascus, Homs, Hama and Aleppo were part of the independent Arab state, the Hejaz.

There was much reference to the map annexed to Sykes–Picot. On that map the Blue Zone is to the north and also includes a coastal strip now occupied by Lebanon. In the Blue Zone France was 'to establish such direct or indirect administration or control as they may desire and as they may think fit to arrange with *the Arab State or Confederation of Arab States*'.[5] The emphasis has been added to show how concrete was the idea that there would be a sovereign Arab presence. But the Blue Area would not include Damascus, Homs, Hama or Aleppo.

To the south, and including Mosul in the east and Damascus in the west is 'A' Zone, destined for French influence: France was to recognize and uphold an independent Arab state or confederation. To the south of that is 'B' Zone, British Influence, and to the east was Red Zone, what is now Iraq. There was also an Allied condominium on the Mediterranean coast, containing Jerusalem and Gaza.

Until now France had relied rigidly on the inviolability of Sykes–Picot, but faced with the fact that some of its implications might not be to her liking, Pichon changed tack and argued that Sykes–Picot had been overtaken by events. Since then the League's mandatory system had been devised. That being so, Clemenceau suggested that France be given not the excluded vilayets outright, but rather a mandate over them. Lloyd George's response was that 'the League of Nations cannot be used for putting aside our bargain with King Hussein'.

Whether Lloyd George was animated by a love for the Arabs or distaste for France, he put the Arab case very strongly. He emphasised that Britain was bound by McMahon–Hussein: on the strength of it Hussein 'had put all his resources into the field which had helped us most materially to win the victory'. Britain could not break faith with the Arabs. She would be breaking faith if Damascus, Homs, Hama and Aleppo were included in the sphere of direct French influence.

He challenged Pichon. Did France intend to occupy Damascus? – because that would be a breach of the treaty with the Arabs. Pichon said that France had no treaty with the Arabs. Lloyd George's response was again that France had in effect assented to Britain's commitments under McMahon–Hussein by signing Sykes–Picot. He read out part of Sykes–Picot. Britain and France had agreed to an independent Arab state or confederation in A Zone and B Zone, the 'influence' zones. His argument was that Damascus, Homs, Hama and Aleppo were included in A Zone, A Zone was an independent Arab area, and the fact that the vilayets were in that zone and not the Blue Zone showed that France had in practice recognized Britain's agreement with Hussein.

Pichon's principal response was very simple. How could France recognize a treaty of which in 1916 she was unaware? He also made the point that although France accepted the existence of an independent Arab state or confederation, she had never made any undertaking in relation to the Hejaz or the king of the Hejaz.

A fairly tense meeting concluded with Wilson breezily reminding everyone that the mandate system had already been agreed. Was it accepted that Britain got Mesopotamia and France got Syria? It seemed to be.

Wilson, according to Nicolson sticking to his Principles for almost the last time, 'said it was a matter of complete indifference to him what France and Great Britain had decided in the form of Secret Treaty: they had since then accepted the Fourteen Points: they were thus obliged, whatever their previous engagements, to consider only the wishes of the populations concerned'. There was some doubt about these wishes: 'according to M. Chukri Ganem (a Syriac poet of Paris, who, although he had not set foot in Syria for twenty years, had been produced by M. Pichon as the spokesman of the Syrian Arabs), the whole heart of Syria was pulsating with but one hope – that of a French mandate. According to the Emir Faisal the Syrians had no partiality for anything other than their own independence: these divergences could only be reconciled by an "Enquiry"'.[6]

An enquiry was exactly what Faisal had wanted. He was confident that it would work against France. His main proposal to the council had been that a commission should ascertain the wishes of the populations concerned. This chimed in with Britain's Declaration to the Seven and an address which President Wilson gave at Mount Vernon, George Washington's estate. Wilson was attracted by the proposal. Lloyd George was not enthusiastic and Clemenceau was very much against it, but at the secret Rue Nitot meeting Wilson and Faisal got their way and the president undertook to draft the terms of reference.

That decision was endorsed at a meeting of the Council of Four on 25 March and when Faisal heard the news, he drank champagne for the first time in his life (and drank it copiously). He and Lawrence flew over Paris and he dropped cushions on the capital, regretting that he had no bombs to throw. He had already thrown cushions from his car at the headquarters of the American and British delegations and the Quai d'Orsay. Lawrence and Faisal had latterly become bored and frustrated during their time in Paris. Lawrence's frustration was relieved by throwing rolls of lavatory paper at Lloyd George and Balfour. At the end of April, Faisal sailed to Syria.

The Zionists and the French were distinctly hostile to the idea of the commission. Even some of the Americans were against it, not on principle, but simply because they thought that there was enough information available in Paris. The full commission never materialised. What was technically the 'American section of the International Commission on Mandates in Turkey', and became generally known as the King–Crane Commission, consisted of just two Americans: Henry King, the president of Oberlin College in Ohio, and Charles Crane, a Chicago businessman who contributed to Democratic Party funds. They arrived in Jaffa on 10 June and spent some six weeks in Palestine and Syria. When the commissioners were in Syria and Palestine, which were under British control, the local British officials were in a position to vet those whom they met. France was unhappy.

The commissioners visited 40 towns and received over 1,800 petitions. They lodged their report in Paris on 28 August 1919. The commissioners reported in favour of the mandatory system for Syria, Palestine and Iraq. They found that the Syrians, while not in favour of the concept of mandate, did want 'assistance', preferably from the United States or Britain, but certainly not from France. While the commissioners started off in favour of Zionism, they ended by concluding that the Jewish inhabitants intended to take over almost all of Palestine by purchase in various forms. None of the British officers whom they had consulted could see how Zionist aims could be carried through except by force of arms, and the whole thing they felt to be inconsistent with Wilsonian principles.

Later Churchill, as Colonial Secretary, tried hard to reconcile Arabs and Jews, but he had some sympathy with King–Crane: 'Whereas in Mesopotamia we have been able to study the wishes of the people and humour their national sentiment, we are committed in Palestine to the Zionist policy against which nine-tenths of the population and an equal proportion of the British officers are marshalled.[7]

By the time a copy of the report was handed in at Washington by Dr King, the president was back in the United States on the speaking tour during which he became seriously ill. It is thought that he never read the report in full. The King–Crane Commission had been boycotted by Britain and France and its conclusions were ignored by the other powers.

The cardinal principle of awarding the mandates 'chiefly to consider the wishes of the inhabitants' was totally ignored. Balfour said that in the case of Syria there were only three possible mandatories: England, America and France. England had said that she did not want the mandate, and America said that she did not want it. 'So that, whatever the inhabitants may wish, it is France they will certainly have. They may freely choose; but it is Hobson's choice after all.'[8] Not only were the wishes of the natives not consulted; both Britain and France managed opinion to make sure that the wishes were frustrated.

21

FAISAL AT VERSAILLES

1. The Perfume of Frankincense

Prince Faisal emerged from the war as the heroic, romantic figure who helped Britain sweep to victory over the Turks, and his standing was enhanced by the dignity of his appearances at the conference, moving through the ranks of bureaucrats in flowing silk robes, attended by Lawrence in khaki but wearing his *kafeeyah*. The physical impact was reinforced by his moral conviction that the Arabs had earned the right to be rewarded.

After the event Lawrence painted an idealised picture of his first meeting with Faisal during the war in *Seven Pillars of Wisdom*: 'I felt at first glance that this was the man I had come to Arabia to seek – the leader who would bring the Arab Revolt to full glory'. At the time his reaction had been less romanticised: 'Hot-tempered, proud, and impatient, sometimes unreasonable.'[1]

Before Faisal got to Versailles he travelled to London on HMS *Gloucester*. On the way he had a brief and disquieting excursion ashore at Marseilles, where he was met by two senior French officers who told him that he was a welcome visitor, but could not be received in any representative or official capacity. The French were not treating Faisal as the British did. He was not a head of state in waiting. Would he like to tour the battlefields of the Western Front?

In London he was treated with more ceremony, but he had a difficult three weeks. He was told that the French objected to the idea that he should represent the Hejaz at the conference. While he was in London, so indeed was Clemenceau, but Faisal took no part in the Lloyd George–Clemenceau talks. Lloyd George wanted to annul Sykes–Picot on the grounds that it had been denounced by Russia, but Clemenceau did not agree. The niceties did not concern Faisal. He spoke neither French nor English, and understood little of Western diplomacy. He felt himself alone and isolated, and relied largely on Lawrence, whom he knew already. He moved to Paris in the middle of January 1919, convinced that his best chance of success against France lay in support from Britain. He was right: under British pressure, France allowed the Hejaz delegation official representation, and with not just one seat, but two. In all other respects, the French were resistant to all that Faisal sought.

On 29 January 1919 he submitted a written statement, setting out the Arab claim to independence. He wanted an independent state for Arabs from the Alexandretta Line southwards, including Syria. He was prepared to leave the fate of Palestine to be determined by those interested in it.

When he appeared in person before the council for the first time, the effect was a piece of theatre that dazzled the Peace Conference. US Secretary of State, Robert Lansing, was carried off to the Orient: 'He suggested the calmness and peace of the desert, the meditation of one who lives in the wide spaces of the earth, the solemnity of thought of one who often communes alone with nature.' Even General Allenby, 'the Bull', was moved by 'a keen, slim, highly strung man. He has beautiful hands like a woman's . . .'[2] Dressed in white and gold and carrying a scimitar, Faisal held the council spellbound. He spoke in Arabic, which Lawrence, in white robes, his headdress braided with gold for the occasion, translated. Some said that Faisal recited the Koran and that the speech was truly Lawrence's.

Faisal's *de facto* government was already installed in Damascus but he had to convince the Allies, the French in particular, that he should now be confirmed as king of Syria. Whatever it was that he was saying, he said it in a low confident voice without notes. His audience was captivated by this exotic character in golden robes. One observer said that 'his voice seemed to breathe the perfume of frankincense and to suggest the presence of richly coloured divans, green turbans and the glitter of gold and jewels'.

Faisal and his colleague, Rustem Haidar, thus attended the conference as the representatives of the Hejaz. They sat sixth and seventh from the bottom of the inside of the delegates' U-shaped table. The seating arrangements are informative. The important representatives sat at the top and outside shoulders of the table. The delegates who sat further down the outside of the table became increasingly less important, and those who sat on the inside of the table were less important still. The South American nations had the most ignominious seats of all.

The great powers had five seats each. Clemenceau, as chairman, sat at the centre of the top of the U. He was not technically part of the French delegation, but France could not be allowed to dominate the seating plan, so the French delegation itself was placed beyond the top of the shoulder. Back at the top, Clemenceau was flanked by the American delegation on his right and the British delegation on his left. One has to remember the peculiar status of America and Wilson to understand why America, which had hardly figured in the fighting of the Great War, should have been represented at the conference as it was. It is crass and unappealing to measure contributions in terms of body counts, but the fact is that the United States casualties totalled 365,000, 8.2 per cent of personnel enlisted, while the French Empire had 6,161,000 casualties, 76.3 per cent of personnel enlisted.

Including Clemenceau, France effectively had six delegates. In fact it did even better, because Foch, as Allied Generalissimo, had a seat all of his own. That would have made France seven and Britain five, but Britain was able to add in a further nine imperial representatives, two for Canada, two for Australia, one for New Zealand, two for South Africa and two for India, and the five Japanese representatives could almost be counted with the British. Japan's contribution to the war had not been huge, but they had been Britain's main ally in the east. Lloyd George managed somehow to obtain for Japan the status of a great power. Japan's casualties totalled 1,210 men, some 0.2 per cent of her mobilized troops. There were 300 dead, 907 wounded and three taken prisoner. Without minimizing so many individual tragedies, one can reflect that comparatively Japan's seats at the council table were cheaply bought.

Gertrude Bell arrived a few weeks after Faisal. She met him for the first time and was impressed by him. He was less impressed: 'Miss Bell has a poor mind. You should not attach any importance to what she says'.[3] That was unfair: Gertrude Bell's mind was certainly not poor. Later Faisal would come to have a more generous and more accurate estimate of her abilities.

Bell came to see her role at the conference as being dedicated to promoting Faisal's cause in Syria. She saw the future of Mesopotamia as inextricably linked with the Faisal venture, and she worked tirelessly with Lawrence to advance it. She had had some brief doubts about Lawrence (an 'introverted megalomaniac'), but he was now in favour again.

She had time to dine with Harold Nicolson. She had known him and Vita since 1914. Vita was now in the middle of her romance with Violet Markham. She refused to leave her, but did make a brief visit to Versailles. 'Mrs Vita was over for a day. She is a most attractive creature and would be more so if she didn't whiten her nose so very white.'[4]

The fate of Iraq and Syria at Versailles was, then, being determined largely on the basis of British and French self-interest with, on the British side, a strong romantic element mixed in, the attraction of 'the perfume of frankincense'. Britain also felt some sense of obligation to make sure that the liberated parts of the Middle East did not fall back into the clutches of the Turks, and to this extent their views were consistent with American notions of the inviolability of self-determination. For cohesive philosophy, that was about it.

2. Faisal and Syria

Faisal did not wait for the Allies to make up their minds in Paris. Before the conference reached any conclusions about the future of Syria, he was already settling in at Damascus. Although there was no doubt that Sykes–Picot had envisaged a French Syria, it was difficult to ignore the fact that the charismatic Faisal was established in Damascus, heading what was effectively an Arab state, militarily occupied not by the French but by the British. Would France accept this practical amendment to Sykes–Picot? Would she accept it alongside a British mandate in Palestine, and alongside a British Mesopotamia which included Mosul and its oil?

Clemenceau had not initially been very much interested in the Middle East. He was much more concerned about Alsace and Lorraine. Pretty soon after the war ended, however – and to an extent even before it ended – he had come into conflict with Lloyd George and the British, and as we have seen was also under pressure from interest groups and public opinion in France. And Britain could not maintain an army in Syria for long. By the end of 1919 she had left Syria. The Arabs were in control of the inland territory. Gertrude Bell spent some time there in October 1919 on her way back from London and Paris to Baghdad. By then Faisal's government had been in place for a full year. The French still refused to recognise him but that had not stopped him settling down with an entourage of black Abyssinian eunuch slaves. The Arabs in Syria met in congress in July 1919 and declared for an independent Syria, explicitly rejecting any sort of control by France.

France was strongly aware that the British had not delivered their part of the bargain they thought had been made at the Downing Street meeting. In February 1919 France tightened up its position. It now wanted a mandate over the whole of area 'A'. The Blue Zone was to be included, with Mosul cut out of it only if a guaranteed percentage of oil revenue was secured for France. Britain by now was feeling the military and economic pinch and could not contemplate a full-scale rupture with France. In September, Lloyd George was authorised to agree to handing over Syria to the French Army and, under pressure, Faisal bit the bullet. In December 1919, he said that he would agree to a French protectorate. But when he returned to Syria, the Syrian distaste for France had not abated, and the General Congress in Damascus in March 1920 insisted on declaring for independence, with Faisal as their king.

Faisal accordingly proclaimed that the country was independent and included Lebanon. He made his proclamation from the balcony of Baron's Hotel in Aleppo. The hotel catered for belligerents with splendid impartiality. Before the war, Bell and Lawrence stayed there (though not of course together); during the war it was occupied by German soldiers, and Liman von Sanders, the German commander of the Ottoman forces (winner at the Dardanelles, loser in

Palestine) and Kemal both stayed there before their adversary, Faisal, who is still referred to in the hotel as King Faisal I of Syria, which he only briefly was.

For France this was a British conspiracy. Briand claimed in the French Assembly on 25 June 1920 that Britain had engineered Faisal's election to sabotage France's legitimate right to Syria. 'From England he returned tranquilly to install himself in our zone, to which the English had appointed him.'[5]

But Faisal's position was militarily weak. His army had wandered away. He was dependent on Britain and indeed he wanted a British mandate for Syria. But Britain did not want that. She was strapped for cash and urgently reducing expenditure. Without British military support, and with much diminished British subsidies, Faisal had no alternative but to come to terms with France.

Unlike Britain, France had been unimpressed by Faisal, and they were unimpressed by Arab declarations. They intended to stand on their rights under Sykes–Picot. For the moment, France recognised Syria's right to self-government, but it was a limited form of self-government: France would be Syria's sole foreign ally and would advise on military matters and have favourable economic treatment.

The relationship did not work. The Syrians hated the French and pressed Faisal to declare war on them. He resisted the pressure, but equally he did nothing to discourage violence by some of his supporters. The French speedily lost patience and on 14 July 1920, less than three months after the San Remo Conference, which Faisal ignored as studiously as the deliberations at Versailles, his French masters told him to cancel a planned trip to Europe and served an ultimatum requiring compliance with five very onerous conditions. He was to hand over railways to French control with consequent occupation by the French of various towns and villages, abolish conscription and reduce the strength of his army, accept the French mandate in unqualified terms, adopt the French currency system, and punish those implicated in anti-French action.

The aim was to ensure that Faisal could not comply, but to everyone's surprise he did. The French army advanced on Damascus all the same. There was a popular rising and much violence in the course of which the young minister of war was killed leading his troops into French machine-gun bullets. Faisal was expelled on 28 July. He retreated to Lake Maggiore in Italy, until he was invited to London at the end of the year.

The French were satisfied that they were quashing a British plot. Their cynicism was reinforced when Britain picked up the deposed Faisal and saw to it that he was installed as king of Iraq. The independent Arab state had lasted just five months. Faisal had never appealed to the French. To them he was merely a cat's paw, the puppet of the devious and perfidious British. In reality, the British were slightly in awe of him in the early years, and never more so than when he dazzled them at Versailles.

22

THE MIDDLE EAST DEFEATS PARIS

Negotiation of the mainstream, European elements of the treaties consisted of self-interest tempered by Wilsonism. There was much less restraint on self-interest where the Middle East was concerned.

During the early discussions, Wilson, Lloyd George and various senior French representatives, principally Pichon, were involved. Wilson was much less interested in the Middle East than in Continental Europe. He saw what Britain and France were up to, and tried to restrain them, but almost nothing had been agreed by the time he went back to the States for his break, and not much more by the time he left for good. Self-interest was less trammelled thereafter, but huge areas were still not agreed when the conference broke up finally. These areas had to be disposed of at a number of seaside venues and pleasant watering holes over the next few years. By then America had withdrawn from European involvement, Turkey was revived, belligerent and re-expanding, and old-fashioned diplomacy was back in vogue.

The importance of Versailles so far as the Middle East was concerned was that it left almost every issue unresolved. For the senior negotiators, consideration of European frontiers and the distribution of German and Austro-Hungarian territories was much more important. By the time these matters had been disposed of, the leaders of the powers were anxious to return home. President Wilson was exhausted, sick and disillusioned. Differences between the parties chiefly interested in the Middle East – the British and the French – were so extensive that there was no possibility of their early resolution. It is hardly surprising that the conference proper established so little for Britain's interests since Britain's policy for the Middle East was in complete confusion as the war ended. Confusion and fluidity was nowhere more evident than in Mesopotamia. In October 1918 Arnold Wilson said that he was amalgamating the legal administrations in Basra and Baghdad. A month later, he said he intended to revive the local administrative council. Later that month he was going to occupy Sulaimaniyah in Kurdistan. By the end of November he was in favour of an independent Kurdistan. He told London that the Arabs had no wish for an independent Iraq on the Anglo-French model.

Against such a background, the Eastern Committee had to try to create a specific British policy. The chairman, Curzon, did not feel his task aided by the 'embarrassing' McMahon pledges or the Sykes–Picot 'millstone round our necks'.[1] He took out a metaphorical blank sheet and asked Arnold Wilson to find out whether the population of Iraq wanted the country to be protected by Britain and whether they wanted Faisal's son, Abdullah, as their king. Wilson sent on the request to his political officers on 30 November. He framed his question pretty tendentiously. It was clear what the answer to the enquiries would be. Public meetings were only to be called if it was certain that the response would be positive. Favourable decisions would be recorded and sent to Baghdad.

Wilson completed his enquiries by about the end of 1918, with predictable results. He forwarded a long report, 'Self-Determination in Mesopotamia', to London. Gertrude Bell had written the report, and she went off in person to catch up with it at the Paris Peace Conference, to give Arnold Wilson more purchase at the council tables.

Part of the report was a memorandum, 'A review of the civil administration of Mesopotamia'. It is a remarkably full and informative summary of the recent history of Mesopotamia – and not all that recent: there are references to Xenophon's account of the Campaign of the Ten Thousand. It runs to 149 pages and is written in a pleasing style that has literary merit. It is very different from most official documents.

Unfortunately for Wilson, Hubert Young, a Mesopotamian adviser who had recently arrived at the Foreign Office, picked up and highlighted the loaded instructions which Wilson had given to secure the answer he wanted. Curzon was shocked: 'When the French do this sort of thing we are up in arms. But when our man does it, because it is marked "Secret and Confidential", it is proposed that we should wink at it'.[2] Arnold Wilson did not come from the same branch of the family as President Wilson.

A feline official at the India Office put a delicious gloss on the matter. Possibly Arnold Wilson 'in his anxiety to guide his officers in ascertaining the real drift of public opinion – a very intangible and uncertain factor in an oriental population – had unconsciously erred, but he had erred for the very best of reasons'. But the Foreign Office knew that the India Office was to blame, and Curzon liked 'the idea of Col. Wilson being in a state of unconsciousness when he overstepped his instructions'.[3]

The question of whether there should be a king and who he should be was not settled. Wilson's enquiries revealed no great support for Abdullah, but the

India Office was far from certain. Neither was Lawrence, who grandiloquently said that after the Syrian question had been settled 'I will make up my mind whether I will put Abdullah up for Mesopotamia or not'. The presumptuousness of this junior adviser was astounding, and Hirtzel squashed him neatly: 'I apprehend that H.M.G. are at liberty to do this whether or not Col. Lawrence makes up his mind'.[4]

But Lawrence, in his inappropriate Arab headdress, had a role at Versailles that was opaque but far more important than his status would suggest. Officially, he was at Versailles only as Faisal's interpreter. He was not an official representative in the British delegation, and indeed the Foreign Office had little time for him. 'And,' said Nicolson, 'Colonel T.E. Lawrence the while would glide along the corridors of the Majestic, the lines of resentment hardening around his boyish lips; an undergraduate with a chin.'[5]

He achieved more than might have been expected, and he did so because he knew what he wanted, whereas the Foreign Office officials did not. As Faisal's supporter and adviser, he was *parti pris*, but he was treated as if he were impartial. Arthur Hirtzel, the senior India Office official, was unimpressed by the Lawrence charisma. 'I have a great admiration for Col. L, but the F.O. made a bad mistake when they handed themselves over to him – showed him all their papers & admitted him to their most secret deliberations.'[6]

Arnold Wilson followed Gertrude Bell to Paris, arriving there on 20 March 1919, to find that the India Office approved most of his administrative recommendations. As well as senior advisers and leaders (Gertrude Bell, Crowe, Mallet, Lloyd George, Balfour, Cecil, Faisal, Weizmann), he met Lawrence for the first time. '[He] seems to have done immense harm and our difficulties with the French and Syria seem to me to be mainly due to his action and advice.'

Back in London, the Eastern Committee remained in business until early 1919, now working hard on Anglo-French relations unaware that Lloyd George was covering much the same ground direct with Clemenceau in Paris. The committee had met for the forty-seventh time on 26 December 1918. It concluded that Sykes–Picot would require to be cancelled. There would be no Allied annexation, and self-determination would require some sort of European supervision. Its remaining conclusions were embarrassing and banal. It disbanded on 7 January 1919. Senior politicians and officials were now at Versailles and there was nothing more the committee could do.

Arnold Wilson was horrified to find how little the delegates at Paris knew about the region whose future they were determining: 'Experts on Western Arabia, both military and civil, were there in force, but no one, except Miss Bell, had any first-hand knowledge of Iraq or Nejd [the upland part of Arabia] or, indeed, of Persia. The very existence of a Shiah majority in Iraq was denied as a figment of my imagination by one "expert" with an international reputation, and Miss Bell and I found it impossible to convince either the Military or the Foreign Office Delegations that Kurds in the Mosul Vilayet were numerous and likely to be troublesome, that Ibn Saud was a power seriously to be reckoned with or that our problem could not be disposed of on the same lines as those advanced for Syria by the enthusiasm of the Arab Bureau.'[7]

He still thought well of Gertrude Bell. But she was starting to go native, convinced by the arguments of Faisal and Lawrence about Arab independence. She hoped the French might accept an independent Syria, with Faisal as king. Wilson clashed violently with Lawrence. He was delighted when he heard that Lawrence planned to return to England and retire.

This lack of policy and lack of direction from London made for fluidity and vagueness in the British position at Paris. The Secretary of State for India, Montagu, complained to London that he did not know what to tell Gertrude Bell and Arnold Wilson to do – and this at the very time that unrest was spreading in Mesopotamia.

The military reality was that while the talking continued in Paris, substantial numbers of British troops were still stationed throughout the Middle East, and there they remained when the statesmen left Paris and the ink started to dry on the treaties. Only the broadest indication of what the shape of the region would be emerged from the discussions. Some officials in the Foreign Office and the India Office were of course very interested in what that shape would be. So were administrators such as Bell, Wilson and Cox, and the Turks, and Faisal and Abdullah and numbers of Frenchmen. It is probably fair to say, however, that for the mass of the British electorate, what happened in the Middle East was of little interest or importance.

23

MANDATES

Mandates were unfinished business at Paris. They were the children of Versailles and Wilsonism, but they received very little thought while Wilson was around.

Even after his departure, no firm decisions were made by the statesmen who remained. Neither the final shape nor even the concept in principle of the mandate system was agreed until the series of resort conferences that followed the Paris Conference and which will be considered in the next section. Even then there was no model mandate. Each one was different, established on an *ad hoc* basis, by treaty here and agreement there, with no major common feature except the connection with the League.

The Peace Conference had to do some original thinking. Mandates were a new concept. The idea had come from Smuts, who elaborated it in concert with Hankey. The United States were never really involved, and viewed with suspicion something that looked pretty like imperialism. President Wilson was particularly suspicious of Australian designs in the Pacific. America eventually accepted the concept with reluctance, as her interest in events in Paris diminished. Wilson could reassure himself that at least protectorates, the traditional vehicle for clandestine acquisition, had been replaced by something ostensibly more ethical.

In fact, the United States rather liked *some* mandates. They liked those that affected the former German Pacific Islands, because they made it impossible for Japan, Britain's ally, to use the islands as military bases. The annual reports that would go to the League would keep Japanese activity documented. On the other hand, in the case of Iraq, America was concerned that a British mandate would give Britain and the Turkish Petroleum Company, which Britain controlled, not only a strategic advantage in the area, but also a commercial one. In 1920, and before the mandates were formally in existence, when the San Remo Oil Agreement was concluded, splitting the oil revenues between Britain and France, the US State Department complained that Britain was not keeping an 'open door', and was violating free trade principles.[1]

But generally America took little part in the evolution of the mandates, and after the tensions of the negotiations among the Big Four, the construction of the mandates generated less heat and involved less rigour. Not only was America semi-detached; the discussions were also sabotaged by France, which refused to discuss the matter until the areas in question had been decided on. French delegates did not even attend the mandate meetings.

So, how bogus was the whole concept of the mandates? The mechanism by which they were awarded was itself open to criticism. They were assigned not by the League, in its democratic entirety, but simply by the victors themselves, the Supreme Council. With America and Wilson's Principles out of the way, the Supreme Council consisted of France, Britain and Italy, who picked up for themselves the territories they had chosen during the war.

While the Americans saw mandates as 'a sacred trust on behalf of civilisation',[2] some have argued that Britain more cynically regarded them as a means of disguising 'the crudity of conquest . . . in the veil of morality'.[3] Sykes had said in 1918 that 'Imperial annexation, military triumph, prestige, white man's burdens have been expunged from the popular political vocabulary'.[4] Nobody had told George V about the new vocabulary: 'We are the victors. We are the Top Dog,' he said.[5]

Back in London in December 1918 there had been an interesting exchange about mandates in the Eastern Committee. Curzon wanted Britain to be the mandatory for the Caucasian Republics:

Balfour: Why should there be a mandatory? . . . Of course the Caucasus would be much better governed under our aegis . . . But why should it not be misgoverned?
Curzon: That is the other alternative – let them cut each other's throats.
Balfour: I am in favour of that.[6]

Of course Balfour as usual is being flippant and enjoying teasing a far from facetious colleague; but the exchange illustrates evolving views about world governance. And just as Balfour's joke disguised a more serious attitude, the superficial similarity of mandates to protectorates should not obscure the differences or lead to the assumption that, at least as far as Britain was concerned, imperial business was going on as usual. Britain indeed considered herself an exemplary imperial power. She was the primary sponsor and defender of the mandate system and reckoned that she would benefit from the publicity the mandate system gave to her ethical system of administration. Britain regarded the regulatory body with approbation, and the approbation was generally reciprocated.

That regulatory body was a Permanent Mandates Commission of the League of Nations at Geneva and the authority administering a mandate was required to report to it every year. There was also a right of petition to the commission by those governed under mandate. That right was often used in the case of the Middle East. The Permanent Mandates Commission convened in Geneva for the first time on 4 October 1921. It consisted of eight men, seven European and one Japanese, and one woman. What they had to administer was divided into 'A', 'B' and 'C' mandates.

The 'C' mandates were geographically remote and largely awarded to Japan and the dominions. Smuts described them to his countrymen as 'annexation in all but name'. 'B' mandates were in Africa. They contained no promise of any early move to independent rule. Smuts had originally wanted to exclude Africa from the mandate system on the grounds that the territories there were too barbarous and that self-determination would be impracticable. The 'A' mandates were component parts of the Ottoman Empire, and in theory the populations affected were to receive no more than 'administrative advice and assistance' on their route to self-government: those former Ottoman possessions which could be considered as 'independent nations' could be provisionally recognised as such, receiving simply limited assistance in regard to administrative matters. This sort of *quasi*-mandate was applied in the case of Iraq and Northern Syria, although not to Palestine.[7]

The Permanent Mandates Commission had moral authority, but few powers. France bluntly told the Assembly of the League in 1929 that the 'B' and 'C' mandates could be described as permanent so far as France was concerned. Even if the commission, which only met twice a year, had been minded to be more positive, its reports were no more than advisory. Real responsibility rested with the Council of the League. When in 1926 the commission asked for more powers, including the right to interview petitioners from the mandated territories, it was immediately rapped over the knuckles by the Council for seeking to arrogate authority from the mandatory powers to itself.

But if the commission was toothless, that did not mean that it did not bark. The commissioners were experienced administrators who enjoyed security of tenure and were supplied with an abundance of information about what was going on. Although the commission met in private, the grievances that came to its attention were communicated to the Assembly, where the small nations (as opposed to the mandatory powers, who dominated the Council) had a voice. Petitioning and publicity affected the culture in which the mandates were exercised. When Nazism threatened German Jews, for instance, Britain was urged to facilitate Jewish immigration into Palestine. There was also criticism of her failure to repress civil disturbances in Palestine. How far the essentially moral influence of the commission through the League affected the conduct of the mandatory depended on who the mandatory was.

France paid little attention. Britain paid more, but the influence was only on the margins of events.[8]

While the imperialist element in the mandates was ostensibly tempered by the supervisory role of the League of Nations, that monitoring was less significant than it might have been, with the United Nations outside the League. This has led to claims such as this of Elizabeth Monroe: '[T]he mandate system of the League of Nations was converted by victorious Empires into a cloak for a good measure of imperialism.'[9]

That is too simple. The mandates in Iraq and Palestine cost Britain millions of pounds. Indeed, in 1922 the Beaverbrook and Rothermere newspapers opened a campaign against retaining the mandates. In 1923 *The Morning Post* conceded with regret that Mesopotamia had to be retained to keep it away from Turkey; but Palestine should be disposed of while it still could be. Even Churchill in July 1923 argued against 'fumbling with Mesopotamia and reaching out for Persia'.[10] In financial terms at least, Britain was not motivated by self-interest. Britain did not want the Palestine mandate. She would have been delighted if Palestine had been placed under international control, or if the United States – or indeed any country other than France – had been the mandatory power.

A final judgement on Britain's Middle East mandates is not easy to arrive at. They have to be considered individually, as they will later be. But a broad judgement on the mandates in general as Britain operated them cannot be avoided.

At a constitutional level, Jordan and Iraq became at least nominally sovereign states fairly speedily. France only reluctantly instituted power-sharing after revolts in Syria and Lebanon, and independence was delayed till it was impossible to withhold it any longer. In Palestine, Britain was never able to move the mandate to independence. Indeed she was unable even to set up consultative institutions. In Palestine, a gulf widened between Britain and the Mandates Commission. As the Arabs became more vocal, the commission became more Zionist.

On the other hand, the Middle East mandates lacked moral authority. They had been established in contravention of the wishes of the local populations. Iraq and Jordan would have liked to be independent. Syria and Lebanon would also rather have had anything than French rule. Article XXII of the Covenant of the League, in addition to containing particular provisions regarding the scope of the mandates, expressly provided in the case of Arab countries that the wishes of the populations were to be taken into consideration. San Remo ignored that; such expression of the wishes of the populations as had been obtained by the King–Crane Commission was also ignored. The proposition that the countries in question were not fit 'to stand by themselves' was questionable. Truly representative and democratic regimes were not established.

For Britain, an overarching and lasting Empire was not established as a force for good in the world as a result of the post-First World War settlement. The ideals of the League of Nations, in which many Britons passionately believed, were not realised. But from the point of view of *realpolitik* the mandates did a great deal for Britain. They gave her economic, military and political power in the region for half a century. They even worked to her advantage in a crisis which had never been foreseen: they gave her a vital base in the Second World War. Does that vindicate British policy? Not in itself, because taken as a whole, the mandate exercise was not essayed for purely selfish reasons.

The reality was that neither Britain nor the League and the Mandates Commission could move uncohesive tribal groupings, which were more characterised by internecine rivalries than by their interest in the rule of law and the sovereignty of parliament, towards the democratic ideal. But Britain at least did the best she could with what was available. To say of Iraq, for instance, that the British 'managed to locate a class of collaborators . . . on whom they could devolve authority without jeopardising British strategic interests'[11] fails to acknowledge that Britain had to rely, as the Turks had done, on those who would make governance possible. Examination of the individual mandates will reveal the rivalries that frustrated the hopes for moving Iraq and Palestine in particular towards objectives that Britain honourably sought to promote.

Palestine stands apart from Iraq and Jordan. Britain always saw Palestine more as a burden to be dutifully carried than as a resource to be exploited. Jordan was regarded as a fairly unimportant attachment, first to Palestine and later more to Iraq. In the event, Jordan, the unconsidered trifle among the mandates, can be said to have been a success, and has endured strong, moderate and on the whole a force for peace in the region. Iraq was the only acquisition which was assumed to bring Britain material advantage, chiefly in strategic terms rather than for its mineral resources; and Britain certainly sought to create a lasting nexus over the country, which would subsist after independence. But that did not mean that independence was delayed. On the contrary, the mandate was pushed past the staging posts on the road to sovereignty at full speed.

Britain can regard the period of the mandates without any sense of shame. In all the heat and passion and violence of these years – particularly in Palestine and Iraq – soldiers and administrators frequently failed to attain ideal levels of self-restraint and humanity. The disparate elements of the Ottoman Empire were suddenly removed from its systems of controls and coercion, systems that had been condemned for centuries. Whatever replaced them would still be less than perfect. In the institutions of politics, the habits that have characterised the practice of politics throughout history were not abjured. Perhaps those who criticise the mandatory power are less than realistic.

24

PALESTINE AND ZIONISM

President Wilson appeared to have little difficulty in squaring self-determination with a Zionist state. But he paid little attention to Palestine, and indeed little was done at Paris regarding Palestine. There were many practical problems. Palestine's borders had to be addressed. Lloyd George wanted them to run from Dan to Beersheba. The French were worried about whether Dan included the Litani River and threatened Syria and its water supplies. The borders were eventually agreed, but little more. Britain was not awarded the mandate until the 1920 San Remo Conference (and even then there was a last-minute attempt by the French to retain the right to protect the Christians). The details of the mandate were not agreed for another two years.

The Zionists were one of the many unofficial delegations at the Peace Conference. They were unofficial only in the sense that they did not represent a country. They were received by the Supreme Council as early as 27 February. Among those who spoke was Nahum Sokolow, the great Zionist advocate and writer who had come from Poland to London and went on to be president of the Jewish Agency for Palestine and president of the World Zionist Conference. His successor in the latter role was Weizmann, who observed him closely at Paris: 'I could see Sokolow's face and without being sentimental it was as if 2,000 years of Jewish suffering rested on his shoulders.'[1]

During the war, France had half-heartedly supported the idea of a Jewish home. Now they were steadfastly against the idea. They recalled, instead, their traditional role as protector of the Christians in Palestine. When Weizmann addressed the Supreme Council at Versailles on behalf of the Zionists, completing his peroration by saying that his demand was 'in the name of the people who had suffered martyrdom for eighteen centuries', he was congratulated by all the delegates of the great powers, other than the French.[2]

Right from the start of discussions in Paris, there was Arab antagonism and opposition towards the British concept of Palestine and of a Zionist home. The Balfour Declaration had always been hateful to the Arabs. The phrase that was so often used, 'The land without people – for the people without land' was good propaganda but untruthful. The British view, and the Jewish view, was contemptuous of the indigenous Arabs who formed the majority of the inhabitants of Palestine and who were regarded as uncivilised Orientals who could not fail to benefit from the civilising effect of Jewish immigration. Balfour could seem to dismiss the Arab inhabitants of Palestine as if they were no more than an insignificant presence.

Weizmann visited Palestine in 1918 and, encouraged by the British, did his best to dispel Arab concerns. It was then that he met Faisal. He wore an Arab headdress for the occasion. He said there was room for Jews and Arabs to work together until they were ready for joint autonomy. Faisal got on well enough with Weizmann: they were both united in their dislike of the French.

Faisal did caution that Arab opinion had to be kept in mind. From the start, the Zionists did not do that. Their attitude was aggressive in a way that their Gentile supporters had not expected. At a conference in Jaffa, they demanded that the name of the territory be changed to Eretz Israel, the Land of Israel. But even Faisal was dismissive about the indigenous Arabs. After his meeting with him Weizmann wrote back to his wife: 'He is the first real Arab nationalist I have met. He is a leader! He's quite intelligent and a very honest man, handsome as a picture! He is not interested in Palestine, but on the other hand he wants Damascus and the whole of Northern Syria. He is contemptuous of the Palestinian Arabs whom he doesn't even regard as Arabs!'[3]

'After "the War to end War" they seem to have been pretty successful in Paris in making a "Peace to end Peace"' said the future Field Marshal Wavell (who served under Allenby in the Palestine campaign). Though the Great War did not prove to be the war that ended war, the Peace Conference that followed it has proved to be the Peace Conference that ended peace conferences. As the Second World War drew to a close, a number of decisions were deferred to the Great Peace Conference which Churchill expected to attend. No such conference ever took place. The reason in part was the lessons that were drawn from Versailles.

Versailles concluded little so far as the Middle East was concerned. A series of further conferences would be needed before it was put into even preliminary shape. Cambon said that the peace treaties that were settled at Versailles had in them the seeds of 'a just and durable war'. In retrospect at least Versailles can be said to have sown the seeds of wars that would certainly be durable whether or not they were just.

All the participants at Paris, not only the senior statesmen, but perhaps even more the diplomats and the secretariat, were exhausted by the time their work was concluded. The freshness of spring had given way to a long, hot summer. The dust of the city and the heat of the pavements had become wearisome. The delegates agreed that it would be much more congenial to meet in future in luxury resorts, and we shall now follow their example.

V

DIPLOMACY BY CONFERENCE

25

RESORT DIPLOMACY: SAN REMO, SÈVRES, LAUSANNE AND CAIRO. INTRODUCTION

The Turkish question had not been disposed of at Versailles. Indeed, it was scarcely addressed. There was broad acceptance of the general principle that the Straits and Constantinople should be internationalised and that the Ottoman Empire was to be partitioned in accordance with secret treaties. But great complications had been stirred up by the publication of those treaties and by Wilson's objections to them.

Accordingly, the Allies left Paris in December 1919 with nothing substantial agreed about Turkey and with Lloyd George saying that the final decision would be postponed 'till we know what the United States are going to do'.[1] It was still hoped that the United States would play an active part in administering the mandates; but it would soon emerge that they were increasingly uninterested in running the Middle East and increasingly irritated as they saw Britain and France cornering the region's oil.

The Long–Bérenger Oil Agreement seemed to the United States to be an example of that process. A tentative step towards reconciling French and British interests, which were already conflicting, was made in April 1919 when France and Britain signed the agreement (later incorporated into the San Remo Oil Agreement of 24 April 1920). French investors received 25 per cent of the investment in the Mesopotamian oilfields – or 25 per cent of crude oil output if the fields were in the event given up by the British government. The United States were fiercely hostile. While they did not want any political responsibility for the Middle East, they very much did want to exploit the economic opportunities.

But the Americans were no longer on the scene, so Europe was left with a largely free hand to award mandates and carve up the Middle East. The victors were far from business-like as they sought to redraw the world map. Britain's problem was that she did not have a clear view about what she wanted. Her main motivation continued to be a distrust of the French and a dislike of the Turks.

At Versailles, Nicolson said what he thought of the Turks, and his views were typical of those of his colleagues: 'For the Turks I had, and have, no sympathy whatsoever. Long residence at Constantinople had convinced me that behind his mask of indolence, the Turk conceals impulses of the most brutal savagery. This conviction was not diminished by his behaviour towards the Kut garrison or towards the Armenians within his borders. The Turks had contributed nothing whatsoever to the progress of humanity: they are a race of Anatolian marauders.'² By 25 June 1919, Nicolson had come to the conclusion that it was unlikely that a peace treaty would ever be signed with Turkey. 'It will just drag on.'³

There was no consensus whatsoever about what should be done with the Turkish Empire. Its collapse had been long foreseen, but precipitation of the collapse was not a British war aim. On 19 May 1918, Nicolson was separated only by a glass partition from a meeting of pretty well the whole Cabinet in the Rue Nitot and through it he heard Curzon arguing for the ejection of the Turks from Europe, Montagu and Milner not wanting to disturb the Turks at all, Churchill keen to leave them as they were but with America getting a mandate over Constantinople and the Straits. Balfour was happy with that solution for Constantinople, but Smyrna was to go to Greece and the rest of Turkey was to be an independent kingdom controlled by the powers. Lloyd George expressed no view.⁴

The Eastern Question was finally tackled at a series of gatherings in agreeable resorts where the statesmen could relax when they were not conferring. 'Diplomacy by Conference' was how Hankey described the three years which Lloyd George spent after the war, avoiding the humdrum necessities of domestic politics and visiting a series of bathing places and spas with his golf clubs. It is not easy to picture the austere Hankey making the most of the amenities that such surroundings offered.

The conferences began in San Remo on the Italian coast between 19 and 26 April 1920, after a preliminary meeting in London in February. The decisions that were reached there were embodied in the treaty of 10 August 1920. The signing ceremony did not take place at the seaside, but in the Paris suburb of Sèvres, from which the treaty takes its name.

26

SAN REMO AND SÈVRES

1. The San Remo Conference

Curzon did not much like San Remo: 'a very poor sort of place confined in a very narrow strip between the hills and the sea, much less tidy and spick-and-span than the French Riviera' with 'an eternal twitter of the engines of Italian motors, which seemed to make a quite different noise from any other'. Italian gendarmes in heavy black uniforms and cocked hats irritated him: '[T]here are 600 walking about and dogging us as though we were criminals'. What others regarded as the jewel of the Italian Riviera, Curzon saw as 'a second-hand English watering-place'.[1]

He did not think much of the deliberations either. Balfour was less interested in the discussions than in a book he was writing. 'Lloyd George has fits of impetuosity at the Conference which sometimes take him in the right direction, sometimes in the wrong. The French are depressed and take little part.'[2] The conference concluded with much business still undone.

What happened at San Remo was that the Allied powers simply divided up the mandates among themselves on the basis of the secret wartime negotiations. The League of Nations, the supervisory authority, was not even consulted. The United States had turned their back on Europe, and never joined the League. Britain drafted peace terms which could be offered to Turkey, and the Allies agreed them. The substantive work at the conference consisted largely of questions about boundaries and railways. The northern frontier of Palestine was adjusted to secure territory from Syria at the headwaters of the Jordan and the Litani.

San Remo ignored promises of Arab independence, which annoyed Arabs. It annoyed the French too, because while Sykes–Picot was supposed to be honoured, Britain seemed ready to accept the fact of Faisal's position as king of Syria. But British support for Faisal in Syria, as we have seen, was only temporary. Lloyd George did not wish alienation of the French to interfere with the establishment of British direct rule in Mesopotamia. In these circumstances he could forget wartime promises to Hussein.

France confirmed her agreement to the inclusion of Mosul Vilayet in the British area – with the important proviso that the terms of the Franco-British San Remo Oil Agreement were not prejudiced. The lines of the railways and oil pipelines were so agreed as to allow Britain, among other things, to get her oil to the Mediterranean through Syria.

The essence of the San Remo Agreement was that the whole of the Arab rectangle between the Mediterranean and Persia was placed under mandatory rule with a rider declaring that the mandate with Palestine would contain an obligation that the Balfour Declaration should be applied.

The Arab reaction was to regard what the West had done as a betrayal, a denial of promises of independence and unity. 'It was on the strength of those promises that the Arabs had come into the War and made their contribution and their sacrifices; that fact alone sufficed to turn the corresponding obligation into a debt of honour. What the San Remo Conference did was, in effect, to ignore the debt and come to decisions which on all the essential points, ran counter to the wishes of the people concerned.'³

By this stage, Britain had secured all she wanted from the Ottoman Empire. She had secured it largely at the expense of France. She had gained Mesopotamia, including Mosul and Palestine. Her positions in Cyprus and Egypt were recognised. The Straits were open to all but were effectively controlled by the most powerful navy in the world, the Royal Navy. Russia was vulnerable in the Black Sea as never before. India and the oil of the Middle East were secure. None of this was what Britain had gone to war for, either against Germany or Turkey, but it was a wonderful prize.

2. The Treaties of Sèvres

There were really two treaties of Sèvres. One was a treaty with the Turks. The other was a secret treaty between France, Britain and Italy, 'The Tripartite Agreement'. Both treaties were signed on the same day. The secret treaty confirmed British oil and commercial concessions and put the former German enterprises in the Ottoman Empire in the hands of a Tripartite Corporation. This agreement was the completion of negotiations which had taken place over 15 months, beginning at the Paris Peace Conference, continuing in London and concluded at the San Remo Conference.

The other Treaty of Sèvres was the crystallisation of the terms agreed at San Remo for offer to the Turks. The terms were put to the Turks on 11 May 1920. They were bitterly denounced by the Turkish delegation, but in the event agreed to on 10 August 1920. The terms were, first, that the sultan would remain at Constantinople. Secondly, the Allies were entitled to occupy the

Straits and European Turkey. Thirdly, an Armenian state was to be created, excluding Trebizond and Erzincan, but with access to the sea. Finally, Turkey was to be deprived of Syria, Palestine, Mesopotamia, Arabia and the Aegean Islands.

Armenia, which floated in and out of the consideration of the great powers as they rearranged the world, was given independence at Sèvres but an independence which was not guaranteed. Promises, but no more than promises were also made to Kurdistan.

America was asked to assume a mandate or delimit state boundaries. The Senate rejected the mandate on 1 June 1920.

27

LAUSANNE

1. Background

Mustafa Kemal, later Atatürk, became president of the new Republic of Turkey in 1922. The Empire was abolished. The caliphate, an office which had been only in intermittent existence since the death of Muhammad in 632, was abolished in 1924. The sick man was in robust health. In August 1922, Turkey finally attacked Smyrna: 'Soldiers, your goal is the Mediterranean.' On 10 September, Kemal entered the town on horseback. Whether it was another white horse I do not know.

At San Remo and at Sèvres the victorious powers had dismembered Turkish possessions at the very moment the Turkish army was reviving and starting to recover what the Allied delegates were disposing of. The result was a further conference at Lausanne at which the Turks took part as a rehabilitated major power and not as a vanquished victim. By the time the resulting treaty was signed on 24 July 1923, there was a mood of much greater hostility between the former allies, Britain and France, than between either of them and Turkey.

At San Remo, France's cordiality towards Turkey disquieted Britain. In October 1921 France signed a treaty with Kemal, in exchange for which they got important concessions. Britain was very angry. Now, at Lausanne, the last vestiges of goodwill between France and Britain evaporated. Tragically the two countries were propelled apart, and the divergence that opened up left a space that could be filled by a resurgent Germany. The Entente was broken, and hopes for the League were undermined.

The conference lasted 11 weeks scattered through the period from November 1922 to July 1923. Events outside the conference chamber did not stand still and indeed exacerbated the tensions within, fuelling the reciprocated distrust between the British and French delegates. The conference spanned the triumph of Mustafa Kemal and the crushing of Greece. It was a conference from which France was expected to emerge the winner, but from which she achieved little and by which she was diminished. Britain's success at San Remo appeared to be fatally threatened throughout the conference, but at the last moment that success was triumphantly consolidated. The retrieval of the situation was due entirely to the diplomatic skills of George Nathaniel Curzon, first Marquess Curzon of Kedleston.

2. Curzon at Lausanne

Curzon was not without his problems at Lausanne. Some, as will emerge, were objectively serious ones. Others were less so, but disquieting all the same for a man of such gravity. His steel back brace broke. His valet got drunk and hid his dress trousers.[1] Mussolini attended Lausanne in an unlikely combination of white spats and black shirt, but at least he did not part company with his trousers.[*]

Curzon's greatest contribution to the state which he served so long was during his first, five-year term as Viceroy of India. He was a great, reforming proconsul, who took no account of his political self-interest in doing justice to the native population, and equally little account of his own health and comfort in visiting the areas affected by plague in 1899 and 1900 and seeking to alleviate famine by extending the irrigated areas.

His second, shorter term was less happy, undermined by scheming on behalf of Kitchener, the commander-in-chief, and not supported by the government. When he returned to Britain the trajectory of a brilliant career was checked. He joined Asquith's coalition cabinet in 1915, but was given nothing much to do. Even today he tends to be remembered for just two things: his viceroyalty and the fact that he did not become prime minister in 1923 because he was a peer.

In fact the period from December 1916, when he became a member of Lloyd George's War Cabinet, was one of the most fruitful of his political career. As well as leading the House of Lords, an important office in those days, he was intimately involved in the direction of the war. He was the only man to remain in the cabinet throughout Lloyd George's leadership, a measure of his utility.

In January 1919, as well as continuing with a range of other duties, he was asked to mind the shop at the Foreign Office while Balfour, the Foreign Secretary, was with the prime minister in Paris. In October of the same year he took over from Balfour. Before and after October, Lloyd George interfered in any aspects of foreign policy that interested him – mainly European issues. But the system worked reasonably well. The only matter they differed on was the peace terms for Turkey. That make Curzon's task at Lausanne more difficult, and his success all the more remarkable.

---

[*] British Foreign Secretaries have had problems with their trousers. Sir Geoffrey Howe, as he then was, lost his in the course of a sleeper journey in the United Kingdom some 60 years later.

One of the points of difference between Britain and France was that France did not share a commitment to the protection of minorities, particularly the Greeks, against the Turks. By 13 December, Curzon was threatening to walk out: 'When we go away – and we may go quicker than you think – the whole world will look at what we have been saying and doing here during the last two days. When the world hears that we have been fighting the battle of these minorities and have received nothing in return from the Turkish Delegation but platitudes, the general impression will be deplorable.'[2]

French opinion was very critical of Britain. When Curzon threatened to leave the conference, *Le Temps* said that 'While France has always remained faithful to her policy of disinterestedness, England has changed her attitude accordingly as it appeared easier and more profitable for her to extend her possessions in the east'. On 21 December, *Le Temps* again 'regretted deeply that the question of the Straits had become the pretext for a new incident at the Lausanne Conference'. The paper also resented the fact that France was being carried along in Britain's imperialist, anti-Turkish wake. It deprecated a collective threat against the Turks, a common position which was being adopted only because 'England has been unable to agree with the Turks on the question of the Straits and Mosul'.[3]

It was all very different from Sèvres. Turkey was in a position to dictate and deny. The Turkish delegation was now led by Inö Ismet, a member of the new nationalist regime. Ismet could be difficult. He was deaf and pretended to be deafer than he was. He switched off his hearing aid whenever something was said with which he disagreed. Curzon told him he was like a music box, playing the same old tune all the time. Curzon was aware of his own weakness. 'Hitherto we have dictated our peace treaties. Now we are negotiating one with the enemy who has an army in being while we have none, an unheard-of position.'[4]

On the face of it, everything Britain had secured by the end of the San Remo Conference was at risk. Mosul was threatened. The Turkish victory over the Greeks had reopened almost everything that had already been settled. The question of the Straits had to be considered afresh. The position of minorities in the old Empire arose again. The capitulatory regime needed to be renegotiated, and the negotiations were now with a confident, reinvigorated Turkey. Britain and France were clearly at odds with each other, and there was no question of a united front against the Turks, though Curzon did his best to pull the wartime allies together at the pre-conference meeting in London. He had already made it clear that if he could not achieve some sort of agreement with the French, he would not go to Lausanne at all.[5]

The fate of Mosul was not determined at Lausanne. The Turks said that the

Kurds, a substantial part of the inhabitants, were Turks. The *Encyclopaedia Britannica* said so too. Curzon: 'It was reserved for the Turkish Delegation to discover for the first time in history that the Kurds were Turks. Nobody has ever found it out before.' Mosul was referred to the League, which ultimately gave it to Iraq, which is what Curzon had wanted.

Britain, so far as Lloyd George spoke for the country, was robustly hostile to expansion under Mustafa Kemal. He said in the House of Commons on 21 July 1920 that the government's policy 'consists of rescuing all non-Turkish populations from the Turkish yoke'.[6] On 22 November 1920, at the first sitting of the League, Balfour described Mustafa Kemal as a 'bandit' insensitive to the very principles of the League.[7]

France, though deploying troops in Syria to defend Cilicia, took a much more conciliatory view. Conversations between France and Turkey took place in London. The conversations, embodied in the Franklin Bouillon Agreement of October 1921, caused great problems between Britain and France. France recognised the nationalist regime in Angora, as Ankara was then called in the West, as the legitimate Turkish government. Kemal was delighted, but Britain was appalled by what she regarded as treachery. France was making a separate peace and leaving Greece and Iraq at Turkey's mercy. Indeed, France had not only stopped fighting the Turks; she was now supporting them financially in their war against Britain's allies, the Greeks. France could almost be regarded as being at war by proxy with her former Entente ally.

Churchill sent a memorandum to the Cabinet saying that if the stories of the Franklin Bouillon Agreement, the Angora Accord, were true (which they were) the information 'would unquestionably convict the French government of what in the most diplomatic application of the phrase could only be described as an "unfriendly act"'.[8] Churchill was well versed in the technical language of diplomacy, as Sir Alexander Cadogan, the most professional of diplomats, Permanent Under-Secretary at the Foreign Office from 1938 to 1946, was to discover to his surprise during the Second World War. 'An unfriendly act' has a technical meaning: it defines an action on the part of one country that would justify another country in going to war with it.

The French prime minister, Aristide Briand, was not hostile to Britain. Briand had, in fact, been trying to repair relations with Great Britain. But French public opinion was out of sympathy with this approach, and Poincaré was ready to take a much harder line. The Supreme Council of the League met in Cannes, another congenial resort, in January 1922. Briand was photographed by the press being taught by Lloyd George to play golf. Golfing with the Anglo-Saxons (a Celtic leader of the Anglo-Saxons, at any rate), hastened Briand's fall and his succession by Poincaré.

Briand had not understood how the Angora Accord would appear to Britain. Indeed he was so unaware of the anger aroused that he innocently asked Britain to join with France in a defensive alliance against the revival of Germany which France increasingly feared. Britain was certainly not prepared to enter into an alliance with France unless they abrogated the Angora Accord. The rebuff and the golfing were too much: on his return to Paris and despite appealing to the Chamber for support, Briand had to tender his resignation.

With Poincaré's succession real hostility began. The significance of the change of regime was immense. Instead of remaining close to Britain and working together to safeguard the future of Europe against the revival of German militarism, Poincaré went off on his own to look for support from a web of alliances with minor, Eastern European powers. This alienated Britain, who interpreted France's policy as a renewed desire for Continental domination. The straggle of minor alliances that France made, for instance with Poland and Czechoslovakia, meant that there was no substantial protection against the eventual Nazi menace. The collapse of the Franco-British alliance led to the debacle of 1939–40.

The tensions that the Angora Accord caused contributed to a crisis in September 1922, when the Turks threatened to attack the Turkish town of Chanak and the troops – French as well as British – that were guarding the neutral Dardanelles zone. Despite the fact that there were French troops there, France encouraged the Turks to resist Britain's reaction to the Chanak Crisis, and indeed Poincaré soon ordered the withdrawal of the French detachment giving the Turks a freer hand against Britain.

Lloyd George, surrounded by a small inner Cabinet (which included the Conservative Austen Chamberlain) was extraordinarily belligerent. The Cabinet Secretary, Hankey, thought that Lloyd George and Churchill positively wanted a *casus belli.* Lloyd George told his friends that he thought that the country would be behind him if Britain again went to war. But he had made serious mistakes. He had issued an ultimatum on behalf of Britain and the dominions. The dominion prime ministers, particularly Canada, took exception to the assumption that they would automatically fall in behind Britain as they had done in 1914. He had also misjudged public and parliamentary opinion. Despite Austen Chamberlain's complicity, the crisis led to the Carlton Club meeting at which the Conservatives voted to end the coalition, and thus Lloyd George's political career.

After Chanak, French outrage became even more pronounced. On 19 September 1922, the day on which Poincaré ordered the French contingent to withdraw from its support of British troops at Chanak, Curzon left for Paris to confer with Poincaré and Italy's Count Sforza. In the course of the next few days, the negotiations between the three men contained 'scandalous recriminations' which Churchill, who could recall the Agadir crisis, described as the 'worst moment' of the 'worst years of Anglo-French relations which the twentieth century with all its stresses has seen'.[9]

The exchanges reduced Curzon to tears, stiffened though he was by his steel corset. Poincaré's reproaches were so bitter that at a break in the sittings Sforza claimed Curzon, walking up and down with him in the *Salon de l'Horloge*, suddenly 'burst out sobbing (I learned later on from Curzon's friends that he had *la larma facile*)'. He pulled a silver hip flask from the depths of his frock coat and 'swallowed an invigorating mouthful of brandy'. Sforza was sympathetic and tried to reassure Curzon with a white lie 'of the kind one tells children when they have a fit of nerves, and told him that I had myself been obliged to put up with like discourses from Poincaré'.[10] Tears did come surprisingly easily to the marmoreal Curzon – he had for instance been reduced to tears by Lawrence's bad temper at the Paris Conference – but this was an embarrassingly public display of weakness for A Most Superior Person.*

Sforza may be thought to be enjoying himself a little too much, but Ronaldshay's biography of Curzon pretty well confirms the episode: '[The] Council Room was resounding with charges and counter-charges, with recriminations, attacks and retorts, until Lord Curzon could stand the strain no longer and rising from his chair, shaken with emotion, left the room.'[11]

It was said of Keynes that 'he began life as a Roman; he ended it as a mere Italian'.[12] *A fortiori*, the same could be said of Curzon, and here he was, reduced to tears by a mere Frenchman. This was a low point for Curzon, but Lausanne had not ended, and Curzon was not defeated.

3. Curzon's Triumph

Briand had tried to brush the Angora Accord aside as a *'tractation locale'*, just a local deal, but the agreement can be seen in hindsight as a discernible staging post in the diverging paths of the wartime allies, France and Britain. It was frequently said in these days that there might still be an Entente, but that it was no longer Cordiale.

---

* In 1880, seven undergraduates at Balliol College, Oxford, published 40 quatrains of doggerel lampooning various members of the college under the title *The Masque of B-ll--l*, now better known as *The Balliol Masque*, in a format that has come to be called Balliol Rhyme. It is funny, benevolent and harmless, but the college authorities suppressed it fiercely, which may be why it is well known 150 years later. The quatrain about Curzon ran:

> My name is George Nathaniel Curzon.
> I am a most superior person.
> My cheeks are pink, my hair is sleek.
> I dine at Blenheim twice a week.

France was inclined to talk of the new Turkish Republic as a daughter of the French Republic, with shared ideals and aspirations, but there was more to it than that. In the accord, France ceded about 18,000 square kilometres of territory, including an evacuated Cilicia, but in a covering letter the Turkish negotiator said that France would receive iron, chrome and silver concessions for 99 years in the Kharshut Valley. Other concessions would be considered sympathetically. France was well on the way to establishing an important new sphere of influence, which might counterbalance some of Britain's gains in the Middle East. Britain saw the accord as aimed directly at her, and Curzon made a vigorous complaint in an exchange of notes, 'the Curzon–St Aulaire Correspondence'. He was understandably exasperated: he had been assured by Briand himself that Franklin Bouillon had not gone to Turkey on an official mission. Indeed Briand had assured Britain 'that no general engagement had been or would be entered into by France on the general question of peace between the Allies and Turkey without a close agreement with the Allies, and especially the British government'.[13] Then France had gone and concluded a separate peace.

The French response was largely to defend its actions on the basis of necessity and to assert, fairly limply, that 'without claiming in any sense to have assured herself of England's agreement to her plans, France can legitimately maintain that she warned her Ally of the necessities which she had to take into account'.[14]

France was pretty well admitting that she had made a separate peace. This issue was only one of a range of issues between Britain and France. They were separated over disputes about the Rhineland, occupied by the Allies under the terms of the Versailles Treaty. On this matter, Britain was leaving France to fend for herself. Differences over Turkey were just part of the Middle East competition between the two countries in Mesopotamia, Arabia, Palestine and specifically in relation to Constantinople.

The decorous language of the diplomats expressed the tension between the two governments in relatively moderate words; press opinion in both countries was more outspoken. *The Morning Post*, usually strongly hostile to Lloyd George, deprecated France's support for Mustafa Kemal[15] and *The Times* regretted that the governments had not been able to work together over Cilicia and work out a plan together.[16] More violent criticisms of French policy were expressed by other newspapers on both sides of the political divide, such as the *Pall Mall Gazette* and the *Daily Telegraph*. In France, *Le Temps* defended the French government against 'the fanciful suppositions' of the *Guardian* and *Daily Herald*.

The background to Lausanne, then, was that the separation of Britain and France over Turkey continued to widen and that France was increasingly seen as the friend of Turkey, Britain as her enemy – particularly after a strong speech by Lloyd George in the House of Commons on 4 August 1922. Lloyd George was always suspicious of the French, and his speech hinted that Turkey was being reinforced from France in her conflict with Britain's Greek allies. Correspondingly strong anti-British feeling was expressed in the French Chamber.

Relations degenerated further: France wished to move reinforcements to Silesia. Britain did not. Because the necessary joint approach to Germany for permission to move troops across the frontier could not be made, Germany was able to refuse the French demand and did so publicly. France was humiliated, and French public opinion strongly questioned the value of an alliance with such an unhelpful ally. Anglo-French relations were at their worst since 1918, and Curzon listened to a note from the French ambassador which threatened an open rupture between the two countries. The matter was referred to the Supreme Council: Lloyd George told the House of Commons that 'there were questions here which menaced the solidarity of the Alliance'.[17] Silesia in the summer was followed by the Washington Naval Conference in the autumn, where France regarded her treatment as a further humiliation.

British policy over Turkey could not be formulated without taking account of the Indian dimension. There was a lack of consensus between London and India. From the perspective of the viceroy, the views of 70 million Indian Muslims had to be taken into account in handling the Turks. India wanted a much less robust line against the Turks than the Foreign Office. The viceroy sent the Secretary of State a strongly worded memorandum to this effect. Strangely, he asked for authority to publish it and, even more strangely, the Secretary of State for India, Montagu, consented on 4 March 1922 without even obtaining the sanction of his colleagues. Curzon, always sensitive to the notion that he was unappreciated and ignored, complained to Austen Chamberlain, the leader of his party in the House of Commons,

Look at the position in which it has placed me. I am about, by desire of the Government, to enter into negotiations of the utmost difficulty in Paris [in connection with Lausanne] in which the dice are already loaded heavily against me and in which my chances of success are small. Just at this moment, on the eve of the Conference, my pitch is queered, my hand is shattered by the declaration from a branch of the British Government claiming far more for the Turks than even in their wildest moments they have dared to ask for themselves, or than it is possible for any British statesman to concede. When I argue to Mustafa Kemal or to Poincaré about Adrianople or the Straits they have merely to brandish against me this fatal declaration. I have now no desire to go to Paris at all . . .

> If the policy of H.M.G. is the policy for the Viceroy and Montagu, then
> let Montagu go to Paris in my place, and fight to obtain Adrianople and
> Thrace and the Holy places for his beloved Turks. He will then have the fail-
> ure which his own action will have rendered inevitable instead of thrusting
> it upon me.[18]

Lloyd George supported Curzon, and Montagu resigned.

Curzon wrote his letter in bed, ill. His recovery was retarded by insomnia, a
frequent problem for him. To deal with it he resorted on this occasion to
a hypnotist: 'He stood at the end of the bed, made me look at a gold ring on his
finger, talked hard all the time about the certainty that I would have a quiet
night, a tranquil night, restful sleep, no more worry, the sub-conscious self
fulfilling itself; then told me to close my eyes; went on chattering; declared I
could not open them (which I found not the slightest difficulty in doing);
announced that in half a minute, one minute, two minutes I should be fast
asleep, and finally after half an hour of this foolish chatter, left me far more wide
awake than when he came.'[19]

There was a minor crisis on 31 December when Curzon came to London to
consult with Bonar Law, who had succeeded Lloyd George as prime minister
following the Chanak Crisis. Bonar Law was not well and seemed to have an
attack of cold feet. Curzon found that the prime minister was anxious to give
up Mosul, the Straits and Constantinople rather than have a row.[20] Fortunately
the prime minister's defeatism did not persist.

France faced quite different problems after the collapse of the Conference on
Reparations in Paris on 4 January 1923. A week later, French troops occupied
the Ruhr in consequence of missed payments. France's attention was no longer
focused on Lausanne. Curzon's was. He produced heads of agreement, which
were intended to serve as the draft of a preliminary treaty. The result was to
reveal that he had already achieved agreement on most of the matters which
concerned him. The French concerns were with financial and economic issues
which had not fully been discussed, let alone agreed. On other issues, Britain
was actually close to being in a position where she could make a separate peace
with Turkey.

The main outstanding issue was Mosul. Curzon attempted to negotiate the
issue directly with Turkey through a private exchange. Negotiation led to
nothing, except perhaps to develop the capacity for practical dialogue between
the two countries. Various schemes were discussed but no agreement was
reached. The Allies accordingly delivered an ultimatum to the Turks on 29
January 1923. It was a joint ultimatum, but the French negotiator, Bompard,
met the Turks on the following day and indicated that, whatever Britain might

say, France was still prepared to talk. France had occupied the Ruhr in defiance of Britain's opposition, and had developed a taste for an independent policy. But there was a flurry of diplomatic activity as a result of which Bompard's initiative was disavowed.

4. Tactics and Brinkmanship

When he arrived at Lausanne, Curzon was irritated to find that the Swiss hosts required that the presidency would rotate through the hands of Great Britain, France and Italy. This was not at all what he wanted and his solution was very neat. He accepted his hosts' requirements in relation to plenary sessions, but then arranged that there would be *no* plenary sessions. The conference proceeded at the level of a committee, with Curzon chairing all the meetings of that committee.

He chaired it outstandingly well. He was in much better form at Lausanne than he had been at Paris with Sforza and Poincaré. His approach was masterly. The outcome of a pre-conference meeting was reasonably satisfactory, although Curzon found Poincaré formal and precise.

There was, all the same, continuing friction between Britain and France. Turkey, breaking an undertaking, had started taking over Constantinople. The sultan fled. He did so on a British warship, which worried the French until they were reassured that the British government had not authorised the action.

Curzon's brinksmanship was a little like Disraeli's at the Congress of Berlin. Both let it be known that their special train was ready. But Curzon's bluff was called. Strengthened by the French declaration that they did not regard the text of the treaty as final, the Turkish representative, Ismet Pasha, declined to sign the treaty that was presented to him. He said that he could accept those portions which had been dealt with by Curzon, but objected to the provisions in the economic and judicial clauses. They were those which were of interest only to the French. The debate went on for two hours. Just before 8 p.m., Curzon announced that he must be on his train shortly after 9 p.m. Just after 9 p.m., his train pulled out. The conference stalled until 24 April.

During the break in negotiations two things happened. The National Assembly in Ankara rejected the draft treaty but recognised that dialogue must continue and authorised further negotiations, with the economic clauses detached and considered separately. The second thing was that the French, seeing how little progress they had been making with their new Turkish friends, decided that they were not so friendly after all. Franklin Bouillon had got it wrong. So when the negotiations resumed, France was seen as obdurate and Turkey's enemy, and Britain as constructive and Turkey's friend.

Distinguishing between the 'French' and the 'British' clauses of the treaty proved to be a productive manoeuvre. In fact Curzon had been doing his best for both the allies, and his relationship with the French representative, Barré, was a good one. It was not Curzon's fault that the outcome was a failure for France. His own conduct of the negotiations was a political triumph, carried out just three months before Baldwin, and not he, became leader of the Tory Party, more or less ending his political life. ('The cup of honourable ambition has been dashed from my lips . . . I could never aspire to fill the highest office in the service of the Crown.'[21]) J. St Loe Strachey, the hugely influential editor of the *Spectator*, wrote to him at the end of the conference, speaking about what he had done at Lausanne: 'It was one of those miracles of statesmanship which deserves to stand with the work that Talleyrand did at the congress of Vienna. You went into the Conference without a single trump in your hand and with everything against you, and yet, by sheer power of management, good sense and integrity of purpose and knowledge of facts, you soon gained complete predominance . . . [Y]ou have recovered our diplomatic status which had fallen so low.'[22]

When the Turks said on 24 July that they were ready to sign an agreement, Britain emerged clear winner. The conference had been expected to seal France's success in achieving a special relationship with Turkey. On the contrary, France suffered an immense blow not only to her financial interests, but also to her general prestige in the Middle East. Britain continued to control the international regime at the Straits, with her fleet in the Bosphorus and her troops at Gallipoli. The oil of Mosul was still in her hands. Her Middle East defence system was intact.

By the time Curzon returned from Lausanne, France and Britain were separated by what is euphemistically called in diplomatic language a *rupture cordiale*. The cause was the increasing divergence of British and French policy, and in particular, France's occupation of the Ruhr. Britain recognised economic realities and wanted to reduce German indebtedness to the Allies, rather than to attempt to enforce payment. Though technically Britain's position was one of benevolent neutrality towards France and what France was doing, public opinion would have been glad to see rather less benevolence. The strains between Paris and London were exacerbated by the fact that diplomatic relations between France and Germany had now been broken off and that Germany was therefore dealing only with Britain. This reinforced the French perception that Britain was scarcely her ally.

The purpose of Lausanne was to settle Turkey. It came too late for the Armenians, and the Kurds were also abandoned. Major Noel, 'The Kurdish Lawrence', had been sent out in 1919 to stir up an independence movement.

He reported enthusiastically: the national movement was 'so virile that I do not see much difficulty in setting up a Kurdish state under our protection'. Arnold Wilson was not convinced. He did not see that the Kurds would unite behind a single leader. He replaced Noel with Major Ely Soane, 'one of the most remarkable men,' he said, 'it has ever been my lot to meet . . . [H]e had the power which no man in my experience has possessed in anything approaching the same degree, of dominating by sheer force of personality.' Soane had famously travelled incognito through Kurdistan before the war, and became a Shiite Muslim.

Soane tended to the same conclusion as Wilson, and the claim of Kurdish solidarity seemed even more spurious after the prospective leader, Sheikh Mahmud, attempted to take control, his men wearing copies of President Wilson's Fourteen Points on their sleeves. His rising was not supported by other Kurds and was suppressed by the British.

Britain was far from committed to setting up an independent Kurdish State. Lloyd George complained that he had not been able to find a single representative Kurd. There was talk of fomenting Kurdish dissent to discommode Turkey, but eventually after drift and confusion, and despite commitments in the Treaty of Sèvres and the personal preferences of men like Churchill and Curzon, it seemed that the best thing that could be done with the Kurdish territories was to use them to bolster Iraq.

28

PREPARING FOR CAIRO:
CHURCHILL TAKES THE REINS

By 1922 the war had been over for four years. But British troops were still in Baghdad. No mandate had been awarded to Britain, and it was not certain that one ever would be. But the cost of Mesopotamia was enormous – over £16 million a year, according to the Colonial Office, of which revenues from the territory only defrayed £4 million. The War Office estimated the cost even higher at £18 million.

Churchill inherited responsibility for these costs when he became Colonial Secretary in February 1921. Even before then, at the War Office, he had become concerned about costs and ordered that military expenditure be halved in the fiscal year 1920–21. He wanted the military authorities to dump their responsibilities on to the civil administration. Troops that could be used to garrison large areas of India were being used in Iraq to police 'a score of mud villages, sandwiched in between a swampy river and a blistering desert, inhabited by a few hundred half-naked native families, usually starving'.[1]

Arnold Wilson was taking an increasingly pessimistic view of the situation in Mesopotamia. He maintained that a strong military presence was necessary if any semblance of law and order were to be preserved, and he attributed the state of affairs to the Anglo-French Joint Declaration and the promise of *quasi*-independence to a country that was not ready for it. All the same, in the light of increased nationalist pressure following San Remo, he considered that a constitutional assembly would require to be called. He was increasingly criticised, both by the Foreign Office and by the wider public. He was attacked in *The Morning Post*, *The Guardian* and *The Times* which, on 15 June 1920, referred to the government's policy in terms of 'evasions, concealments, and half-truths' and to Wilson himself as a civil commissioner trying to Indianize Mesopotamia.

He was accused of lack of judgement as well as simply being too young; but his assessment of the precarious state of affairs was vindicated by events. By the autumn of 1920 the uprisings in Mesopotamia involved the whole of the middle Euphrates region. Half of three companies of the 3rd Manchester Regiment were lost and by October British forces had suffered nearly 2,000 casualties.

Press reaction was bitter. The administration of Iraq was compared critically with that of India. Lawrence even said that the Ottomans had done better: 450 British officers were required to administer an area that had been run by the local inhabitants under the Turks. It was particularly galling that the Arabs were revolting against a policy designed to create an Arab state.[2]

Lawrence was always ready to talk to the papers. He gave interviews to *The Observer*, the *Daily Herald*, and the *Sunday Times*. They attracted a lot of attention as continuing unrest cut off garrisons and threatened to require evacuation. He complained there was an 'empty space which divides the Foreign Office from the India Office' and that in that space Wilson was able to pursue his own policy. He returned to the idea that Wilson's policy was worse than that of the Turks. They killed about 200 people a year. Britain had killed 10,000 in one summer.[3]

While Wilson did not enjoy London's support, on the spot he was respected by his political officers and by the GOC, Mesopotamia, Aylmer Haldane. Haldane had been in prison in South Africa with Churchill – and indeed his escape plan was scuppered when Churchill pinched it. Now Churchill had sent him out to Mesopotamia with the task of reducing the garrison. Haldane was his own man. He suggested that the chief political officer should go to London for consultations so that he could get the problem into his chiefs' heads.

But the stirrings of nationalism could not be subdued simply by force, and the techniques that were applied in India would not work in Mesopotamia. From London, Hirtzel, for example, could see that. He told Wilson, 'As regards Arab nationalism, I think you will find yourself in pretty deep water, and to be frank I do not feel that you are going the right way to work with it. You appear to be trying, impossibly, to stem the tide, instead of guiding it into the channel that would suit you best . . . You are going to have an Arab state whether you like it or not, whether Mesopotamia wants it or not.' In September 1919 he tried again, still using the tidal metaphor: 'We must swim with the tide which is set towards the education and not towards the government of what used to be called subject peoples. They won't have good drains of course, but the drains of India are nothing to boast of.'[4] And so on, over many months, but he was advocating policies which would not be congenial to a hero of the Indian Mutiny, and Wilson had never totally let go of his reflections in that P&O saloon.

On 29 July 1920 Wilson sent a cable to Cox: 'An Arab state though not on the lines desired by His Majesty's Government, may yet come, but it will be by a revolution and not by evolution.'⁵ Two days later he had a new idea. He cabled London to ask if they would consider Faisal, now being expelled from Syria, as king of Iraq. That proposal would eventually save Iraq, though it came too late to save Wilson.

Cox replaced him. On 4 October 1920 he became High Commissioner of Mesopotamia. He continued the Wilsonian policy of installing Faisal. France, which had expelled Faisal from Syria, indicated that they would regard his installation in Iraq as unfriendly, so Cox was instructed to see that there was a 'spontaneous' desire for Faisal from 'a sufficiently representative body of public opinion in Mesopotamia'.⁶ While Faisal was canvassed, the new High Commissioner was left with a very wide discretion. That was hardly surprising. London had no real ideas of its own.

One thing on which London did have strong views was the matter of expense. As the revolt died down, Churchill sent a telegram to Haldane, asking whether it might be possible to limit the military occupation to part of Mesopotamia. On 1 December he told colleagues that he would require to ask for supplementary estimates of £33–34 million, largely because of Mesopotamia. On 7 December the Director of Military Operations prepared a memorandum spelling out the detail of the cost and suggesting that Britain's true objectives for having Mesopotamia in the first place – acquisition of oil supplies and control of the Gulf – could be achieved by controlling Basra and defending a line Ahwaz–Qurna–Nasirya. A single division at a cost of £8 million a year would do.

The General Staff in London did not support the view that India should be defended in Iraq – as India charged particularly high fees for the use of its troops. Cox's estimate for the coming year was £25 million. Churchill argued at a Cabinet on 13 December that the troops should withdraw to cover only Basra. He reminded his colleagues that the General Staff considered that Mesopotamia and Persia were 'of no importance from the point of view of the defence of India'.⁷

But there were wider considerations. Some held that it would cost just as much to defend the smaller area if it were under attack. In any event, what about the mandate and the commitments to an Arab government? Cox was consulted. He was against withdrawal for various reasons. He still thought that Faisal was worth trying, although he recognised the implications of the fact that he was a Sunni while Iraq was predominantly Shiite. He was confident that Iraq could more than pay for itself because of its irrigation possibilities and its oil resources.

When Churchill moved from the War Office to the Colonial Office at the end of 1920, responsibility for the Middle East was entrusted to his new department. Churchill hesitated about the move, and about having direct responsibility

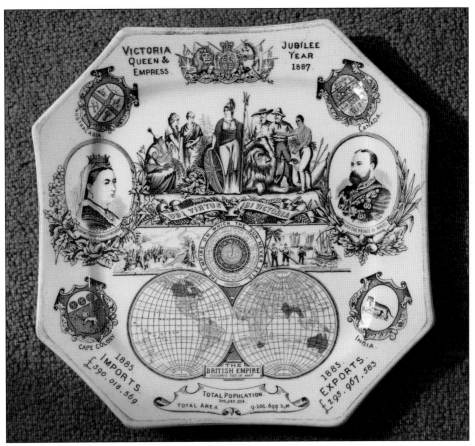

Above. The extent of Victoria's empire was celebrated at the time of her Jubilee in 1887, but informed opinion believed that the age of expansion had ended and that decline might well follow. Yet by 1922 there were 150 million more inhabitants in an empire which was 5 million square miles bigger. Most of the expansion took place in the Middle East. (Author's Collection)

Left. Turkey by Partridge. Before the First World War, Britain tolerated the Turkish presence in the Middle East – as long as Turkey was there, France and Russia were not. But she had to remember her place. (Punch Ltd)

Above. General Townshend and his staff as prisoners of the Turks after the fall of Kut. Townshend, centre, looks understandably downcast, but was to enjoy a comfortable imprisonment. His opposite number, Khalil Pasha, is on his left. (Imperial War Museum Q 79344)

Right. Key members of the Arab Bureau in Cairo. T. E. Lawrence left, Commander D.G. Hogarth centre and Alan Dawnay, who liaised with Faisal's forces on behalf of Allenby. The photograph was taken by Lowell Thomas, who shared with his subject the responsibility for creating the Lawrence myth. (Imperial War Museum Q 59595)

Gertrude Bell. A remarkable woman. When this picture was taken, around 1900, she was already a celebrated traveller and explorer. She went on to be an outstanding colonial administrator. She is still remembered in Iraq with admiration and affection. (Getty Images)

T.E. Lawrence in a prickly situation. An understandably self-conscious pose. (Imperial War Museum Q 12629)

Ibn Saud, Sir Percy Cox and Gertrude Bell meet in the desert in March 1917. Even in these circumstances, Gertrude Bell's turnout is elegant. The jovial staff officer to the right has not been identified. (Getty Images)

Right. Allenby and Faisal.
(Getty Images)

Below. Camels bringing up
ammunition during action on the
Palestine Front, July 1917. The
Middle Eastern War, apart from
Gallipoli, is overlooked in favour of
the Western Front. It was a hard-
fought campaign that ended with
outstanding British victories. These
victories hardly affected the
outcome of the larger war, but
they had a huge influence on the
division of the spoils.
(Imperial War Museum Q 79444)

The capture of Jerusalem, December 1917. The mayor of Jerusalem (with walking stick and cigarette) attempts to deliver the Turkish governor's letter of surrender to two British sergeants who were scouting ahead of Allenby's main force. The sergeants refused to accept the letter, which was eventually handed to a senior British officer. The white flag of truce was a sheet taken from one of the beds in the Italian hospital in Jerusalem and nailed to a broomstick by the photographer.
(Imperial War Museum Q 13213B)

From the steps of the Citadel in Jerusalem, at the entrance to King David's Tower, General Allenby reads his proclamation on 11 December 1917 'to the inhabitants of Jerusalem the blessed and the people dwelling in its vicinity'. He promised to protect the interests of all religions in the City, and declared the establishment of a military administration.
(Imperial War Museum Q 55529)

The capture of Damascus. Faisal leaves the Hotel Victoria after an interview with Allenby at which he was warned that Arab influence was not to extend to conflict with French claims in the west. (Imperial War Museum Q 48222)

The Paris Peace Conference. The Big Four (or perhaps Three and a half), 27 May 1919: from the left, Vittorio Orlando, the Italian Prime Minister, Lloyd George, Clemenceau and President Wilson. (Imperial War Museum Q 12364)

Arthur Balfour arrives at the Peace Conference, looking as if he is ready for an agreeable weekend in the country. (Imperial War Museum Q 70058)

The British Empire delegation at Lloyd George's house in the Rue Nitot, where so many critical Peace Conference decisions were taken. Broadly, from left to right, excluding unidentified figures in the background, Sir Joseph Ward (New Zealand), General Smuts (South Africa and UK War Cabinet), Lord Milner (Colonial Secretary), Sir Joseph Cook (Australia), George Barnes (War Cabinet), Arthur Balfour (Foreign Secretary), Edwin Montagu (Secretary of State for India), Lloyd George (Prime Minister), Austen Chamberlain (War Cabinet), Billy Hughes (Australia), Lord Birkenhead (Lord Chancellor), Winston Churchill (Secretary of State for War and Air), General Sir Henry Wilson (Chief of the Imperial General Staff), Louis Botha (South Africa), William Massey (New Zealand), Philip Kerr (Lloyd George's Private Secretary). (Imperial War Museum Q 14993)

Right. The seating plan at the Peace Conference. The number and situation of the seats of each delegation are an interesting guide to the dynamics behind the deliberations. China was a 'small power' and had just two seats. Japan was a 'great power' and had five. Poor Bolivia.

Below. Faisal at the Peace Conference, where he 'breathed the perfume of frankincense'. Behind his left shoulder is Lawrence in British army dress and inappropriate headgear. (Getty Images)

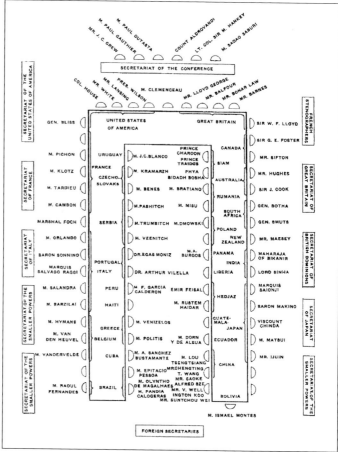

Not the final curtain at a Gilbert and Sullivan opera, but the British Commission to the Cairo Conference in 1921. Gertrude Bell, second from left, second row, T. E. Lawrence, fourth from the right, second row and Churchill – of course – centre stage. Gertrude Bell was the only female member of the Commission. (Getty Images)

Winston's Durbar. The photograph was taken during the Cairo Conference. The Conference has been the subject of criticism from a variety of sources, but after a matter of just weeks as Colonial Secretary Churchill was able to settle a range of urgent practical issues, and the regimes he created proved capable of survival. The photograph was achieved at a cost: Churchill slid off his camel several times before the shutter clicked. Mrs Churchill in white robe and hood. To her left Churchill, Gertrude Bell and T. E. Lawrence. For once Lawrence's headgear looks more boring than Gertrude Bell's. (Churchill Archive Centre, Broadwater Collection, BRDW 1/2/83)

The Emir Abdullah greets Churchill
and Mrs Churchill at the Cairo
Conference. Abdullah looks every
inch a Prince in search of a kingdom.
(Imperial War Museum Q 60172)

Sir Percy Cox in 1936. More than anyone else, Cox created Iraq in the years after the First World War. He was highly
intelligent, a very able colonial administrator and personally brave. Here he faces up to an evening of cards with Lady Cox.
(National Portrait Gallery)

France flirts with Turkey and John Bull is upset by his war-time friend's inconstancy. In fact, France had more grounds for complaint about Britain's perfidy. (Punch Ltd)

HER NEW FANCY.

Turkey. "WHO'S YOUR FRIEND?"
France. "OH, JUST SOMEBODY I KNEW IN THE WAR."

Balfour in Jerusalem, 1925. Ronald Storrs, Civil Governor of Jerusalem and Judea, beside Balfour. The City's Arab inhabitants were on strike in protest against Balfour's visit. Insouciant as ever, he said that he had seen much worse demonstrations when he was Chief Secretary in Ireland. (Getty Images)

British soldiers patrolling in Jerusalem in 1925 during the Arab strike in protest against Balfour's visit. (Getty Images)

A British Army convoy ambushed in Palestine in 1936 during the Arab Revolt of 1936–1939. (Imperial War Museum HU 56369)

Left. British soldiers searching Arabs during the Revolt. (Imperial War Museum HU 38376)

Below. Sleeves rolled up for action, the Peel Commission at Victoria station on the way to Palestine. The original newspaper caption read, 'Brits to the Rescue'. From left, Professor Coupland, Sir Laurie Hammond, Sir Horace Rumbold and Lord Peel. (Getty Images)

" ... The Party's shoulder to shoulder behind me, Herbert ?"

Ernest Bevin is widely regarded as having been one of the greatest British Foreign Secretaries of the twentieth century. At the time, however, his policies did not enjoy the unqualified support of his Party. (Author's Collection)

Jewish refugees arrive at Haifa Harbour on 1st July 1946, packed tight on the *Josiah Wedgwood*. A banner runs between the mast and the funnel: 'We survived Hitler – Death is no stranger to us – Nothing can keep us from our Jewish homeland – The blame is on your head if you fire on this unarmed ship'. (Imperial War Museum E 31953)

The King David Hotel, Jerusalem, blown up on 22 July 1946. (Imperial War Museum E 319713)

A Jewish boy is sprayed with DDT before being taken to a British troopship in August 1946. Most illegal immigrants were placed in a camp in Cyprus. The propaganda effect of such photographs was enormous. (Imperial War Museum E 32001)

The End. Women and children forming part of the first wave of British civilians to leave Palestine, photographed by an RAF officer as they left Agir Airfield for Egypt. (Imperial War Museum E 32219)

for an area he wanted to abandon. 'I feel some misgivings about the political consequences to myself of taking on my shoulders the burden & the odium of the Mesopotamian entanglement.'[8] Ahead of his formal appointment, he became chairman of the committee charged with implementing the Middle East transfer.

On 8 January 1921 Churchill wrote to Cox:

I have been entrusted with the general direction of the Cabinet policy in Mesopotamia. At the moment of taking up this task I wish to define it precisely for your guidance and in order that you may be able to assist me to the full.

It is impossible for us to throw upon the British taxpayer the burdens for military expenditure in Mesopotamia which are entailed by your present schemes for holding the country. Unless some better method can be devised and brought into operation within the financial year 1921–22, retirement and contraction to the coastal zone is inevitable and must be accomplished as rapidly as possible . . .

I will address you at an early date upon the selection of an Arab ruler.[9]

Cox responded on 13 January 1921. He was taken aback by what Churchill had said about a reduction in the military establishment of Mesopotamia. He was so astounded that '[i]n order to obviate possible misinterpretation arising, mutilation or otherwise, I beg to repeat back salient points of your message as understood by me'. He ended by saying that if the earlier telegram conveyed the government's decisions, 'I am constrained to let you know at once that I am not prepared to associate myself with [the policy and plans], and if pressed to do so, must, with deep regret, ask His Majesty's Government to accept [my] resignation.'[10]

Hirtzel forwarded Cox's reply to Churchill with the understated comment, 'I am afraid it will not please you'. He went on to argue Cox's case: he had gone out, against his own wishes, to carry out a policy with which he was now associated:

If the policy were changed, through the denial of the means of executing it, he cannot face the charge of breach of faith. That can hardly be called unreasonable, & would I venture to think acquit him of the charge of resigning 'because he could not get his own way.' . . . . It may be that you would not be unwilling for him to resign. I should be sorry if that were the case, because I do not think there is anyone else with sufficient prestige in Mesopotamia to initiate a policy, which – not over-easy at any stage – must in its first stages

depend almost entirely on the confidence which the personality of the High
Commr inspires. Cox has a wonderful hold over most of the very disparate
elements of the Mesopotamian population, & they will take things from him
which they will take from no one else. If he goes, we shall want more troops
& not less![11]

Churchill had a good deal of confidence in Cox. He was prepared to leave to
him the detail of how policy was implemented. On 9 July 1921 he told
Shuckburgh not

to bombard the High Commissioner with all these elaborate instructions . . . There is too much talk about 'mandates', 'mandatories' and things
like that. All this obsolescent rigmarole is not worth telegraphing about. It
is quite possible that in a year or two there will be no mandates and no
League of Nations . . . Do let us keep the practical salient points of a policy
in our minds and only check Sir Percy Cox when he diverges from them:-

   To get another large wave of troops out of the country and so reduce the
expenditure to the British taxpayer.

   To get Feisal [*sic*] on the throne as soon as possible.

   To make whatever arrangements are most likely to conduce to the above
objects in regard to Basra (about which I have a perfectly open mind) or
Kurdistan (about which the only principle is that we do not put Kurds under
Arabs).[12]

On the same day he did think it worth telegraphing Cox, but fairly briefly:

The main thing is to secure the early choice of Feisal and other questions
should be handled in subordinate relation this. We still adhere to the principle of not putting Arabs over Kurds but we have no wish to hamper Feisal's
candidature at this juncture. Cannot therefore question of Kurdistan areas be
left over for a final decision by the new Assembly?'[13]

Cox was a good friend to Iraq, and to Faisal as long as he behaved himself.
But he had no illusions about either. In a telegram of 23 July 1921, after sensitive words of sympathy about the death of Churchill's mother, he allowed
himself some general observations: 'I think things here are going as well as can
be expected, & more or less according to plan, and I hope that before this
reaches you I shall have been able to let you know that our Royal fish is safely
ashore. The Iraqi is an unstable & self-seeking creature and Faisal's job will not
be an easy one, but he starts with a great asset, in his personal charm.'[14]

Responsibility always refined Churchill's ideas. With typical panache he had accepted his new post subject to high-handed provisos, among them the understanding that, limited only by general Cabinet policy, he would have the authority to direct both civil and military affairs. He would also like an early visit to Iraq. Equally typically, as soon as he was established in power, he moderated his position: 'I must feel my way and make sure of my way.'[15] He would need to think a good deal, too, about Faisal. He entered into lengthy discussions in correspondence with Cox. Less wisely, he reverted to consulting Lawrence. The outcome of this period of reflection was acceptance of the policy of non-withdrawal and the decision that a major conference should take place in Cairo.

He loved being out and about. His immediate reaction had been to go to Iraq; that was shelved in favour of Cairo and the ambitious plan of sorting out not just Iraq, but the whole of the new Middle Eastern territories.

But the essential motive for calling the Cairo Conference was largely to address the financial costs of Iraq and the need to reduce British commitments abroad, not wider and more elevated issues. Churchill's mission statement was not exalted: 'I'm going to save you millions'. In a memorandum to the Cabinet of 10 February 1921 he asked for guidance on what might be a suitable grant-in-aid for Mesopotamia 'after the present evacuation of the main body of the troops has been effected and the reduced force is holding the country . . . Unless the Cabinet can see their way to authorise plans to be made on the basis of about 7,000,000 *lakhs** a year for three years after the present year, I doubt very much whether it will be possible to discharge the conditions of the mandate.'

His telegrams to Cox display an impressive grasp of the technical situation, and are very different from the woolly generalisations that Cox received from other Cabinet members. Cox and General Haldane were pinned down with detailed and rigorous enquiries:

Why should you assume that ordinary regular troops organised in divisions and brigades, with their lavish and ponderous staffs, are the only form in which the requisite element of force can be supplied? Surely it is worthwhile considering whether a smaller number of men of much higher individual quality would not be just as effective and less costly to maintain? Again, Air Marshal Trenchard, who has great experience not only of the air, but of the Mohammedan population of West Africa, has established in full detail a scheme for maintaining control once peace and order have been re-established . . . If all alternative methods fail and we have to choose between an indefinite recurring charge of

* A *lakh* is 100,000 rupees.

12,000,000 *lakhs* or 14,000,000 *lakhs* a year, or retirement to Basra and the immediate coastal zone I have no doubt whatever that the retirement will be ordered. You would take a great responsibility if, before any such decision has been taken, you deprived His Majesty's Government of your local knowledge and influence, and thus diminished gravely the chances of a satisfactory solution.[16]

At the Colonial Office, as at the War and Air Ministries, Churchill made economies his central priority. By September 1922 he had reduced Britain's Middle East expenditure by 75 per cent. Inevitably he made himself unpopular with his military advisers. Sir Henry Wilson, the chief of the Imperial General Staff, talked of 'arbitrary reduction of garrisons for financial reasons . . . Winston . . . is playing the fool and heading straight for disasters'.[17]

At the War Ministry and afterwards at the Colonial Office, Churchill worked closely with Wilson. They got on well. Wilson, a delightful gossip and schemer, always got on well with politicians. It was said that he had an erection if he came within half of mile of one. All the same, he could be genially exasperated by Churchill. He recorded in his diary on 28 January 1921

> a wire from Philip Chetwode [commander-in-chief in India, and John Betjeman's father-in-law] tonight giving Winston's instructions about Mesopot: i.e. remove Haldane at once, put in Ironside, hold Mesopot: (I presume the 3 Vilayets?) with 15,000 men, find Haldane another billet owing to some promise made by Winston a year ago!
>
> Winston appears to be coming over here [Paris] tonight in which case I shall see him tomorrow. The man is a fool, and, as I wrote to Philip yesterday it will be very necessary to get our relations with him & his new office clearly defined.[18]

The central element in Churchill's cost cutting was the use of aircraft and armoured cars rather than infantry. In taking that option, he recognised that all Britain would be able to do was to police Mesopotamia, not to defend it against invasion.

Churchill might have approved of Lloyd George's acquisitiveness in the Middle East if he had not been responsible for military finances. As it was, he stated, again and again, that Britain neither had the troops nor the money to control the Middle East. His thinking was also influenced by his study of the pre-war balance of power, and the established spheres of influence that had been at the heart of the classical diplomacy of the nineteenth century. He argued that Britain and the other European powers should renounce their claims to the different parts of the Middle East. 'Instead of dividing up the [Ottoman] Empire into separate territorial spheres of exploitation, we should combine to preserve the integrity of the Turkish Empire as it existed before the war.' His only acknowledgement of the changed circumstances that flowed from Turkey's choice of allies in the war was that the Turkish Empire, though re-established, should be subject to some form of international control.[19]

Churchill loved being the man on the spot with extensive independence. By the time he went to Cairo, one of the flaws in British policy had been repaired. India, like Cairo, now accepted that the Middle Eastern possessions should be ruled through proxies and not directly. This allowed Churchill the opportunity of redrawing the map of the Middle East. He made the most of that chance.

29

CHURCHILL'S DURBAR: THE CAIRO CONFERENCE

1. The Stage is Set

During the conference, Churchill stayed at the Mena House Hotel. It was the sort of hotel that he loved. The building had been a palace, built by the Khedive Ismail as his hunting lodge. It was now the 'hotel to end all hotels', situated in Giza, about 12 kilometres south-west of Cairo. Churchill made the most of its surroundings, close to the Great Sphinx and the Giza Pyramid. He painted so many pictures that he was able to hold an exhibition. He brought Clementine with him.

According to Lawrence, the London delegates arrived at Cairo with many decisions already taken by him and Churchill 'over dinner at The Ship Restaurant in Whitehall'.[1] If indeed the decision to create a Kingdom of Iraq and an Emirate of Transjordan had been taken over dinner it would have been a momentous meal, but he was fantasizing.

When they reached Cairo, Lawrence and Gertrude Bell were glad to meet again. Lawrence bounded on to the Cairo stage like a *jeune premier*: 'Gertie!' he cried. 'Dear Boy,' she trilled in that Mayfair accent. 'Everyone Middle East is here,' he said.[2] Miss Bell was the only woman among the 41 members of the British party.[3]

Not everyone was so pleased to see Lawrence. The Civil Service officials did their best to limit his influence, and after the conference Cox vetoed a visit to Faisal in Baghdad. Churchill's Under-Secretary of State, Sir James Masterton Smith, questioned Lawrence's presence: 'Are you sure that Col Lawrence should come? I had gathered the impression (but perhaps wrongly) that he did not wish to hold a Government appointment in connection with the Arab problem. He is not the kind of man to fit easily into any official machine . . . I gather that Col Lawrence has got used to dealing with ministers – and ministers only – and I see trouble ahead if he is allowed too free a hand.'[4]

Despite Civil Service resistance, Lawrence was pretty near the centre of the stage. He had a lot to do with the conference. He had always been a Churchill protégé, and he had been consulted in London ahead of the meeting in Cairo. He was very gratified to feel that the wartime pledges to Hussein in which he had been involved were at last being made good. Before the conference was out, one of Hussein's sons, Faisal, was to be well on the way to being king of Iraq, and another, Abdullah, to being the emir of Transjordan, a new region, detached from the British mandate territories on the east bank of the Jordan river.

Lawrence hugely exaggerated the Cairo achievement: 'we were quit of the war-time Eastern adventure, with clean hands, but three years too late to earn the gratitude which peoples, if not states, can pay.'[5] That is pretty disingenuous. The Cairo Conference may have been satisfactory in many ways, but if Lawrence had been truly concerned about the promises to the Arabs, he would have found it difficult to imagine that the conference really put things right. Kedourie summed up Lawrence's self-seeking insincerity and the overstatements of *Seven Pillars* rather well. 'When Colonel Lawrence renounced the world his ambition, as readers of his *Letters* know, was to become a great writer, to exchange the uncertain and treacherous triumphs of war and politics for the sure and lasting reward of artistic creation. The attempt does not come off, and *Seven Pillars* is a work seething with rancour and resentment, full of advocacy and rhetoric, firmly imprisoned in the world of practice from which its author ceaselessly proclaimed his yearning to escape.'[6]

Lawrence presented a copy of *Seven Pillars of Wisdom* to Churchill with two inscriptions, written 11 years apart. The first was to 'Winston Churchill who made a happy ending to this show'. Eleven years later he added words which Churchill acknowledged as having gone 'far beyond the truth at the time': 'And eleven years after we set our hands to making an honest settlement, all our work still stands: the countries having gone forward, our interests having been saved, and nobody killed, either on our own side or the other. To have planned for eleven years is statesmanship.'[7]

Lawrence did resign after Cairo. He wrote to John Shuckburgh, who had been seconded from the India Office to the Middle East Department. He recalled that his had been an emergency appointment, 'made because Churchill meant to introduce changes in our policy, and because he thought my help would be useful during the expected stormy period'. He was, unusually for him, fairly happy with the way things had turned out. There had not been a British casualty in Palestine or Arabia or the Arab provinces of Iraq. 'Political questions there are still, of course, and wide open, there always will be, but their expression and conduct has been growing constitutional . . . While things run along the present settled and routine lines I can see no justification for the department's continuing my employment – and little for me to do if it is continued. So if Mr. Churchill permits, I shall be very glad to leave so prosperous a ship. I need hardly say that I'm always at his disposal if ever there is a crisis, or any job, small or big, for which he can convince me that I am necessary.' Churchill replied in generous terms and offered him an honorary position as adviser on Arab Affairs.[8]

A month later, Lawrence enlisted in the RAF. His recruiting officer was Captain W.E. Johns, the man who created Biggles. Lawrence and Johns had something in common, each the creator of a character of fiction.

A great deal of preparatory work for the conference had been done in London, and the discussions at Cairo tended therefore to follow on from conclusions already reached. At the same time, in innumerable subcommittees a lot of very detailed work was done in the course of five weeks. Some of the decisions that were arrived at were big ones on which Middle Eastern structures and notions of today still rest. Others were smaller ones, such as provision for the rates at which officers in the Palestine Defence Force and their messes could purchase items from civilian contractors.

The main members of the Political Committee were Churchill, Cox, Gertrude Bell and Lawrence. The participants at the conference included Generals Trenchard, Radcliffe, Ironside and Haldane, Wilson, Sir Herbert Samuel, the High Commissioner of Palestine, representatives from Iraq, Palestine and Jordan. No Indian Office representative was there.

The conference took place in the Semiramis Hotel, now the Intercontinental, 'a marble and bronze hotel, very expensive and luxurious', Lawrence told his brother. '[H]orrible place: makes me a Bolshevik.' The mood in the hotel cheered up whenever Churchill appeared, followed by an Arab carrying a bottle of wine in a bucket and undisturbed by the Egyptians in carriages carrying placards that proclaimed '*À bas Churchill*'. Indeed he sat at his easel in the road, painting as the carriages drove past him. His skin was never particularly thin. On the other hand, he did not like Arabs coming into the hotel garden, let alone the hotel itself.[9]

The British team posed for a photograph on camelback. Churchill was an experienced horseman but new to camels. He slithered off and was offered a horse. 'I started on a camel and I shall finish on a camel, he said, and so he did, although he looks dangerously lopsided in the photograph. Gertrude Bell is mounted beside him, looking rather more secure, but wearing a rather matronly hat and an improbable mammal, perhaps a fox, round her shoulders. Behind Bell, Churchill, various civilians and military men and their camels and Arab attendants stand the Pyramids and the Sphinx inscrutably regarding the passage of yet another caravan.

Churchill's claim that he created the new Kingdom of Transjordan in an afternoon and then went off to paint pictures of the desert makes the proceedings at Cairo sound effortless. They were far from that. There were many tensions between Churchill, the man on the spot, and the government in London. Churchill was aware all the time of his difficulties with the Cabinet – and especially with Curzon. He threatened to resign at several points in the course of the conference and took particular care to keep in touch with Lloyd George, making much of their personal closeness in the past and of his gratitude to the prime minister for providing him with a fresh horse after his fall at the Dardanelles.

Despite these sentimental allusions, he was privately very angry with Lloyd George. When he returned to London he had an interview with the editor of the *Daily Mail* during which he said 'how fed up' he was with the prime minister and how wrong he felt the spending on Mesopotamia and Palestine to be. He took no responsibility for Britain's presence in Mesopotamia and Palestine: 'He did not initiate any of the liabilities there; the pledges were given and he is obliged to carry them out at the least possible cost. Mesopotamia and Palestine are twin babies in his care but he is not the father.'[10]

The sort of problems he had at Cairo related, for instance, to the fact that Lloyd George was uneasy about the appointment of Faisal as king of Iraq because of the reaction there would be in France. So far as Lloyd George was concerned, any initiative for Faisal's appointment had to come from Mesopotamia, and not from London. Churchill said that he was aware that there had to be a spontaneous movement for Faisal but '[u]nless we have a mind of our own on the subject it is by no means certain that this will occur'.[11] One can sense the frustration at both ends: Churchill surrounded by his specialist Arab advisers, and Lloyd George facing the deteriorating relationship with the French, very much against Faisal, their old enemy.

2. A Ruler for Iraq

Churchill could be pretty irritated by Faisal, too. He felt Faisal was getting ideas above his station. On 15 August 1921 he contemplated but in the event refrained from telling Cox to say to him that he was

> to manage the country with [your] assistance & advice. If he manages it so well that in a few years we can withdraw our forces, he will become a Sovereign with plenary powers subject only to treaty obligations with the Mandatory. But as long as we have to spend many millions a year to ensure the maintenance of order & to support his government, we must expect him to rule in general conformity with the advice tendered to him by you.[12]

Three months later, 'I am getting tired of all these lengthy telegrams about Faisal and his state of mind. There is too much of it. Six months ago we were paying his hotel bill in London and now I am forced to read day after day 800-word messages and questions of his status and his relations with foreign powers. Has he not got some wives to keep him quiet?'[13] He had seen the appointment of Faisal as the solution to problems. That was why 'the main thing is to secure the early choice of Faisal'.[14] Now Faisal was proving to be a nuisance.

Before he left for Cairo, Churchill had not been certain who the new ruler should be. In an early message he asked Cox what he thought:

Do you think that Feisal [*sic*] is the right man and the best man? Failing him, do you prefer Abdullah to any local man? Have you put forward Feisal because you consider, taking a long view, that he is the best man or as a desperate expedient in the hopes of reducing the garrisons quickly? If you are really convinced that Feisal is necessary, can you make sure that he is chosen locally?[15]

But the tone of the enquiry was partly just to keep the local men on their toes. On the same day he told Curzon that he himself though that Faisal was the best man. 'We must certainly see that we get "turtle" and not "mock turtle" . . . I cannot think that if this matter is handled in the proper way it will be difficult to persuade the French to acquiesce.'[16]

Ibn Saud was mentioned, an appointment which would have given the Middle East a dramatically different shape. Ahead of the conference, Churchill had meetings with Faisal. He gradually warmed to him rather than any alternative.

Cox pressed for Faisal. His main rivals were the Naqib of Baghdad, the most eminent notable of the city, and Sayid Talib, a prominent politician. Cox ruled out both of them. But it was important from the point of view of Iraqi reaction and also that of the French that Britain should not be seen to appoint Faisal. Equally, Churchill did not think it fitting that a king should be elected by the new Iraqi Assembly. Instead, a gathering of notables, including former rebels, would make a more decorous nomination. Faisal would withdraw his earlier suggestion of his brother Abdullah, and would announce his own candidacy.

Of course Lawrence supported Faisal. As well as referring to his personal knowledge of the emir, he contrasted his energy with Abdullah's laziness. Faisal would energise 'a backward and half-civilised country'. Churchill's approach was more sophisticated. He saw a great merit in Sharifian policy, the policy of supporting different members of the Hashemite family, in that 'it enabled His

Majesty's Government to bring pressure to bear on one Arab sphere in order to attain their own ends in another. If Faisal knew that not only his father's subsidy and the protection of the Holy Places from Wahhabi attack, but also the position of his brother in Transjordan was dependent on his own good behaviour, he would be much easier to deal with. The same argument applies *mutatis mutandis* to King Hussein and Emir Abdullah.'[17]

A balance had to be maintained between the Hashemites and Ibn Saud. The professionals did not lose sight of the threat from Wahhabism. Cox recognised Ibn Saud's capacity to upset British interests and argued for a doubling of his annual subsidy from £60,000 to £120,000 a year. Gertrude Bell supported him. She was concerned that if two new Hashemite kingdoms were created, one in Iraq and one in Transjordan, Ibn Saud might well take offence. Churchill compromised: £100,000 a year, but paid monthly, in order to keep Ibn Saud on a short rein. Hussein, who was unhappy at having been let down, as he saw it, in Palestine and Syria, would receive a similar figure.

It was finally agreed that Britain would use her influence to secure Faisal's nomination as the king of Iraq, following which the existing mandate arrangements would be replaced by a treaty. Cox and Churchill approached the issue of the election with some elegance. Cox thought that Faisal should arrive in Mesopotamia before the election. Churchill responded that this could be done 'as a result of appeals and invitations to him from local notables' and proposed that Lawrence should send a private telegram on a very low key and unofficial basis.

Lawrence did not keep the key very low: 'Things have gone exactly as hoped. Please start for Mecca at once by quickest possible route . . . I will meet you on the way and explain the details. Say only that you are going to see your father, and on no account put anything in the press.'[18]

Lawrence was gratified to think that Britain was honouring her wartime commitments. He was able to continue helping this process along, because Churchill now took him with him to Jerusalem, to meet the Emir Abdullah, who appeared unexpectedly in November 1920 at the head of a large number of supporters. It was here in Jerusalem that the initial, tentative discussions took place about establishing him in Transjordan.

3. A Ruler for Jordan

The second substantial area of dissent between Churchill and London was in relation to Transjordan. The Cabinet did not want it to become a separate kingdom. It was thought that Transjordan was too small to be viable and would serve better as a defensive adjunct to Palestine. There was also some concern about the French and whether an unhappy Abdullah might become their protégé.

The congress that elected Faisal as king of Syria had also elected Abdullah as king of Iraq. As it was clear that Britain would not support Abdullah's claim, Abdullah set off instead with 2,000 followers to take possession of Transjordan. He had no great difficulty in doing so, as Britain had left no garrison, only a handful of civilian administrators. His intention was to continue north and advance on Damascus. When he arrived in Ma'an, in southern Jordan, the British representative there, Alec Kirkbride, a pro-Arab who had fought along-side the Arabs in the revolt, displayed some ingenuity and astutely welcomed Abdullah in the name of what he chose to call 'the National Government of Moab'. Abdullah was amused and asked, 'By the way, has the National Government of Moab ever been recognised internationally?' Kirkbride replied, 'I am not quite sure of its international status. I feel, however, that the question is largely of an academic nature now that Your Highness is here.'[19] They became firm friends until much later, when Kirkbride began to worry about Abdullah's ambitions. Even so, Kirkbride remained in Jordan until after Abdullah's assassination. He was British Resident and then Minister from 1939 to 1951.

In March 1921, Abdullah reached Amman, and set up his headquarters. He still intended to raise a larger force and march on Syria, but his arrival in Amman coincided with Churchill's arrival at the Cairo Conference, which settled Abdullah's future, as well as much else.

Churchill thought the best way of bolstering Iraq at the same time as controlling the roaming Abdullah was the Sharifian policy, the separation of Transjordan with Abdullah at its head. London had reservations about this, as had Sir Herbert Samuel. Samuel was Commissioner for Palestine, and from his standpoint Jordan was an essential defensive buttress for the Palestine mandate. But Churchill had no doubts, and he steamrollered the policy forward.

When Allenby gave a ball in Cairo on 16 April, Churchill had only danced a few times before his evening was interrupted by Samuel's arrival from Jerusalem to argue for the retention of Transjordan. Samuel, and Wyndham Deedes, who was now his Chief Secretary, claimed that it was not possible for Britain to detach Transjordan from the rest of Palestine: it had been included by the League of Nations as a single mandated territory. But as far as Churchill was concerned, the Jordanian arrangement was an essential part of Iraqi, not Palestinian, policy.

The following morning, at the first meeting of the Cairo Conference's Palestine Political and Military Committee on 17 March 1921, business started with the reading of a memorandum drawn up in London by the Middle East Department prior to the conference.[20] Samuel immediately asked for a chance to read the paper over by himself. He was prepared to agree that Transjordan should be administered on different lines from Palestine, partly because of the Zionist issue. But Transjordan should not be treated as an independent Arab state. In particular, what was to be done about Abdullah, now at Amman? 'It was necessary for us to combine our Sharifian with our mandatory policy.' Stability was required for Palestine, and he was inevitably concerned that instability in Jordan would impact on Palestine and that Transjordan might be used as a base from which disaffected Arabs would seek to destabilise the Palestinian regime.

Churchill handled the matter very smoothly. His main concern was that he was committed to installing Faisal in Iraq and did not wish his position there weakened by enmity from a difficult ruler in Transjordan. He put his case very well: 'to support the Sharif in Iraq and not in Trans-Jordania would be courting trouble . . . If we were to curb the activities of Abdullah, while allowing him to remain in Trans-Jordania, we must obtain the goodwill of the Sharifian family and place them as a whole under an obligation to His Majesty's Government in one sphere or another.' This implied installing Abdullah in Amman at one end of an axis of which Faisal was at the other. A lot of thought was given to French policy and French reaction, most of it based on unsubstantiated speculation. Lawrence reported some hearsay to the effect that France might come round behind Abdullah and install him in Damascus.[21]

The offer of the Emirate of Transjordan to Abdullah was conditional on the renunciation of his plans for invading Syria. That was for the French. It was also conditional on his recognition of the British mandate over Transjordan and of the fact that this mandate was part of the Palestine mandate. Abdullah agreed to both conditions without any difficulty. So far as Syria was concerned, he would have had great difficulty anyway in conquering it by force, and in return for disavowing violence which would upset the stability of the region, Churchill said that Britain would do what they could to persuade the French to accept an Arab Syria with Abdullah as its king. That came to nothing. Abdullah did try for a little more than Transjordan, suggesting that he could be king of Palestine as well. Churchill summarily dismissed the request, on the basis that it conflicted with the promise of a Jewish national home.

Churchill's role at Cairo has been criticised.[22] He has been accused of not knowing the difference between a Sunni and a Shiite. There is no evidence that this is true. Even if it were, he would not, alas, be the only British official to fail to recognise the significance of the different identities. He sympathised with the Kurds, but has been criticised for not creating an independent Kurdistan. The military successes of the new Turkey put an end to a free Armenia or Kurdistan. He accepted reality, but he did not welcome it: he said, 'In the

Lausanne Treaty, which established a new peace between the Allies and Turkey, history will search in vain for the name Armenia.' With Turkey in control of Northern Kurdistan, the Kurds in the south were lumped in with Iraq. His concern about cost has been emphasised. But cost was a consideration that could not be ignored.

Overall and within the operating constraints could much more have been done? For all Lawrence's simplifications and self-aggrandisement, the decisions of the conference were not prearranged over an agreeable dinner. The conference was a formidable assembly of expert opinion, indeed a triumph for Churchill, both in its pre-planning, and in its speedy execution. Churchill himself is said to have called it the meeting of the 'Forty Thieves', and it was a rough and ready settlement that left many questions unanswered, including the real nature of the states it created. But it was at least a settlement of some sort after the years of drift and indecision that followed the declaration of war against Turkey.

VI

ALTERNATIVE MODELS: EGYPT, PERSIA AND SYRIA

30

EGYPT

1. *Middle Eastern but not a Mandate*

A later and final part of this book is principally concerned with the British mandates in the Middle East: Jordan, Iraq and Palestine. But to appreciate fully what was done there it is helpful to look in this part at what was not done, by considering briefly Syria, which was a French mandate, Persia, which was informally run by British influence, and Egypt, which was a British protectorate.

The history of Egypt is not the history of a mandated territory, or indeed of a part of the Middle East in which Britain came to have an interest as a result of the Great War. But it had much to do with Britain's Middle Eastern policy for most of a century. Egypt was central to the evolution of British Middle Eastern policy during the Great War. That policy rested on first, Egypt and the Canal, secondly, India and, thirdly, the nexus between the first two.

Because its strategic significance was thought to be so great, Egypt had to be yoked more closely to Britain than any mandated territory was. Its institutions were certainly not the model for the new territories. It was treated differently from anywhere else. The role of Egypt seemed so intimately connected with the preservation of the Empire that nationalism could not be tolerated. Any hints of real independence were crushed. The British Army was on the spot, and British warships could be called in when they were needed.

The First World War taught Britain the importance of Egypt as a base for the Middle East. It had been critical for the launching of the Gallipoli and Mesopotamian campaigns. There was no question of voluntary withdrawal. In 1929 Lord Lloyd, the High Commissioner in Egypt between 1925 and 1929, said that 'the only place from which the Suez Canal can be defended is from Egypt'. This view informed British policy before, during and after the Second World War.[1]

Such views were rarely questioned. Balfour, for example, was clear that Egypt and the Canal ('the wasp waist of our Empire') must remain British. His pronouncements, the product, as they seemed to be, of more elevated thought than others could aspire to, were treated with possibly exaggerated respect. In the Commons in 1919 he said that Egyptian nationalism would damage Britain and the world – and especially the Egyptians. 'British supremacy exists, British supremacy is going to be maintained: let nobody either in Egypt or out of Egypt make any mistake on that cardinal principle.'[2]

2. Events

For a long time, for geographical reasons, Egypt had been of interest to the Western world in general. Napoleon's conquest of Egypt in 1798 wrested part of the Ottoman possessions from Muslim control. That French incursion was important in cultural as well as political terms. It brought to popular attention the statuary, the antiquities of the country, the Rosetta Stone. Hieroglyphics were deciphered. Napoleon took with him scholars who opened up the history of Egypt to Western learning. What was taken to be Egyptian style influenced architecture and design.

The period of French rule came to a speedy end after Nelson's victory at the Battle of the Nile, but Ottoman control in Egypt had been challenged, and after the British left in 1803, following an equally brief period of occupation, Egypt was seized by Muhammad Ali, an Albanian Muslim.

In the course of the nineteenth century, Egypt's status changed frequently. By the end of the century, it was only nominally and tenuously connected with the Ottomans. The governance was ill defined and opaque. Muhammad Ali's dynasty remained in power, the ruler known as the Khedive, but only as puppets – puppets largely of the British, who were the dominating power. The 'Sirdar' was the British commander-in-chief of what was only nominally an Egyptian army.

France, however, had not in the least accepted that Egypt was a British sphere of influence. The Suez Canal was jointly owned by Britain and France, and British and French financial controllers sat in the Egyptian Cabinet. At an educational and cultural level, French influence remained powerful in the country, and the fact that France felt herself deprived of her true rights in Egypt was a source of friction until 1914 and beyond.

Before the war, Egypt's limited 'independence' scarcely amounted to the usual 'Empire by Treaty': it was more disguised direct rule. The outbreak of war in 1914 did nothing to loosen the grip: it meant that there had to be much tighter control over territories so intimately linked to the Indian Empire. Accordingly, when Turkey, nominally the overlord of Egypt, declared war on Britain in 1914, Britain brought rule through the Khedive to an end. Egypt became a protectorate, part of the Empire.

France took this badly. The generosity of Sykes–Picot, as Britain saw it, was intended to assuage French sensibilities. Egyptian nationalists also took annexation badly: the Declaration of the Egyptian Protectorate represented a breach of many promises that Egypt would be allowed to go her own way. Milner said that 'a witch's cauldron had been brewing almost since Cromer left'.[3] Cromer had been Agent and Consul General until 1907. This brew of nationalism was kept off the boil for the duration of the war. Substantial numbers of British troops remained in Egypt, some units with splendid nicknames like the Jordan Highlanders and Pharaoh's Foot. Martial law was imposed. Camels were requisitioned, and 'volunteers' were forced to labour.

But in Egypt, unlike Arabia, there was a genuine nationalist movement, and the demand for independence was still there when the war ended and the independence party, the Wafd, was formed in 1918. The nationalist leader, Said Zaghloul, asked for an interview with the High Commissioner, Sir Reginald Wingate, and demanded complete autonomy. Indeed he was now able to base the demand on the Anglo-French Declaration and its promise of self-determination to the Arabs. In a matter of months, huge petitions demanding independence were being signed.

Zaghloul was old and frail, but wily and charming. He had been a minister under Cromer, and he was a shrewd and experienced politician. He had a white moustache, and the Americans talked of him as Egypt's Theodore Roosevelt. After popular unrest in March 1919, he and three of his colleagues were arrested, charged with sedition and sent to Malta. It was a bad mistake: the country united behind the Wafd. Women engaged in politics for the first time. Crowds did enormous damage to property, and Europeans were attacked in the streets. The peasantry, the Fellaheen, who had never shown an interest in politics, rose up. The rising took Britain by surprise. It seemed horribly reminiscent of the Indian Mutiny. The reaction was extreme. By the end of 1919, 800 Egyptians had been killed and 1,400 wounded. There was excessive violence, extending to bombing and machine-gunning, imprisoning and flogging. Imperial troops from India and Australia, who had always despised the Egyptians, took the opportunity of demonstrating their contempt ferociously.

Wingate had warned of a difficult mood, but he had not been taken seriously in London. He did not impress Curzon, and he received the usual reward for correctly predicting the undesirable. He was replaced. Allenby, fresh from his victories in Palestine, was appointed High Commissioner. His instructions were to crush the demonstrations. But, for a soldier who was renowned for his bad temper, he was a surprisingly moderate and diplomatic administrator. He decided to release the nationalist leaders, including Zaghloul, who went to the Peace Conference in Paris where he was conveniently ignored. President Wilson privately reminded the Egyptians of what the Americans had done in 1776, but in public he could do nothing other than accept the situation. British protectorates had nothing to do with the conference.

Allenby also lost no time in announcing that the old imperial wizard, Lord Milner, was coming out to assess the situation. But the release of Zaghloul and the promise of Milner were not enough to pacify the Wafd. Violence continued and Milner's mission was boycotted. Pickets outside the mission's hotel, the Semiramis (where the Cairo Conference would take place) prevented Arab witnesses from giving evidence except in secret. Zaghloul was offered an opportunity to attend under cover of darkness, but declined. Despite all that, Milner was able to form a fairly realistic view of the state of affairs and the extent of Egyptian nationalism.

Milner's conclusion in December 1920 was pretty much the same as Allenby's. His report contained some criticism of British policy in the past and a prescription for liberalism now: Egypt would have to be given self-government. But he was quite clear that it would only be a semblance of self-government: 'The difficulty is to find a way of making Egypt's relation to Great Britain *appear* a more independent and dignified one than it ever really can be without our abandoning the degree of control which, in view of native incompetence and corruption, we are constrained to keep.'⁴

When the Cabinet read the report but continued to prevaricate, Allenby came home to confront them. He complained about the number of occasions on which his advice had been rejected, and when he saw he was getting nowhere, he interrupted Lloyd George's objections: 'Well, it's no good disputing any longer. I have told you what I think is necessary. You won't have it and it is none of my business to force you to. I have waited five weeks for a decision, and I can't wait any longer. I shall tell Lady Allenby to come home.' The prime minister put his hand on Allenby's arm: 'You have waited five weeks, Lord Allenby. Wait five more minutes.'⁵

In 1922, Britain announced that Egypt was 'an independent sovereign state' ruled by a king. On paper that is what she became, but the version of independence which Egypt received was ideal from a British point of view. The defence of Egypt was in British hands and Britain was responsible for protecting minorities, and for foreign affairs together with imperial communications to and from Egypt.

Zaghloul and other local politicians recognised a façade of self-government when they saw one. The Wafd took exception to the degree of control which Britain still exercised. Zaghloul said although Fuad was 'the King of Egypt, I am the King of their hearts'. The Wafd opposed the settlement because it did not go far enough; others, including Lloyd George and Churchill, because it went too far. Tory imperialists thought it was a concession to violence. But Zaghloul was silenced by exile in the Seychelles, and Lloyd George and Churchill by Allenby's threat of resignation. The king of Egypt and the British Resident kept the Wafd in check and after Zaghloul died in 1927, his successor, Mustafa Nahhas, was unpredictable and ineffective.

Fuad had been sultan. As a result of the constitutional change of 1922 he became king. He had been shot by his brother-in-law and a bullet was left in his throat. He sounded like a barking dog. When the Prince of Wales met him in 1922 he could scarcely control his giggles at 'the royal yappings'.[6] Despite the sound and sight of the monarch – his moustache was waxed into tusks – he was as effective as he could be in the circumstances, amassing both wealth and power.

What limited him to doing little more than generally making himself unpopular was the power of the British High Commissioner. Some High Commissioners were good, like Sir Miles Lampson, still in place when the Second World War broke out, and some were bad, like Lord Lloyd and Sir Percy Loraine, who regarded the Egyptians as 'wretched brutes'. But good or bad, the High Commissioner had the key to the Citadel, where a British battalion guarded all the ammunition for the Egyptian army. They had access to other resources too. Lloyd said that when he looked out on the Gezira Golf Course and 'I see these jacarandas in bloom, I know it's time to send for a battleship'. So Fuad complained that the Egyptian prime minister 'dared not move a pencil on his desk without Residency advice'.

Tensions between Britain and Egypt continued, but always beneath the surface of a period of ostensible democracy which lasted until 1936, and the Italian invasion of Ethiopia. Then, to sweeten the connection, Britain relaxed her hold and substituted an Anglo-Egyptian Alliance Treaty for the 1922 Declaration. Britain continued to enjoy much the same advantages as before – unlimited presence in the Canal zone and the right to defend India – but some indignities disappeared: capitulations were abolished and the mixed courts, which dealt with disputes involving foreigners, applying a largely Roman jurisprudence, with some Islamic and Egyptian elements, were to be phased out. Yet in a sense Britain was in a stronger position than before: the treaty was signed by a representative government and therefore appeared to be a true agreement rather than a unilateral declaration. The Wafd had become increasingly unpopular and a developing political vacuum was filled by a variety of Islamic bodies, notably the Muslim Brotherhood. Signature of the treaty coincided with the death of King Fuad and his succession by his son Farouk.

In later years, Farouk seemed a figure of fun, an ageing and corpulent playboy, out of touch with the new mood of nationalism that would ultimately sweep his dynasty from power. But he was initially a popular monarch, and in his time he had to be kept in his place. When he started corresponding with the Italians, he was confronted by Sir Miles Lampson, a huge man who towered over the king. The palace was surrounded by British tanks. He was presented with an instrument of abdication and told that he could either sign it or install a government that would cooperate with Britain. He chose the latter. During the Second World War, Egypt was an essential base for Britain's efforts. Until D-Day it was a more significant base than Britain itself. It seemed to be part almost of metropolitan Britain.

The tragedy was that in 1945 Britain did not realise how much had changed. In terms of the 1936 Treaty, Britain's troops should now have been out of the Valley of the Nile and into the Suez Canal zone. They were not, because Britain failed to notice the new mood, a mood of self-confident nationalism. The relationship between Britain and Egypt was very different now. Britain was a major debtor nation, many of her debts owed to her own colonies.

Egypt felt bold enough to go to the United Nations Security Council in August 1947 asking for a declaration that the Anglo-Egyptian Treaty of 1936 was invalid. Because the approach was unsuccessful, Britain remained entitled to retain a base on the Suez Canal until 1956. King Farouk fell in the Egyptian Revolution of 1952, and Egypt was then represented by General Naguib and his more important junior officer, Colonel Gamal Abdel Nasser. Naguib, the figurehead, declared, 'Let every Egyptian consider himself on the battlefield.' The Suez crisis of 1956 was the last example of Britain's assumption that it had special rights in Egypt.

31

PERSIA

1. William D'Arcy

Persia, which officially became Iran in 1935, was not brought within Britain's imperial ambit as a result of the war. It was not a mandate. But Britain was interested in Persia. At least part of Persia had been very much within the imperial system from about 1908, and that remained the case until 1945.

Before and after the First World War there was in some ways a remarkable continuity of outward circumstances, of dual British and Russian control. But the war did make a difference to British policy and revealed, as elsewhere, how undecided policy was.

In the first decade of the twentieth century, during a period of constitutional reform, Persia, ostensibly an ancient and independent kingdom, surrendered huge oil rights to a Briton, William D'Arcy. D'Arcy was a solicitor turned financier who had become enormously rich after exploiting the discovery of gold on the Queensland coast in Australia. He never, ever, visited Persia, but in 1901 he invested in a concession that entitled him to any oil he could find anywhere in the country except the five northern provinces, which adjoined Russia. After three years he had found nothing. He was close to writing off his personal investment of £250,000. 'Every purse has its limits, and I am beginning to see the bottom of my own.' He staved off defeat by bringing in the Burmah Oil Company and operations continued, but still without success. Burmah and D'Arcy were about to give up when major deposits were found in May 1908. In the following year the Anglo-Persian Oil Company was established.

2. Oil

Relations with Persia would never be the same, but it is important not to allow hindsight to obscure the position at the time. The importance of the Middle East in relation to oil was rather in its potential than in actual production. By the early twentieth century, it was pretty clear, although not scientifically proved, but it was only during and after the Second World War that the supplies were vigorously exploited. In 1938, 57 per cent of British oil imports came from the Americas and only 22 per cent from the Middle East.[1]

What was important was that the oil discoveries in Persia came along just as the Royal Navy was considering how to fuel the fleet. Admiral Jackie Fisher was proud of the fact that he had been known as an 'oil maniac' since 1886. Now he was First Sea Lord, and in a position to press for the use of oil as a proper naval fuel, and not just for spraying on coal to make it more combustible. Nothing was achieved directly during his term as First Sea Lord, but he did engage the enthusiasm of his civilian master, Churchill, First Lord of the Admiralty from 1911 until 1915.

Churchill made a critical decision. He concluded that the Royal Navy must have a fast division, which could outmanoeuvre the German fleet and steam at 25 knots. The only fuel that could generate that speed was oil. *Queen Elizabeth*-class battleships were commissioned. They could burn only oil, and it soon became clear that this was the fuel of the future.

The navy had to decide on its source of oil. A mission was sent to Persia to look at oil fields. D'Arcy's Anglo-Persian Oil was not the obvious candidate. It was smaller than Royal Dutch Shell. But Churchill persuaded his colleagues, first, that competition would best be encouraged by favouring Anglo-Persian, and, secondly, that supplies would best be secured by taking control of the company. The British government invested £2.2 million and took 51 per cent of the company's stock. In a secret contract the company undertook to supply the Admiralty with oil for 20 years.[2] The Anglo-Persian Oil Company (APOC) continued under that name until 1935, when it became the Anglo-Iranian Oil Company (AIOC). In 1954 it became, more frankly, British Petroleum. Britain was its biggest shareholder.

Britain was more successful than any other foreign country in homing in on the oil of the region. Germany had secured some rights in 1903, but at a fairly insignificant level. By the end of the First World War, America had convinced herself that she had sold so much oil to Europe during the conflict that she was now running out of supplies and felt excluded from the riches of the Middle East. The only commercial fields to which Britain had access were those in Persia, but Cabot Lodge, the Republican who more than any other man ensured that America never participated in the League of Nations, said 'England is taking possession of the oilfields of the world'.[3] Tension was only relieved in 1929 when two American oil companies joined in a consortium with APOC, Shell and a French company to form the Iraq Petroleum Company, with a 5 per cent share for Calouste Gulbenkian, 'Mr. Five Per Cent'. The United States now had their corner of Iraq, although Britain, through APOC, was the biggest shareholder in the Iraq Petroleum Company.

The importance of oil is nowadays so great that it is important to remember that by 1914 no navy in the world apart from the Royal Navy and the United States' navy had gone far in the direction of oil, and even for the Royal Navy coal remained the normal fuel. But the consequence of D'Arcy's finds and the decision that Churchill and Fisher came to was that for 40 years Britain remained intimately interested in Persia though without the formal political control she exercised over, for instance, Iraq.

3. Policy

Britain's main policy preoccupation in Persia was the threat from Russia, with whom she shared effective control of the country. The Entente with Russia in 1907 aimed at a resolution of competing claims in Persia as elsewhere. The mechanics were crude. Russia was given free rein for influence in the north, and Britain in the south. Four years later Britain actually entered the south and Russia the north. Later in the century there was another interested party, but for the moment Russia was able to secure the dismissal of an American financial adviser and put a stop to interference from that source.

When Curzon officiated at the Foreign Office on an informal basis prior to succeeding Balfour as Foreign Secretary on 24 October 1919, Britain began to evolve an articulated policy towards Persia. His experience in India and his very considerable knowledge of Persia itself disposed him to take a particular interest. He had made a famous journey to Persia in 1889, and the book he subsequently wrote, *Persia and the Persian Question*, was regarded as the definitive study of the region. He tended to regard Britain's interests as peculiarly bound up with the areas he knew. 'The integrity of Persia must be registered as a cardinal precept of our Imperial credo.'[4] That was pitching it a bit strong, even if it was desirable to keep Russia out. But as he was acknowledged as the expert on Persia, he was given a largely free hand in relation to what he saw as an essential link in the chain of defence that ran from the Mediterranean to the subcontinent.

In an address to the Imperial War Cabinet on 25 June 1918, he stressed the importance of Persia and reminded his colleagues of the interest that the Kaiser had shown in the country before 1914. In these last months of the war he perceived Germany as still threatening India. India was the centre of British power in the east, 'and it is at India, along these lines of advance that I have been describing, that Germany is striking'.

When the war ended, he still felt that Persia must be strengthened for Britain against a resurgent Germany and indeed Russia. He did not think that the answer lay in a mandate – indeed it would have been difficult to argue the case for one – but rather in a Persia with the British Army in place, the country's policy shaped by British advice.

Not everyone agreed with him. Montagu, the Secretary of State for India, recorded his dissent from Curzon's Persian policy in a letter of 6 January 1919 in which he pointed out that most of the members of the Eastern Committee had been absent from its most recent meeting 'and therefore the Committee consisted of the Chairman [Curzon]; and the Committee, of course, not unnaturally agreed with the Chairman'.[5]

Despite that dissent, Curzon's policy was embodied in the Anglo-Persian Treaty of 1919. Curzon was for an independent Persia, but one that was clearly subservient to Britain, which is exactly what the treaty delivered. It was negotiated for Britain by Sir Percy Cox, who had been Resident in Persia for many years. Cox was well disposed to Persia. Harold Nicolson described him as 'a silent Apollo, . . . inclined to take the realities of the Persian temperament more seriously than their aspirations'.[6]

British interests in Persia were now Cox's responsibility. British political advisers, army officers, munitions and equipment and a loan of £2 million secured control of the country. Dual control had disappeared with the 1917 Revolution, when Russia withdrew. But Britain recognised that the withdrawal might only be temporary and from 1918 onwards was concerned to protect her oil interests against Bolshevism. There was consequently greatly increased British involvement. But the military presence (Churchill called it 'reaching out for Persia') was expensive and was indeed soon contested by Soviet Russia. Curzon's policy of controlling Persia became increasingly difficult.

In February 1921 Reza Khan, a colonel in the Cossack Brigade, entered Teheran with 3,000 men and required the ruler, the shah, to appoint Sayyid Zia, a young civilian reformer, as prime minister. In return Sayyid Zia appointed Reza Khan as army commander. Reza Khan almost immediately obliged Sayyid Zia to resign and he himself became prime minister. He told the shah to go for a holiday. Three years later he himself became shah, founded a new dynasty and ruled until 1941.

The change of regime in Persia was paralleled by that in Turkey. There were similarities between Reza Khan and Atatürk, who became president of the new Turkish Republic in 1922. Reza is sometimes referred to as the Iranian Atatürk. In reality he was not a true reformer, but he strengthened the armed forces, surrounded himself by a large bureaucracy and enjoyed great wealth and patronage.

The role of the *ulama*, the Muslim scholar class, was reduced, and sharia law and the sharia judicial system were minimised. Men were required to wear European dress and it was compulsory to wear a hat. Small villages bought one communal hat, to be worn by anyone who might be visited by central government.[7] The wearing of veils was outlawed in 1936 and sexual segregation was forbidden.

But despite the economic reforms under the new shah, the Anglo-Iranian Oil Company, an *imperium in imperio*, remained unchallenged and invulnerable, by far the largest industrial employer in the country. The shah would have liked to seize the treasure. He tried to renegotiate the D'Arcy concession of 1901 but had little success. Eventually, in 1933, he negotiated an increase in the royalty payments from 16 per cent to 20 per cent, but in return he had to extend the concession from 1961 to 1993.

What he did do was to counterbalance Britain's role in the economy by establishing economic and political ties with Germany. Germany became Iran's largest trading partner. When the Second World War broke out, although the shah proclaimed neutrality, it was clear that his sympathies were with the Axis. The consequence was pre-emptive invasion by Britain and Russia in August 1941. Reza Shah abdicated in favour of his son, Mohammad Reza Shah.

Despite its new confidence and revitalisation, Iran was back, in the Second World War, to the same position as it had been in the First: ignominiously occupied by Britain and Russia. The affront to her self-esteem did as much as foreign control of her oil wealth to build up resentment for the future.

Iran's problem was that although she sat on a great deal of oil and next to a great deal more in the Persian Gulf, she remained politically and militarily weak. The dynamics of change lay in the fact that the country offered an overland supply route to the Soviet Union. To make use of that route to supply Russia with oil, American troops now arrived in significant numbers. The United States also increasingly supplied military and civilian advisers to the Iranian government and started to interfere in financial and military matters. The pattern of what was to come was being established.

When the war ended, Mohammad Reza Shah faced problems at home and abroad. He had been educated in Switzerland and then schooled by his father: he seemed in some ways detached. He had succeeded to a country that was formally occupied by the United Kingdom and Russia and informally controlled by the Americans. These three powers supported different elements. As always, Britain favoured cooperation with the local ruler, here the shah, and others, such as landowners, who supported the status quo. Russia put her weight behind the Marxist party, the Tudeh. The United States, increasingly concerned about Soviet power, put her support behind the Iranian armed forces.

Inevitably there was resentment about the degree to which Iran had been subject to foreign control throughout the century. This resentment and the spirit of nationalism came to be expressed by Muhammad Mossadiq. Mossadiq came from a privileged background, a landed, aristocratic family. He was educated at universities in Paris and Switzerland and obtained a doctorate in law from the University of Neuchâtel. History has remembered his doctorate: he is invariably referred to as Dr Mossadiq. He was regarded as an incorruptible supporter of democratic institutions. Indeed he opposed Reza Shah's authoritarian rules to such an extent that he was placed under house arrest.

The National Front, which he formed, challenged the power of the Anglo-Iranian Oil Company. He campaigned for cancellation of the concessions it enjoyed and nationalisation of the oil industry. The power and privilege of the AIOC was enormous, and it is easy to see why it engendered resentment. It owned the town of Abadan, the largest oil refinery in the world, which, with its own municipal services, was almost an independent city-state. It built its own roads and airports, entered into arrangements with local tribes and was run entirely by non-Iranians. The 'company' was in reality its largest shareholder, Britain.

In 1951 Mossadiq became prime minister and the Majlis, the assembly, legislated for nationalisation. The AIOC responded by calling for a boycott of Iranian oil. Britain agreed to enforce the boycott and also imposed economic sanctions. The West had Iran by the neck: the United States was as concerned as Britain by events in Iran, not so much because of the nationalisation of the oil company as by fears that Iran was looking to Soviet Russia for protection.

In October 1952, Mossadiq reacted by breaking off diplomatic relations with Britain and took emergency powers. At the same time he attacked the shah's position and transferred control of the armed forces from the shah to the government. He purged the officer corps and introduced land law reforms.

But the country's economic problems together with the clergy's fears about secularisation were eroding support for the National Front. It was crumbling away in two directions. At the same time as it was deserted by the right, the left was moving to the Communist Party. An unhappy army conspired against Mossadiq, and the CIA with help from Britain sent agents to assist in his deposition. A first attempt failed and the shah, who had been complicit in it, fled to Rome. A second attempt three days later on 19 June 1953 succeeded, and the shah returned.

Two years later, Iran joined the Baghdad Pact and became substantially the puppet of the United States, receiving large sums in military aid. In the years that followed the shah consolidated his position. He was determined to avoid a repeat of the wing-clipping that Mossadiq had inflicted on him. The oil issue was settled, with Iran receiving 50 per cent of the oil revenue. The shah tied himself to the West. He received $500 million in military aid in the decade after his return in 1953. His was a repressive regime, with the exception, under

American pressure, of a brief period of liberalisation between 1960 and 1963. America encouraged the shah to use the wealth of his country to buy advanced weapon systems – pretty well anything that was not nuclear, and all of it from America. Between 1972 and 1976 Iran spent more than $10 billion on arms and had the fifth largest military force in the world.[8]

The Ayatollah Khomeini appeared on the scene about 1963. The presence of American military instructors, and their lifestyle, was resented. It fuelled the criticisms articulated by the Ayatollah and contributed to his support. The West had bought Iran's compliance, but not her heart. Indeed the Western presence served rather to alienate the country, and British and American association with the tyrannical regime of the shah did the West no good in the long term. The shah fell in 1979.

Britain's involvement in Iran was different from her role in Egypt or the mandated territories. There was not the complication of promises made and broken or the drawing of new frontiers. In some ways the failure of Western policy in Iran is therefore particularly inexcusable. Britain and Russia simply continued to exploit the country for their own benefit, and in Britain's case all that the First World War did, despite Wilson's Principles and the idealism of the League, was to offer an opportunity to formalise and intensify the pre-existent policy. The role of the United States did nothing to improve matters. The West made no effort to acknowledge Iranian self-respect. The consequences are those of selfish, short-sighted and insensitive policies.

32

SYRIA

Syria, taken here to include Lebanon, was France's reward for being on the winning side. It was a prize France was determined to have, and a settlement which the Arab population, as has been seen, did all it could to avoid. A brief outline of what happened in Syria after the granting of the mandate to France is relevant as a contrast to what happened in the British mandates.

The French regime was based not on any treaty with the Syrians, but on military power. There was not the respect for Arab institutions and culture which Britain attempted in Iraq. The insensitivity of the French in Syria and the Lebanon, where the aim was to replace Arab culture as far as possible with French, was marked and flawed. School children were taught to sing the *Marseillaise*. School textbooks rewrote the history of the area. Freya Stark said, 'It is ridiculous to call [what the French established in Syria] a mandate, for I believe there is not a Frenchman in the country who intends these people to govern themselves.'[1]

Rule was direct and French administrators were used. France saw Syria as her possession as of right because of her traditional role as a protector of Christian communities in the Levant, especially the Maronite Catholics of Mount Lebanon. Further, she had invested heavily in the area and she believed that a Middle Eastern possession was part of the central equipment of a Mediterranean power. In 1920 she created Greater Lebanon, by putting into it, among other things, part of Syria. Syria itself was divided into a series of separate units to inhibit the development of a separate Syrian political identity, a process of institutionalised fragmentation.

A number of uprisings were suppressed. There was a major revolt in 1925–27 in which very many people were killed and which damaged French authority considerably. France used great severity to quell the rebellion. Looting and killing were tolerated.

France blocked, thwarted and vetoed attempts to move Syria towards independence, with only a temporary break in 1936 when Léon Blum's Popular Front Coalition proposed a draft treaty, which subsequent French governments refused to ratify. In 1939, on the outbreak of the Second World War, the High Commissioner suspended the constitution and dissolved parliament.

Lebanon was treated slightly differently in that the local population was involved in government to some degree. The Maronites were included in Greater Lebanon to ensure that they were not swamped in Muslim Syria, but even in Lebanon the Maronites were only 30 per cent of a predominately Muslim population. Lebanon, unlike Syria, moved fairly speedily towards self-government. In 1926 the Republic of Lebanon was established on the basis of representation by religion. But there was still no question of independence. The mandate was still in force. A 1936 treaty with France did promise independence, but, as in the case of the draft treaty with Syria, the French Chamber blocked any further progress, and in 1939 the constitution was suspended and parliament dissolved.

With the outbreak of war, Syria and Lebanon were taken over by Pétainist officials and run as part of the Vichy administration. Britain and Free France invaded both Syria and Lebanon in 1941. Ahead of the invasion, de Gaulle had agreed to immediate independence, but once the invasion had taken place he abjured his agreement.

Under British pressure there was restoration of the constitutions, with elections in 1943 which resulted in a strong vote against France and for independence. But France continued to resist claims to independence, and immediately the war in Europe ended she brought in troops to crush resistance. Britain was required to intervene to achieve an armistice. De Gaulle summoned Duff Cooper, the British ambassador: 'I admit that we are not in a position to wage war against you at the present time [June 1945!]. But you have insulted France and betrayed the West. This cannot be forgotten.'[2]

French troops did not leave Syria till the spring of 1946 and Lebanon in December of that year. Nowadays there are still vestigial signs of the French epoch in Lebanon. Although the colonial architecture of Beirut disappeared in the civil war, some Arabs still choose to have their children educated with French as the language of instruction. But in Syria, apart from the museums which were created by a generation of tireless and able archaeologists, scarcely a trace of France remains, and such memories as linger are of a hated and oppressive occupier.

Having looked at what were not British mandates – Egypt, Iran and Syria – let us now look by contrast at the British mandates themselves – Jordan, Iraq and Palestine – and see what the British made of their new Middle Eastern possessions.

VII

JORDAN UNDER THE MANDATE

33

JORDAN

1. Background

Churchill enjoyed saying that he had created the Emirate of Jordan by the stroke of his pen one bright Sunday afternoon, with time left to make several paintings of Jerusalem before the light went.[1] The reflection of more censorious observers was that 'Transjordan was an artificial State created to accommodate the interests of a foreign power and an itinerant prince in search of a throne.'[2]

Abdullah, the least reliable of the Hashemites, self-indulgent and wayward, could indeed be tethered by implantation in Jordan. But Jordan also required a legitimate government, and Abdullah supplied it. In the process of finding a role for Abdullah, Britain had created a kingdom. But in the long run – certainly not immediately – he turned out to be quite a good king, and the central purpose, of policing the area, was achieved.

Jordan turned out to be a good thing, but it was achieved more or less accidentally. The idea of making Transjordan into a geographical unit, even linked to Palestine, was unplanned and improbable. No one had ever thought of constituting it as a unit. It had never been one. There was no great enthusiasm for Herbert Samuel's plan for incorporating it into Israel. The reason the British wanted it was on the whole negative. The War Office, for instance, did not want it, but it was on the route from the Mediterranean to the Gulf and it was important that it did not go to France. It was for these insubstantial reasons Britain found herself in possession of Transjordan.

The steps taken to deal with it, once it was there, were very haphazard. Britain had no intention of spending much on Jordan's defence. All that was provided was a small military force, which in time became the Arab Legion. Some political advisers were appointed to guide local notables.

The most important of these was St John Philby, who came out as Chief British Representative. He deserves to be properly introduced, and his introduction is a suitable moment to deal with what happened to the Hashemites' rivals, the Saudis, and also with the sad decline of Abdullah's father, Hussein.

2. Philby

In the years with which this narrative is concerned, the two pre-eminent English Arabians, in the sense of those who physically knew the land best, understood those who lived there and were most accepted by them, were Gertrude Bell and St John ('Jack') Philby. Philby is now remembered chiefly as the father of the spy Kim Philby, but in his time he was very much more, taken very seriously as an explorer and Arabian expert. He came to think of himself pretty much as being an Arab. English Arabists frequently fell into this trap, and thought that wearing robes and adopting an Arab lifestyle gave them insight into the Arab psyche; but some Arabs did think that Philby understood them at any rate as well as any European could do. He had a formidable degree of self-regard, which made him an impossible colleague, finally rejected by the British Civil Service, and at the end only tolerated by his Arab hosts.

When Gertrude Bell joined Cox's staff in March 1916, she met Philby for the first time. She liked what she saw, and he respected her experience. There was, however, an element of jealousy in his reaction. He recognised that her private means had enabled her to travel more than he and that her knowledge of the Arabs was greater than his.[3] The extent of her pre-war travelling was prodigious. The Foreign Office had recognised that fact in sending her to Cairo and India to investigate how Arab opposition to the Turks could best be developed, an extraordinary role for a woman in those days.

Philby's jealous reaction was typical of the man. He was arrogant, an egotist without self-awareness, dynamic, stubborn, intemperate and without finesse. He irritated more people than he pleased and when people thought well of him they did so because of his brusque efficiency and not because of any hint of geniality of temperament. Generally any recognition that his efficiency engendered was eventually eroded by the irritation which his deficiencies generated. Within a short time of meeting him, Gertrude Bell lectured him 'like a sister' for being domineering and difficult. Arnold Wilson did not like him, nor did Samuel. Percy Cox, on the other hand, who was both tolerant and capable of considerable insight, thought reasonably well of him. Even he, however, took care to tell Philby no more than he needed to, and eventually he, too, found it impossible to continue to work with him.

When Arnold Wilson arrived in Baghdad in October 1917, he complained to Cox that his activities in Basra were being frustrated by Philby. According to the latter, and his account may be suspect, Philby undertook to clear out and take over the Storrs mission to Arabia: 'If I could be sent on that it would leave the field clear for you. If you could fix it up with Cox, I am prepared to hand over to you straightaway.'[4]

There was never any opposition when Philby said he would like to go away. What he now undertook was an extended journey across Arabia – partly because he wanted to make the journey, but also on the pretext that he would be able to report on the extent of Ibn Saud's control of the deserts. The journey across Arabia from east to west made him famous. He received the Founders' Medal of the Royal Geographical Society. The crossing had only been made once before by an Englishman, Captain Forster Sadlier in 1819.

The journey changed Philby's life. It was now that he took to wearing Arab clothes and grew a beard. His respect for Arabia and Ibn Saud, not always reciprocated, lasted for the rest of his life. His mission of bringing the Saudi court onside was successful. Ibn Saud became an ally. He was invested as a Knight Commander of the Indian Empire in 1916. He received material and monetary rewards, not so much to keep him out of the hands of the Turks as to deter him from attacking Hussein. But Ibn Saud remained adamant in his hatred and contempt for the Sharif of Mecca.

After his great trans-Arabian journey and his meeting with Ibn Saud, Philby met Hogarth of ARBUR at Jeddah. There they met the Sharif of Mecca, Philby for the first time. Coming as he did from Ibn Saud to the man who was the king of the Hejaz and wanted to be known as the king of the Arabs, Philby had a critical role to perform in reconciling the ambitions of the two Arab princes on whom Britain depended. Hogarth's task was to 'try to smooth over the difficulties between the King [Hussein] and Ibn Saud and to secure a working arrangement between them in the interests of Arab unity'.[5] With Philby around, Hogarth's task was not an easy one. He sized Philby up accurately and succinctly: 'Mighty intelligent but very impracticable [*sic*] from an imperial point of view'.[6]

Philby handled the meeting with the old King Hussein predictably badly. He made too much of his time with Ibn Saud, and he did not even understand what he had done, writing to his wife, 'It is not often one gets the chance I have had of making a fool of a King.' Observers criticised 'a certain lack of respect in Mr. Philby's manner', and his insistence on referring to his contact with Ibn Saud.[7] The very fact and nature of Philby's arrival from the court of Ibn Saud annoyed Hussein. It was unannounced, but public knowledge, and Hussein considered that it reinforced Turkish allegations that Britain intended to annex Arabia. Eventually Hogarth judged it wise to keep Philby away from many meetings with the Sharif.

By 1919 Britain was clear that there was a role for the Saudis, as well as for the Hashemites. The government invited a member of the Saudi royal family (and also one from Kuwait) to Britain to consolidate the links and acknowledge their services during the war. To his delight, Philby was chosen to be the host. Any connection with Ibn Saud was welcome. His guest was Ibn Saud's 14-year-old son, Emir Faisal, later King Faisal of Saudi Arabia.

Philby met the party at Plymouth, but found that no hotel accommodation had been booked. The royal guests were hastily put into a hotel at Upper Norwood, where the other guests were awakened on the following morning by the Muslim call to prayer. Swords were exchanged with King George V, and woollen underwear was obtained from the Royal Ordnance Department when the guests complained of the cold. They saw *Chu Chin Chow* and *The Mikado*.[8]

Philby's views about the Arabs were ambivalent. In his diary for 8 January 1924, waiting to meet Hussein, he confided that, 'the days of idleness in company with these Arabs serves better to give one an insight into their natures than anything else . . . With nothing to do they are dreadful . . . They lie about sprawling and livery . . . [E]xaggeration is a natural feature of their ordinary conversation . . . [S]ighs and groans are common, silences frequent'.[9] On the other hand, he adopted Islam. His sincerity in this regard was questioned by the Arabs, who still thought of him as English for all his dressing up in Arab costume. Although he remained married to his English wife, Dora, he was given a number of Arab wives as well.

After he had been abandoned by the British government, he made a series of great voyages of exploration. But as time went by, he became dangerously anti-British and pro-Hitler. The Second World War was a bad time for him. He was arrested in Karachi in August 1940 and charged with 'activities prejudicial to the safety of the Realm' and then detained under Section 18b of the Defence of the Realm Act in Bertram Mills's circus ground at Ascot. He was finally released on the view that he was a harmless fanatic. He returned after the war to Saudi Arabia, but was temporarily banished from the kingdom after he annoyed even his protector, Ibn Saud.

St John Philby was suspected by the British of being a spy. He was not, but his son, Kim, was. It was Kim who chose the inscription for his father's tombstone: 'Greatest of Arabian Explorers'.

3. Hussein and Ibn Saud

The rivalry between Hussein and Ibn Saud had threatened to come to a head at the end of 1918, when Hussein claimed that Ibn Saud was advancing on Khurma. Hussein saw that Ibn Saud's Wahhabist extremists were a threat to him. It seemed possible that in a conflict between Hussein and Ibn Saud one would be using British tanks and the other British poison gas, one against the other.[10] The financial implications were also absurd. Hussein was spending £12,000 per annum out of his total subsidy on defence against the threat from Ibn Saud, also subsidised by Britain.

London tried to adjudicate between the claims of the two kings, but no clear policy arose out of innumerable committee meetings and deliberations. Financial compromises of various sorts were suggested as well as boundary commissions, but they did not do much good. Allenby reported that Hussein was threatening to abdicate – not for the first time – because he could not operate without more effective British aid. Allenby's recommendation was an ultimatum to Ibn Saud to withdraw or face the stoppage of his subsidy. Even though the advice came from Allenby, the man on the spot refulgent in the glory of victory, it was not acted on. By the end of May, fighting was actually taking place and the Hashemite forces were facing defeat. The integrity of the Hejaz was at risk and there was panic in Mecca, where there was the added element of the safety of 11,500 Indian pilgrims.

Hussein attempted to crush the Saudis at Turaba in 1919. Abdullah headed his army, an army of 5,000 men, equipped with all that Britain had given the Hashemites during the war. Turaba was occupied on 21 May 1919. Before Ibn Saud's main forces had engaged Abdullah's army, his camel-mounted scouts carried out a pre-emptive swoop on 25 May. They were only armed with the most primitive of weapons, but they destroyed Abdullah's army and killed most of his men. Abdullah was lucky to escape in his nightshirt.

Britain could not stand aside. They sent in aircraft to reinforce Hussein. Ibn Saud immediately claimed that he offered no threat to the Hejaz and that he had been trying to restrain his followers. Hussein was hungry for vengeance, but Britain held him back. Ibn Saud was told that if he did not withdraw from Khurma and the Hejaz, the 1915 Anglo-Saudi Treaty would be abrogated. His reply was that Britain could not unilaterally disavow the treaty. Arnold Wilson's response to this stand-off was interesting: he was quite prepared to see Hussein abdicate and his unitary regime replaced with a series of systems acceptable to local populations.

It was proposed that Philby be sent to Ibn Saud to mediate, but Hussein – 'a pampered and querulous nuisance' according to Curzon – refused to allow him to travel through the Hejaz. Britain did not press the point and, as Arnold Wilson complained, preferred to let things drift.[11] For the moment and by chance, rather than by clear-sighted design, drift at least appeared to work.

But some more formal arrangements were needed, and after the Cairo Conference, negotiations over a treaty opened. Churchill persisted in his confidence in Lawrence, and it was Lawrence who arrived in Jeddah in August 1921 with a draft. Hussein was normally at pains to treat Lawrence with courtesy, but on this occasion he found it difficult to do so. He was being asked to accept as the essential basis for the treaty Britain's special position in Iraq and Palestine resulting from the mandates conferred at San Remo. That was too much salt to be rubbed in the wounds that Arab aspirations to independence had suffered. Hussein resisted, and his confidence in Britain was diminished.

Fresh negotiations took place in the spring of 1923, but also proceeded unsatisfactorily. Hussein was not prepared to accept the position in Palestine and in particular the implications of the Balfour Declaration. When he had spoken with Hogarth, he had required that the safeguard for Arab civil and religious rights contained in the declaration should be widened to include political and economic rights. This had not been done. This issue went back and forward between London and Iraq till August 1924.

Hussein had declared himself king of the Hejaz and of all Arabs in 1917. In 1924, following the abolition of the Ottoman Caliphate, he named himself caliph of the Muslim world. But by now he was ridiculed in London and a discredited figure in the Arab world. Hussein's final letter to the prime minister, now Ramsay MacDonald, was dated 4 August 1924, the tenth anniversary of the outbreak of the First World War. In it he appealed for implementation of the promises made in that war. Before a reply could be received, he had been deposed. The Saudis took over Mecca, Medina and Jeddah. Britain let them, though they allowed Hussein to take refuge in Cyprus, before moving to exile in Amman.

4. Establishment of Jordan

Transjordan was, like Iraq and Palestine, a creature of treaty. It began as a metaphysical concept rather than a territory. Its borders had not been defined. It was somewhere between the Hejaz on the south, and Palestine on the west. It was indeed only a part of the larger, but equally ill-defined Palestine. Even its name was not clearly established: Trans-Jordan, Trans-jordan, even Jordania and Trans-Jordania. Only in 1949 did it emerge simply as Jordan, more properly the Hashemite Kingdom of Jordan.

Under the Ottomans it had been part of Syria, inhabited by Bedouin tribesmen over whom the Turks exerted little control, largely left to its own, ungoverned devices. Amman, which under the British became the capital in 1921, was just a village of some 2,500–5,000 inhabitants.[12] The population of the city is now in the region of 2.5 million, many of them refugees still living in the camps they set up when they fled from Israel in 1948 and enlarged after the Six-Day War of 1967. The country, if it can be called that, was virgin territory for British policymakers, inhabited by tribes accustomed to survive by raids on what were now becoming Syria and Palestine.

While Faisal was on the throne in Syria, he effectively ran Transjordan under a British flag. After his defenestration in July 1920, more formal arrangements had to be made. The raids on Palestine were destabilizing, and the High Commissioner requested a defensive military occupation. That was vetoed by the War Office. But something needed to be done. For the moment the desert area of the territory was almost abandoned, with just six British officers, aged between 19 and 35, exercising a light control over established settlements, and encouraging local self-government. Conditions were far from stable.

Allenby had expelled the Turks, but thereafter the area had been policed, so far as policed at all, by Faisal from Damascus. With Faisal gone from Syria, the French could arguably maintain that it fell to them, as his successors, to rule the territory. Britain was neither in a position to police the country nor to expel the French if they marched in to establish order.

Fortunately they did not march in. They might well have done. In 1920 there were heated negotiations between Britain and France over drawing a border between Palestine on the one hand and Syria and Lebanon on the other. France was hostile both to a British Palestine and to the notion of a Zionist Palestine. France considered that she had long-standing links with Palestine, both religious and commercial, which were now under attack. There was a good deal of French anti-Semitism, and Zionism was associated for some Frenchmen with Bolshevism. The French government subsidised anti-British propaganda both in Palestine and in Transjordan. France was as anxious to gain control over Transjordan as over Palestine. Transjordan made up some 75 per cent of the Palestine mandate. So far as the border itself was concerned, France wanted to gain control of the upper reaches of the Rivers Jordan and Yarmuk. This they succeeded in doing.

At this stage Hussein's second son, Abdullah, appeared in the territory, roving about, ostensibly punishing the French for deposing his brother, burning telegraph poles for fuel as he went. His romps coincided with the Cairo Conference, to which Churchill had gone with what were truly weightier problems to solve. As we saw, Churchill dealt with the matter very neatly. He invited Abdullah to Jerusalem and was reasonably impressed by what he saw. Lawrence had been sent out to see what was happening. He concluded that Abdullah was not as bad as he had expected, but that he needed a strong British adviser to keep him in order and show him what to do. As usual Churchill took Lawrence's advice seriously, and Abdullah was installed in the way we have seen.

Churchill had no fewer than four meetings with Abdullah in Jerusalem, the last on 30 March 1921. By the end of that series of contacts, he had established what Abdullah's role would be. Abdullah was more or less reconciled to the limited function that he was being given. He was impressed by the fact that, as Churchill pointed out, many would say that Britain's interest would be better served by dividing the ruling houses, rather than having two Hashemite kingdoms. On 5 April, Churchill wrote to Curzon, 'Abdullah turned round completely under our treatment of the Arab problem. I hope he won't get his throat cut by his own followers.'[13]

Both Jordan and Abdullah, then, were Churchill's creations. Colonel Richard Meinertzhagen, who had been in charge of field intelligence under Allenby and thereafter moved to the War Office, was a delegate at the Paris Peace Conference and chief political officer in Palestine and Syria from 1919 to 1921. He was appointed military adviser to the new Middle East Department in April 1921. He was violently opposed to the detachment of Transjordan from Palestine, as being a betrayal of the pledge to the Jews. He considered the Middle East Department to be 'almost 100% Hebraphobe', or anti-Zionist. Meinertzhagen made vigorous representations to Churchill – largely without result, although on the following day Churchill said to Herbert Sidebotham, then a journalist on *The Times*, that he was thinking about allowing Jewish settlement in Jordan. That was no more than musing, but what did emerge from Churchill's conversation with Sidebotham was how impressed he had been by the Jewish colonists in Palestine: 'Splendid open-air men, he exclaimed, beautiful women; and they have made the desert bloom like the rose.'[14]

Transjordan was created not just, as was claimed, to find a throne for the itinerant Abdullah, but also to bring order to a lawless region, to police Transjordan for Britain. To this end Abdullah received a British subsidy and support from some British civilians and soldiers. His stipend was £5,000 a month. He was only on six months' probationary rule. For Abdullah, it was better than nothing, though not as good as Iraq, which he had wanted. But he had a difficult job. He had to keep the Hashemite exiles from Syria in check, and be on guard against his father's claims on Transjordan as part of the Hejaz.

5. Development of the New Kingdom

Philby wrote to Gertrude Bell in February 1922, 'I frankly like Abdullah, a vain but well-read man with excellent ideas, though lacking in initiative or vigour of action. Of course nobody here or in Syria wants him or any member of the Sharifian family, but what matter? He is here and is as good a figurehead as anyone else would be.'[15]

The new set-up was given formal recognition in May 1923, when the British government announced that 'subject to the approval of the League of Nations, His Britannic Majesty's Government will recognise the existence of an independent government in Trans-jordan, under the rule of His Highness the Emir Abdullah ibn Husain [*sic*], provided such government is constitutional and places His Britannic Majesty's Government in a position to fulfil their international obligations in respect of the territory by means of an agreement to be concluded between the two governments.'[16]

In 1924 Philby was replaced by Sir Henry Cox, not to be confused with Percy Cox, who appears more frequently in these pages. Henry Cox was not entranced by Abdullah's ways and was disposed to replace him with someone who could be regarded as more reliable, perhaps his brother Ali. An opportunity to ditch him arose in June that same year when he was away from his kingdom for two months on the *hajj*. There was a serious suggestion that he should not be allowed to return. The Colonial Office thought this was a step too far, but Henry Cox was authorised to present the king with an ultimatum which seriously limited his freedom of movement and in particular ended his profligate control of the kingdom's finances by placing British hands on his exchequer. To everyone's surprise, Abdullah meekly accepted. He did not want to go on his travels again, and he proved surprisingly compliant for the rest of his reign. He was a figurehead. Transjordan was ruled by the British Resident.

Transjordan's army, the Arab Legion, was in effect part of the British Armed Forces. Its role was supplemented by the Transjordan Frontier Force, which was funded from the Palestine budget and commanded by the High Commissioner. In 1930 a Desert Mobile Force was set up under J.B. Glubb, later known as Glubb Pasha. Glubb got on well with Abdullah and in 1939 succeeded to the command of the Legion.

By 1928 Britain decided that the Jordanian experiment was working, and entered into an agreement with Transjordan. It confirmed Abdullah's limited role and subservient status and reserved a great deal to Britain. The agreement was followed by a formal constitution. This procedure was to become the model for moving mandates towards self-government.

In the years that followed, Abdullah behaved much as would have been expected – or perhaps a little better. He was ambitious and could be difficult. He would have liked a larger crown. He continued to look towards Syria and Iraq, and dreamed of being king of a 'greater Syria'. But in the long run he was always brought to heel and supported Britain, which continued to subsidise him and maintain the Arab Legion of 8,000 men under Glubb. At the time of the Rashid Ali crisis in Iraq in 1941 when Britain had to suppress a potentially pro-Axis *coup d'état*, Abdullah allowed Britain to make use of the Legion.

Until the end of the Second World War, Transjordan was part of the Palestine mandate. Abdullah requested termination of the mandate in regard to Jordan in recognition of his support during the war. The country became an emirate in

February 1946, under its new name. It was an independent kingdom, approved by the United Nations but denounced by both Zionists and Arabs, who saw independence as indirect British control of territory which should form part of Palestine, and to which both therefore had claims.

Abdullah, originally a probationary prince, was now king, and an old man. He was of the generation of Hashemites who had moved from Ottoman rule to British rule. His views had not moved in a nationalist direction as the years passed; in fact, he was considerably more pro-British now than he had been when he was first installed. He signed an old-fashioned treaty with the British in 1946 which followed the old pattern of giving Britain the right to keep troops in his kingdom for 25 years.

The Arab League criticised him bitterly. The days for this sort of relationship were long over. Abdullah sought to revise the 1946 Treaty. When he did so, there was resistance from Foreign Office officials, who did not favour steps that appeared to loosen Britain's control, but not from the new Foreign Secretary himself. Ernest Bevin was working to establish a fresh type of relationship with Arab states and agreed to loosen the chains. A new Transjordan Treaty was signed on 15 March 1948.

Novel currents were affecting the flow of events. Abdullah was assassinated at Friday prayers on 1 July 1951. His 15-year-old grandson, Hussein, was with him and chased after the gunman, who fired another round that hit a medal on the prince's chest. Within the year Hussein's father had abdicated because of mental illness and Hussein was king.

In November 1955, Eden sent his foreign secretary, Harold Macmillan, to attend a meeting of the Baghdad Pact in the city that gave the pact its name. Macmillan was impressed by the Turks and at their suggestion attempted to bring Jordan into the pact. He sent General Templer, CIGS, to Jordan in 1955. The Templer Mission was disastrously unsuccessful. Jordan declared that there would be no pacts with foreigners. Shortly afterwards, to demonstrate Jordan's independence, Hussein dismissed Glubb Pasha, the commander of the army for 26 years. In March 1957 when Hussein's rule was threatened, it was an American fleet that came to support him.

VIII

IRAQ

34

STRATEGY

1. Inchoate Plans

The approach to the creation of what was to be Iraq started as easily as the descent into hell. We have seen that at the outset of the war, British policy in regard to Mesopotamia was reasonably defined. This was because it was briefly the policy of largely just one agency, the Indian government, which simply wanted to see Mesopotamia, from Basra to Baghdad, part of the British Empire. Indian troops were assembled at Bahrain even before Britain was at war with Turkey.

By March 1917, 11 months after the siege of Kut, Baghdad was occupied by the British Military Expedition and the captured parts of Mesopotamia were ruled by a British administration composed of military forces and political officers entirely on the Indian model. Mosul, although intended for France's sphere of influence in Syria, was added.

The Indian government had taken care to do nothing to encourage the idea of independence for Mesopotamia. But policy began to fragment towards the end of the war, when London started to interfere rather more. When the British army, under General Maude, stood outside Baghdad, it seemed the time for a proclamation. The proclamation acknowledged the concept of Arab unity, and pointed towards the idea of independence for an Arab nation. The man who drafted it was Mark Sykes, and he let himself go: its contents reflected his dreams, rather than the policies of Wilson, or even Cox. Sykes luxuriated in the glories of Mesopotamian history going back to the time of the Mongols:

Your palaces have fallen into ruins, your gardens have sunken into desolation, and your forefathers and yourselves have groaned in bondage . . . It is the wish, not only of my King and his peoples, but also of the great Nations with whom he is in alliance, that you should prosper even as in the past, when your lands were fertile . . . and Baghdad was one of the wonders of the world.

You, the people of Baghdad, whose commercial professions and whose safety from oppression and invasion must ever be a matter of the closest concern to the British government, are not to understand that it is the wish of the British Government to impose upon you alien institutions. It is the hope of the British Government that the aspirations of your philosophers and writers shall be realized once again. The people of Baghdad shall flourish . . . under institutions which are in consonance with their sacred laws and their racial ideals.

Many noble Arabs have perished in the cause of Arab freedom, at the hands of those alien rulers, the Turks, who oppressed them. It is the determination of the Government of Great Britain and the great Powers allied to Great Britain that these noble Arabs shall not have suffered in vain. It is the desire and hope of the British people and the nations in alliance with them that the Arab race may rise again to greatness and renown among the peoples of the earth and that it shall bind itself to this end in unity and concord.

A worrying number of hostages were being given to fortune with these references to pan-Arab nationalism, but more practical promises followed, with an invitation 'to you to assume the management of your civil affairs in collaboration with the political representatives of Great Britain who accompany the British Army . . . through your nobles and elders and representatives', specifically in order that 'you may unite with your kinsmen in the North, East, South and West in realizing the aspirations of your race'.

The terms of the proclamation which Maude had to deliver had been considered and approved by a committee of the Cabinet which was composed of Curzon, Hardinge, Milner and Austen Chamberlain. One Sykes phrase about the Arabs of Iraq and Baghdad being 'a free people . . . under their own institutions and laws' was rejected as being too explicit a promise of independence, but there was enough left for Wilson to claim that 'few more remarkable documents' had ever received Cabinet approval.[1]

It is almost superfluous to note that there was a total absence of any settled policy. In November 1914, on board the SS *Multan*, Arnold Wilson 'in an idle half hour in a P&O saloon' wrote to Colonel Charles Yate, MP, suggesting that 'in the annexation of Mesopotamia may be found the solution of some of the most difficult questions that must arise in India after the war'. His scheme was a grandiose one, involving irrigating and cultivating huge areas of the desert and peopling them with India's surplus population, to the extent of 25 million colonists. There was nothing in it for the Arabs of whom there would be just one for every ten Indians, but there would be 'no trouble from [them]': they would 'gladly accept British rule as they have done in Basrah'. The scheme was for the benefit of 'Mohammedan India . . ., a *quid pro quo* for its action in the war . . . I should like to see it announced that Mesopotamia was to be annexed to India as a colony for India and Indians, that the Government of India would administer it, and gradually bring under cultivation its vast unpopulated desert plains, peopling them with martial races from the Punjab'.[2] Irrigation in India itself could not be developed further but acquisition of Mesopotamia would permit the irrigation of 'millions' of new acres.

Wilson's proposal was never going to appeal to the government. At this stage Asquith and Grey were against taking over *any* Ottoman territories, even though they had supported Russian annexation of Constantinople – though Asquith noted that the rest of Cabinet were not quite as committed to pure Liberalism as he and his Foreign Secretary. 'Grey and I are the *only* men who doubt and distrust any such settlement, he told Venetia Stanley. Wilson was obliged to disavow his idea, and he never referred to it again. But it had been more than a daydream in the P&O saloon. He had taken care over who it should be shared with. Yate had been a soldier and then an Indian civil servant. In the middle of a confrontation with the Russians in a frontier dispute he had once invited the Russian officers to dine with him between the opposing lines of troops. Champagne toasts were exchanged in no-man's-land, but the Russians seized the disputed territory at dawn the following morning. When Yate returned from India to Britain and entered Parliament, he did so, as he explained to Curzon, 'to join in the fray on behalf of Imperialism as opposed to Little Englandism'; and he was the ideal man to promote Indian expansion.

In March 1917, on the day after Maude's proclamation was issued, Churchill established a committee to consider the position of the Baghdad Vilayet and the Basra Vilayet. Curzon chaired this Mesopotamia Administration Committee, 'the MAC', subsequently the Middle East Committee, said by Lord Robert Cecil to be hated by every Department of State. Cecil was well qualified to judge: he was Assistant Under-Secretary of State for Foreign Affairs right from 1915 to 1919, an office which he combined at one point with being the nicely named minister for blockade, before becoming Assistant Secretary of State for Foreign Affairs, and thus deputy to his cousin, Arthur Balfour. Sir Arthur Hirtzel, Sir Thomas Holderness and Sir John Shuckburgh, all advocates of a forward policy in Mesopotamia, attended. Hirtzel was a grand old man of the India Office whose name has been mentioned already. He had started as private secretary to Morley when he was Secretary of State, and was involved in formulating the Morley–Minto Reforms. He went upwards through the Office to end as Permanent Under-Secretary of State from 1924 to 1930.

Holderness was another India Office man. Shuckburgh started out as one, but when Churchill became Colonial Secretary and asked Hirtzel to work with him there, the latter declined and recommended Shuckburgh. Shuckburgh was transferred to the Colonial Office and the new Middle East

Department that Churchill had established. He was a very effective administrator, particularly involved in Palestine policy, where he accepted the
pro-Zionist bias that the government wanted, writing to Churchill that 'we
are committed to this policy and have got to make the best of it'. He was a
realist: 'We are confronted with two distinct obligations . . . it will be a difficult and dangerous task'.[4]

The MAC's secretary was Sykes. He wanted the Foreign Office to administer
Iraq; others wanted it to go to India, as 'the prize for which the Indian Army is
fighting' and which Chamberlain said 'Indian blood had won'. The decision
was a compromise: London would be responsible, but Delhi would be the executive agency. Basra would be under direct rule, but Baghdad would have a local
ruler. Indian officials should not be employed in Basra, and would not be
employed in Baghdad. The Iraq legal code, based on the Indian model, applied
in Basra but would not be extended to Baghdad.

The men on the spot did not necessarily agree with MAC's conclusions. Cox
did not think Basra and Baghdad could each be administered differently, and
Indian administrators could not be done without. Moreover there was tension
between the men on the spot. Sykes managed to get the Foreign Office to
instruct Maude to promote the Arab policy. This tended to bring him into
conflict with Cox. But there were differences between Maude and London too.
He wanted British administrators. Hirtzel, then secretary of the Political
Department of the India Office, said, 'the existing administrative machinery is
as far as possible to be preserved for the present with the substitution of Arab
for Turkish spirit and personnel. The façade must be Arab.'[5] Stanley Maude had
been appointed GOC in July 1916 at the quite early age of 52. His appointment was part of a military reorganisation in Mesopotamia after the fall of Kut
and the mismanagement that was revealed. He had done well at the Dardanelles.
He was an able and popular commander who got things done – if need be by
getting involved in detail. He had views of his own. He believed that 'before
any truly Arab façade can be applied to [the] edifice, it seems essential that
foundation of law and order should be well and truly laid'.[6] From the point of
view of sound construction principles his opinion cannot be challenged.

In Hirtzel's view, the proclamation ignored existing commitments to
Hussein. Hirtzel argued for an un-Indian regime which would recognise the
Arab character of the country. There would be a minimum number of British
advisers, and the Indian army's enthusiasm for Indian methods would be kept
in check. Iraq was to be run like an Indian princely state, but out of India and
out of the hands of the India Office. Sykes was also prominent among those who
were anxious that Mesopotamia should be under Foreign Office control and not
that of the Indian government. That was all very well, but the people on the

ground, like Cox and Wilson, inevitably came with an approach conditioned by their Indian background.

The government was indecisive. There was much committee work and much discussion, but no really forceful attempt to resolve the competing points of view or to press for a definitive formula. Finally the idea of leaving the India Office as a local executive agency was amended: India would control southern Persia, Muscat and the southern and western sides of the Persian Gulf. The Foreign Office, via Cairo, would control the rest. The government of India was agreeable to this if an 'alternative field of expansion' could be found – otherwise 'bitter and legitimate resentment' would arise![7] No wonder Hirtzel was worried about 'Indianization'.

The War Office was also involved in departmental bickering. Sir William Robertson, chief of the Imperial General Staff, agreed to the appointment of Cox as Civil Commissioner in Mesopotamia, but only on condition that General Maude was to be accepted as 'the ultimate seat of authority'.[8] Poor Cox had to look in several directions at the same time: he was also to report regularly to the India Office to take account of their sensibilities.

But it was worse than that. Apart from the fact that some wanted an Indian Mesopotamia and some wanted an Arab Mesopotamia, there were many – Chamberlain, for example – who did not want Britain saddled with Mesopotamia at all. By 1918 – indeed in the course of 1917 – it was pretty clear that neither Basra nor the Baghdad Vilayet could fail to be retained by Britain, partly to secure the area from a revived Germany or Russia. Even so, right up to the last, there were those, like Churchill, who greatly doubted the wisdom of accepting the mandate for Mesopotamia, Irak or Iraq, as it was successively called.

2. Searching for Policy

In 1917 a French consul was appointed to Baghdad. Apart from other worries, there was concern that the appointment might affect the Red Sea ports to which Britain had so far not appointed officials. There was also concern that a peace treaty might be concluded which would rest on the principle of mutual relinquishment of conquests. The alarming significance of that idea lay in the fact that Britain was the only Entente ally which had made conquests. France and Russia had not; neither had the Central Powers, Germany, Austria, Hungary and Bulgaria. Basra could therefore be at risk. Britain considered nursing local elements which would favour Britain and generally secure Mesopotamia under British influence.

For Mesopotamia the last year or so of the war was then one of great confusion. There was serious hostility between the chief political officer, Cox, and

General Sir Stanley Maude, GOC Mesopotamia until November 1917. Cox came close to resigning. He told Storrs, visiting Baghdad in May 1917, that his position as High Commissioner-Elect was unworkable, not least because of 'an omnipotent and unworkable general'. Maude was a good soldier, but 'purely a soldier', and he did not understand 'the East or Orientals'. Cox wanted his precedence established.

Maude really was quite difficult. He did not want any political officers. All he needed were intelligence officers under his command. After all, there were no political officers with the Army in France. Gertrude Bell despaired: 'That we shall ever be able to pursue a reasonable policy under Maude I don't believe . . . [But] the W[ar] O[ffice] can't be expected to remove the one successful General of the War.'[9]

Cox withdrew his threat of resignation: he was prepared to be High Commissioner, provided this 'did not connote any more extensive introduction of the Arab Administration than was recently agreed upon'. In July 1917 he was made not that, but 'Civil Commissioner', a novel title and a compromise. Cox's authority was enhanced and a hint of eventual superiority was made, but for the moment he continued to report through the GOC.

The conflict was finally resolved when Maude died in November 1917. He was entertaining a visiting American journalist, Mrs Egan, by taking her to a performance of *Hamlet* in Arabic. He was offered coffee, to which he added a 'large quantity of cold, raw milk' which was infected with cholera. He died four days later. His successor, Sir William Marshall, was fully occupied by his military duties, under pressure from the government to push further forward into Persia as Russia collapsed and Ottoman resistance crumbled. He had no time to quarrel with Cox.

By late 1917 Wilson was pressing for an investigatory commission, first mooted a year earlier, to decide on a huge raft of practical issues relating to Mesopotamia, issues on which no decisions had yet been made. He was supported by Cox and Marshall, the new GOC Mesopotamia. On the other hand, there were those at home, like Curzon, who felt that the idea was premature and would present a peace conference with an apparent fait accompli. There was no unanimity on the issue. The commission was vetoed at the Middle East Committee.

In November 1918 the Foreign Office published a memorandum in regard to the settlement of Turkey and the Arabian Peninsula which summarised the whole range of commitments by which Britain was already constrained, starting as far back as the *Règlement Organique* of the Lebanon Vilayet of 9 June 1861, concluding with the Joint Anglo-French Declaration about Syria and Mesopotamia of 9 November 1918, and taking in the Understanding with

King Hussein of the Hejaz ('not embodied in any single instrument . . .'), the Treaty of 1915 with Ibn Saud and the letter of 2 November 1917 from Mr Balfour to Lord Rothschild.

The paper went on to consider Britain's '*Desiderata*' (an archaic word even then); and then 'Policy', 'in which suggestions are put forward for the *revision* [my emphasis]' of commitments 'if and when opportunities offer in the course of negotiations' so that they did not conflict with *Desiderata*. Commitments were not to be allowed to get in the way of *Desiderata*.

Britain's general commitments were interpreted on a fairly restrictive basis: the government had 'declared in a general way that the non-Turkish populations shall be liberated from Turkish misrule and given an opportunity of national life and economic development'. It was stressed in regard to commitments to King Hussein that Hussein had 'claimed the boundaries of Arab independence to which we have assented, not in his own name, but as the spokesman of the various populations, and our pledge was given to him in this capacity only'.

It is interesting in view of what failed to happen later that the paper was more outspoken about Armenia than about most other issues: 'It is clearly incumbent upon us to put an end to these wrongs to humanity [the massacres and misrule] and violations of an international treaty [the Treaty of Berlin, 1878] to which we are a party, now that it lies within our power to do so.'

Overall, the conclusion was that the various commitments made to the Arab rulers, far from tying Britain's hands, had established for her a special position in most of the Arab area, to the exclusion of other outside powers. They were permissive rather than restrictive.

The *Desiderata* varied from the very vague ('maintenance of pre-existing British rights, relations, facilities') to the very specific. The Black Sea Straits were to be under international control. Outside powers were to have as limited a place in the area as possible. Britain already had a role in the Trucial States, some 11 sheikhdoms in the Persian Gulf which were allied to Britain in the Perpetual Maritime Truce of 1852. The Trucial system was at the heart of the pre-war nexus of alliances and zones of influence on which the Empire's safety rested. On the basis of the Trucial system and traditional links with many of the ruling families, like the sheikhs of Kuwait, Bahrain, Qatar and Oman, Britain had been the dominant power in the Gulf in the eighteenth and nineteenth centuries. The paper stressed that 'a Trucial system to be effective must be in the hands of a single Power'.

Where, as in Mesopotamia, the state of the country was so backward that a Trucial system could not operate, Britain should be responsible for an indefinite period for administration – but that emphatically did not amount to annexation, which would carry unwanted responsibilities and might impede an ultimate Arab national revival. The situation in regard to Syria was a little more complicated, and there the matters had to be kept open for the moment.[10]

In terms of Sykes–Picot, part of Iraq was to go to France. France gave that up at the Downing Street meeting and Versailles, as we saw, in exchange for Syria and some of the Mosul oil. The whole of Iraq, the vilayets of Basra, Baghdad and Mosul, would thus become a single British mandatory state. Avi Shlaim put it vividly, though a little unkindly to Churchill, because the whole thing was not really his idea: 'Iraq was created by Churchill, who had the mad idea of joining two widely separated oil wells, Kirkuk and Mosul, by uniting three widely separated peoples: the Kurds, the Sunnis, and the Shiites'.[11]

The three Ottoman provinces in Mesopotamia which were arbitrarily put together to form Iraq certainly had little in common. To the north there was the mountainous Mosul. The central province of Baghdad was agricultural. Basra traded with India and the Persian Gulf. There was no shared political identity, and the different parts were among the most ethnically and religiously diverse of the region. Eighty per cent of the inhabitants were Arabs, of whom rather more than half were Shiites, linked with the *ulama* of Iran. Twenty per cent were Kurds, predominantly Sunni Muslims but ethnically, culturally and linguistically distinct from the rest of Iraq. They resisted centralisation. In the north there was a Syrian Christian minority, and in Baghdad there was a substantial Jewish community.

Confusion in Eastern policy was nothing new. One study of Britain and the Eastern Question ends as follows:

Of all the impressions left by a study of the Eastern Question, perhaps the strongest is of the awesomely slender strands on which great powers were obliged to base major policy decisions, of the entire inaccuracy of using the terms 'Britain', 'Russia', 'Austria', 'France', 'Germany' to describe the two or three worried but hopeful men who usually took decisions in their country's name. The statement 'Britain decided to discontinue support for Turkey' might really mean 'the Prime Minister persuaded by two slightly better informed Cabinet Ministers, a newspaper proprietor and an awkward Admiralty report, reluctantly agreed to abandon all that he had previously stood for' – or, alternatively, 'The Foreign Secretary, impressed by a memorandum from a young F.O. adviser, and by the arguments of a deputation of Liverpool merchants, has informed the Prime Minister that previous assumptions about British interests had been false, and that new instructions must therefore be sent to the ambassador in Constantinople'. Equally, the statement 'Britain decided to *continue* support for Turkey' might mean 'The Prime

Minister has been unable to think out any better election-winner than to resurrect the policy of one of his predecessors. He hopes public opinion, or at least the London mob will be impressed'. There is not much exaggeration in these paraphrases. The decision-making apparatus of all the great powers was exceedingly informal, flexible, and by design almost, amateurish.[12]

The fluidity of policy-making cannot really be overemphasised. The different agencies, with their different objectives, never combined to agree on a settled policy. Committees were established almost on a whim. Despite their resonant titles, they could be insubstantial creatures. Their existence depended largely on the strength of the personality of the chairman and secretary. Some met regularly but their decisions meant nothing. Others simply stopped meeting and functioning. If there was not a dynamic behind the committee it disappeared very quickly. All of these new bodies were created as a reaction to new circumstances, desperate attempts which often failed to address desperate situations.

Curzon said to Robert Cecil on 6 January 1918, 'There is or was a Committee of the Cabinet of which I am or was Chairman and of which Sykes is or was Secretary. We used to have frequent meetings and all the earlier Mesopotamian and Hejaz policy was formulated by us. The Foreign Secretary was of course present whenever he desired. Now I have observed that no questions are referred to us. We have not been summoned for some 2 months & the Foreign Office policy as regards these countries is formulated and published without any reference to us at all.'[13]

Cecil responded by writing to Balfour:

George [Curzon] holds strongly to [the Persia Committee] as he does to another body called the Middle East Committee: the function of which appears to be to enable George Curzon and Mark Sykes to explain to each other how very little they both know about the subject. An attempt by me to smother decorously both Committees was detected by George and had to be abandoned. They are now to meet regularly on Saturday mornings: a time fixed with the hope that it may ultimately prove discouraging to their existence.[14]

So as the war entered its last stages, no one in London or in Mesopotamia knew what would happen to the huge new territories which Britain found herself controlling. At the Trades Union League meeting at Caxton Hall on 5 January 1918, which has been mentioned already in connection with the doctrine of self-determination, Lloyd George seemed to be moving to a

Wilsonian position. He departed entirely from schemes of protectorates and spheres of influence: the constituent parts of the Ottoman Empire – including Arabia, Syria, Palestine and Mesopotamia – were 'entitled to a recognition of their separate national conditions'.[15] Sykes was moving in a similar direction. In his memorandum, 'The Position in Mesopotamia in relation to The Spirit of the Age', he made proposals for Arab development which Hirtzel dismissed as a scheme 'evolved from the inner consciousness of Sykes or others without any contact with the facts on the spot (which are very imperfectly known to us)'.[16] Sykes may have meant what he said; Lloyd George did not.

Those on the spot, and Hirtzel who was not, were not keen on self-determination. They reached that conclusion by different routes. Hirtzel did not want to see Basra, acquired as a matter of policy by Britain at some cost, thrown away. If self-determination were to be applied it could be applied, in Shuckburgh's delightful phrase, 'speciously, at any rate'.[17] Gertrude Bell, on the other hand, whose motivation was a more unselfish concern for the Arabs, did not see that their interest would best be served by leaving them to look after themselves. Cox went back to London to consult, leaving Arnold Wilson as Officiating Civil Commissioner. Local policy was the synthesis of tensions between Allenby in Cairo and Arnold Wilson in Baghdad.

35

ESTABLISHMENT

1. Early Years

In 1918 Cox left Baghdad to be ambassador to Persia at Teheran. Arnold Wilson was left as Acting Civil Commissioner. But Cox continued to be very influential. His opinion was repeatedly requested, and in no time at all he was brought back to deal with Iraq again. For the next two years, Wilson, an active and practical man, had the frustrating experience of being refused any guidance from London, despite his repeated requests, on how he should run his country. He made innumerable suggestions, none of them silly, but London would simply neither endorse nor reject them. The Foreign Office wanted nothing done until peace had been made with Turkey and a mandate awarded.

As the year came to an end Gertrude Bell was enjoying herself hugely, revisiting the ground she had extensively traversed, drawing frontiers where none had existed before. Her remit ranged from designing flags to educating the women: 'We must give the girls an opportunity for self-expression. If you only knew the harems as I do, you would have pity upon the women.'

In London there were those who were thinking of an independent Mesopotamia; not everyone in Iraq wanted independence. The Naqib of Baghdad, the Sunni religious leader, deprecated even the idea of a poll, which he considered to be a personal folly of Arnold Wilson, a man to be contrasted with Sir Percy Cox: 'There are a hundred and a thousand men in England who could fill the post of ambassador in Persia [where Cox now was], but there is none but Sir Percy Cox who is suitable for Iraq.' The Naqib asked Gertrude Bell to tell London that 'we wish to be governed by Sir Percy Cox'. He had no time for the unrealistic notion of self-determination, the dream of the American president, 'Sheikh Wilson'. 'Does Sheikh Wilson know the East and its peoples? Does he know our way of life and our habits of mind? You English have governed for three hundred years in Asia and your rule is an example for all men to follow. Pursue your own way.'[1]

Gertrude Bell returned to London for consultations in 1920. In her memorandum, *Self-Determination in Mesopotamia*, she had argued that prior to the

Anglo-French Declaration of Arab Liberation, most Arabs expected to remain under British rule. The declaration had accelerated the demand for independence. That acceleration, in turn, had alarmed conservative elements so that there was now a direct confrontation between the supporters and opponents of independence.

The Wilson–Bell relationship was always dodgy. He did not miss her while she was in London and took the opportunity to dismantle the Arab Bureau office in Baghdad. He was apprehensive when he heard that she was returning to Baghdad in the autumn of 1920: 'I shall be interested to know what Miss Bell is going to do when she comes here. She will take some handling.'[2]

Wilson was right to be apprehensive. Gertrude Bell was starting to reverse her previous views, and during her time away, as a result of her contact with Faisal and Lawrence at the Paris Peace Conference, she had become convinced of the need for Arab independence. *Self-Determination* itself foresaw Arab self-rule. Wilson repudiated this view, but he was increasingly out of touch with developing policy. *The Times* described him as 'a sun-dried bureaucrat set on Indianizing Mesopotamia'.[3] That was a bit extreme for a newspaper of record, but it is certainly true that Wilson did not approve of the idea that Iraq should gently move towards independence. Since Gertrude Bell spoke for the policy of Arab independence, her efforts to promote it brought her into increasingly open conflict with him. He believed that Gertrude Bell was intriguing behind his back with Edwin Montagu, who was Secretary of State for India from 1917 to 1922. She was not truly intriguing, but she certainly sought to press her views at every opportunity.

Wilson complained to Montagu. Bell received a rap over the knuckles from Montagu: 'I should be glad if you would either ask the Civil Commissioner [Wilson] to communicate [your views] or apply for leave and come home and represent them. You may always be sure of consideration of your views but Political Officers should be very careful of their private correspondence with those not at present in control of affairs.' Miss Bell submitted gracefully: 'With regard to correspondence except for private letters to my Father I cannot recall letters on political subjects to unofficial persons which have not been previously submitted to Colonel Wilson. Your remarks are however a useful warning.'[4] In any event she and Wilson were now permanently estranged.

2. A Mandate?

Even after the Peace Conference, Britain was far from convinced that she should remain in Mesopotamia. In 1920 her presence in the region required 17,000 British and 44,000 Indian troops. A further 23,000 troops were in Palestine, and the total cost was £33.5 million a year. Asquith, among others, argued that

Britain needed no more than Basra with its port. Lloyd George was now the strongest opponent of abandonment. He was particularly aware of the oil resources of Mosul. The government view prevailed, although not without opposition and internal debate; a commission was formed to request a British mandate.

When the news reached Baghdad on 1 May 1920, Wilson sought to remove any sting by issuing a communiqué saying that the objective was no more than to create 'a healthy body politic' with Britain as 'a wise and far-seeing guard-ian': there would be in due course, an independent Arab state of Iraq.[5] Despite his efforts, there was much opposition. The mandate seemed to betray the Anglo-French Declaration and the promise of self-determination. Wilson was at a loss. He had not wanted an Arab government, but he found himself obliged to talk about an independent Arab state. He did not want an immediate consti-tution, but was obliged to ask the Foreign Office if he could publish proposals for one. He asked London if he could be replaced by Sir Percy Cox. London would neither let him go nor let him have his constitution.

The news of Britain's application for the mandate had been unhelpfully formal in its tone. No thought was given to public relations. What Britain was doing sounded to the Arabs pretty like annexation. When the mandate was actually awarded on 28 April 1920, London announced that steps would be taken to draw up proposals to create 'a form of civil administration based on representative institutions which would prepare the world for the creation of an independent Arab State of Iraq'.[6] That did not sound too imperialistic, but the damage was done, and the consequence was the Euphrates Revolt of 1920.

3. The Year of Catastrophe

Nineteen-twenty is known in Arab history as the Year of Catastrophe. It was marked by risings in protest against the settlements in various Arab countries. Indeed during the whole decade of the 1920s Arab resentment at the loss of Palestine, Syria, Lebanon and Mesopotamia was expressed in outbreaks of violence throughout Mesopotamia. Those who sympathised with Arab aspira-tions, such as Gertrude Bell, pointed out that they had always predicted this. Britain did not know what to do. Churchill said there were no troops available. The reaction of many was to question the worth of the new possessions.

The rebellion was akin to *jihad*, precipitated by a number of causes: the replacement of Ottoman informality by what Wilson called the 'steel frame' of British rule, with its inflexible tax collection and rigid, official methods. They jarred with the new concepts of nationalism and the unity of Islam.

General Coningham halted the rebel seizure of Rumaitha, at the cost of the lives of five British officers and 30 Indian soldiers. Wilson was alarmed by the extent of the rebellion. He sent a telegram to Churchill asking for a division, rather than a brigade 'to give those Arabs on the lower Euphrates a good lesson'.[7] He was disappointed that Churchill's reaction to his demand was to talk of expense.

Between June and October there were some 10,000 casualties. Arab casualties totalled 8,000, which included perhaps 4,000 Arabs killed. The military commander, General Sir Aylmer Haldane, told his men to 'be as rough as nutmeg graters'. The risings were suppressed brutally. Villages were burned, crops were destroyed, ringleaders were summarily executed. Huge numbers ignominiously disarmed and passed 'beneath the Caudine Forks', as the classically educated general put it.[8] Britain lost 426 British and Indian troops dead, 1,228 wounded, 615 missing. Some political officers were killed. Initially the participants were mainly tribal chiefs and those who had fought in the Arab revolt, but a religious dimension developed as Shiites joined the struggle.[9]

Among those killed was Colonel Gerard Leachman. Leachman was another of the courageous and hardy officers, travellers, spies and political advisers that the region seemed to attract. He covered huge areas in his travels across the desert, and in 1909 found himself in Mesopotamia along with some of the other larger-than-life characters of the region, like Shakespear and Lawrence, who were amassing information for Britain in her competition with Germany, combining scholarship and espionage. In March 1915, he was involved in setting up an intelligence network behind enemy lines. He was not impressed by the irregular Arab cavalry, 'careering impertinently' around.[10] Later he was formally designated 'O.C. Desert'. His meeting with Faisal and Lawrence at Wajh in May 1917 was described by one who was there: 'Lawrence in sumptuous Arab clothing, and Leachman in his army khakis: Faysal's [sic] aristocratic charm, Leachman's straightforwardness, Lawrence's condescending superiority'.[11]

Leachman had not been impressed by the Arab Revolt, and he was sceptical about the post-war campaign for Arab independence. His bravest of many brave exploits was at Kut. As a result of his courage in entering the city, some 5,000 troops were able to escape, avoiding the terrible fate that awaited those who were captured.

36

CHURCHILL AND MESOPOTAMIA

There was some splendid doggerel about the loot and money, *lakhs*, that Mesopotamia would provide:

> L is the Loot we hope we shall seize –
> Wives and wine and bags of Rupees,
> When the Mayor of Baghdad hands over the keys
> To the British in Mesopotamia.[1]

Another piece was enclosed with a letter from Hirtzel to Chamberlain on 8 October 1920. It referred to Karind in the Zagros Mountains in Persia, where the British High Command established their hill station:

> Half a lakh, half a lakh squandered,
> Up to the Persian Hills GHQ wandered . . .
> Think of the camp they made.
> Think of the water laid
> On, and the golf links made.
> Think of the bill we paid.
> Oh, the wild charge they made!
> Half a lakh squandered.

The truth was that taking on Mesopotamia cost money and did not make it, and it fell to Churchill, first as Secretary for War, and then as Colonial Secretary, to control that cost.

As he prepared to take over responsibility for colonial affairs in 1919, and particularly for the Middle East, Churchill found himself moving apart from the prime minister, Lloyd George. He still felt himself bound to him by ties of gratitude and because of their long friendship, but things were not the same as before. Some differences could be ignored, but it was impossible to ignore them all. There was a direct divergence between the two in the area of Churchill's new departmental responsibilities.

Churchill was entitled to consider that he knew a thing or two about the Colonial Office. His first ministerial office, in 1905, had been Under-Secretary at the Colonial Office. He was never accustomed to stand back in the shadows, and as the Colonial Secretary was the Earl of Elgin, it was Churchill who spoke for the department in the Commons. Indeed, overall, he had a far wider experience of office than the prime minister. But since the Peace Conference, Lloyd George had found it much more interesting to deal with broad issues of foreign policy than with the details of domestic politics. Now he tended to a hawkish approach to the Turks. Churchill took a more conciliatory view for reasons of grand strategy – to preserve a balance of power – and for the pragmatic reason that Britain, with all her Muslim subjects, should not antagonise a leading Muslim power. In 1920 there were nearly 87 million Muslims in the British Empire, 600,000 in Palestine, 250,000 in Jordan and 3 million in Iraq. The total was more than six times the population of Turkey.[2]

Churchill's relationship with his chief was still a relaxed one. They met at several house parties over the 1920 Christmas recess and got on well. Indeed Churchill could still be amazed by Lloyd George's brilliance. It was in predominantly a sense of benign reflection that he wrote a letter of 4 December 1920:

My dear Prime Minister,

I am vy sorry to see how far we are drifting apart on foreign policy. No doubt my opinions seem a vy unimportant thing. But are you sure that about Turkey the line wh you are forcing us to pursue wd commend itself to the present H of C? I feel vy deeply that it is most injurious to the interests we have specially to guard in India & the Middle East . . .

In the military circles whose opn it is my duty to understand there is universal disagreement and protest. These circles exercise much influence on the Conservative Party . . . It wd be quite easy for you to be vexed with me & to override any counsels I may offer in all goodwill & sincerity. It wd be vy easy for me to sit still & let events take their course. I do not often trouble you with letters; but I feel I owe it to you & to yr long friendship & many kindnesses to send a solemn warning of the harm wh yr policy – so largely a personal policy – is doing to the unity & cohesion of several important elements of opinion on wh you have hitherto been able to rely.

Moreover it seems to me a most injurious thing that we, the greatest Mohammedan Empire in the world, shd be the leading Anti-Turk power. The desire you have to retain Mosul – & indeed Mesopotamia – is directly frustrated by this vendetta against the Turks.[3]

It is interesting to see that although he was so often characterised as extravagant and imperialistic, Churchill was at this time so strong for financial and territorial retrenchment. He was convinced that 'the burden of carrying out the present policy at Constantinople, in Palestine, Egypt, Mesopotamia and Persia is beyond the strength of the British Army and is producing [the] most formidable reaction upon the Indian Army'. He was for making peace with the Turks, and did not welcome the fact that 'we, the greatest Mohammedan power in the world, should] be the leading Anti-Turk power'. He did not share Lloyd George's appetite for Mesopotamia. When he could not lobby Lloyd George, he attacked Cox: 'It is impossible for us to throw upon the British taxpayer the burdens for military expenditure in Mesopotamia which are entailed for [*sic*] your present schemes for holding the country'.[4]

At the War Office Churchill's personal inclinations were in general reinforced by the advice of his professional adviser, the chief of the Imperial General Staff, Sir Henry Wilson, who advocated withdrawal from most of Palestine, Mesopotamia and Persia.[5] As well as military logistics and the constraints of finance, inept administrative arrangements niggled. Churchill complained that there could be no sensible administration of the Middle East when the Foreign Office, the Indian Office and the Middle Eastern Department all had hands in it.

For the moment order had been re-established by severe retribution and the discovery that aircraft were the cheapest way of policing the new possessions. At a time of serious economic constraint in Britain, the cost of the military exercise was substantial, over £40 million. The Royal Air Force could bomb and strafe the rebels at no great risk to aircraft and crew and at relatively low cost. In his anxiety for efficiency and economy, Churchill, surprisingly for a man of such humanity, rejected advice that poisoned gas was undesirable because of its horrible effects and the risk to civilians: 'I can't understand why it shd be thought legitimate to kill people with bullets, and barbarism to make them sneeze.'[6]

Low-flying skeletal De Havilland biplanes, which flew at no more than 114 miles an hour, dropped 20-pound high explosive bombs to keep the peace and to ensure that the taxes flowed. When Glubb stayed with Sufran tribesmen, he was asked why he was working on a map. He 'candidly told them I was preparing the map to be used for the bombing, and that I myself would have to be in the leading aircraft'.[7]

The RAF was perfectly frank: 'We rely on "frightfulness" in a more or less severe form'.[8] The Labour MP George Lansbury spoke for a tiny minority of aware and humane people in Britain when he complained about 'this Hunnish and barbarous method of warfare against unarmed people'.[9]

The humane alternative to frightfulness was to replace Wilson with Cox and to install an Arab figurehead, in the shape of Faisal.

37

NATION-BUILDING

1. Sir Percy Cox Returns

For the moment, and in the absence of other voices, Arnold Wilson had more influence than anyone else on the future of Mesopotamia. The creation of Iraq, the idea of bringing together Basra, Baghdad and Mosul was in large part his. He envisaged the creation of a single and valuable possession for Britain rather than foreseeing the tensions and centripetal forces. It is easy to caricature Wilson – a supporter of Hitler in his later life – but the reality was much more complex and his opponents never really understood him.

Cox was much more comprehensible, and people generally liked what they saw. The Arabs were pleased when 'Kokkus' returned as High Commissioner to replace Wilson. He arrived on 11 October 1920. Gertrude Bell was delighted and moved. She had always liked Cox. She had been charmed by the daily tea parties on the deck of his boat at Basra in 1916. Now she was weak at the knees. 'When he came into the enclosure Sir Edgar [Bonham Carter] presented me [and] while I made my curtsey, it was all I could do not to cry.'[1]

He arrived very soon after the risings in the Baghdad Vilayet. As soon as the presentations were over, he, Bell and Philby sat down. 'He said he intended to set up an Arab Ministry at once as a temporary expedient without waiting for a complete pacification of the country. His scheme was to call on someone to form a cabinet and he himself would appoint British Advisers to the Ministers.' Cox and Philby did not have a relationship that lasted. Cox found Philby's views diverged too much to be able to work with him. He never lost confidence in Bell, and she never lost her admiration and affection for him: 'From the first moment [of his return] I saw that all was well.'[2] How different from Arnold Wilson.

Cox's policy had not been authorised without considerable debate in London, where cutting losses, abandoning the mandate and evacuation had not been ruled out. Cox had argued against abandoning £7 million or £8 million worth of assets, breaking wartime promises to the Arabs and

subjecting them to 'chaos and the hated yoke of the Turk as soon as we left'.[3]
While he was far from confident that a national government would necessarily work, he saw it as a risk worth taking and preferable to evacuation. The attractions of Iraq for Britain were the communications link with India and the opportunity to exploit the oilfields. The difficulty was how to secure these benefits without the cost of direct government. The answer appeared to be a mandate, leading to a treaty with a subservient Iraqi government which would be left to run the place.

Churchill, as Secretary of State for War from 1917 to 1919 had two associated and essential aims. There had been breakdowns of discipline among soldiers who were desperate to return home. His response was to devise a humane and speedy system of demobilisation. It was also essential for the country, indebted as it was, to scale down its military expenditure. So far as Mesopotamia was concerned, Churchill wrote to the local commander, Sir George MacMunn, on 30 August 1919 saying that 13,000 of the 25,000 British troops there had to be sent home within the following three months; 45,000 of the 80,000 Indian forces were also to be repatriated. Churchill's priority was to concentrate available troops against the Bolshevik threat.[4]

So, after the risings the drive was first to keep Iraq governable and secondly to do so at reduced cost. When Churchill became Colonial Secretary in February 1921 he set up the conference in Cairo to sort out the Middle East which we have already attended. For Iraq one of the consequences of the conference was that he got his way in the matter of reducing the British military costs. Both British and Indian forces were greatly scaled down, and Churchill accepted Sir Hugh Trenchard's suggestion that Iraq could be kept in order by use of the Royal Air Force. The utility of the Royal Air Force in this sort of role had already been demonstrated in Somaliland.

Cox was as conciliatory as possible in the circumstances. He was careful to create an Arab façade. He set up a council, which he said was the provisional national government. An electoral law was planned to establish a constituent assembly and a constitution. There would be a national army. Behind the façade there would be a High Commissioner with a veto on council proposals and a British adviser shadowing and controlling each Arab minister.

But the pivotal means of achieving the combined objective of keeping the peace and doing so at reduced cost was to be the creation of a local government under a planted king. That would be the Emir Faisal. Why Emir Faisal, the commander of the Arab Revolt and the son of Sharif Hussein? A combination of a sense of responsibility to a protégé and a lack of alternatives.

2. The Insertion of Faisal

Kings for the countries of the new Middle East were a bit of a problem. Faisal had already been proclaimed king of Syria on 8 March 1920 by a congress set up by him or at least with his connivance. Britain suspected that France (whose allergy to him was not yet evident) might have engineered Faisal's nomination, and declined to accept the legitimacy of the nomination by an unrepresentative body which was not entitled to arrogate to itself the powers which were vested in the victorious powers. On the other hand, Allenby, on the spot, urged Curzon that Faisal should be recognised as the head of a confederation of Syria, Palestine and Mesopotamia. In the meantime the Damascus Assembly named Abdullah king of Mesopotamia. Arnold Wilson said that his nomination was unwelcome in Baghdad. In any event, he said, there was no support for the Allenby idea of one king for the whole region.

All this confusion about kings serves to emphasise that even in March 1920 there was no certainty that there would be a separate Iraq, or that it would be peculiarly Britain's responsibility. The decision to apply for a mandate was not made until several weeks later. Curzon realised that time was running out and Britain needed to make up her mind about what was to happen to Mesopotamia. There were widely differing views on what should be done. A decision was needed between the Direct Rule School and the Native State School. When Curzon reviewed the whole matter at an interdepartmental meeting on 13 April 1920, and a future constitution was considered, the India Office and the Foreign Office produced their own separate drafts.

Cox had returned to the question of a king in a telegram to the Secretary of State for India on 26 December 1920. The telegram was one of many in which Cox pointed out that misunderstandings were arising because the government had not been reading his telegrams carefully. He reminded the Secretary of State that when Faisal's candidature had been discussed in August 1920 the project had to be abandoned because of 'such a storm of opposition' from the French. Accordingly, he and his staff had been dodging questions about the future ruler of Mesopotamia. Now, however, he was confident that Faisal's candidature could be promoted, and he recommended opening the matter by inspiring 'a Reuter to the effect that the French had now withdrawn their opposition to Faisal's candidature . . . the placation of Mesopotamian candidates needs a little strategy, but I will submit my views on that point if occasion arises'.[5]

The emergence of Faisal, which was dealt with briefly in the context of Cairo, was quite a subtle affair. The Secretary of State replied to Cox on 31 December

1920 asking whether Faisal would be likely to be elected by notables. It is clear that what mattered to the government was their understanding that if Faisal were so elected, Cox would be able to reduce the army of occupation to one division and one brigade within 12 months. Cox replied two days later. Before he could get to grips with the question he had been asked, he had to dispose of a discrepancy between the Secretary of State's telegram and a War Office telegram to the General Officer Commanding in Iraq. He had thought that there had been a proposal from the War Office, and the War Office only, to withdraw to the Basra Vilayet. Now he had found that the Cabinet itself had taken a provisional decision to withdraw. He made it very clear that if the mandate were to be undertaken, Mosul and Baghdad had to be held as well as Basra. He considered that that could be done with one division and one brigade. If Baghdad and Mosul were not to be held then he considered that the mandate must be refused altogether and Basra retained under traditional British administration.

Having made his position clear on that point he turned to Faisal. It was 'extremely undesirable that I should queer the pitch by consulting notables of various elements of the population at this stage. His Majesty's Government must therefore accept or reject my personal opinion on the subject, and the initiative as regards Faisal must come from your side.' He saw the only other candidates inside Iraq as being Sayyid Talib and the Naqib. He counselled that Faisal should announce his candidature and immediately tell the Naqib that if elected he would hope that the Naqib would become the first president of council or prime minister. The Naqib would then tell Sayyid Talib that if he were appointed president of the council he would appoint Talib minister of the interior. Talib and the Naqib would ask Cox if Faisal had British support. Cox would reply that if the people of Iraq wanted him and the French did not oppose him, Britain would accept. He was confident that an announcement of such a fait accompli would be enough to ensure Faisal's installation, possibly without even the need for elections.[6]

But this smooth sequence of events was put at risk: Sayyid Talib started campaigning for appointment of the Naqib as king or emir. Now, fearing that Britain was backing Faisal, he briefed against not Cox, with whom he said he was 'wholly satisfied' but 'British officials in H.E.'s entourage [probably Gertrude Bell] who were known to be partisans and who were exercising undue influence'. He openly threatened armed insurrection by the Naqib, and an appeal 'to Islam, to India, Egypt, Constantinople and Paris'.[7]

By 24 January 1921 Cox was concerned by a growing 'no mandate' faction, and a significant swell of opinion for the appointment of a Turkish prince.[8] At the second meeting of the Political Committee of the Cairo Conference on 13

March 1921, Gertrude Bell argued all the same that Faisal would have an easy run. 'Sayid Talib might be expected to offer a certain amount of opposition, but it was probable that this would be negligible in contrast with the acclamation with which it was anticipated the Sharif would be received.'

So it was agreed at Cairo that Britain would back Faisal's nomination as the first king of the new kingdom. At the same time, Cox reported that things were moving in Baghdad and that there were suggestions that the Naqib should be the monarch, with the reversion for Talib. Ibn Saud had also thrown his hat into the ring, but was bought off by suitable British bribes. There was growing support for Talib with his slogan of 'Iraq for the Iraqis'. Faisal, it must be remembered, was not an Iraqi, nor did the Iraqis know anything about him. He was an exotic creature implanted by occupying forces. Cox produced a timetable for the process of choosing the monarch, and Churchill noted that it was generally thought that it was unnecessary for the proposed Council of Notables to be asked for its views on the appointment of the Sharif. '[I]t was felt that his presence in Irak would have such an inspiring effect upon the majority of the population that there was little to fear of any opposition to his candidature. It was impossible to give the Sharif a definite assurance to this effect, but he must take his chance.'[9]

But his chance could be improved by removing Talib from the scene, and his removal was like something from Sapper. He was invited to Lady Cox's Saturday tea party. When he left, Gertrude Bell escorted him to the front door and said good-bye. He had scarcely left the Embassy before his car was halted by a broken-down truck on a bridge. A British officer, acting on Cox's orders, arrested Talib and placed him in an armoured car. Philby said that 'the wiliest man in Arabia had walked into the simplest of traps'.[10] Talib was deported to Ceylon. This was Talib's final deportation: he had already been dumped out of the way in India early in 1916, shortly after the capture of Basra, as had been Nuri al-Said. This was Cox's way with difficult local leaders. Now, with Talib removed, he worked on the less threatening Naqib, convincing him that he was too old and frail for leadership. One result of this sort of policy was to deprive the new country of a generation of able and ambitious politicians.

Philby was Talib's British adviser, his monitor. He was loyal to Talib and hostile to the idea of a monarchy. He had already threatened to resign, but Cox had told him that the British had no intention of installing Faisal. Philby resented Gertrude Bell's support of Faisal. He snubbed her whenever they met and their long-standing friendship only just survived, and not for long. Now, with the arrest of Talib, Philby, like many others, was outraged. He protested to Cox and was dismissed.

There was no serious attempt to disguise the manipulative role of the British government. Lawrence discouraged Faisal from making any announcement about a modification of the mandate 'until he delivered his speech from the throne'. Churchill 'trusted that immediate signs of the approval of the people would be manifested'.[11]

Faisal arrived in Iraq in the summer of 1922. Gertrude Bell designed a flag for him and ceremonial for his court and together with Cox surrounded him with supporters. The British worked hard to ensure an overwhelming degree of support for his candidacy, and he became king on 23 August 1921. The malleability of complaisant officials is illustrated by the prefect in Kirkuk. He dutifully prepared a petition of support for Faisal, but when, wrongly, he heard that Britain had had a change of heart, speedily prepared an alternative duly signed petition against Faisal. He supplied both to his superiors, leaving them to choose which they wanted.

As between Faisal and the local pretenders, Britain had been very clearly in favour of the Sharifian, and had maintained the flimsiest illusion of neutrality. Despite that, Faisal was not nearly as grateful as Churchill thought he should be. Faisal opposed the mandate. Churchill wanted no nonsense about mandates. Faisal was to be told to come to heel and if he did not then Britain would simply clear out. Lloyd George discouraged this line of thinking. He was against scuttle generally and he was particularly concerned in the case of Iraq that if Britain pulled out the Americans or the French might find that the territory was full of oil.

The installation of Faisal, the outcome of great manipulation and persuasion, with the improbable claim that 96 per cent of those consulted had favoured him, meant that not only had Britain got a king for Iraq, but had it got a king who was, as they thought, Britain's creature. Gertrude Bell said, 'We have carried him on our shoulders.'[12] Since he had no national anthem of his own, he was crowned to the tune of the British national anthem. The spirit of Britishness continued. The Organic Law of 1925 would say that Iraq was a hereditary constitutional monarchy with a bicameral legislature, all as British as could be. Britain would then try to distance itself, so that Faisal did not appear to be their puppet; but he depended ultimately and always on the British Army and the Royal Air Force.

The choice of Faisal as king of Iraq has sometimes been described 'as a consolation prize for his eviction by the French from the throne of Syria'.[13] But if Britain was to choose a king of Iraq, it was pretty obvious that the choice would be Faisal. His links with British decision makers – and not only Lawrence and Churchill – were far closer than those of any other candidate, and he was as safe a choice as Britain could expect to make.

When Faisal was crowned, Gertrude Bell wrote 'It was an amazing thing to see all Iraq, from north to south, gathered together. It is the first time it has happened in history.'[14] It did not occur to her to consider whether it was a good thing that 'all Iraq', whatever it was, had been gathered together for the first time in history.

The beneficiary of the construct, Faisal, was committed to attacking it. Churchill found it very tiresome:

> I have come to the conclusion that Feisal [*sic*] is rather too prone to raise difficult constitutional and foreign questions. He has only just been installed . . . In a few years all these points will doubtless be satisfactorily settled, but meantime why instead of fretting and fussing can he not live quietly and do his practical work as a ruler? . . . All the time he takes our money, he will have to take our directions . . . Faisal should be under no delusions in the matter. He will be a long time looking for a third throne.[15]

Gertrude Bell loyally claimed that he was simply trying to show that he had not sacrificed his independence: 'From the very beginning the King told us with complete frankness that he would fight the mandate to the death.'[16] Like Faisal, the United States did not recognise the mandate, and encouraged the Arabs to claim their independence. They may have done so for altruistic reasons or, as Gertrude Bell believed, because of oil: 'Oil is the trouble of course, detestable stuff.'[17]

38

BRITISH IRAQ

1. Structural Flaws

Critics of Britain's role in Iraq have no shortage of points to make, and Kedourie makes them well:

> British action then, from 1920 until the end of the mandate in 1932, worked powerfully to create in Baghdad a centralised government ruling over a population disparate and heterogeneous in the extreme, whom no ties of affection, loyalty or custom bound to its rulers. To establish the authority of these rulers, therefore, the British, following the logic of their choice, had to exert their power and their influence and eliminate all potential and actual resistance to them; and the fortunate Baghdad government found at its disposal the Royal Air Force to coerce and to inhibit all opposition . . .[1]

But, subject to the premise that Ottoman control had to end, could anything very different or better have been done? On the face of it, a Shiite leader for a predominately Shiite country seems an obvious essential. In reality, the Shiites would not have coalesced spontaneously and there was not an obvious figurehead who would have been acceptable to them and to the British. Bonds of a sort bound Faisal to the London government, which is more than can be said in relation to a Shiite alternative.

Iraq did not greatly want Britain or a mandate, but without homogeneity it could not do very much about it. There was no semblance of homogeneity. The composition of Iraq was half Shiite, who were close spiritually to Iran. The rest were Sunnis and Jews, Christians and Kurds, who were distinct from the mainstream Sunni community. The geographical spread of the different groupings was of course not even. There were concentrations in particular areas.

A British survey of Baghdad in the 1920s showed that the biggest single ethnic group was Jewish.[2] The Jewish community was a significant part of Mesopotamia's population. Indeed it was the most significant element in Baghdad, not only in terms of numbers, but also by reason of wealth and eminence. The Jews traced their roots in Mesopotamia back to the destruction of the temple in 587 BC. Babylon was the birthplace of Abraham. There the Talmud had been written and Jewish law codified.

The Jews feared the prospect of Arab rule. They petitioned against it in 1918 and again in 1919 when they said 'that the nomination of an Emir for Mesopotamia is inadmissible. Direct British government is indispensable for the future administration of this country.'

It is sometimes said that under the Ottomans the Jews were subjected to indignities and oppression and that the concept of Muslim tolerance was a myth. There is little to support that. Jews were members of a *millet*, a legally protected minority religious group. They accordingly paid a higher rate of tax, but in return they enjoyed a lifestyle that was secure and comfortable. In the case of many of the families it was very comfortable indeed.[3] The Jewish élite in Baghdad, an élite which contained some high-profile dynasties – the Sassoons, for example, and the Kedouries – was at the heart of the community, to the extent that the markets closed on the Jewish Sabbath and not the Muslim day of rest.

This secure community, controlling trading empires that linked east and west, was unimpressed by the Balfour Declaration. Balfour told the Foreign Office that the local Jewish notables thought that Palestine was a poor country and Jerusalem a bad town. Zionism had no appeal for them. Neither had an independent Iraq. They viewed the prospect of majority rule with misgiving. They regarded the bulk of the Muslims as unfit to govern, and their wish was for direct British rule.

When Faisal was installed, the Jews attended on Sir Percy Cox and asked that they should be British subjects: 'They based their claim on the fact that their country had been conquered by British troops, and that they were actually at the moment Turkish subjects under British control . . . They were eventually appeased by the personal influence of the High Commissioner, and by his assurance that ample guarantees would be afforded them by the British Government against any form of local tyranny.'

Faisal tried to unite his new country, telling them that the words 'Jews, Muslims and Christians' were meaningless and that there was simply a country called Iraq populated by Iraqis. In fact, he and Nuri al-Said, the man who installed the Arab governor in Damascus in 1917 before Allenby got there and who was the Anglophile prime minister for much of the time until he was assassinated in the revolution of 1958, continued to recognise the Jews' value to the state and their sophisticated skills, and to allow them a privileged role in the administration of the country.

Despite that role, they were never seen as being *part* of the country. They were regarded as pro-British, and associated with the mandate. They were also, though quite wrongly, associated with British policy for Palestine, with which they had no sympathy. Thus, when Britain invaded Iraq in June 1941, one reaction was a massive attack on Jews and their property in the *Farhud*, a pogrom associated with a general breakdown of law and order that lasted for two days, leaving very many Jews and a number of Muslims dead.

After the *Farhud*, Jews started to move from Iraq. Things might have settled down, but did not. The proclamation of the State of Israel on 15 May 1948 put an end to any prospects of an integration of the Jewish community in Iraq. Two years later, the Denaturalisation Act was passed, allowing Jews to leave Iraq if they renounced their citizenship. They had a year to decide. They did not need it. Encouraged by the detonation of a bomb in a Jewish area, they fled.

Operations EZEKIEL and NEHEMIA, as Mossad called the exit, meant that by the end of 1952 almost nothing was left of the Iraqi-Jewish community which had been established in 587 BC.

2. Racial Conflict

A heartfelt commentary on the problems of dealing with a heterogeneous population was contained in a letter to the *Nation* from a young British officer who was later killed in a rising in 1920 when he was in charge of a district in the Middle Euphrates:

> You, Sir, and your correspondents want to see 'national aspirations gratified . . . and the absolute prevention of any further additions to the already over-weighted British Empire'. The problem is, of course, how to provide a native government with the force required to govern a wild and very mixed race divided by the bitterest religious hostilities and tribal feuds, and containing in its midst also colonies of fiercely hated Jews and Christians . . . [T]hat you allow your correspondents to proceed airily in the assumption . . . that, if left alone, these people could govern themselves and freely employ European advisers, is almost Tolstoyan in its view of human nature . . . We are dealing with people who have lost all consciousness of nationality in the political sense, who have from time immemorial been governed by foreigners, and among whom indeed the very word 'arab' is used scornfully.[4]

The Revolt of 1920 was to a significant extent incited by Shiite leaders. They looked to an end to Sunni domination. They were consequently not pleased by the establishment of the Sunni Faisal and his supporters. The Shiite grievance – that they, the majority, were controlled by the Sunni minority – persisted and manifested itself in repeated risings in the Euphrates basin. Faisal was well aware of their position. His parliament of 1933 contained a Chamber of Deputies in which there were 28 Shiites, 16 Kurds and 36 members of his Sunni supporters in a country largely consisting of Shiites and Kurds.

The Khatun, as the Arabs called Bell, was a mixture of emotion and steel. When the Kurds showed signs of independence in 1921 and Kirkuk refused to swear allegiance to Faisal, Gertrude Bell's reaction was that 'since Kirkuk is in the middle of Iraq [its independent line] can't be countenanced. We must regretfully inform them that if they come they'll have the warmest welcome they have ever met with. The guns they've heard; the Levies are ready and behind them aeroplanes enough to obscure the light of the sun.'[5] Not only was the integrity of Iraq to be protected, but the Kurds, who were mostly Sunnis, were needed to balance the Shiite majority in Iraq, taken as a whole. The juggling reflected the artificiality of the construct.

Britain is often accused of having failed to acknowledge the significance of the Shiite preponderance. But Arnold Wilson, and then Percy Cox, was as conscious as Gertrude Bell of how difficult it was to draw a circle in the desert and call it Iraq.[6] He had to use what agencies he could where the population was tribal and without any tradition of obedience to a central government. The Sunnis had experience of administration under the Ottomans, who had excluded the Shiites from power. The Shiites were also tainted by their participation in the Euphrates Revolt. It was pretty inevitable that Britain would rely on the Sunnis as the Turks had done.

The British approach was arbitrary and paternalistic, but that approach was consistent with the India Office's way of dealing with tribal interests. For instance, the frontier separating Saudi Arabia from Iraq remained in dispute. It was settled by Sir Percy Cox in 1922. He had long known Ibn Saud. For 18 years he had been his mentor and paymaster. He was received with great ceremony and luxuriously appointed tents awaited him, filled with everything he could need, including Cuban cigars and Johnnie Walker whisky. All the same, after five days of intensive debate between the various representatives, nothing was settled, and Cox castigated Ibn Saud so roundly as to bring him close to tears. Ibn Saud collapsed: Cox was his father and mother: he would surrender 'half his kingdom, nay the whole, if Sir Percy ordered'.[7] Sir Percy took a map and drew a red line to award part of the Nejd to Iraq and two-thirds of Kuwait to Arabia. He then created two neutral zones, the Kuwait Neutral Zone and the Iraq Neutral Zone. One of the

Saudi delegates argued that there should not be a Kuwait Neutral Zone. When asked why he replied, 'Quite candidly, because we think oil exists there.' 'That,' said Sir Percy, 'is exactly why I have made it a neutral zone.' The lines that Cox drew were those that Gertrude Bell had already devised.

The borders which were chosen for the new construct restricted access to the Persian Gulf. There were only 36 miles of coastline and the lack of deepwater ports there was to cause ongoing friction with Kuwait. Iraq resented its restricted access to the sea then and later and maintained that, in terms of former Ottoman territorial divisions, they were entitled to Kuwait. That resentment led to the First Gulf War.

3. The Model of Government

British policy was to prepare Iraq for independence within a timescale that was uniquely short in British imperial history. She did so almost entirely for financial reasons. But in the country which Iraq had become there had been no experience of representative government above local council level until 1908. There was no real middle class. In the countryside, there were sheikhs, local potentates known as *aghas* and tribal chiefs. In the town, there was an urban aristocracy. The country people were Britain's supporters. They were hostile to the urban politicians and to the army. The sheikhs were accordingly elevated to an importance that they had not had under the Ottomans, indeed to a greater role than Faisal, who wanted to see a strong central government, would have wished. Prior to the war, their role had been diminishing. Britain restored an *ancien régime* that had been decaying. Now it staggered on until 1958. Alongside the sheikhs was an élite administrative class, an aristocracy of families who had held powers for centuries. Their role persisted under the British.

There were also some 300 ex-Sharifian officers. They had been with Faisal in Syria and gradually found their way to Baghdad, *arrivistes* and adventurers who were resented by the sheikhs. Faisal necessarily favoured them, and they had a powerful role under his rule.

Basra sat slightly apart from the rest of Iraq to begin with. Britain had seized it in 1914, and the Iraqi state was not established till 1920. In the interim, Basra received a fairly rough-and-ready military administration under the British.

Some have represented British rule in Iraq as a victory for democratic institutions. Others, notably Kedourie, have taken a very different view:

Whether it is British officials in Cairo and Khartoum seeking to build a regional policy on Sharif Husain and his sons; or Allenby prohibiting his troops from entering Damascus in order that the Sharifians should claim to have conquered it themselves; or Samuel being persuaded to appoint, in an irregular manner, Hajj Amin al-Husaini as Mufti of Jerusalem and affording him unchallenged and unaccountable control over all Muslim institutions in Palestine; or Allenby, Milner, and Lloyd George allowing themselves to be out-manoeuvred by Egyptian politicians whom Cromer and Kitchener had known how to control; or the success of Ministers who set up the ramshackle, sanguinary, and ill-fated Kingdom of Iraq; or Eden, Spears, and Altrincham elbowing the French out of the Levant and seeking to preserve control over the middle east by the promotion and encouragement of pan-Arabism; all these episodes show successive and cumulative manifestations of illusion, misjudgement, maladroitness and failure.[8]

The arguments that Kedourie put forward in *The Chatham House Version* were attacked when it was first published, notably by Professor Arnold Toynbee and by Sir Alec Kirkbride, the diplomat who welcomed Abdullah to Jordan, on the basis that when the new Middle Eastern Empire was acquired, Britain's imperial ambitions were in decline and colonies were untenable in the face of nationalism. In the 1984 edition of his book, Kedourie attacked these arguments on the grounds that they were anachronistic and founded on the imputation to the years following the First World War of views which were not current until after Suez. 'In fact, during this earlier period there is no evidence that policy-makers were guided in their decisions by a belief that the Empire was on the decline, or that nationalism was an uncontrollable force which rendered the Empire ungovernable'.[9]

Well, up to a point. But Kedourie does concede that military expenditure was scaled down enormously after the First World War. He attributes that to the fact that governments thought there was little prospect of another major conflagration. But much of the reduction in military expenditure was the involuntary and inescapable consequence of Britain's weakened economy as she came out of the war. At the level of popular and press opinion there was no jingoistic momentum on the platforms of the political parties. David Pryce-Jones, in his introduction to the 2004 edition goes even further than Kedourie:

The violence and tyranny suffered by others was a cause of self-congratulation for socialists, and some conservatives went along with it as well. Never mind law and order, they liked to argue, the British should never have had an Empire in the first place and had rightly got out of an exploitative and immoral enterprise about which they ought to feel nothing but guilt. The intellectual vapidity of that era was captured when Harold Macmillan, British Prime Minister no less, in a speech which set its stamp on events, spoke of 'the winds of change' as though the end of Empire blew in from something vague to do with climate, unrelated to the wilfulness, inconsistencies and folly of those who made decisions.[10]

Without necessarily accepting such a full development of Kedourie's arguments, it is possible and correct to agree, as some have not done, that the policymakers during and after the First World War had choices. Kedourie's conclusion is that they could have done better. My view is that while they could sometimes indeed have done better, very often they could have done worse.

It was a fundamental principle of the time that dependencies would cover their own costs. It followed that there could be no question of holding on to Iraq by continuous military activity. From that, in turn, it followed that Britain would, as so often in India, rely on local princes or, in this case, sheikhs. The Tribal Criminal and Civil Disputes Regulations of 1914 were based on the India Frontier Crimes Regulations and later embodied into Iraqi law in 1924. It gave the tribal leaders judicial powers with responsibility also for collecting taxes. They were like feudal barons.

But there was no real parallel with India, where a multiplicity of local potentates could rule on the British behalf, and where taxation allowed the imperial power to subdue a docile subcontinent. It is therefore unfair, but great fun, for Kedourie to say that

When we consider the long experience of Britain in the government of Eastern countries, and set beside it a miserable polity which she bestowed on the populations of Mesopotamia, we are seized with rueful wonder. It is as though India and Egypt had never existed, as though Lord Cornwallis, Munro and Metcalf, John and Henry Lawrence, Milner and Cromer had attempted in vain to bring order, justice and security to the east, as though Burke and Macaulay, Bentham and James Mill had never addressed their intelligence to the problems and prospects of oriental government. We can never cease to marvel how, in the end, all this was discarded, and Mesopotamia, conquered by British arms, was buffeted to and fro between the fluent salesmanship of Lloyd George, the intermittent, orotund and futile declamations of Lord Curzon, the hysterical mendacity of Colonel Lawrence, the brittle cleverness and sentimental enthusiasm of Miss Bell, and the resigned acquiescence of Sir Percy Cox.[11]

Even in the vilayets of Basra and Baghdad it does not do to overemphasise the strength of the local rulers or their institutions. What was to be done with these disparate municipalities? It was inconceivable that the pieces of

Mesopotamia that Britain found herself in possession of would not be brought together for efficient administration or that the loose and corrupt Ottoman model would be preserved. It is not easy to see what other model could successfully have replaced it. The influence of the Ottoman Empire in any event was confined to the large cities and had not touched the tribal confederations which had been left alone, almost autonomous. They were resentful of interference, as the 1920 rising of the tribespeople on the Euphrates showed.

A test of British rule is to contrast it with what followed. With the British departure in 1932 any control of the corrupt mechanism of government disappeared and the élite who manipulated government for their own advantages were unchecked. Policy now was entirely to favour the Sunnis and to take no account of the peasants or non-Arabs. Land rights and education policy were applied to these ends. The Sunni political élite was, however, regarded with contempt by the army, which aspired to replace them. In the army, the role of the ex-Sharifians, whom the British had never effectively controlled, was dominant.

4. Faisal

Faisal was the best Britain could find. He was not ideal. Part of the reason that the French had thrown him out was that they had found him devious and indecisive. Even Lawrence, his promoter, described him as weak and empty.[12] Lloyd George agreed with Berthelot, the French foreign minister, that Faisal was 'a weak man, a very feeble character, of considerable prestige, but dangerous' but said that 'the Sheikhs' liked him and that if the French were prepared to agree to his candidature, Britain could bring home 70,000 soldiers.

When Faisal got to Baghdad, he performed pretty much as everyone had expected. He proved unreliable. Gertrude Bell admitted that he was indecisive, not prepared to disavow his supporters in their extreme moments and ready to support unsuitable individuals. She faced up to confrontation with the king but was not clear that he would mend his ways: 'He embraced me with great fervency and we parted on rather unsatisfactory terms of close sentimental union and political divergence.'

He had an impressive number of mistresses, with some of whom he disported himself in Europe under the alias of Prince Usama. He was understood to seduce the wives of his ministers and staff. He attempted to supplement his meagre resources by seizing assets for himself.

Cox had a difficult time. When he called on the king on 23 August 1922 to congratulate him on the first anniversary of his accession, he was confronted by contrived anti-British demonstrations. This was no way for puppets to behave.

Cox demanded punishment for the obstreperous protestors and, when Faisal chose to be ill and unable to take these steps, Cox took them for him.

Faisal attempted to undermine his prime minister, al-Maquib, as well as pro-British notables. Gertrude Bell returned for more hugs and kisses. She asked Faisal if he accepted her sincerity. He did. She told him she 'was extremely unhappy. I had formed a beautiful and gracious snow image to which I'd given allegiance and I saw it melting before my eyes . . . I did not think I could bear to see the evaporation of the dream which had guided me day by day.' Her hands were repeatedly kissed and at the end of the interview she kissed his hands too. But little lasting good came of it.

39

MOVING FORWARD

1. Mandates and Treaties

Formal award of the various mandates was a slow business. There were three stages to the establishment of a mandate. The principal Allied and associated powers had to agree on conferment; the draft mandate had to be submitted to the League; and the League had to approve it, after being satisfied that its terms were in accordance with the provisions of the Covenant.

The powers assigned the various 'A' mandates at San Remo in April 1920. They came before the Council of the League on 21 February 1921. Balfour moved a postponement of the question till more settled times, a characteristic Balfourian manoeuvre. Part of the trouble was American disquiet. In a note of the same date, the United States Secretary of State, Bainbridge Colby, complained that as far back as 20 November 1920 he had asked for a draft mandate to be submitted for approval by the United States. On 1 March 1921 the Council replied evasively and suggested that the US discuss the matter when it again came before the Council. There the matter ended. The State Department neither responded to the invitation nor expressed its views on the subject to the Council.

Final drafts of the Mesopotamian and Palestinian mandates were published in August 1921, but the usual indecisiveness prevailed. The United States locked themselves in to a Gilbertian circle and declined to consider the mandates without previously approving their terms. And by now there was considerable instability in the Middle East, arising from the war between the Greeks and the Turks and the dispute between Britain and Turkey over the Mosul Vilayet.

It was not until 19 July 1922 that the 'A' mandates again came before the Council of the League. After some squabbles between Britain, Italy and France about the Syrian mandate, the mandates were approved. The United States' approval was constituted by treaties with Britain in relation to Palestine and with France in relation to Syria. There was a strange discrepancy between the mandates. Britain had 'full powers of legislation and administration save as they may be limited by the terms of this mandate' for Palestine, but France had no counterpart for Syria.

Iraq's mandate is often taken as dating from 10 August 1920, because Britain's status was regulated by her treaty with Turkey of that date, the Treaty of Sèvres. Iraq was a little like a protectorate: Britain undertook to give armed support and assistance; the British High Commissioner and staff would reside in Iraq and guide the country's government. In international affairs and finance, the role of the High Commissioner was more extensive: his advice was binding on the Iraqi government. Britain would use her good offices to secure Iraq's admission to the League, and the treaty would terminate on Iraq's admission to the League, failing which it would last for 20 years. A protocol of 30 April limited the endurance of the treaty to the earlier of Iraq's entry into the League or four years from the ratification of peace with Turkey.

France was of course never happy about Britain's role in Iraq. She felt after all that she and not Britain should have been there. Beyond that, Britain's wide powers there and in Palestine contrasted with France's narrower powers in Syria. France had herself to blame here: the terms of the mandates were largely drafted by the mandatory powers themselves. France had been opposed to the whole notion of mandates from the start, and a mandate was much less than she had wanted in Syria. The French representative to the Permanent Mandates Commission complained about 'certain errors inspired by the democratic Wilsonian ideal'.[1]

The next stage in the preparation of Iraq for ostensible independence was a treaty with Britain. Negotiations began in 1922. In 1924 the Treaty, Protocol and Subsidiary Agreements were being debated by the Constituent Assembly in Iraq and the British Cabinet had to consider whether Britain should ratify them.

The Colonial Secretary, James ('Jimmy') Thomas, circulated a memorandum. He had a little difficulty in explaining why Britain was in Iraq at all. It was because Britain had been required to send an expeditionary force to Basra:

We could not abandon without a struggle our one hundred years' predominance in the Persian Gulf; nor could we, for strategic reasons allow the head of the Gulf to remain in hostile occupation. Had we done so, the Gulf might have been converted into an enemy lake, with hostile submarine bases etc. The effect upon our communications with India would have been disastrous. A further consideration was the need to protect the Persian oil-fields (nothing to do with Mosul oil . . .)[2]

There was an even bigger question about why the wartime advance had gone beyond Basra. The matter 'may be open to dispute. In war it is never easy, and may be perilous, to sit still. At any rate, we did not sit still.' Britain's presence in Iraq was admitted to be a matter of accident, compounded by 'various pledges, undertakings, etc. to the local Arabs' and McMahon's 'famous promise to the Sharif of Mecca'.

Although the memorandum was presented by Churchill's successor, following the fall of the coalition government, Thomas acknowledged his predecessor's success at the Cairo Conference and the importance of his transfer of military control in Iraq from the War Office to the Air Ministry, with a consequent reduction in the size of the garrison and its attendant expense.

The recommendation was that the agreements and protocol should be ratified; as they were. The memorandum ends on a note of resignation: 'There is no use in idealising the Arabs, whether King or peasant, or in attributing to them qualities which they do not possess. The best of them are shifty and unreliable from the western standpoint. We have to work with the material that lies to hand, and shall gain nothing by pretending that it is better than it is.'[3]

The terms of the treaty were offensive to Iraqi nationalists and created an unacceptably colonial system. Faisal developed appendicitis so he could not sign it. While he was indisposed Cox imposed direct rule, and sent some opponents of the treaty off to exile. Faisal recovered and signed.

2. Mosul. The Kurds

The League was concerned about what an independent Iraq might do to the Kurds and other minorities. It decided in 1926 that a new treaty between Iraq and Britain should be signed, to last for 25 years. Less heat was generated by the negotiations this time. Britain was very anxious to bring the mandate to an end and stop subsidising Iraq and accordingly did not dig her heels in over the treaty provisions. The Lausanne Treaty had left the future of Mosul to be dealt with later. Turkey wanted it and so did Faisal and Iraq. The issue was remitted to the League of Nations. Iraq was content to have Britain involved in its future at least until the future of Mosul had been decided.

Negotiations with the League on the line of the Iraqi–Turkish frontier – essentially about Mosul – were thrown in jeopardy by one of these minor accidents, the want of a nail, that can shape the course of history. Answering a supplementary question in the House, Baldwin bluntly dismissed the idea that Britain would be prepared to give Iraq ongoing protection. Amery, fighting Britain's case at Geneva against an aggressive Turkish delegation, found the ground cut from under his feet. He had no doubt what had happened: Baldwin simply had not known what British policy on this crucial issue was. Amery drafted the answer the prime minister should have given and asked him to confirm that that was what he would have meant if he had thought about it.

Baldwin agreed with Amery's 'interpretation' of his response, and Amery and Austen Chamberlain rushed round to advise the Council on the following morning. There had been panic in the League and it continued for a little time further, until the verdict was announced on 16 December, in favour of the frontier for which Britain and Iraq were arguing. Mosul went to Iraq.

The Foreign Office had prepared interesting memoranda about the Iraq frontier dispute, which Chamberlain circulated on 21 October 1925. The documents were severely realistic: 'For all practical purposes Mustafa Kemal is both the Turkish Government and Turkey. He is a practical idealist and a constructive patriot with far-reaching ambitions which have already attained a considerable degree of realisation. His aim is to create a new, modernised, independent Turkish State which will be recognised as an equal by the civilised States of the world. His model is Japan and his methods are those of Mussolini.'

Kemal's commitment to obtaining Mosul is assessed as being important in terms of prestige, rather than for its practical value. Kurdistan, however, had a more practical value for him: 'The Kurds are essential, both racially and militarily, as breeders of citizens and as defenders of the State.' The memoranda are well written and balanced and do not underestimate the limits on Kemal's room for manoeuvre in regard to Mosul. But it was noted that he had called off agitation against Britain in the Turkish press and that his representative had spoken to the British Ambassador at Constantinople about the hope of a resolution of the dispute about Mosul by diplomatic discussions. The best hope of resolving the matter was thought to be some sort of face-saving manoeuvre, possibly coupled with some cash and perhaps 'a flattering invitation, conveyance on a British warship, etc.'[4] Beads for the natives.

Terms were finally agreed with Turkey in 1929 and signed in 1930. Turkey accepted the Mosul settlement. Britain had what she wanted. She would recommend that the mandate be ended and Iraq allowed to join the League in 1932, if all went well. Iraq would thereafter have its foreign policy dictated by Britain. Britain had the right to move troops across Iraq and to use two airfields free of rent. There would be an alliance of 25 years from the date on which Iraq was admitted to the League. Even so, there was criticism in Britain that not enough was provided by Iraq to guarantee imperial communications. Iraq obtained its independence at a cost in terms of oil. In 1925 Britain was given a 75-year concession through the Iraq Petroleum Company. Iraq received royalties but did not own any part of the company.

The lack of steps taken by Britain to protect the Kurds after the end of the mandate is a reproach to her history. The international community did no better. The treaty did not repeat the promise that had been given in 1922 of autonomy for the Kurds, or other safeguards to Kurdish interests. The Mandates Commission spent most of the sessions on Iraq agonising over the likely fate of the Kurds and Assyrians, but in the end the League did nothing concrete to protect them.

Iraq was the first mandate territory to be given independence, and remained the only one until 1945. What was apparently the least viable of ex-Ottoman Empire states was the first to shed its mandate. Iraq was duly admitted to the League on 3 October 1932, and the treaty came into effect on that date. Now Iraq wore many badges of self-government. Britain's role as an administrator has been criticized by some,[5] but the purpose of this study is to consider whether Britain did her best for the mandated territories by her own lights, or did no more than create stable client states for her own benefit. On that test, Britain had come to administer Iraq reasonably sensitively and to try to create a stable regime. Britain knew that the country had to be stable when independence came. She also took care to achieve a reconciliation between Faisal and Ibn Saud and thereafter to ensure that good relations between Iraq and Saudi Arabia were maintained.

Iraq was fortunate in that the British officials were particularly able and conscientious.[6] There are even today Iraqis who regret that these administrators were not available after the invasion of 2003. Distinctions can be drawn between the British administration in Iraq and the French administrations in Syria and the Lebanon.

3. Endgame

Faisal's reign ended with his death from natural causes on 8 September 1933, the year after Iraq joined the League of Nations. His successors' ends were more violent. His 20-year-old son Ghazi succeeded him and was less circumspect. He ruled from 1933 to 1939. He was nationalist and anti-British. He ran a private broadcasting station from the palace and used it to attack British policy. The British ambassador accused him of 'total irresponsibility'. He dallied with Hitler. He was killed when he drove a racing car into a lamp standard in 1939.

Overall, Faisal did his best for the country in which he found himself planted. His son's views were in tune with those of his generation, as those of Faisal had been in tune with those of his contemporaries. In 1936 the government was overthrown and the army was in effective control. There were six more coups between then and the end of 1941, but each time all that happened was that another member of the old élite was installed. When war broke out in 1939,

Iraq was gripped by militarism and there was a powerful fascist youth organisation.

There was tension between those who wished to use the war to achieve true independence and those who thought that their positions could be enhanced by retaining the British connection. The country soon fell into the hands of a clique of former Ottoman officials and ex-soldiers, corrupt and conservative. Despite the Shiite majority, they were all Sunnis. Many people in the country, especially younger army officers, were disaffected and like Ghazi resented the accommodation of the political élite to Britain.

In 1940 a group of military officers – 'the Four Colonels' – effected a *coup d'état* and installed Rashid Ali as prime minister. His government appeared to be distinctly pro-German. There was disagreement about whether Iraq was entitled to deny Britain the use of a base. When Britain expanded the base all the same, the Four Colonels surrounded the British airfield at Baghdad.

The regime was strongly pro-Nazi. Britain could obviously not accept a German threat to the oilfields. A British relief force marched from Palestine to Iraq, and by the end of May the revolt was crushed. British troops stopped on the outskirts of Baghdad. Abd al-Ilah, who acted as regent during the minority of Faisal II, had fled in the first stages of the *coup d'état*, but the Foreign Office and the Middle East commander-in-chief, Wavell, felt that the regent's dignity would be compromised if they interfered in the governance of his capital.

British forces were obliged to watch at a distance while looting, disorder and massacre went on within the town. The principal victims were Jews. During the *Farhud* of 1–2 June 1941, it is estimated that about 900 Jewish homes were destroyed, with 175 killed and perhaps 1,000 injured. Britain remained in full military control of the country for the rest of the war and re-established political control through Nuri al-Said who displaced Rashid Ali, the ambitious, nationalist and pro-fascist prime minister. This is the same Nuri al-Said who had been present at the entry to Damascus; he was also thought to have been implicated in the death of King Ghazi at the wheel of his racing car.

So in 1941 Britain was back in the position of 1920, running the country. From 1941 until 1946 Britain ruled as she had done under the mandate. The army was run down – as indeed were the soldiers, who received 1,000 calories a day less than the medical requirement. The Iraqis resented their military weakness, which was revealed when they attempted to deal with a Kurdish rising between 1943 and 1945.

After the end of the war the new British Foreign Secretary, Ernest Bevin, was keen to maintain influence in Iraq, and there was an attempt to create a fresh long-term relationship. But Britain was by now far too discredited in Iraqi eyes, and the move was unpopular even though most of the British framework

was removed in the course of 1946–47. The vehicle for the long-term relationship was to be the Treaty of Portsmouth, but the terms of the treaty prompted
violent response in Iraq and the regent refused to ratify it. From 1948 to 1958
British influence reduced and Britain's formal rights were given up with the
establishment of the Baghdad Pact in 1955.

The memories of humiliation by the British in 1941, and of the displacing
of Rashid Ali, now seen as a national hero, were not forgotten. Britain's negative image was not helped by her support of Israel. This perception of the
British role contributed to the change of regime in 1958 and the rejection of
Britain as a continuing ally. The 1958 coup destroyed the monarchy and with
it the British connection.

IX

PALESTINE

40

'MANDATORY OF THE WORLD'

In November 1918 the Foreign Office memorandum on *Desiderata*, considered already in relation to Iraq, concluded so far as Palestine was concerned that the strategic consideration was that the country adjoined the Sinai Peninsula, the Canal and Aqaba, and that a railway from Akka–Haifa to Iraq would run through the country. It followed that Palestine should be independent, administered by America or preferably Britain, with special transit facilities. It is very interesting indeed that the Zionist dimension and the impact of the Balfour Declaration played very little part in policy-making. Just how important did policymakers consider the declaration to have been?

The government wanted to 'ensure reasonable facilities in Palestine for Jewish colonisation, without giving Arab or general Muslim opinion an opportunity for considering that Great Britain has been instrumental in handing over free Arab or Moslem soil to aliens'. In terms of policy, the problem was addressed in a little more detail. The Jewish colonists 'for special reasons will be entitled to a position more than mathematically proportionate to [their] numbers at the start . . . Moreover, in Palestine there are international religious interests so important, and so difficult to reconcile, that they almost overshadow the internal problems of the native inhabitants. For these reasons, the desires of the inhabitants, or of the several sections of them, will have, to some extent, to take the second place. The assisting Power will be bound to act not merely as their mandatory, but as the mandatory of the world, and in cases where local and international interest conflict, the former may often have to give way.'

These sentences are very important. In them lay the assumptions that suggested that the conflicting elements of Palestine policy *could* be reconciled. This easy resolution of the problem, the assumption that the local population would accept a second place to minority colonists, was at the centre of Britain's policy in Palestine at its start.[1]

Everything about Palestine was novel and artificial. It was the child of the Balfour Declaration and the exigencies of the war. Palestine had not been a distinct entity in Ottoman times. It had been composed of provinces that formed part of South Syria. At the San Remo Conference in 1920, when the mandates were allocated, the precise boundaries of Palestine, as of other mandated territories, were left 'to be determined by the Principal Allied Powers' – but it was understood that Palestine was to extend as far east as the western boundary of Mesopotamia, thus taking in what are now Jordan, Israel, the West Bank and the Gaza Strip. Its frontiers were arbitrary, and it lacked natural cohesion.

Before the mandate, British intelligence had been very poor. Little was known of conditions in Palestine. There may have been a 'willed ignorance', deliberate evasion of fact-finding which has been compared to policy in the run-up to the 2003 invasion of Iraq.[2] In the case of Palestine, but not of the invasion of Iraq, that judgement seems unfair.

At any rate, it soon became clear that the particular problem of Palestine – what made it distinct from any other mandated territory – was the commitment to a Jewish home. While that seems a banal understatement today, at the time it was not unreasonable to hope that Jews and Arabs could live together amicably in Palestine as they had done in so many parts of the Ottoman Empire. Palestine would be the Jews' national home, but the home also of the indigenous Arabs who made up 85 per cent of the population.[*]

That hope of Arab–Jewish amity was reflected in the discussions, already described, between Weizmann and Faisal in 1919. Weizmann said that he would cooperate with the Arabs economically. Faisal recognised the Balfour Declaration. He accepted Jewish immigration, though he insisted on protection of the rights of the Arabs in Palestine and recognition of the Arab claim to Greater Syria. The Weizmann–Faisal dialogue might have been the basis for a happy future for Israel, but it came to nothing: France occupied Syria in violation, in Arab eyes, of it. Arab opinion was further alienated by the San Remo Conference and approval of the mandates by the League.

The Weizmann–Faisal agreement did not, as sometimes has been suggested, commit Faisal to the concept of a Jewish national state, but then the question of whether Palestine was to be a national state or a national home, or indeed what was quite meant by a national home, was never clear. There was ambiguity and deliberate fudge right from the start.

There is no doubt that Britain was cavalier in the way it regarded the indigenous Arab majority. They seemed to be unadvanced and inconsequential in

---

[*]   The problems of the declaration were inherent also in the mandate. On the one hand, the San Remo Treaty incorporated Article 22 of the Covenant, referring to the rights of indigenous peoples. On the other, Articles 2, 4, 6, 7, 11 and 22 of the mandate obliged Britain to foster and support the concept of a national home for the Jews.

comparison with the great justice of restoring the destiny of the Jews. Balfour said that they were a trifling factor compared with the rights of the Jewish people. Behind this judgement, there was an additional factor: even Balfour, and certainly more committed Zionists, treated Palestine right from the time of the declaration as if the Jewish community throughout the world were already in Palestine. They were a metaphysical majority.

But the real majority was Arab, and in the Arab view the wartime British government perpetrated a conscious fraud. That judgement does not take account of the fluidity of policy under the stress of war and its diplomatic ramifications. Even when account is taken of these factors, Arabs will say, with Antonius, 'This cannot exonerate Mr. Lloyd George's government from blame, for nothing can excuse – or for sheer duplicity, surpass – the message sent through Commander Hogarth to King Hussein in January 1918 about the safeguards of the Balfour Declaration, or that other message which was sent to him a month later over the Foreign Secretary's signature to bamboozle him into believing that the Sykes–Picot Agreement was a figment of Turco-Bolshevist imagination.'[3]

That is to give too much stress to what were no more than some of innumerable conflicting emphases that circulated in the course of the war, and which can look so damaging when brought together afterwards to substantiate the idea of a concrete scheme, when all indeed had been fluidity. The reality lay not in Antonius's elegant rhetoric and its translation of cock-up and confusion into duplicity and bad faith. If Arabs and Jews had wanted to, they could have lived together in peace and harmony. Arab–Jewish hostility was not a given in 1917. There were many examples of Arab and Jewish communities happily coexisting. The model only appears flawed in the light of later events which need not have taken place. Jews throughout the world could indeed have looked to Palestine from afar as their legally recognised national home. There was no reason to think that they would flood in to live there. Very many assimilationist Jews had been at pains to emphasise that they would not do so. The fact of the Arab majority in Palestine was not cynically ignored. On the contrary, it was thought to be a check on appetites that might be whetted by the peculiar status of Palestine so far as the Jews were concerned. If Jews had a titular advantage, Arabs had a numerical one. Coexistence was guaranteed by this balance.

What was new, unexpected and eventually terrible was, first, the novel and huge desire for Arab self-rule throughout the Middle East, and, secondly, the scale of the Jewish ambition not just to live in Palestine, but to dominate it and control the whole of its territory. These aspirations may seem natural enough today, but in 1917 they were not foreseeable. Balfour could never be described as naive, but even he could not know what genies would emerge from the bottle he opened. It did not take long for them to be discerned.

At the Peace Conference in Paris, Weizmann said that the object was to make Palestine as Jewish as England was English. And while the declaration talked about upholding the rights and privileges of 'existing non-Jewish communities in Palestine', the Jews accorded these communities neither respect nor dignity. The Arab policy of non-cooperation was equally negative.

The men on the spot in Palestine did not immediately recognise the impasse. They tended to be fairly pro-Arab. They wanted to buy in Arab participation and establish Arab representation in the same way as the Jews were represented by the Jewish Agency. The Arabs appealed for application of the Fourteen Points and referred to the various wartime promises. Britain's response was to require as a pre-condition that the Arabs accepted the mandate. Not unreasonable, but this they would not do, and their decision to stand on their principle, rather than to participate and seek to change the structure of Palestine from within is at the centre of the development of mandated Palestine into modern Israel. The Arab position was logical, but the Jews were pragmatic, prepared to participate, trying all the time to improve their position. The result was that, despite the best intentions of officials, the Arabs tended to be marginalised.

As a consequence, while by 1932 Iraq had become independent and Syria, Lebanon and Jordan had assemblies with powers for the mandated peoples, no such representative government was developing in Palestine. Far from it: there was an imbalance between the rights of the minority, the Jews, who through the Jewish Agency enjoyed diplomatic representation at the Geneva League of Nations Permanent Mandates Commission, and the majority Arabs, whose representation was only through the British. The Arabs were not attending to their own best interests.

The men on the spot were frequently overruled from London, where sympathies were generally for the Jews. Anthony Eden, Foreign Secretary 1935–38 and 1940–45, was unusual in being pro-Arab. The bulk of those in high office in London were often called Gentile Zionists. The Gentile Zionists were able to overturn, for instance, the Passfield White Paper of 1930. Sidney Webb, recently ennobled as Lord Passfield and appointed Colonial Secretary, had considered the reports of the Shaw and Hope-Simpson Commissions into the Wailing Wall riots, of which more later. He accepted their conclusions that unchecked immigration and land acquisition could not fail to exacerbate tension. The response was formidable resistance organized by Balfour's niece, Blanche Dugdale, and the outcome was a formal letter from Ramsay MacDonald to the Zionists which abrogated the White Paper.

Despite the Gentile Zionists and benevolent sentiments towards the Jews, there was no hostility to the Arabs. Oscillation and fluidity, though it may indicate weak policy or poor policy, demonstrates that there is little in the idea that there was a consistent and devious anti-Arab programme.

Balfour was inclined to throw out observations that attracted attention but did not really reflect his settled and serious views. One of these was, 'In short, so far as Palestine is concerned, the Powers have made no statement of fact which is not admittedly wrong, and no Declaration of Policy which, at least in the letter, they have not always intended to violate.' Avi Shlaim describes this statement as 'one of the few honest remarks on the subject [of Palestine]'.[4] But Balfour's epigram was unfair to himself and to others. The history of British administration shows that the government was always prepared to reverse its policy and depart from its previous positions. It did so in a genuine and well-meaning attempt to cope with interests that proved to be irreconcilable.

41

ADMINISTRATION IN PRACTICE

1. Sir Herbert Samuel

In 1917, Palestine was occupied under the Military Occupied Enemy Territory Administration. In 1920 there was a change to civilian control. Administration of the mandate started in effect with the appointment of the first High Commissioner for Palestine. In 1920 Sir Herbert Samuel signed a receipt for the benefit of the outgoing military administrator. The receipt was for 'one Palestine, complete'. Samuel insisted on adding 'E & OE', Errors and Omissions Excepted.

Samuel was Jewish, and his commitment to a Jewish state had been evident from the time that he submitted his memorandum on the subject to Grey in November 1914. Because of this, he hesitated before he accepted the appointment. In his memoirs, he said that the government had known of his Zionist sympathies and that it was indeed perhaps on account of them that he had been appointed, but that he 'was there to administer the country, not for the benefit of one section of the population only, but for all: not commissioned by the Zionists, but in the name of the King'.

He kept to that impartial position. In May 1921 he set out his interpretation of the Balfour Declaration. It meant 'that the Jews, a people who are scattered throughout the world, but whose hearts are always turned to Palestine, should be enabled to found here their home; and that some among them, within the limits which are fixed by the numbers and interests of the present population, should come to Palestine in order to help by their resources and efforts to develop the country to the advantage of all its inhabitants.' The distinction between that limited number of Jews who would physically live in Palestine and that far greater number who would found Palestine in their hearts as their home is the formula that enabled British administrators to believe that they could honourably discharge their duties both to Zionists and to the native Arab inhabitants of Palestine. Was it naïve to hold to that belief? Might the formula have been workable but for Nazism?

In the report he published in August 1921 reviewing his first year as High Commissioner, Samuel was already pointing to Zionists 'who sometimes forget or ignore the present inhabitants of Palestine'. They were to do so throughout the term of the mandate. In the House of Lords in May 1939 Samuel said that whereas immediately after the end of the First World War he and others had thought that at some stage a Jewish state might be set up, he and those others, like Chamberlain, Churchill and Smuts, later became convinced that the whole of Palestine could never be turned into a Jewish State.[1] He was flexible, his judgement fair and balanced.

His report began with a Churchillian flourish: 'When General Allenby's army swept over Palestine, in a campaign as brilliant and decisive as any recorded in history, it occupied a country exhausted by war.' He had no illusions about the need for Jewish self-control: 'In a word, the degree to which Jewish national aspirations can be fulfilled in Palestine is conditioned by the rights of the present inhabitants.'[2]

The traditional view of Samuel as a carefully impartial arbiter between Arab and Jewish interest groups has been subjected to careful scrutiny and sometimes challenged.[3] The traditional view deserves to survive, pretty well intact. The Arabs regarded him as both a Jew, which he was, and a Zionist, which he was not. He was high-minded and liberal; he expected others to be so too. Life for him was said to be 'one Balliol man after another'.[4] He very soon realised 'the irritating effect of an alien body in living flesh'.[5] When the Arabs resorted to violence in 1921, his response remained sympathetic: he restricted Jewish immigration. Goodwill towards the Arabs was also shared by the army and its commander in the Middle East, General Congreve, and by civilian administrators. There was a fairly widespread view in the army and among those administrators that the indigenous Arabs were the victims of an unfair policy which the British government was pursuing at the behest of international finance.

If there was an element of anti-Semitism in the criticism of the Jews, it could be balanced by an objectionable racism of which the Arabs were the victims. Administrators did not greatly distinguish between the elements of 'a tiresome gaggle of yids and wogs'.[6] But though immoderate observers, like G.K. Chesterton, could always find caricatures to denigrate in either community, overall the pushy Jew, who came with skills and was resistant to authority, was less acceptable to the British than the Arab, resigned to a culture of oppression. The wife of a British official put it thus: 'When an Arab is dirty he is picturesque. When a Jew is dirty he is filthy.'[7] The romantic appeal of Arabia was still powerful. The novelty of Zionism made it difficult to understand, and the tradition of anti-Semitism did not help.

Samuel had to deal with a situation that was already degenerating. At the outset, as early as November 1918, the Jews proved demanding and triumphalist, parading in Jerusalem to celebrate the anniversary of the Balfour Declaration. The Arabs, for their part, pointed out that they had occupied Palestine since the conquest of 634. There were 512,000 Muslims in Palestine, compared with 61,000 Christians and 66,000 Jews. The Jewish population of Palestine had reduced during the war: they now constituted just 7 per cent of the population and owned only 1 per cent of the land.[8] Politics in the Middle East continues to be bedevilled by the length of the parties' memories. There are not many parts of the world where actions and responses are conditioned by population movements 2,000 years in the past. Where is the starting-point of settlement to be?

In order to secure Arab goodwill, Samuel tended to favour the Supreme Muslim Council, which he set up in 1920 as the official Arab representative body with responsibility for managing Islamic institutions within the mandate and as a counterbalance to the Zionist executive. It was anti-Zionist but reasonably moderate until the outbreak of violence in 1936; all the same, unruly demonstrations were more or less endemic. Balfour insouciantly brushed some aside in March 1925 when he visited Palestine during an Arab strike and hostile demonstrations: 'Oh, I wouldn't worry about that – nothing compared with what I went through in Ireland'.[9]

After serious riots in 1920 and 1921, it was seen as essential that Arab opinion be placated. Samuel did his best to integrate Arabs into the system. He pardoned Arabs involved in the 1920 riots, and set up an advisory council, in which the Arabs had a majority (four Arabs against three Christians and three Jews). He was prepared to put the executive committee of the Arab Congress on terms of parity with the Zionist executive and commission. But the Arabs would not be pragmatic: they would not pay the price, which was acceptance of the mandate.

In 1921 Samuel set up a court of enquiry consisting of Sir Thomas Haycraft, the Chief Justice of Palestine, and two others to report into the disturbances of May 1921, notably into what were called the Khedara raid and the Jaffa riots. The enquiry's conclusion was that the trouble started with a demonstration by Bolshevik Jews who made use of slogans such as 'Long Live the Communist International!', 'Long Live the Socialist World Revolution!' and, my favourite, 'Long Live the Free Women of the Communist Society!'.[10] There was a clash between the Bolshevik demonstrators, who were unofficial, and an official Jewish Labour Party demonstration. The problem then developed into a general anti-Jewish riot which was badly handled by the police, 'with few exceptions half-trained and inefficient, in many cases indifferent and in some cases leaders of or participators in violence'.[11]

On 4 October 1923 the Secretary of State for the Colonies, The Duke of Devonshire, told Samuel to try to establish the Arab Agency on similar lines to the Jewish Agency. On 11 October Samuel met 26 eminent Arabs. He started by making it quite clear that the question of promises to Hussein had been dealt with once and for all in the 1922 White Paper. There was going to be no more discussion of that. As far as the Balfour Declaration was concerned, it was a twofold obligation 'each side of it as sacred as the other'.

After his speech, he withdrew to allow the Arabs to debate. 'On His Excellency's return, Musa Kazem Pasha [the president of the Arab delegation], on behalf of those present, stated that the meeting was unanimous in declining to accept the offer of an Arab Agency which would not satisfy the aspirations of the Arab people. He added that the Arabs, having never recognised the status of the Jewish Agency, have no desire for the establishing of an Arab Agency on the same basis.'[12]

The early years of the new state were reasonably quiet – at least in comparison to the later years. Immigration proceeded fairly slowly and in one or two years in the late 1920s there was even a net emigration of Jews.[13] Britain could control Palestine with a small garrison initially from a castle of Bavarian appearance on the Mount of Olives, and later from a newly built Government House, with its ball-room and minstrels' gallery, established inauspiciously on the Hill of Evil Counsel. British administrators relaxed in the Jerusalem Sports Club and in pink coats hunted jackals with the Ramleh Vale Hunt. Since 1948 Government House has been the United Nations Headquarters. It sits unhappy and ineffective, isolated behind its defences, looking towards the soaring steel wall that separates Jerusalem from Palestinian-controlled Bethlehem, just 8 kilometres away. In front there is a new road, named after concord. It is a cul-de-sac.

With Jews and Arabs refusing to cooperate and administering their communities in parallel, the British tried to deal with practical matters like health, education and agriculture, making Palestine, as Storrs, now governor of Jerusalem, said, 'cleaner, richer and duller'.

2. Immigration

Jewish immigration was to be one of the great issues. Waves, *aliyahs*, of immigration took place regularly, two before the First World War. The third was in 1919–23, the fourth in 1924–26, the fifth in 1933–36. The fifth was stimulated by Hitler's persecution of the Jews in Germany, and brought 170,000 new Jewish inhabitants into Palestine, doubling the size of the Jewish community.

The significance of these demographic changes was self-evident to the Arabs. In 1922, there were 93,000 Jews and 700,000 Arabs. In 1936, there were

382,000 Jews and 983,000 Arabs. In that period the Jewish element rose from
11 per cent to 27.7 per cent of the total population.[14] Both communities were
growing, but the Jewish community was growing faster. The changes in population created competition for arable land and the Jewish National Fund bought
such land, largely from absentee Arabs, but even from Arabs, sometimes indeed
notable Arabs, who were resident in Palestine. The British system of taxation
in terms of money, rather than goods as in Ottoman days, created a need to
liquidate investment in land in order to generate cash.

The demographic dynamics were not static. In the 1920s taken as a whole
there was significant Jewish immigration, and after the Nazis came to power in
Germany in 1933 it became yet more marked. Legal and recognised Jewish
immigration figures from 1929 to 1936 were as follows:[15]

1920	5,514	1929	5,249
1921	9,149	1930	4,944
1922	7,844	1931	4,075
1923	7,421	1932	9,553
1924	12,856	1933	30,327
1925	33,801	1934	42,359
1926	13,081	1935	61,844
1927	2,713	1936	29,727
1928	2,178		

Jewish *land purchases* were no less important. In 1914 Jews owned some
650,000 *dunams* (a *dunam* was 919.3 square metres till 1928 and 1,000 square
metres since, about a quarter of an acre). In 1939 they owned perhaps
1,420,205.[16] In terms of total areas the Jewish landholding was not significant.
The total area owned by Jews was only about 5 per cent of the whole of Palestine
in 1940; but from 1928 onwards, the sales were increasingly of fertile farmland
by native Palestinians, as opposed to poor quality ground by non-Palestinians.

Glubb cites an example of an area of 50,000 acres on the Plain of Esdraelon
which was sold by a Christian family in Beirut to the Zionists for £726,000.
Within the area there were 21 villages with 8,000 Arabs dispersed among
them. They were evicted and received derisory compensation of £28,000, some
£3.50 per head.[17] It is estimated that 90 per cent of the land acquired by
Zionists up to 1929 was acquired from similar absentee landlords.[18]

42

CHURCHILL'S WORK

As Colonial Secretary, Churchill visited Palestine in March 1921, after the Cairo Conference and following the Arab riots of 1920 and 1921. He was presented with a memorandum by the president of the Executive Committee of the Arab Palestine Congress, 'the Haifa Congress'. It is an emotive, unsophisticated and anti-Semitic document. 'Jews have been amongst the most active advocates of destruction in many lands . . . We have seen a book entitled "The Jewish Peril" which should be read by everyone who still doubts the pernicious motives of the Jews . . . The Jew, moreover, is clannish and unneighbourly, and cannot mix with those who live about him . . . The Jew is a Jew all the world over.' Samuel was unacceptable because he was a Jew. The tone is rhetorical and uncompromising. The conclusion is a blunt demand for the recall of the principle of a national home for the Jews, and an end to Jewish immigration until an Arab-dominated government had been established, associated with the other Arab states.[1]

He also received a memorandum from a deputation of representatives of the Jewish community.[2] It was different in every respect, Western and not Arab in its tone, shorter, factual and pragmatic. Samuel minuted 25 factual errors in the Arab memorandum. He minuted no errors in the Jewish memorandum. If accepted at face value, it was bound to create a much more favourable impression on the Colonial Secretary: 'It is our constant endeavour to assist the High Commissioner in establishing cordial relations between all sections of the population, and our Jewish and Zionist programme lays special stress on the establishing of sincere friendship between ourselves and the Arabs. The Jewish people returning, after 2,000 years of exile and persecution, to its homeland, cannot suffer the suspicion that it wishes to deny another nation its rights . . .' In 1921 it was possible for Churchill to hope that coexistence could be achieved.

His replies to the two deputations deserve to be read carefully. They are sensible, practical and expressive of good faith. He frankly told the Arabs that

in the very able paper which you have read, there are a great many statements
of fact which we do not think are true, and I think everyone of you knows in

his heart that it must be taken as a partisan statement and on one side of the case rather than as a calm, judicial summing-up of what is best for all of us to do in the difficult circumstances in which we find ourselves.

He told them that he could not repudiate the Balfour Declaration and even if he could, he would not wish to do so.

> [I]t was a declaration made while the war was still in progress, while victory and defeat hung in the balance. It must therefore be regarded as one of the facts definitely established by the triumphant conclusion of the Great War . . . Moreover it is manifestly right that the Jews, who are scattered all over the world, should have a national centre and a National Home where some of them may be reunited. And where else could that be but in this land of Palestine, with which for more than three thousand years they have been intimately and profoundly associated?

He did his best to reassure the Arabs that they faced no threat from the Jews. He drew their attention to the part of the Balfour Declaration which promised the inhabitants of Palestine the fullest protection of their civil and political rights. 'I was sorry to hear in the paper which you have just read that you do not regard that promise as of value'. He stressed the precise words of the declaration and the distinction between *a* national home for the Jews, of which Balfour had spoken, and *the* national home for the Jews.

He promised that Britain would implement the two parts of the declaration equally carefully. 'If the one promise stands, so does the other; and we shall be judged as we faithfully fulfil both.' If one reads the history of the mandate years unburdened by bias, one must conclude that despite the efforts of both sides, Britain did not do her best to discharge both promises.

He contrasted the prosperity which could be achieved by peaceful coopera-tion between the two communities with the neglect and starvation that had been the hallmarks of Turkish rule.

> The paper which you have just read painted a golden picture of the delightful state of affairs in Palestine under the Turkish rule. Every man did everything he pleased; taxation was light; justice was prompt and impartial; trade, commerce, education, the arts all flourished. It was a wonderful picture. But it had no relation whatever to the truth, for otherwise why did the Arab race rebel against this heavenly condition?

Not that he thought much of the Arab Revolt:

> I thought, when listening to your statements, that it seemed that the Arabs
> of Palestine had overthrown the Turkish government. That is a reverse of the
> true facts. It has been the armies of Britain which have liberated these regions.
> You have only to look on your road here this afternoon to see the graveyard
> of over 2,000 British soldiers, and there are many other graveyards, some
> even larger, that are scattered about in this land.[3]

His response to the Jewish delegation was much shorter, just as their memorandum was the shorter of the two. It was the headmaster talking to the prefects,
rather than to the unruly junior school.

> I have just been making a statement to the Moslem deputation which I am
> afraid was not very agreeable to them. They will not expect me to make a
> statement to you which will be very agreeable to you. It is my duty to try to
> reassure and encourage both.

He stressed that he was aware of the alarm among the Arabs, the fear that they
might be dispossessed because of a flow of immigrants, some of them imbued
with communist doctrine. He stressed that the Jews must dispel these fears. He
was treating his audience as a sophisticated one:

> It would be easier for me to speak in terms of ardent enthusiasm of the cause
> which you have at heart, but I should only be speaking to those who are
> already convinced. It is more important for me in these words which I address
> to you to counsel prudence and patience, and to endeavour to strike a note
> which will make your path more easy, while allaying the alarm, however
> unjustified, of others.

Later he spoke at the Hebrew University site, where he thanked the rabbis 'for
the precious gift you have presented to me, the scroll of the Law, which, as you
have said, contains all the truth which has been accepted by the greater part of the
enlightened world, and which is the heritage of Christians and Jews alike'. He
referred again to the double promise contained in the Balfour Declaration:

> Every step you take should therefore be . . . for the moral and material bene-
> fit of all Palestinians. If you do this, Palestine will be happy and prosperous,
> and peace and concord will always reign; it will turn into a paradise, and will
> become, as it is written in the scriptures you have just presented to me, a land

flowing with milk and honey, in which sufferers of all races and religions will find a rest from their sufferance. You Jews of Palestine have a very great responsibility; you are the representatives of the Jewish nation all over the world, and your conduct should provide an example for, and do honour to, Jews in all countries . . . I am now going to plant a tree, and I hope that in its shadow peace and prosperity may return once more to Palestine.[4]

As the tree was handed to Churchill for planting, it broke. There was no spare and after some hunting all that could be found was a palm tree, which alas would not thrive on such a site.[5]

Churchill was a romantic, and had been in favour of Zionist settlement in Palestine as far back as 1908,[6] , but he was not discernibly partial. He did his best to reassure the Arabs that they faced no threat from the Jews. 'The Jews have a far more difficult task than you. You only have to enjoy your own possession; but they have to try to create out of the wilderness, out of the barren places, a livelihood for the people they bring in.' He pointed out that they only bought land that people chose to sell to them. Above all, he tried to impress on the Arabs that they had to negotiate: 'It is not fair to come to a discussion thinking that one side has to give nothing and the other side has to give large and important concessions.'[7] Churchill could understand the Jews, who appeared to try to conciliate Arab opinion. The Zionists supported Arab claims to Syria against those of France, they accepted that there would be areas of Arab autonomy within Palestine and they offered economic concessions to the Arabs. The Arabs on the other hand were uncompromising and immoveable.

Churchill's point about the existence of willing sellers of land was a good one. While the poor peasants struggled, rich landowners fell over themselves to sell to the Jews, who did not have enough money to buy all the land that was offered to them.[8]

Back in London, Churchill and his staff in the Middle East Department tried to bring the Arabs in to the structure of administration. But the Arab delegation which came to London in June 1921 did not feel a need to make concessions. In Palestine there was little sympathy for Zionism among officials and officers. The Arab leaders had scented this lack of commitment.

On 14 June 1921, Churchill made a historic statement to the House of Commons on policy in the Middle East, in the course of which he said, 'We cannot, after what we have said and done, leave the Jews in Palestine to be maltreated by the Arabs who have been inflamed against them, nor can we leave the great and historic city of Baghdad and other cities and towns in Mesopotamia to be pillaged by the wild Bedouins of the desert.'[9]

He said that there were two choices when it came to dealing with the Arabs.

One was to keep them divided, discourage their aspirations and make use of provincial notables, as the Turks had done. The alternative was to create an Arab state around Baghdad that was vital and viable. This was the policy that the government had decided to adopt. In implementation of that policy, Faisal was to 'present himself to the people' of Mesopotamia, and Abdullah was to be placed 'in charge' of Transjordan. The cost of keeping Ibn Saud happy with this Sharifian policy was an annual subsidy which was not more than 'the cost after all of a single battalion of Indian Infantry'. For that he would keep the peace in the Nejd.

The speech was a huge success. Austen Chamberlain, Lloyd George and Curzon all congratulated Churchill. Herbert Sidebotham reported in the *Palestine Weekly* that 'I have never known a House more interested in any speech, or a speaker more easy and confident in his power'. In the course of the debate, Lord Winterton managed a good intervention: 'The Right Hon. Gentleman who has just spoken gives an impression of power and grandeur which is possessed by few persons and institutions with the possible exception of the Pyramids or Lord Northcliffe.'[10]

By the time Churchill met the Palestinian Arab delegation on 22 August 1921 he was clearly exasperated by their reiterative and unconstructive approach:

Churchill: The British Government mean to carry out the Balfour Declaration. I have told you so again and again. I told you so at Jerusalem. I told you so at the House of Commons the other day. I tell you so now. They mean to carry out the Balfour Declaration. They do. What is the use of looking at anything else? The Government is not a thing of straw, to be blown by the wind this way and that way. It is bound to carry out the Declaration. It contains safeguards for the Moslems, just as it contains clauses satisfactory for the Jew.

You are not addressing your minds to the real facts of the case. You think that by coming over here and asking that the Balfour Declaration should be set aside, that is all you have to do. I have told you that is useless; you cannot do it. We have taken up our position before the world, and with the support of the great victorious powers gathered in counsel. That is the fact. I was trying to suggest ways in which this could be carried out, which would not be injurious to you in any way.

Secretary of the Arab Delegation: If you will allow us to say a few words about this subject.

Churchill: Yes, but say words not on the principle, because really I cannot discuss that with you. I am only a servant of higher powers. In the first

place, I have told you again and again that the Jews will not be allowed
to come into the country except in so far as they build up the means for
their livelihood according to the law. They cannot take any man's
lands. They cannot dispossess any man of his rights or his property or
interfere with him in any way.[11]

He reiterated the assurances he had given to the Arab delegation in Jerusalem
about a year earlier. On 21 February 1922, the Palestine Arab delegation wrote
to him in London from the Hotel Cecil. Churchill replied on 1 March. Although
conciliatory, he pointed out that he could not treat them as a recognised authority as they had not agreed to any official machinery for representation. They
were still requesting the disavowal of the Balfour Declaration. When they
replied on 16 March, they added nothing to their often repeated position, that
Palestine had already been promised to the Arabs before the declaration.[12]

Churchill's substantive response was a 'Statement regarding British Policy
in Palestine' which he sent with a letter of 3 June 1922. He was at pains to say
that expressions like 'Palestine will be as Jewish as England is English' were
untrue and unhelpful. 'When it is asked what is meant by the development of
the Jewish National Home in Palestine, it may be answered that it is not the
imposition of a Jewish Nationality upon the inhabitants of Palestine as a whole,
but the further development of the existing Jewish community, with the assistance of Jews from other parts of the world, in order that it may become a centre
in which the Jewish people as a whole may take, on the grounds of religion and
race, an interest and pride'.[13] Unfortunately for Britain and the Palestinian
Arabs, the Zionists wanted very much more than that.

Churchill argued that the pledges to Hussein excluded the country to the
west of the Vilayet of Damascus and therefore excluded the whole of Palestine
west of the Jordan. The Arabs, in response, founded on the fact that the term
'district' and not 'vilayet' had been used in the correspondence, stated that
there was no Vilayet of Damascus and that what was meant was Vilayet of Syria.
Unfortunately their general approach could not fail to give the impression of
hair-splitting and obstructive pedantry. Their response to the Statement of the
Policy runs to seven pages. Weizmann, on behalf of the Zionist Organisation,
limited himself to less than a page. His tone is businesslike and cooperative and
contained welcome reassurances about working with the Arabs. The cultural
differences between the two ways of negotiating with the British Department
of State could not fail to operate to the disadvantage of the Arabs.[14]

Churchill's important Palestine White Paper of 3 June 1922 was embodied
in an Order in Council in August of the same year. It was a simple and honest
attempt to implement the Balfour Declaration, made before the full extent of

the hostility between the two populations was evident. Palestine would not become a Jewish state, though a commitment to a national home was confirmed. A legislative council would be set up. Immigration would be controlled by the legislative council, and the British government, and would be confined to what could be absorbed by the economy. Pending the election of a legislative council, the British High Commissioner would be assisted by an executive council containing senior British officials and an advisory council made up of British officials and Arab and Jewish members.

Churchill's approach in the White Paper was based on Samuel's advice. It assumed Arab–Jewish cooperation, which would pave the way to independence in which the Arabs, by virtue of their numerical superiority, would clearly play the larger role. The White Paper was realistic. It offered a wonderful opportunity for harmony. The Jews were prepared to participate; the tragedy was that the Arabs were not.

Samuel went ahead with elections. But because the Arabs boycotted them, the proposed constitution was dropped in 1923. He then attempted an advisory council with 10 Arabs and 2 Jews. The Arab policy of non-participation killed this. Whether Arab negativism was wise must be in doubt. The result at any rate was that there was no popular government. Samuel and his officials were left to run the place. There was no building of a community.

That is not to say that the Arabs played no part whatsoever in the polity of the country. The local élite continued to be used, as in Ottoman days. A Palestinian Arab Congress was formed and met annually. At the third conference, in 1920, an Arab Executive was formed but Britain did not formally recognise it or work with it and it came to an end in 1934.

Jewish institutions were better organised. The mandate had authorised the formation of a public Jewish body to consult with the mandatory. In 1921 the World Zionist Organisation created the Palestinian Zionist Executive, which in turn became the Jewish Agency in 1929. The Histadrut was founded in 1920 to promote Jewish trades unionism. It expanded its role greatly into that of an Entrepreneur Agency and worked with the Kibbutz Movement, stressing the dignity of labour. The Haganah, the Jewish Defence Force, was controlled by the Histadrut. It was set up in response to the Arab riots in 1920 and became in effect an underground army – which the British made no effort to disband.

In 1929 Passfield attempted to revive the idea of a nominated council, but the attempt failed, as did a further attempt in 1935. Unable to achieve Jewish–Arab cooperation, Britain did her best by attempting to work with separate Zionist and Arab bodies. The senior Arab representative was Amin al-Husayni, who was appointed as mufti of Jerusalem, the senior Sunni cleric in charge of the city's Holy Places, when the Mufti Kamil-al-Husayni died on 21 March 1921. Amin al-Husayni was a strange appointment, selected largely because the preceding mufti, who was his brother, had worked well with the British. Amin was not otherwise obviously qualified for his role. As mufti he was also president of the Supreme Muslim Council.

Whatever his brother might have been, Amin had not been pro-British. He had been active in the anti-Zionist riots and had been sentenced to ten years' imprisonment, escaping to Syria and only returning after Samuel's general pardon. But his family, the al-Husayni, had been supporters of the British, and Amin promised Samuel that if he were appointed he would cooperate with the mandatory power. He now led the Arab community in Palestine, despite rivalry between his family and the Nashashibi clan.

Formerly there had been many muftis, men of learning and authority, in all the provinces of the Ottoman Empire. No one of them was superior to the others, unless that superiority was earned by evident pre-eminence. But the British wanted to define who they were dealing with and it was convenient to treat the mufti of Jerusalem as head of the whole Muslim community in Palestine and to dignify him by the title of the Grand Mufti. Samuel was trying hard to win Arab goodwill, and tended to favour the mufti and the Supreme Muslim Council as the official Arab representatives, to balance the role of the Zionist Executive which had replaced the Zionist Commission. After the riots of 1920 and 1921 it was seen as essential that Arab opinion was placated.

But Samuel could not bring the Arabs together. Their political activity was frag-mented. There were at least six political parties. Arab opinion in its fragmentation contrasted with the more cohesive and expanding Jewish element in the country. Arab opinion radicalised, and from 1936, and the General Strike of that year, there was a move from the mere expression of political views to physical action. There were assassinations in a number of towns, including Tel Aviv and Jaffa in April 1936. Unofficial councils were established in some towns and a strike developed.

Jewish opinion and Jewish institutions were far more coherent than Arab ones, but there was a division between Weizmann's moderate gradualism and the 'Revisionist' position of Vladimir Jabotinsky. He was of the non-religious right and spoke for those who rejected the 'practical Zionism' of Weizmann and David Ben-Gurion. Jabotinsky claimed that the British might at any moment abandon Zionism. He wanted to secure the Jewish future of Palestine by encouraging 50,000 new inhabitants to immigrate and by making an immedi-ate proclamation of a Jewish state, which would include Transjordan. The Revisionists set up the militant Irgun, independent of the Haganah and the Jewish Agency.

43

DISTURBANCES AND COMMISSIONS

1. The Early Commissions

The Wailing Wall, or Western Wall, of the Temple of Herod had been a holy site for Jews since the Middle Ages. It was, however, also very important to Muslims, forming part of the sanctuary that contained the Dome of the Rock and the al-Aqsa Mosque. At the time of the mandate, the Wall was designated as a *Waqf* and enjoyed the legal protection thus conferred. The Jews were entitled to visit the Wall but were not entitled to set out chairs or screens to separate men and women at prayer.

The British, correctly, enforced these Arab requirements as part of the maintenance of the existing religious arrangements. The consequence was the Wailing Wall Disturbances of 1929. In response, the British government sent in the Shaw Commission in that year. Sir Walter Shaw recommended a more sensitive treatment – not of the existing Jews, but of the Arabs. He argued, for instance, that Arabs should not be evicted after land sales and pointed to the establishment of a landless class of discontented Arabs.

The Shaw Report on the Wailing Wall Disturbances extended to around 202 pages plus graphs. Its essential conclusion was unremarkably that tension had been caused by conflict between the Balfour Declaration and McMahon–Hussein. But not so much because of an *inherent* conflict: rather because 'many of the leaders of either race placed the widest possible construction upon these promises'.[1] The commissioners considered that the Jews were as disappointed with the limitations placed on the Balfour Declaration promises as the Arabs by the limitations on the McMahon–Hussein promises. In each case, they had allowed themselves to ignore qualifications that were always present. The detailed enunciation of British policy in the 1922 White Paper had brought reality home painfully.

To this had been added economic competition from immigrant Jews. 'The Jewish immigrant of the post-war period . . . is a person of greater energy and efficiency than were the majority of the Jewish community of pre-war days.'[2]

In response, Passfield emphasised the delicacy and difficult nature of the problem and announced that Sir John Hope-Simpson had been sent to Palestine to confer with the High Commissioner on land settlement, immigration and development. At the same time H.L. Dowbiggin of the Ceylon Police had gone out to report on policing in the mandate.[3]

If the number of commissions that came out to Palestine and the number of White Papers that governments published was a measure of commitment, Britain deserves congratulation. There were no fewer than 19 Palestine commissions and enquiries.

Shaw's recommendations were enshrined in the Passfield White Paper of 1930. This stressed the obligation of the British government to set aside land for dispossessed Arabs, and it also proposed limits on Jewish immigration. But the attempt to reduce immigration coincided with the beginning of Nazi atrocities and was soon abandoned. Now, between 1933 and 1936, 177,000 Jews joined the Palestine community in the fifth *aliyah*, bringing the Jewish share of the population to more than one quarter.[4] Tension increased as Britain had to choose between on the one hand excluding Jews, who could not find sanctuary in Britain or the United States and faced extermination if they remained in central Europe, and on the other alienating the Muslim inhabitants of the Empire by seeing the Arab community crushed.

When the State of Israel was established, Arab opinion tended to represent Britain as having been unequivocally friends of the Jews. It is impossible to sustain that argument given the efforts of the British government in the interwar years to treat both sides fairly. Certainly the Jews, not least Weizmann, were greatly disappointed by the Passfield White Paper and were hostile to its conclusions. As has been seen, it was finally repudiated by Ramsay McDonald as a result of the pressure from Blanche Balfour and the Gentile Zionists in a letter which became known as the Black Letter of 1931. The whole episode shows how the government was being pulled in different directions at the same time.

Arab opinion was hardening, and resentment against Britain and Zionism, now increasingly supported by America, was coming to a head. The moderate Jewish leadership was also under attack. The arrival of significant numbers of European Jews added to the pressure, and the General Strike of 1936 and widespread associated risings were the result.

The British administration had almost no army in the country to deal with the unrest. Palestine was militarily under the command of the Royal Air Force, which had only one squadron of aircraft. Larger contingents of British troops were sent out, and firmer measures were attempted. At the same time a carrot, in the shape of a further Royal Commission, was promised, but only if violence had ended.

In the meantime by May 1936 the country was in a state of paralysis. Telephone wires were cut, and roads were blocked. There was support from Syria and Transjordan. Iraq protested against British policy. British officials and soldiers were attacked, as were Jews. The British reaction was heavy-handed. Much of the old city of Jaffa was destroyed to root out terrorists. Collective punishments were imposed.

Finally Britain sent out both a Royal Commission of Enquiry, the Peel Commission, and still more troops. As the unrest which brought the commission to Palestine had largely been provoked by the level of Jewish immigration, it was not helpful for the Palestine government to announce, on the very day that the Royal Commission left London, that a further schedule of permitted immigration had been issued. The announcement was intended to balance the concession to the Arabs which the Royal Commission represented. But this desire for balance resulted in disastrous imbalance. The Arab Higher Committee, which had been established on 25 April 1936 by the Mufti Amin al-Husayni after the start of the revolt, and comprised the leaders of Palestinian Arab clans under the mufti's chairmanship, responded to the immigration announcement by boycotting the Royal Commission, a boycott which only ended at the request of the Arab kings: the Arab royal families in Iraq, Saudi Arabia and Transjordan appealed to the Higher Committee to call off the strike and end the disturbances.

The disturbances ended on 12 October 1936, and the boycott was finally lifted – but so late in the day as to damage the presentation of the Arab case to the most important of all the Palestine commissions: the Peel Commission.

2. The Peel Commission

The commission was immensely strong in terms of its personnel. Lord Peel had been Secretary of State for India for two spells and had been chairman of the Burma Round-Table Conference and a member of the Joint Select Committee on Indian Constitutional Reform. The vice-chairman, Sir Horace Rumbold, was an experienced diplomat who had filled many public roles including serving as chief delegate at the second Lausanne Conference. The other commissioners were Sir Laurie Hammond, a former governor of Assam and a member of the Joint Committee on Indian Constitutional Reform, Sir Maurice Carter, who had presided over the Tanganyika Territory and was chairman of the Kenya Land Commission of 1932–1933, Sir Harold Morris, the president of the Industrial Court, and Professor Reginald Coupland, the Beit Professor of Colonial History at Oxford.

When the commissioners attended a concert in Jerusalem at which Toscanini conducted, one of them is supposed to have said that they could have been in

Paris or London. The remark suggests a half-baked approach. That is unfair. It does not reflect the commissioners' serious purpose and awareness. The commission's recommendations followed detailed discussions. There was extensive debate among the commissioners. A number of important proposals, as well as the headline ones, were made. The analysis of the Palestine Question was very wide-ranging.

The commission did its homework thoroughly. Before it had even left for Palestine it had received extensive written evidence; and once in Jerusalem in the course of three months it heard 62 witnesses at 31 public meetings (some people giving evidence in more than once session) and 35 closed sessions at which an unknown number of witnesses was heard. The commissioners examined matters of detail, such as the type of marker used to plot land for settlement. They looked at broader questions too, relating to land and immigration, economy and labour, education and health. And they looked at the biggest and broadest issue of all: what the mandate meant and how it was to be interpreted.

The exceptionally wide terms of reference given to the commission reflect the government's honest readiness to try anything to deal with a problem that was proving intractable. The commission was to

> ascertain the underlying causes of the disturbances which broke out in Palestine in the middle of April; to enquire into the manner in which the Mandate for Palestine is being implemented in relation to the obligations of the Mandatory towards the Arabs and the Jews respectively; and to ascertain whether, upon a proper construction of the terms of the Mandate, either the Arabs or the Jews have any legitimate grievances on account of the way in which the Mandate has been or is being implemented; and if the Commission is satisfied that any such grievances are well-founded, to make recommendations for their removal and for the prevention of their recurrence.

The commissioners were faced with the fact that the mandate prescribed that there was to be a Jewish homeland. That had to be respected. Equally, there patently was an Arab nationalist movement which could not be ignored. The commission's answer was ultimately to be partition. But initially there was no unanimity among the commissioners about the concept. It was Professor Coupland who argued for it, and he slowly won the others round. He emphasised that the problem lay in the mandate itself, rather than in the size of the Jewish community or the speed at which it had grown.

While the commission had not come out to Palestine already committed in any sense to a partition solution, partition had been discussed in the Palestine government and the Colonial Office for some years. Partition of a sort had been adopted in Bengal and population transfer in the dispute between Greece and Turkey. Peel and Rumbold both had direct experience in such areas.

The Jews in Palestine were far from unanimously in favour of partition. Those who were elaborated a plan which was put to the commissioners. It was known as the Northern Plan, giving them Galilee, as opposed to the Southern Plan, which gave the Jews the Negev Desert.

The commissioners did not dig deep into the background. Their report made no reference to the Declaration to the Seven of June 1918. Arab historians have criticised them for not studying a list of grievances. But that was not their remit. Their remit was a practical one, directed towards the future. Indeed, they specifically recorded that they had not undertaken detailed research into what had happened 20 years previously: 'We think it sufficient for the purposes of the Report to state that the British Government have never accepted the Arab case.'[5]

The commissioners were perhaps inevitably impressed by the professional way in which the Jewish case was presented, in contrast to the presentation of the Arab case. The Arabs did not assist their cause by the boycott, which did not end until just a few days before the commissioners were due to leave Palestine. By the time the Arab kings persuaded the Higher Committee to give way, only five days were left for a presentation of the Arab case. Those five days contrasted with seven or eight weeks taking evidence from British officials and Jewish representatives. To that extent, the commission worked under a huge disadvantage, a disadvantage that operated to the prejudice of the Arabs, and that they themselves had created.

The outcome of the commission's deliberations, delivered on 7 January 1937, was the recommendation that the coastal strip of Galilee and a sizeable chunk of Palestine west of the Jordan should form a Jewish state. Partition was thought to be a workable device. It had worked elsewhere, as the commissioners knew. There were to be zones of permanent British mandate around Jerusalem, Bethlehem and Nazareth to protect the holy places and with a corridor to the sea; the rest of the country would be merged with Transjordan as an Arab state. The issue of whether the Jewish unit was to be a Jewish home or a Jewish state was addressed: it was to be a Jewish state.

The report was presented as unanimous and concealed doubts and differences that had existed among the commissioners. A year after the report was published, Rumbold complained that he had had no time for partition and only agreed to it to avoid a split among the commissioners. The report has been referred to as 'one of the great State Papers of the inter-war period', 'a work of lucid and compelling power'. It confidently concluded that 'while neither race can justly rule all Palestine, we see no reason why, if it were practicable, each race should not rule part of it.'[6]

The Zionists saw the importance of keeping onside with the mandatory power. Ben-Gurion had already told the High Commissioner that the Jews wanted Palestine to be part of the British Empire. Weizmann contrasted the constructiveness of the Jews with the Arabs, 'a destructive element. We build!'[7] Now it was politic to appear to accept the Peel Commission's conclusions, although both Weizmann and Ben-Gurion were far from enthusiastic about partition. The Arabs reacted differently.

44

ARAB REACTION AND THE BRITISH RESPONSE

It would have been better politics to see the proposals as something on which to build, rather than to reject them out of hand as the Arabs did: riot and disturbances revived in 1937. Some 3,000 active terrorists attacked buildings, police stations, oil pipelines and all the means of communication. Britain established 'Arab investigation centres' where police resorted to torture and reprisals. One British policeman described the retribution he and his fellows wrought, following the murder of some of their colleagues: 'We . . . descended into the sook & thrashed every Arab we saw, smashed all shops & cafes, & created havoc and bloodshed . . . [R]unning over an Arab is the same as a dog in England, except we do not record it.'[1]

Militant Arabs not only killed Jews; Arabs whose commitment was regarded as doubtful were killed in even greater numbers. In the violence that followed, Britain lost control of large parts of the country, including parts of Jerusalem. As well as the heavy-handed British military reaction, Jewish forces were deployed.

By the summer of 1938, Palestine was scarcely governable. Much of Galilee and Judea, together with major towns such as Bethlehem and Jerusalem, were effectively out of Britain's control. In March 1938, in succession to Sir Arthur Wauchope, Sir Harold MacMichael was appointed High Commissioner and commander-in-chief in Palestine, a post he would occupy until 1944. He was pro-Arab, but pragmatically he came to the conclusion that partition was the only way forward for Palestine. He could not have been appointed at a less propitious time. Seven months after he arrived, he was obliged to hand civil power over to the army.

The army re-established control, but at a frightful price. Arabs were placed in something pretty close to concentration camps. They were attacked from the air as Spanish republicans had been attacked by Hitler's warplanes. Over 100 Arabs were hanged. Much of the terrorist activity took place at night: this was addressed by the use of Orde Wingate's Special Night Squads or Squadrons, many of them making use of men nominated by the Haganah, an illegal organisation.

Initially British forces in Palestine consisted of a single brigade. Tactics were improvised with what resources could be found, such as armoured cars and lorries mounted with naval pom-pom guns. Very soon, however, following the biggest British troop movement since the end of the Great War, the garrison was raised to 80,000 men with the arrival of a two-division-strong Palestine Expeditionary Force, under Lieutenant General John Dill, Chief of the Imperial General Staff during the Second World War. Dill's force was supported by four squadrons from Bomber Command. These conventional forces went on the offensive along with less conventional units. They operated under instructions to Dill by the Army Council and a number of Orders in Council, all of which required stern measures and authorised severe punishment under martial law.

As well as military forces, the government could deploy the civilian police. The Dowbiggin Reforms of 1930, intended to improve the efficiency of policing, were designed to maintain an equal number of British and Jewish policemen on the one hand and Arab on the other. British policing was largely carried out under senior officers from police forces in India, Africa and other parts of the Empire. Dowbiggin, for instance, was brought in from Ceylon. But by the time of independence a very high number of Jewish men were employed at subordinate levels in the police force. They were armed, and many are known to have been members of the Haganah. Latterly indeed the Arab element of the police force was disbanded. The British element of the Gendarmerie, subsumed into the Palestine Police in 1926, was largely from the Black and Tans. There is no doubt that they were pretty rough in Palestine, as they had been in Ireland in the 1920s.

From December 1937 to June 1938 Sir Charles Tegart, a former commissioner of police in Calcutta, advised on police organisation and methods. He recommended the use of specialist counterinsurgency units. There were precedents for this in the Palestine Gendarmerie, which had been formed by Colonel Wyndham Deedes in 1921. Tegart now argued for the use of 'the tough type of man, not necessarily literate, who knows as much of the game as the other side'.

Tegart was a Zionist, one of those incredible, larger than life characters for whom the Empire appeared to have been created as a playground. In Calcutta he put on a false beard and a turban, and drove around the city at night, posing as a Sikh taxi driver. Tall, lean and with blue eyes, he can have fooled no one. During the day, he drove an open car with his Staffordshire bull terrier perched on the hood. Radical politicians thought him insolent; but he was good for the morale of Europeans caught in a campaign of terror. 'He appear[ed] to treat the whole thing as a game',[2] and his courage, insouciance and enthusiasm created the legend of 'Tegart of the Indian Police'. Before he left Palestine in 1939 'Tegart's Wall', a two-metre-high barbed-wire fence, ran the length of the frontier with Lebanon and Syria, and some 50 'Tegarts', fortified police stations, had been built.

There are widely different judgements about the nature of Britain's reaction to the terrorism. For some, the British response was draconian, and Wingate's Special Night Squads brutish thugs. For others the Special Night Squads are invested with the sort of Arabian nomadic romance that Philby and Lawrence enjoyed.

Orde Wingate was a cousin of Sir Reginald Wingate, whom we have frequently met. He was sometimes called 'the Lawrence of Judea', and like Lawrence, he was a favourite of Churchill's. He became an ardent Zionist. He was a charismatic leader. He was also outstandingly eccentric, surviving for long periods on nothing but onions, conducting business while he lay naked on his bed combing his body hair with a toothbrush.

Wingate was, however, one of the few Britons – particularly few within the army – who both understood the Jews and was sympathetic to them. The British had already been using Jewish personnel. Wingate built on this, following the nineteenth-century military prescription for small wars. His methods have influenced the Israel Defence Force's combat doctrines. David Ben-Gurion, Moshe Dayan and Ariel Sharon all recorded their admiration for him. There is a Wingate Street in Tel Aviv, and Wingate Square in Jerusalem is appropriately at the junction of Balfour and Jabotinsky Streets.[3]

Myth had it that Wingate, pretty much on his own, checked the Arab Revolt and did so in the face of opposition from anti-Semitic British officers, who were choosing to ignore the use of Nazi money and weapons by the Arabs in their fight against the Jews. The reality, rather, is that Wingate and his Special Night Squads were only part of a counter-insurgency strategy that did not depart from established practice. The Special Night Squads were not the Anglo-Jewish death squads they have sometimes been portrayed as, fighting terror with terror. Again in contradiction of the myth, Germany and Italy supported the insurgents with nothing more than propaganda. Wingate operated the Special Night Squads for the brief period from March to December 1938. When he went on leave to London, he met Basil Liddell Hart, then acting as a special adviser to the minister for war, Leslie Hore-Belisha, who in turn introduced him to Churchill, describing Wingate as having 'a Lawrence-like role' in Palestine. Churchill was impressed and remembered Wingate later. As a result of his subsequent role in Burma, more prominence has been given to his time in Palestine than it deserved. His Night Squads did play their part in controlling terrorism, but they did so in the context of a British military success which had reduced the rebel numbers very considerably. As a result, rebel activity had switched to clandestine deeds of sabotage or of terrorism against Arab individuals suspected of supporting the government.

There were many British Army officers who sympathised with the Haganah and cooperated with its intelligence officers. There was little opposition to a fierce prosecution of the battle against the terrorists. That is not to suggest that the military or civilian command was fiercely illiberal. It was not. Major-General Sir Arthur Wauchope, the High Commissioner who preceded Sir Harold MacMichael was particularly tolerant. He was a cultivated and artistic man, appointed by Ramsay MacDonald, who wanted a High Commissioner who used his head and not his feet.[4] Wauchope argued that the Arabs had genuine grievances, and that the issue was a pan-Arab one, which should be resolved by the Arabs themselves. Thus he attempted to involve the three Arab kings, as the mufti had advised him he must do.

Different British commanders took different views about brutality. Wingate approved of savage methods, including lashing villagers on their bare backs. He appears frequently to have participated in the brutality himself, shooting and killing Arabs. He forced suspects to swallow oil-soaked sand as a form of torture.[5] Major-General Richard O'Connor, who commanded Sixth Infantry Division in Southern Palestine, wrote to his wife, 'There is definitely a certain degree of Black & Tan methods about the Police . . . I have issued stringent orders against harshness & unnecessary violence on the part of our own soldiers & I am sure they will be obeyed apart from the odd few, who there will always be. Jack Evetts has always (between ourselves) encouraged his men to be brutal, as being in the end more humane. I disagree with him over this.'[6] While O'Connor disapproved of Evetts's methods, Montgomery did not: 'Jack Evetts require[d] no urging . . . During the ten days ending today we've killed 100 in my divisional areas.'[7] There was some support both at home and on the spot for the beleaguered minority regime – 'Brave little Jewish Ulster'.

Not only did the attitude and therefore policy of officials and army officers vary depending on whether they were for or against Zionism or for or against the Arabs; within each group there were further gradations of prejudice. Some, for instance, approved of British, American or German Jews, but not those from Eastern Europe. Others were sympathetic to Jews fleeing from persecution in Europe, but were hostile to the second or third generation Jews who had moved into Palestine from elsewhere in the region. As far as Arabs were concerned, very many Britons distinguished between the noble, rural *Bedu* 'warriors' and urban 'so-called Arabs'.

Britain was simultaneously attacked for using excessive force and applauded for not using it. At the time, she certainly did not think that she was being brutal. The requirements of military law were meant to be observed. The 1929 Manual of Military Law was reduced to two pamphlets which could be carried by an officer on active duty so that he could be sure to act within permitted parameters. These instructions did, however, permit group punishments, and reprisals were allowed.[8]

45

MORE COMMISSIONS AND THE APPROACH OF WAR

Throughout the 1930s Britain was inclined to backtrack on her promises to the Zionists. Almost immediately after Peel, the government started to back away from its recommendations. There was a growing apprehension that greater account had to be taken of Arab views.

Britain never much liked the idea of partition. In 1937, following Peel, the Secretary of State for the Colonies, William Ormsby-Gore, told the Permanent Mandates Commission that carrying on the existing mandates was impossible if there were not to be repression, friction and hostility both within the two communities *inter se*, and between each of them and the Administrator. The Permanent Mandates Commission recognised that partition might have to be the way forward. But in the Statement of Policy of 1937[1] the government described itself as having 'been driven' to partition to resolve deadlock. Partition was not the preferred option.

Ormsby-Gore was an able Colonial Secretary, one of the ablest and best-qualified men to hold the office. He had been Sykes's assistant at the Cabinet Office in the First World War. He appointed Peel. He persuaded the government, but failed to persuade Parliament, to accept its proposals. The proposals thus went to the Permanent Mandates Commission (on which Ormsby-Gore had been the first British representative) without official British endorsement. Ormsby-Gore was convinced that partition had to work. He was impressed by what he saw of Zionism, and was horrified by what he knew of Nazi anti-Semitism. The policy of conciliating the Arabs as war approached by curtailing Jewish immigration was not congenial. When he succeeded to a peerage he offered his resignation as Colonial Secretary to Chamberlain, though he need not technically have done so. It was accepted, and that is regrettable.

The Peel Commission had operated under constraints of time, and its recommendations were expressed in fairly general terms. A new commission, the Woodhead Commission, ostensibly concerned with *how* partition should take place, arrived in Palestine on 27 April 1938 to go into matters in more detail. In reality, the commission was to rewrite Peel. It concluded fairly swiftly that the original proposal would not work: the proposed Jewish state would have been 49 per cent Arab. The Arab state would have contained only 7,200 Jews against 485,200 Arabs.[2]

The new commission accordingly considered 'Plan B', in which the Arab area in the Jewish zone of Galilee would go to the Arab state. This would reduce the percentage of Arabs in the Jewish state to 38 per cent. The configuration of the Jewish state would, however, have been unsatisfactory. The commission went on to propose a 'Plan C'. There would be a substantial retained mandate, with a Jewish state on the coastal plain and a larger Arab state comprehending Samaria, Hebron and Gaza. A number of subsidiary issues arose; but none of this mattered very much as the Arabs rejected entirely any sort of partition.

But by now Britain too was against partition: partition was dead in the water. The Government Statement on Policy of November 1938 concluded 'after careful study of the Partition Committee's Report . . ., that the political, administrative and financial difficulties involved in the proposal to create independent Arab and Jewish States inside Palestine are so great that this solution of the problem is impracticable.'[3]

The next attempt to address the problem was not a further commission, but a Round Table Anglo-Arab-Jewish Conference in London in February 1939. When it reached no agreement, Britain had to make decisions for herself. The result was the last White Paper, the White Paper of 1939. It briefly considered alternative Jewish homes: Tanganyika, Madagascar, British Guiana, even satellite settlements in Eritrea and Tripolitania. It was the only White Paper that committed Britain to a definite policy. Even that was not all that definite.

Yet it was a radical document, and an entirely new policy departure, a departure conditioned by the perception that in the context of the coming war Jewish support could be relied on, but not Arab support. Arab support had to be bought. Palestine was not to become a Jewish state. Immigration was to be limited and then stopped, unless the Arabs consented. Palestine was to be given independence within ten years. Britain had now distanced herself from a Zionist interpretation of the Balfour Declaration and something close to the principle of Arab self-determination appeared to be accepted.

The White Paper imposed limits on Jewish immigration and land purchase. Various formulae for immigration were considered: what was clear was that Jewish immigration would be severely checked. One suggestion was a maximum limit of 40 per cent after ten years, with future levels of immigration only as agreed between the communities. In the end, a further five years of Jewish immigration, involving 75,000 people in total, would be permitted. After five years, there would be no immigration without Arab approval. Land sales would also be curtailed. The High Commissioner would have power to control or prohibit land sales to Jews. By way of some sort of balance, there would be no independence without Jewish approval.

Britain often appears unsympathetic to the plight of persecuted Jews in Nazi Germany, but the statement did declare that 'above all, Her Majesty's Government are conscious of the present unhappy plight of large numbers of Jews who seek a refuge from certain European countries, and they believe that Palestine can and should make a further contribution to the solution of this pressing world problem'.[4] It was for this reason that in addition to permitting 10,000 immigrant Jews per year for five years, an additional quota of 25,000 was allowed. The overall consequence at the end of the five-year period would be to bring the Jewish population of the country up to one third of the total population.

The White Paper underlay British rule for the remainder of the mandate. It stressed that it had never been British policy that Palestine should become a Jewish state. Equally it denied that there had ever been any idea of subordinating 'the Arab population, language or culture in Palestine'. What Malcolm MacDonald, the Colonial Secretary – Ramsay MacDonald's son, but rapidly establishing that he deserved the appointment on his own merits – wanted from the White Paper was to secure that there would be no Arab or Jewish state, simply a single territory which Britain would for the moment continue to rule. Poor MacDonald: his achievement was widely seen as overtly pro-Arab. Jewish Zionists described him as 'so anti-Semitic as to be almost demented'. Churchill described the White Paper as a retreat in the face of force, and Ben-Gurion called it 'a new edition of Munich'.[5]

Relations between the Jews and the British were never the same. The easy association was at an end. In 1936 Wauchope, the High Commissioner, had complained that whereas Weizmann had access to the prime minister in London whenever he wanted, he himself had never even met the prime minister.[6] There had been a very cosy relationship between the Zionists and those at the top in British government. This ended with the 1939 White Paper. The Zionists were in disarray as well as alienated. Many, such as Ben-Gurion, despaired of Weizmann and his policy of working with the British.

The campaign against the White Paper was intensive. Zionists in Palestine and elsewhere, including the United States, were aghast. Irgun began a terrorist campaign. There was a complaint to the League's Mandates Commission that the White Paper conflicted with the terms of the mandate. But the war put an end to any further action by the League, and the subsequent history of Palestine was dictated by the events of the war, and much less by the terms of the White Paper.

The British authorities did their best to begin the implementation of the White Paper. In 1940, regulations were issued to govern land sales. Arabs who had been in custody or exile were pardoned and released. The Arabs seemed to have gained a great deal and there was some relaxation of tension, but they did not welcome the White Paper. It did not go far enough for them, and was officially rejected.

The reaction of the Jews is more comprehensible. They had more to complain about in the White Paper, and they were wholly alienated. At Evian-les-Bains in 1938, a conference of international powers had agreed that they would close their doors to Jewish victims of persecution. Palestine was all that was left to them, and Palestine Jews now felt they had no option but to have recourse to violence. They also did all they could to get the Jews who were being chased out of Germany safely into Palestine. They came in unseaworthy craft at great risk and found their way into Palestine through the crossfire between the Haganah and the British. Events in Palestine could no longer be viewed in isolation from what was going on in Europe.

Not only the Palestine Jews regarded the White Paper as ungenerous;[7] it was not much liked even in Britain, where it was felt to offer little support to the Jews, whose plight in Germany was becoming known. The decision to limit immigration was made just as the world was learning something of the horrors of the Nazi persecution of Jews. The dynamics of Zionism were changing critically. By the time the Second World War had ended, the consciousness of the fate that the world had allowed European Jews to suffer had created an atmosphere of collective guilt which irreversibly and critically altered the way in which Palestine was seen.

46

WAR

The war altered everything and in very many ways. Not the least important was that the American influence on events became much more significant. Britain's larger concerns in the Middle East during the war meant that the Arabs were to a degree left alone. The Jews fought with the British against Hitler, but they also fought against the White Paper. Ben-Gurion famously said, 'We shall fight with Great Britain in this war as if there was no White Paper, and we shall fight the White Paper as if there was no war.'[1]

The Jews had every reason for wanting Britain to defeat the Axis powers. In February 1941, 88 per cent of the Palestinian Arabs were in favour of Germany and only 9 per cent for Britain. *SS Obersturmbannführer* Walter Rauff and his *Einsatzkommando* were already detailed to liquidate the Jews in Palestine.[2]

The concurrence of local and world politics meant for example that the Haganah, although technically illegal, was openly tolerated by the British who wanted to have it ready, against the event of Axis invasion. Britain was aware that Jewish gun-running was going on to establish the Haganah. Churchill said, 'We won't mind it, but don't speak of it.'[3] But as the war went on, Jewish military strength was increasingly used against Britain and her institutions.

During most of the war the geopolitical significance of Palestine was very real. Colonel Wedgwood* described Palestine as 'the Clapham Junction of the

---

* Josiah Clement Wedgwood, first Baron Wedgwood (1872–1943), is yet another of these vigorous, highly motivated young men for whom the twentieth century opened doors to possibilities and adventures that would never otherwise have been available. Wedgwood had been turned down for a military career on medical grounds, but the South African War enabled him to see service with a field-gun battery manned mainly by men from the family pottery works. That led on to becoming a member of Milner's Kindergarten and resident magistrate of Ermelo, in the Transvaal, administering an area the size of Wales at the age of 30. He reminded Milner that he knew no law. 'That doesn't matter. Just keep them happy.' In 1914 he was made a lieutenant commander in the Royal Naval Volunteer Reserve. He commanded a squadron of armoured cars in Belgium and was awarded the DSO at Gallipoli. He played a prominent part in the famous landing from HMS *Clyde* at V Beach, was hit and invalided home. In the course of the rest of the war, he served with Smuts in German East Africa, sat on the 1916 Royal Commission on Mesopotamia, was sent on a goodwill mission to the United States, and after the 1917 Revolution investigated the situation in Russia with the rank of colonel. Between the wars, he

Commonwealth'.[4] In the course of the 1920s the Haifa–Baghdad route had been developed as an alternative approach to India if the canal were unavailable. A deepwater terminal was created at Haifa, and oil pipes were laid from Kirkuk. There was talk of establishing a strategic reserve at Haifa and using it instead of Malta.

As the war progressed and an increasingly pro-Zionist America became involved, the 1939 White Paper began to be looked at more critically. Churchill, always a Zionist, had never liked it and now he wanted to ditch it. It did not sit with the nature of the war Britain was now fighting. Duff Cooper said that what the Nazis were doing required that Britain 'do more rather than less for the Jews than she ever promised or intended'.[5] In 1943 a subcommittee of the Cabinet began to look again at partition plans. Amery produced such a plan, although it was opposed by Wavell for strategic reasons and by Eden, the Arabist who had studied Oriental languages at Oxford. When the Arab dimension was taken into account, the decision, despite all that had been happening to European Jewry, had to be to support the *status quo*. Relations with the Jews deteriorated, and those with the Arabs did not improve.

There were important developments in the United States. In May 1942, a Zionist conference took place at the Biltmore Hotel in New York and produced what was known as 'the Biltmore Program', a Zionist demand for a Jewish state. The program was accepted by the Committee of the Zionist General Council in Jerusalem in 1942, and its adoption gradually resulted in a sustained propaganda campaign directed against Britain. The resolution adopted, that 'Palestine be established as the Jewish Commonwealth', was Ben-Gurion's. It was pretty well endorsed by Roosevelt's administration. In Britain, the Labour Party Conference in December 1944 went even further, requiring immigration of Jews to be coupled with emigration of Arabs. Even Ben-Gurion thought this went too far.

The atmosphere was increasingly poisoned. There were the tragic incidents involving the *Patria* and the *Struma*. The first was a ship on which Britain embarked illegal immigrants with a view to sending them away from Palestine to a non-European destination. The ship was blown up, possibly by Jews themselves, while still in Haifa harbour. The incident was described as one of mass suicide. The *Struma* sailed from Romania to Palestine in February 1942, with 769 Romanian Jews held in cages. The refugees had no permission to land. At Britain's request, she was stopped by the Turks in Constantinople. The ship sank in a storm in the Black Sea. There were only two survivors. The tragedy is often – though wrongly – described as the greatest civilian maritime loss of the war.

sat in Parliament, successively Liberal, ILP and Labour. It was wholly in character that in 1939 at the age of 63 he was the first MP to join the Home Guard, then the Local Defence Volunteers.

Zionist determination 'to fight the White Paper as if there were no war, and the war as if there were no White Paper' eroded after the threat of attack by the Afrika Korps diminished and the news of what was happening to Jews in Germany began to arrive. Jewish opinion in Palestine turned even more strongly against the British. There was feeling that more could have been done to save Jews in Germany. While Jews continued to fight bravely in the war alongside British units, in Palestine itself weapons were stolen and British officials were murdered.

There was a serious revival of activity by Jewish terrorist groups. Before the outbreak of war, the Irgun – the national military organisation – had responded to the Arab rebellion chiefly by attacking Arabs in Arab areas. Now the Irgun and the Stern Gang directed their efforts against British officials and servicemen. There was a series of high-profile attacks. In August 1944 an attempt was made on the life of the British High Commissioner, Sir Harold MacMichael. On 29 September Assistant Police Superintendent Wilkin was shot dead, hit by six bullets. On 6 November, Lord Moyne, the British Minister Resident in the Middle East (who as minister for agriculture had invented the British Egg Mark), was shot dead in his car in Cairo by two members of the Stern Gang.*

On each occasion, the Jewish Agency disassociated itself from these events. Even in Palestine there was a degree of revulsion after the assassination of Lord Moyne, and the Jewish Agency purported to cooperate with Britain for the rest of the war. For a time, the Haganah helped to contain Jewish terrorism. But Zionist propaganda in the United States continued to stimulate outrages. To begin with, the dominant militant agencies were Irgun and the Stern Gang, but by 1945 the Jewish Agency and the Haganah were also thoroughly involved.

The assassination of Lord Moyne had a particular and dramatic impact in Britain. With characteristic magnanimity Churchill had overlooked Moyne's dalliance with Clementine when she sailed on his yacht in 1934, on an expedition to find a large reptile known as the Komodo dragon. His death appalled Churchill: 'If our dreams for Zionism are to end in the smoke of assassins' pistols and our labours for its future to produce only a new set of gangsters worthy of Nazi Germany, many like myself will have to reconsider the position we have maintained so consistently in the past.'[6] After Moyne's death, Churchill never again spoke to his old friend Chaim Weizmann.

---

* The Stern Gang broke away from the Irgun with the explicit aim of forcing the British from Palestine, allowing unchecked Jewish immigration and establishing a Jewish state. Its leader, Avraham Stern, said that 'no difference existed between Hitler and Chamberlain, between Dachau or Buchenwald and sealing the gates of Eretz Israel.' (Shindler, *The Land Beyond Promise: Israel, Likud and the Zionist dream*.)

47

THE END OF BRITISH PALESTINE

1. Overview

With the end of the war, the pressures on Britain's control of Palestine became unendurable. The history of the last years of the mandate is savage. Jews and Arabs suffered horribly. Contemplation of the agonies of the Holocaust, of the carnage on the Eastern front, of the misery of the hundreds of thousands of innocent people displaced for ever from their homes, might have prompted thoughts of reconciliation. In fact, they intensified inter-communal hatred. The greatest pity was that those who suffered most were not those committed to violence, but those caught up in events, innocent men, women and children, among them the conscripted British soldiers, whose chief desire was to return to their families.

Here we are concerned with British policy rather than the events of each day, but as we see how Britain struggled to find a way to make the mandate work, it will be helpful to keep in mind how that mandate ended. It ended in the realization that the task was by now an impossible one, and by its surrender to the United Nations, the successor to the League of Nations, the authority that had granted the mandate in the first place. The sequence of events now has a sense of inevitability about it which was absent at the time.

In brief outline, which will later be filled out, what happened was this. In 1946, the British Cabinet sought to share its responsibilities by involving the United States. An Anglo-American Committee of Inquiry was established, which reported on 20 April in terms which were on the whole unrealistic and which Britain rightly considered unworkable. In February of the following year, Britain announced that she would surrender the mandate to the United Nations. A Special Session of the United Nations considered the matter, and on 15 May a Special Commission on Palestine, UNSCOP, was set up.

On 1 September UNSCOP reported, and recommended the establishment of two states, one Arab and one Jewish, with Jerusalem set apart under international trusteeship. The Jewish state would have 498,000 Jews and 407,000

Arabs; the Arab state would have 725,000 Arabs and 10,000 Jews. Jerusalem and its enclave, which would include Bethlehem, would have 105,000 Arabs and 100,000 Jews.

Britain rejected the recommendations and said she would not accept responsibility for their implementation. The United Nations debated the proposals on 29 November 1947, and in remarkable circumstances, which included the surprise announcement by the Soviet spokesman, Andrei Gromyko, that the USSR would support the Jews, voted for partition by 33 votes to 13. Britain abstained.

The UN motion, which was advisory only and not binding, envisaged that the mandatory power would take on responsibility for the preliminary implementation of its terms, but Britain concluded that partition, which she had herself considered in detail, was unworkable. Britain could not accept responsibility for the Assembly resolution, which she knew was unacceptable to the Arabs. On 26 September she announced that, whatever happened, she would renounce the mandate on 15 May 1948, although military withdrawal would not take place until 31 July. In March 1948, it was decided that the military withdrawal could also take place on 15 May.

2. Bevin

In 1945 in the United States Truman succeeded Roosevelt as president, and America became more Zionist than ever. At the British General Election of the same year, the Labour Party replaced the Conservatives in a landslide. A strong foreign policy team was established under a prime minister, Clement Attlee, who proved a much more powerful leader than had been expected and who gave the strongest of support to the Foreign Secretary, Ernest Bevin, who emerged as perhaps the most able member of a very able Cabinet.

Bevin started his time as Foreign Secretary full of confidence about Palestine. He said he would 'stake my political future' on solving the problem.[1] Churchill responded by saying that 'No more rash a bet has ever been recorded in the annals of the British turf.'

Bevin discovered that things were not as simple as he had hoped. There was a huge diversity of views in Britain about what should happen. Bevin originally wanted Britain to stay on in a Palestine which would perhaps be a bi-national state. Attlee was for getting out: he felt strongly that among all those displaced persons who needed to be resettled, a special case could not be made for Jews. Arab and Muslim Indian opinion had also to be considered. The War Office, for its part, wanted to retain Palestine as a key part of Britain's overseas defences. The chiefs of staff stressed the importance of protecting oil, and keeping

Russia's hands off it.² By the beginning of 1947, Bevin was beginning to see the impossibility of achieving agreement between the two communities.

The Foreign Office started out strongly against partition. The Colonial Office, which had direct responsibility for Palestine, took a different view. Arthur Creech Jones, Colonial Secretary from July 1945, favoured partition. The Colonial Office line followed that of the Peel Commission. On the other hand, the Foreign Office could claim continuity with the thinking behind the 1939 White Paper, which was based on the view that there could be no Arab support for a mixed Jewish–Arab Palestine unless it was accepted that Jewish immigration would not continue indefinitely.

Creech Jones had been Bevin's parliamentary private secretary from 1940 to 1945, so the two knew each other well. But Creech Jones was his own man, a man of integrity who took the trouble to inform himself thoroughly before reaching a decision. In time he came to agree with Bevin and the idea of a bi-national state. The chiefs of staff were also for this. Palestine was crucial to their thinking in terms of Britain's strategic defence. The shift in defence policy is intriguing. Quite suddenly the centuries-old view of the Middle East as simply a buttress for India had disappeared. India was about to become independent and did not need to be defended. In both wars, the roles of the Middle East and India had been precisely the opposite of what the Foreign Office and the India Office thought it would be: India had proved to be indispensable for the defence of the Middle East and not the other way round.

An independent India could no longer be counted on to fulfil that role, and the chiefs looked to Palestine as a screen for the defence of Egypt, which they identified as the key position in the Middle East. They wanted to retain a naval base at Haifa, two army garrisons and an airbase, and they were of the view that treaty rights to enable them to do so could more easily be established with a bi-national state than in the context of partition.³

The chiefs and Bevin also saw the vital importance of the Middle East because of its oil. I have stressed that during and immediately after the First World War, the region's oil was not a critical factor and that it is an unhistorical mistake to overemphasise its significance. But by 1945 the mistake would be to underemphasise it.

Bevin accepted the advice of both the Foreign Office and the chiefs of staff that Palestine was an essential component in Britain's policy in the region. He was also influenced by the advice of the relatively junior Foreign Office official in Palestine, Harold Beeley, who was his closest adviser on the issue that 'Abdication in Palestine would be regarded as symptomatic of our abdication as a Great Power'.⁴ Beeley, incidentally, heard his chief say to Ben-Gurion that the Balfour Declaration had been the greatest mistake in

British twentieth-century foreign policy.[5] But although Bevin agreed with the chiefs of staff that British control should be maintained over the Middle East, he differed with them on how that control should be exercised. He wanted to move away from the traditional, dominating role, to one of partnership with the Arabs. There is continuity between his views now, as Foreign Secretary, and what he had come to believe during the second Labour government in 1929, when he served on the Colonial Development Advisory Committee. In justice to the Arabs as well as in Britain's interests, he wanted to work through genuine treaties, rather than influence.

The victory of the Labour Party in the British General Election in 1945 had initially been thought to favour Zionist aspirations. Legal immigrants were to be admitted for the moment at the rate of 1,500 per month. Illegal immigration proceeded faster than ever. The bias did not last. Bevin announced his abandonment of a pro-Zionist policy to Atlee with disarming bluntness: 'Clem, about Palestine. According to my lads in the [Foreign] Office, we've got it wrong. We've got to think again.'[6] His sympathy for the Arab cause ('under the Jews the Arabs would have no rights but would remain in a permanent minority in a land they had held for 2000 years'[7]) was not the product of anti-Semitism but an impartial reaction to the facts. Policy was in turmoil. Keeping the Americans happy pointed to Zionism; maintaining Middle Eastern interest and protecting oil pointed to a pro-Arab position.

Bevin started out as Foreign Secretary from a position of benevolent ignorance, but he was a formidable reader, highly intelligent and very anxious to learn. His principal source of information, of course, was the Foreign Office, and his bias came to be in favour of the Arabs. He was briefed on the importance of Arab oil and of the strategic importance of the Middle East for Britain. He needed no briefing to be hostile to any idea that the Communists might achieve a toehold in the Middle East. Jewish immigration was thought to go hand in hand with the growth of Communist influence. Accordingly he restricted it.

By the time that the decision to evacuate Palestine had been taken, Bevin had come to despair of the Jews. He reverted to the traditional, turn-of-the-century view that there was some conspiracy by 'international Jewry'. His twist to the conspiracy theory was to consider that Russia, with the connivance of the Jews, had established Palestine as a satellite state. He believed that Russia saw immigration as a way of flooding Palestine with indoctrinated Jews. All of this harked back to the idea that revolutionary Jews had helped to overthrow the tsar.

There were parallels, it seemed, between the collective farms of Russia and the kibbutzim in Palestine. Czechoslovakia supplied arms and ammunition to the Jews in 1948. British Intelligence found that there were indeed indoctrinated communists making their way to Palestine.[8] This explains to some extent why Bevin positively encouraged King Abdullah of Jordan to take over what Bevin called 'Arab Palestine'. While he stressed that the parts of Palestine awarded to the Jews in terms of the United Nations partition plans should be left severely alone, he told the Transjordan foreign minister that occupying the West Bank seems 'the obvious thing to do'. Indeed it was so obvious that he repeated that remark.[9]

Bevin is sometimes represented as anti-Semitic, but as early as 1930 he had demonstrated his open-mindedness by intervening to modify the Passfield White Paper to the advantage of the Jews. In his 1937 presidential address to the TUC he commended the achievement of the Jewish settlers in Palestine. In 1940–41 he was regarded by the Zionists as one of their supporters in the British War Cabinet.[10]

His attitude to the Jews hardened, but only as a result of direct responsibility for policy in the area, the change in circumstances in Palestine after 1945, and the increasing aggressiveness of the Haganah, Irgun and the Stern Gang. The Jewish Agency was now ready to mount armed rebellion against Britain if illegal immigration were not allowed, and 50,000 men in the Haganah and 6,000 in the Irgun and Stern Gang had been trained in guerrilla warfare.[11] The gradualism of Weizmann had gone.

Like many Britons of his generation, Bevin could make crass and thoughtless references to Jews and Jewishness. Colleagues like Ian Mikardo and Christopher Mayhew, Bevin's Parliamentary Under-Secretary, commented on his crude and vulgar anti-Semitic observations. Mikardo was of Russian Jewish stock, which stopped Attlee from giving him office in 1945, on the basis that there were already enough Jews in the government,[12] but he was far from thin-skinned. Mayhew was not Jewish, but was a man of sensibility. He was fastidious enough to sack the spy Guy Burgess from his information research department at the Foreign Office on the grounds that he was 'dirty, drunken and idle'.[13]

There is no evidence that anti-Semitism informed Bevin's policy, though he could not fail to react to terrorism and what he considered to be Jewish intractability. He was wholly committed to a thoroughly old-fashioned concept of British imperialism and to the promotion of Britain's greatness in the world. He had consciously rejected the notion of a socialist foreign policy in favour of a more expansive concept, and his policy towards Palestine was entirely consistent with that larger idea.

He was determined that no more British lives would be lost. He tried to block the establishment of a purely Jewish state. A bi-national state, with Jews reintegrated into Europe, even Germany, seemed infinitely preferable. He made policy. He talked, rightly, of 'my foreign policy'. He felt that a continued line of tradition tied him to great foreign secretaries of the past, 'Old Salisbury' and 'Old Palmerston'. 'Last night,' he said to Dean Acheson, the American Secretary of State with whom he established very close links, 'I was reading some papers of Old Salisbury. Y'knowe had a lot of sense.' So Ivone Kirkpatrick, Permanent Under-Secretary at the Foreign Office, and a great admirer, said that 'there was a great deal of the Emperor in Mr. Bevin's outlook'. He was 'Palmerston in a cloth cap'.[14] Stalin did not like the 'cloth cap': he complained that Bevin was no gentleman.

Bevin wanted to safeguard Arab Palestine from Zionist expansionism as the mandate ran out, and to see it preserved thereafter. But it deserves repeating that while he made it very clear that he had no objection to Transjordan's attempts to support or indeed take over Arab parts of a divided Palestine, he also made it clear that no moves should be made against the parts allocated to the Jews. When in the event Transjordan's Arab Legion, commanded by Glubb, officered to an extent by Britons, and supported by British aid, started fighting for Jerusalem, rather than confining its role to the occupation of Arab areas, he insisted on the withdrawal of British officers from the Palestinian operation and cut off further supplies of arms and ammunition, impairing the Legion's capacity for action.

48

BEVIN STARTS WORK

Bevin saw a joint approach by Britain and America as the best hope of finding a solution that would work. It would reassure Arab opinion, as well as helping to reconcile Britain with the United States. He had been perturbed by the deterioration of the relationship with the American government. He failed, however, to understand the extent of support for Zionism in the United States. His view that those Jews who had survived the Nazi atrocities could now be expected to settle down again in Germany was not shared by the Americans. The theme of this passage, his attempt to share the Palestine burden with others, is of a growing disillusionment with America followed then by handing the burden unceremoniously to the wider world community of the United Nations.

He announced that an Anglo-American Committee of Enquiry would go to Palestine to investigate the possibility of further Jewish immigration. It had been thought that America would not want to be involved, and her participation came as a surprise. The Anglo-American Commission of Enquiry or AAC consisted of six Britons and six Americans.

At the very same time as Bevin's plan was approved by the Cabinet, the Jewish leadership carried out a series of concerted raids on British military installations in Palestine. The timing was unfortunate. Weizmann and Moshe Shertok, the head of the Jewish Agency from 1933 until the establishment of the State of Israel, were summoned to Bevin who spoke with 'great anger and tension, a muscle at the side of his mouth giving a warning signal', according to Shertok. '"I cannot bear English Tommies being killed. They are innocent." When Weizmann referred to the millions of Jews who had been killed, and were still dying, in refugee camps, Bevin replied: "I do not want any Jews killed either, but I love the British soldiers. They belong to my class. They are working people."'[1]

The AAC considered the whole future of Palestine. Its report was published on 1 May 1946 and pleased no one. It unanimously rejected making Palestine either an Arab or a Jewish state. There was to be no partition. It concluded for a bi-national state. Bevin was happy with that. On the other hand, it also recommended the immediate admission of 100,000 Jewish refugees; thereafter Jewish immigration would continue without the requirement of Arab acquiescence that had been contained in the 1939 White Paper.

The idea of 100,000 refugees was to be a red-hot political issue. Bevin knew that the Arabs would have none of it, but Truman picked it up at once and unilaterally demanded the immediate admission of 100,000 new Jewish immigrants to Palestine. He was quite frank about the domestic political factors that motivated him. He told an Arab audience: 'I am sorry, gentleman, but I have to answer to hundreds of thousands who are anxious for the success of Zionism; I do not have hundreds of thousands of Arabs among my constituents.'[2]

Bevin later claimed that if Truman had not made this demand, and made it so forcefully, Britain and the United States might have settled the Palestine issue in a satisfactory way. Still in favour of a bi-national state at this stage, he maintained that the influx of 100,000 more Jews would be fatal to his plan. Far from wanting 100,000 more Jews in Palestine, Bevin hoped that some of the Jews already in Palestine might move back to Europe.[3]

He was anxious not to part company with America. He knew that on the United States depended Britain's only chance of preserving her position in the Middle East. But relations were deteriorating. Truman continued to press for his 100,000. Bevin was infuriated that party considerations were being allowed to derail a major geopolitical issue of principle. He proclaimed that Truman wanted Palestine to take the 100,000 because he 'did not want too many Jews in New York'. He was making the point that pro-Zionism was frequently the product of local anti-Semitism. It was not a point that Truman wanted to hear, and the result was to irritate American Zionists and encourage support for the Haganah and the terrorist organisations. At the same time Chaim Weizmann, Britain's friend, was replaced by Ben-Gurion, who took the view that Zionist aims could only be achieved by driving Britain out of Palestine.

Things got worse. Truman was concerned that the Democrat Party would suffer if the Jews were 'ghetto-ized' in a position of provincial autonomy within a bi-national state. On 4 October 1946, on the eve of Yom Kippur, he made an important speech which at least appeared to support 'the creation of a viable Jewish state' even if in reality he was arguing for less than that. The British prime minister, Attlee, who had been trying to prevail on the president not to make any more unilateral statements, was furious. He drafted in his own hand a blistering letter to the president, which even Churchill would not have dared to send:

I have received with great regret your letter refusing even a few hours' grace to the Prime Minister of the country which has the actual responsibility for the government of Palestine in order that he might acquaint you with the actual situation and the probable results of your action.

These may well include the frustration of the patient efforts to achieve a settlement and a loss of still more lives in Palestine.

I am astonished that you did not wait to acquaint yourself with the reasons for the suspension of the conference with the Arabs. You do not seem to have been informed that so far from negotiations having been broken off, conversations with leading Zionists with a view to their entering the conference were proceeding with good prospects of success.[4]

49

EVENTS

It soon seemed pretty clear to Bevin, and to British opinion generally, that the AAC Report would not be workable. In July 1946 he turned from bi-nationalism to think briefly about partition. But the Cabinet was not impressed, and he was not there to argue the case. Bevin was ill or abroad much of this time. Between 22 April 1946 when the AAC Report was signed and the end of the year, he was absent for 46 of the 69 Cabinet meetings.[1] His influence on the development of policy was for a time attenuated. In the meantime, the British secretariat and Army HQ in the King David Hotel was blown up, with 91 dead and 45 wounded. The atrocity and the British response, characterised by anti-Semitic demonstrations, made rational developments difficult.

Bevin's ideas about partition were strangled by assassination and sabotage. The carnage convinced him that partition would not in fact work and he reverted to the belief that bi-nationalism would have to be attempted. He ruled out partition in a bleak but realistic memo to the Cabinet:

> The certainty of Arab hostility to partition is so clear, and the consequences of permanently alienating the Arabs will be so serious, that partition must on this ground alone be regarded as a desperate remedy. The risk cannot be excluded that it would contribute to the elimination of British influence for the whole of the vast Moslem area lying between Greece and India. This would have not only strategic consequences; it would also jeopardise the security of our interest in the increasingly important oil production of the Middle East.[2]

His final position was the 'Bevin Plan' of 2 February 1947: a five-year period of trusteeship to be succeeded by self-government, with immigration at the rate of 4,000 a month for the first two years and a provision for United Nations' arbitration. United Nations trusteeship would lead to an independent bi-national state. Provincial autonomy was replaced by 'cantons' reflecting the preponderance of inhabitants. This was provincial autonomy, a model rather like that of Switzerland. Neither the Jews nor the Arabs liked it; nor did the Americans.

It was clear that none of the different approaches would work. The Arabs rejected anything that implied Jewish self-government or continued Jewish immigration. The Jews rejected anything that did not promise an eventual Jewish state. The independent state that the Arabs wanted would have stirred the Jews into civil war with huge consequent bloodshed. Partition would stir the Arabs into civil war, without even enjoying the support of the Jews.

On 13 February 1947, Creech Jones had told the Cabinet that there should be no question of evacuation, which would amount to abandoning the 'sacred trust' of the mandate and would be a 'humiliating course'.[3] Twelve days later he was still telling the House of Commons, 'We are not going to the United Nations to surrender the mandate.'[4] In between the two statements, on 15 February 1947, the Cabinet had agreed to referral to the UN. Referral did not necessarily mean abandoning the mandate; rather seeking guidance on how it should be exercised. But policy was changing very fast.

On 18 February, Bevin made his historic announcement to the House of Commons. He said that Britain could not accept the proposals of the Arabs or Jews and could not devise a workable solution of their own. The problem would be handed to the United Nations, who would be told that the mandate was unworkable. The curtain was falling on empire: on that same day, the Cabinet fixed a date on which Britain would leave India, whatever the circumstances in the subcontinent might be.

50

SURRENDERING THE MANDATE

Bevin had begun to toy with the idea of handing the problem to the United Nations quite early.[1] But in his desire not to be associated with a policy of scuttle and abdication, he resisted as long as he could. In view of the withdrawal from India, 'the impression seemed to be growing that we had lost the ability, and, indeed, the will, to live up to our responsibilities'.[2] Quite apart from national image, there was the importance of the natural resources and strategic importance of the Middle East.

The decision to quit was made while the War Office was still building up supplies in Palestine for a long stay. Initially indeed Bevin had thought that involving the United Nations need not imply the surrender of the mandate. What he wanted to do was to involve the wider community in the problem. The reality was that Britain had given up the initiative and Palestine was now the world's problem.

The turn-around was apocalyptic. It was an admission of defeat in the face of inescapable political facts. Britain had been separating from America over the issue. Bevin deprecated the fact that American policy was directed by political considerations in New York City; but bankrupt and friendless in a bleak post-war world, Britain could not ignore the reality of American strength and influence. General Marshall, the United States' Secretary of State, warned Bevin that American agreement on Palestine was essential. Britain could not go it alone. Her abdication of responsibility for the mandate she had once accepted demonstrated, just as much as Suez, that British foreign policy was dependent on American support. Bevin's minister of state, Hector McNeil, told him that Britain 'no longer had the means nor the military resources to command this whole area by ourselves. It is essential even when the Jews are the most wicked and the Americans most exasperating not to lose sight of this point'.[3]

Everything came together. From January 1945 to November 1947 running Palestine cost Britain £100 million and in the period 338 British subjects had been murdered by Jewish terrorists.[4] In 1947 Britain had no money, no food and no power in one of the harshest winters of the century. Hugh Dalton, the Chancellor of the Exchequer, wrote to Attlee:

I am quite sure that the time has almost come when we must bring our troops out of Palestine altogether. The present state of affairs is not only costly to us in man-power and money but is, as you and I agree, of no real value from a strategic point of view – you cannot in any case have a secure base on top of a wasps' nest – and it is exposing our young men, for no good purpose, to abominable experiences, and is breeding anti-Semites at a most shocking speed.[5]

It was an extraordinarily difficult decision, an admission of defeat by a Britain which had just emerged victorious from the most terrible of struggles and with the honour and distinction of having been the only country to fight from start to finish against enormous odds in the clearest conflict between good and evil than can be conceived. She was still apparently the greatest imperial power the world had ever known. Her territories spanned the globe, still defended by formidable armed forces. Her people did not know, and even her leaders scarcely recognised, that the cost of victory had been her relegation to the ranks of the second-class powers and that her days of Empire were at an end. The contrast between the glory of victory and the humiliation of impotence was colossal. Even 65 years later many in Britain are still not reconciled to a role as just one member of the European community, with a navy smaller than that of Belgium. How difficult then to be reconciled in 1945 to the change of status. But there was no alternative and for the Opposition Churchill's reaction was simply that the government was taking too long to hand the matter to the United Nations.

Indeed, things went badly in the interregnum. The referral, the admission that Britain could not deal with the matter by itself, stimulated the Jews to increase resistance to the regime. The notorious hanging of two British sergeants in reprisal for the execution of three Irgun men took place on 30 July. Shortly afterwards the *Exodus* reached Palestine, only for the 4,500 Jews aboard to be returned to camps in North Germany. The British convoy was described as a floating concentration camp, and when a baby died at sea the Zionists proclaimed that 'the dirty Nazi-British assassins suffocated this innocent victim with gas'.

The hanging of the two young British sergeants caused particular revulsion in Britain. Bevin was furious. He told General Marshall that the executions of the sergeants 'would never be forgotten' and that 'anti-Jewish feeling in England was now greater than it had been in a hundred years'.[6] His handling of the *Exodus* episode was a direct result of his anger. It was intended 'to teach the Jews a lesson'.

Opinion was revolted by the sight of full-page photographs of the sergeants' bodies and by the knowledge that their corpses had been violated by planting them with booby traps. There was resentment against American funding of Zionism – 'dollars helped to buy the rope' on which the sergeants were hanged.[7] The reaction to the rise of Jewish terrorism, and particularly the hanging of the unarmed sergeants, provoked demonstrations and a breakdown of discipline among British soldiers and policemen in Palestine, and anti-Semitic riots in Liverpool, Manchester, Glasgow and London.

The suddenness of Britain's departure from Palestine permitted Jewish expansion, and the fact that in the last six months before the exit any real attempt at peacekeeping was abandoned meant that Arabs were being pushed off the land. But Britain's role in the mandate experiment was not ignoble, and to the end policy was not dictated solely by self-interest. Self-interest would have pointed towards the creation of a single independent state, dominated by the Arabs, whose support and whose oil Britain wanted.

History has treated Labour's tussles with the Palestinian problem unkindly. The government did not throw in its hand and dump the problem on the United Nations without trying very hard to find a solution. More than 50 years of hindsight reinforces the view that there is nothing that could have been done without consequences that were going to be fairly disastrous.

51

AFTER THE ANNOUNCEMENT

On 2 April 1947, Britain asked the United Nations Secretary General to summon a special session of the General Assembly so that UNSCOP, the United Nations' Special Committee on Palestine, could be set up to consider the Palestine situation. The basis on which Britain did this was the conclusion that Britain 'should not have the sole responsibility for enforcing a solution which is not accepted by both parties and which we cannot reconcile with our conscience'.

When UNSCOP arrived in Jerusalem, Jewish terrorism was becoming even more extreme. There was an attack on the Tel Aviv military headquarters, a raid on the British Officers' Club in Jerusalem, in which 20 Britons were killed, a bombing raid on the Cairo–Haifa train. The immigrant ships arrived one after another. British reaction to terrorism varied from the illicit beating up of Jews to the imposition of martial law, executions, the seizing of immigrants and their transfer to internment camps in Cyprus.

The Jews represented the response to these atrocities as being akin to Nazism. They benefited both from the atrocities and from the propaganda effect of the response. When Bevin arrived in New York in November 1946 he was taken aback by the strength of popular feeling against Britain, based on Palestine. Dockers refused to handle his luggage and when he attended a football game the crowd booed when his presence was announced over the loudspeakers. When he opened the New York papers he was faced by whole-page advertisements which described the British occupation of Palestine as being like a concentration camp run by the Nazis. When the *Exodus* was turned around, the *Christian Science Monitor's* correspondent in Haifa said that 'The Jews here believe that one "illegal" ship may be worth ten million words in helping to convince [UNSCOP]'.[1]

By the time that the members of UNSCOP reached Palestine, there were about 100,000 British soldiers defending a territory the size of Wales, one soldier for every 18 inhabitants, one soldier for every city block.[2] The cost of this presence, almost £40 million a year, was a heavy burden, borne at a time when the economy was close to collapse and convertibility was under discussion.

Britain felt herself beleaguered. The international pressure she faced was not simply a reflection of post-Holocaust sympathy for the Jews, but also of positive dislike for what was seen as continuing British imperialism. Russia and America were brought together in a tacit anti-colonialist alliance against the imperial power.

By now the mandate was scarcely being exercised in any real sense. The British corralled themselves inside barbed-wire enclosures known as Bevingrads. Civilians were evacuated in 1947. The terrorism, the bombings continued. As was inevitable, Britain lost the propaganda war. The Royal Navy intercepted illegal immigrants and sent them to Cyprus. These displaced persons were the skeletal survivors of the extermination camps. They had escaped from the German camps to be imprisoned in camps the victors set up for them. They had no wish to be resettled in the Europe which had treated them so foully; Europe was one vast crematorium. It was easy for Ben-Gurion to say that terrorism was 'nourished by despair' or that Britain had 'proclaimed a war against Zionism' in order 'to liquidate the Jews as a people'.[3]

UNSCOP was given only a few months to submit a recommendation. It reported to the Secretary General on 1 September 1947. Seven out of the eleven UNSCOP members recommended partition (with Jerusalem under direct United Nations control). The United Nations plan, like the Peel Commission, gave the coastal plain, the Plain of Esdraelon and the area to the west and north of the Sea of Galilee to the Jews. But it went further and also gave to the Jews the south of Palestine, the Negev, in which there was only a handful of Jews, but which gave the new state access to the Red Sea at Aqaba. The rest of Palestine was to be an Arab state, apart from Jerusalem and Bethlehem, which were to remain controlled by the United Nations. When the report came before the General Assembly, the Zionists threw themselves into looking for support, while the Arabs resorted to their favourite position of boycott. They would have been well advised to exert themselves.

The final acts in the drama were played out in the United Nations and certainly not in London. The key event had been a sudden demarche in May 1947. The USSR saw the opportunity of denying the British a base in the Middle East and announced that the Jews were entitled to their own state. Gromyko's intervention lent validity to the idea of partition, which earlier in the year it had been assumed the United Nations would veto. Truman for America followed suit and applied huge diplomatic pressure on minor states. The combination of Stalin, Zionist powers of persuasion and American encouragement, a combination of ethics and bribery (votes were said to be going for

$75,000) won a result that was not, however, uninfluenced by a debt of conscience after the Holocaust.

The events at the United Nations were charged with enormous drama. The new world organisation was in its infancy. The dynamics of power had been transformed with the emergence of two superpowers – and in confrontation. It was far from clear whether the League's successor would be robust enough to survive, and right at its birth it had to adjudicate on the most intractable and delicate of geopolitical issues. In the vote on 29 November 1947, by 33 votes to 13, with 10 abstentions, just over the required two-thirds majority, the General Assembly of the United Nations voted for the partition of Palestine and the establishment of an independent Jewish state. Votes of the General Assembly are not binding. The vote was only advisory; the resolution was never adopted by the Security Council. But the tectonic plates had shifted for ever. The Arabs walked out. The United Nations' view, like Peel's, was that two states should coexist in Palestine, one Jewish and one Arab. But because the Arabs refused to agree to partition, no Arab Palestine was ever established.

Palestine was to be the Jewish home. The Jews were still only one-third of the population and owned only 6 per cent of the land. Within a year, the Jewish population of Palestine was in excess of 650,000, as opposed to considerably less than a third of that 20 years earlier.

The detail of the proposal was extraordinarily complicated, dividing each state into three segments. The bias of the plan was distinctly in favour of the Jews, who received the most fertile ground, including most of the fruit orchards, half of which were owned by Arabs. Five hundred thousand Jews would have within their territories 450,000 Arabs. Bevin's reaction was that the plan was 'manifestly unjust to the Arabs'. He had not wanted partition: that was why the problem had been handed to the United Nations. And he had not expected the United Nations to recommend partition. When they did so, they asked Britain to manage Palestine during a period of two years to allow the transition to take effect. The United States endorsed the request, but Britain would have none of it. Bevin had not wanted to alienate the Arabs when it was he who formulated policy, and he had no wish to alienate them now that policy was being formulated by the United Nations. He sought to make it very clear that Britain took no responsibility for what the UN was doing to the Arabs. He recommended that Britain should take no responsibility for enforcing an unworkable and unfair plan on Palestine. The Cabinet agreed, and on 26 September Creech Jones announced that Britain would not be responsible for imposing a solution which neither party wanted.

Bevin expressed his philosophy very clearly in a speech in the Commons in a two-day debate on 11 and 12 December 1947: 'I think that the Arab feeling in this question has been under-estimated. It has got to be assessed at its correct value by everybody, or we shall not get a peaceful settlement. It is because I want it assessed at its proper value that I do not want the Arabs to be dismissed as if they were nobody'.[4]

Britain brought the original surrender date – not later than 1 August 1948 – forward. The United Nations, and in particular the United States, were slow to realise that Britain meant it when she said that she would surrender the mandate and cease to be responsible for Palestine with effect from midnight 14/15 May 1948. The United States argued that as mandatory it was Britain's responsibility to implement the United Nations' decision. But the Defence Committee of the Cabinet continued to work on plans for withdrawal. On 4 December, the Cabinet agreed that 'while HMG should do nothing to obstruct the carrying out of the UN decision, British troops and the British Administration should in no circumstances become involved in enforcing it or in maintaining law and order while the UN Commission enforced it'.[5]

Things were going badly in Berlin, and it appeared that Britain might need to fight a war in Europe. The priority was to get personnel and material out of Palestine as neatly as possible. Britain confined herself to maintaining order in one or two defensive areas and along her own exit routes. Meanwhile the two communities fought with each other, and the Jews extended their areas of control.

The political gap between the Jews and the Arabs was now unbridgeable. The Jews were irrevocably committed to a Jewish state, while the Arabs would only accept the presence of the Jews already in Palestine provided that there was no more immigration and that a democratic and independent state was created. The Arab League, dominated by a nationalistic Egypt, was now the voice-piece of the Arabs. No one wanted the British to be in Palestine, not the Jews nor the Arabs, not the Americans nor the Russians. Britain had no wish to be there either.

It is not easy to see that Britain would have stayed in Palestine however voting at the UN had gone. There were no plans for remaining. On the other hand, there was no preparation for departure; no steps were taken to prepare political institutions to accept the transfer of power. Indeed there *was* no transfer of power. There was no one to transfer it to. 'The Union Jack was lowered and with the speed of an execution and the silence of a ship that passes in the night British rule in Palestine came to an end.'[6]

On 15 May 1948, as the British Army withdrew to Haifa, to embark and withdraw, six Arab armies entered Palestine: the Jordanian Army, the Arab Legion, the Egyptians, the Syrians, the Lebanese and the Iraqis. Israel repulsed the attacks and extended her borders. Outbreaks of warfare and ceasefires succeeded each other. On 15 October 1948, Israel attacked the Egyptian Army and within a week had taken Beersheba. Egypt signed an armistice on 24 February 1949 and Lebanon on 23 March. Hostilities were concluded for the most part not by peace treaties but merely by armistices, some of which are still no more than that today. What these agreements put in place was what Peel had wanted: partition.

It was still far from certain what territory the Jewish state would actually have. But the Zionists were building up their forces for expansion, and they were assisted by the surprising fact that Abdullah of Jordan, with his powerful Arab Legion, made a secret agreement with Golda Meyerson (later Meir) to the effect that he would leave the Jews in the areas that the United Nations gave them, providing he got the central area alongside Jordan.

Even before the State of Israel formally came into existence, Arabs were fleeing from the territory. Violence was sometimes used, but even more effective were rumours and reports of violence that inevitably circulated and precipitated further departures. The Haganah encouraged a further Arab exodus. In 1948 it authorised a campaign, 'Plan D', against potentially hostile Arab villages which protected Israel and Jewish communities outside Israel's borders, by '[t]he conquest and permanent occupation, or levelling, of Arab villages and towns'.[7] Only Jordan gave Arab nationality to the displaced Arabs from Palestine; in the other Arab states they remained and remain stateless and a continuing source of reproach to the Jews and to their hosts.

The movement was two-way. Arabs left Palestine in huge numbers, although more than 100,000 remained within Israel, but hundreds of thousands of Jews were expelled from Iraq and North Africa. The historic coexistence of Jews and Arabs was coming to an end, and cities such as Baghdad, which, while Arab, had always had a substantial Jewish minority, for the first time became overwhelmingly Arab. The character of the Middle East was changing fast and not for the better. Soviet Russia's cordiality towards Israel soon came to an end, and increasingly the USSR supported the militant aggrieved Arab states. Nineteen forty-eight brought Arab nationalism, the Muslim military and Soviet Cold War strategy together for the first time.

So ended British Palestine. It ended in abandonment by Britain, cynical manoeuvres by the United States and the USSR, and a solution from the United Nations which could never work.

X

CONCLUSIONS

52

Tentative Judgements

The judgements that matter are those that readers form on the facts that this narrative contains. I have allowed myself to hint at some of my own views in the course of the narrative. It would be heavy-handed to underline them unduly. It may be permissible, however, to make a few broad observations about British policy in the mandated areas and about the nature of the British mandates, chiefly those in Palestine and Iraq.

The Arabs, the French and to some extent the Jews have accused Britain of deceit and treachery. Some groups continue to do so. Did Britain cynically abuse the trust of her allies to further her interests in the region for strategic reasons and for the sale of oil resources, as is so often suggested? Was she party to a Jewish plot, as conspiracy theorists allege?

My conclusion is that British policy was formulated in good faith, the outcome of a desperate and uncoordinated series of attempts to stave off defeat, much of it at a time when Britain was threatened by starvation as a result of submarine blockade. There was confusion, sloppiness and a multiplicity of competing agencies. Some policy initiatives – the Balfour Declaration is the most egregious – were subsequently assumed to have a significance greater than their authors had intended. Three main promises which jarred with each other were made (one to the Jews in the Balfour Declaration, one to the French in the Sykes–Picot Agreement and one to the Arabs in the McMahon–Hussein Correspondence – arguably with another, conflicting promise to Ibn Saud). They were made under the overriding imperative of finding allies to help win the war, and little thought was given to how they could be reconciled in the event of victory.

Hindsight must not obscure the fact that victory was very far from certain. In 1914, Allied strategy failed to deliver the swift moves on which victory was predicated. In 1915, France suffered huge losses that threatened to destroy the country militarily and morally. For the rest of the war, there was a very real risk that France would collapse. Germany sought to defeat Britain, as Falkenhayn said in relation to Verdun, by knocking the French sword out of Britain's hand. British attempts to relieve the pressure on France in 1916 and 1917 were only partially successful, and the cost in terms of losses left scanty drafts for 1918. The German submarine blockade brought the British Isles to the edge of starvation and the cost of the war had turned the biggest creditor nation in the world into a supplicant debtor. In 1918, Ludendorff almost succeeded in crushing the Allies before America could enter the war. The British and French line very nearly broke. Britain came close to falling back to the Channel ports with the result that took place in 1940. Haig issued his 'Backs to the Wall' Order of the Day. Even though the retreat of spring 1918 was checked and turned into a great series of British victories, it was almost unanimously thought that final victory could not be achieved until 1921 or 1922, when huge American armies would be in the field.

Much policy was created without the knowledge or involvement of government as a whole, by individuals who were motivated by particular enthusiasms, and as stop-gap creations which acquired a dynamic of their own. But there was little or no deliberate deception, little long-term planning of devious strategy. The conflicting ambitions which developed in Palestine during Britain's time there persist in provoking hostility, violence and tragedy in an area where Jews, Arabs and Christians once lived in harmony. But confusion is more obvious than conspiracy.

The country or interest group that can legitimately complain of bad faith is France. France had been Britain's traditional rival for centuries, and around the end of the nineteenth century a number of incidents threatened to result in war. The Entente Cordiale of 1904 was an attempt at rapprochement, and in the First World War there was a close military alliance. But most politicians and senior army officers thought this a brief historic anomaly after which competing interests would again collide.

In the other concessions and promises there was at least an element of generosity towards noble Arabs and ill-treated Jews. What was given to the French in Sykes–Picot was given grudgingly and of necessity. As soon as that necessity was past, politicians started to reflect on how dangerous the French threat had been in the past and was likely to be in the future. The government started to withdraw and qualify much of what France had been promised. The language that was used was remarkably frank, malevolent and ungenerous.

The argument that circumstances had changed really meant that France's help no longer had to be bought. Lloyd George referred to the fact that it had been British arms that had won Mesopotamia from the Turks and had also dominated activities on the Western Front in the Hundred Days, that great, unbroken series of British-led victories that ended the war. But overall, Britain's losses were only a little more than half of France's. France suffered far more than Britain did. She was bled to death to the point that her army's morale and the resilience of her civilian population were close to breaking. Clemenceau, remarkably, allowed Britain to rewrite some of Sykes–Picot, but Lloyd George's ambitions were not satisfied. Finally Britain and France came to *rupture*. France felt let down and badly treated and was entitled to do so.

What did Britain's time in Iraq amount to? On one level, she made many mistakes. She had chosen to rely on the minority Sunnis, mostly from Baghdad and the north, together with the landed interest. She did not buy into the liberal middle class. She has accordingly been criticised for ignoring the structure of Iraqi society. But the lack of viable alternatives has already been canvassed. What else could have been done?

At the very least, Britain's self-interest was well served. At the end of the First World War, Britain found herself the owner of Iraq pretty well by chance. There was never any question of grooming her on a long-term basis for independence, like India. Britain got what she wanted for 40 years: control of a strategically important piece of territory, together with favoured access to Iraq's oil.

Oil had been the least important consideration in 1918. In the event, control of Iraq's oil was of crucial importance, particularly in the Second World War. From a British perspective, the fusion of the three vilayets, however imperfect, and the establishment of a British connection that lasted 40 years, created one of the pillars of victory in 1945. That was an unintentional and unforeseen benefit. It also served to protect the route to India, a *desideratum* that had been consciously identified. To that extent, the creation of Iraq was a good thing for Britain. Whether it was a good thing for Iraq itself or for the world at large is another question. It is a question that cannot be answered unless an alternative way of filling the vacuum left by the Ottomans can be imagined.

Jordan started as a mere appendix to the Palestine mandate, and it is something of an appendix to these concluding thoughts. But if there is little that needs to be said about the country that perhaps suggests that Britain did not do too badly there. What started as an insignificant and unpopulated piece of desert with an itinerant prince, ended up as a very important military power ruled by a dynasty with the capacity to survive. The credit does not lie entirely with Britain. King Hussein was an outstanding ruler who managed to view relationships in the region in more than two dimensions. Egypt has come to adopt a similar approach, and the hope must be that other Arab countries and Israel will one day do so too.

There is no easy conclusion about the Palestine mandate. In *Western Imperialism in the Middle East 1914–1958*, D.K. Fieldhouse begins his chapter on Palestine under the British mandate thus: 'It is arguable that Palestine was the greatest failure in the whole history of British imperial rule.'[1] Elizabeth Monroe's famous assertion that the Balfour Declaration was 'one of the greatest mistakes in our Imperial history' has already been noted.

From the point of view of pure self-interest, was the British presence in Palestine a failure or not? For more than a quarter of a century, Britain was able to consolidate her interests in the Middle East, particularly the Canal, from Palestine and to deny the area to rivals, France before the Second World War and Germany during it. Britain's policy was successful from that standpoint, whatever its effect in the longer-term history of the region.

Secondly, was Britain's discharge of the mandate flawed? Could any power or any policy have avoided the appalling, horrible and enduring inter-communal strife that desecrates the area, given the initial decision to establish a Jewish home? And how wrong, in any event, was that promise?

The Balfour Declaration, made in the circumstances and envisaged in the limited way that has been described, did not commit Arabs and Jews to conflict. They chose that conflict for themselves. The Arabs exacerbated the problems inherent in Palestine by their sulky non-cooperation and obstructiveness, the Jews by their desire for much more than amicable coexistence. The charge that the present-day State of Israel exists as a result of an Anglo-Jewish conspiracy is particularly bizarre. Overall, British policy towards Palestine was much more directed towards Arab than Jewish interests, as indeed demographics would require. Britain's conduct was not perfect, but she sought to exercise responsibly a mandate which she had not wanted in the first place. The United States, which was offered the mandate at the outset, stood aside, without responsibility, to criticise, interfere and inflame.

The mandate had committed Britain to developing self-government, but Palestine never governed itself. Of necessity, it was governed under the least liberal of the British colonial models, without a legislative council. Britain's eventual departure was precipitate, and, on the face of it, irresponsible, a departure for which no one was prepared and which left Palestine without any system of government to accept a smooth transfer of power. The Chief Secretary, Sir Henry Gurney, told journalists that 'I shall put [the keys of my office] under the mat'.[2] He wrote in his diary, 'The Police locked up the stores (worth over one million pounds) and brought the keys to the UN [Commission], who refused to receive them. I had to point out that the UN would be responsible for the administration of Palestine in a few hours time (in accordance with the UN November Resolution) and that we would leave the keys on their doorstep, whether they accepted them or not; which they did.'[3]

Sir Alan Cunningham, the last High Commissioner, says much the same thing, but explains why Britain did what it did: 'In the end the British were blamed for not having handed over to anyone, whereas, in point of fact, there was nobody to whom to hand over.'[4] That vacuum was of the world's making. And it is too simple to single out Britain for creating the disaster that Palestine had become. Remember that Britain had never wanted the mandate – she would have been greatly relieved if the United States had accepted it. The tragedy is indeed that things could have been so different. Palestine could have developed for the benefit of both communities. Churchill's vision, when he planted the tree at the Hebrew University and quoted from the Scriptures he had been given, the vision of 'a land flowing with milk and honey, in which sufferers of all races and religions will find a rest from their sufferance' could have been fulfilled.

It is not to the shame of the mandatory alone that it was not fulfilled. The Balfour Declaration was based on the idea that Jewry dispersed throughout the world by persecution and cruelty was entitled to consideration along with the wishes of the largely nomadic peoples who happened to be in Palestine in 1917. The interests of the two peoples were not, in any case, thought necessarily to be mutually inimical. Nor need they have been. No one saw or could see the immigration that the Holocaust would prompt. No one foretold the appetites that dispersed Jewry would develop. No one could have imagined that the Arabs would strain to put on limited and tentative British undertakings constructions that they were never meant to bear.

The situation that was left was a disaster and a tragedy, a disaster which has begotten further disaster and tragedy for three generations in the land which all three Faiths of the Book regard as holy and in which they had lived for centuries in reasonable amity. The disaster is not of Britain's making. It is a disaster born of selfishness and short-sighted greed. It is a disaster which Britain strove to avoid. It is a disaster that vision and restraint can still remedy.

OUTLINE CHRONOLOGY

1904

8 April	Entente Cordiale with France signed.

1907

31 August	Entente with Russia signed.

1914

28 July	Seizing of *Reshadieh* and *Sultan Osman I*.
4 August	Declaration of War between Britain and Central Powers.
2 October	'Force D' ordered from India to Mesopotamia.
4 November	Declaration of War between Britain and Ottoman Empire.

1915

30 August	Henry McMahon writes to King Hussein.

1916

9–16 May	Sykes–Picot agreement embodied in Grey–Cambon Exchange.
10 June	Start of Arab Revolt.

1917

2 November	Balfour Declaration.

1918

January	Hogarth sent out to deliver the Hogarth Message to King Hussein.
8 January	President Wilson enunciates his Fourteen Points.
March	Zionist Commission for Palestine formed. In 1921 became the Palestine Zionist Executive and acted as the Jewish Agency for Palestine.
16 June	Declaration to the Seven.
7 November	Anglo-French Declaration.
30 November	Armistice of Mudros ends hostilities between the Allies and the Ottoman Empire.

1919

18 January	Paris Peace Conference opens.
28 August	King–Crane Commission reports.

1920

8 March	Faisal proclaimed king of Syria.
19–26 April	San Remo Conference.
25 April	Mandates over Palestine, Jordan and Iraq effectively constituted by San Remo Resolution.
May	Euphrates Revolt breaks out.
10 August	Treaty of Sèvres.

1921

12 March	Cairo Conference opens.
23 August	Faisal crowned king of Iraq.
October	Haycraft Report into Khedara Raid and Jaffa Riots.

1922

28 February	Egypt Declaration: Britain's statement of Egypt's status ends protectorate established under the Khedivate from 1914.

1923

May	Jordan established as an independent country.
24 July	Lausanne Conference concludes.

1924

First Anglo-Iraqi Treaty.

1926

Second Anglo-Iraqi Treaty.

1928

British–Transjordanian Agreement.

1929

25 October	Shaw Commission into Wailing Wall Disturbances in Jerusalem opens its hearings.

1930

1 October	Passfield White Paper giving effect to Shaw recommendations issued.

1932

End of Iraq mandate.

1933–36

Fifth *aliyah*, or wave of Jewish immigration.

1936

15 April	The Arab Revolt in Palestine breaks out and continues until 1939.
25 April	Arab Higher Committee established.
26 August	Anglo-Egyptian Treaty.

1937

7 January	Peel Commission reports.

1938

27 April	Woodhead Commission arrives in Jerusalem.

1939

24 May	White Paper of 1939, 'the MacDonald White Paper', approved by Parliament.
3 September	Britain declares war on Germany.

1942

11 May	The Biltmore Program.

1946

20 April	Anglo-American Committee of Enquiry into Palestine reports.
22 May	British-Transjordan Treaty. End of Jordan mandate.

1947

30 July	Two British sergeants hanged in Jerusalem.
1 September	UNSCOP reports.
29 November	United Nations Debate on Palestine.

1948

Midnight 14/15 May	Britain gives up responsibility for Palestine.

HASHEMITE FAMILY TREE

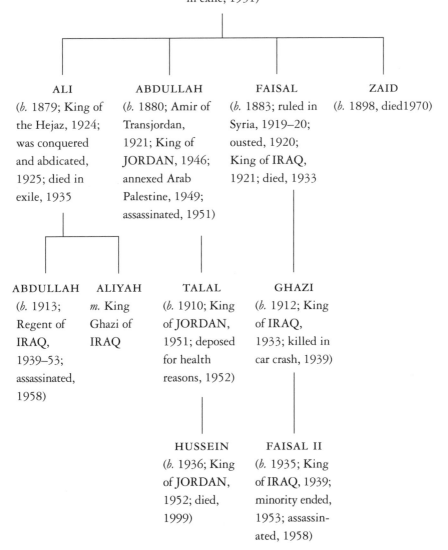

HUSSEIN

Sharif of Mecca

(*b.* 1852; raised Arab revolt, 1916, and
became King of the HEJAZ; attacked
by Ibn Saud, 1924, and abdicated; died
in exile, 1931)

ALI

(*b.* 1879; King of
the Hejaz, 1924;
was conquered
and abdicated,
1925; died in
exile, 1935

ABDULLAH

(*b.* 1880; Amir of
Transjordan,
1921; King of
JORDAN, 1946;
annexed Arab
Palestine, 1949;
assassinated, 1951)

FAISAL

(*b.* 1883; ruled in
Syria, 1919–20;
ousted, 1920;
King of IRAQ,
1921; died, 1933

ZAID

(*b.* 1898, died1970)

ABDULLAH

(*b.* 1913;
Regent of
IRAQ,
1939–53;
assassinated,
1958)

ALIYAH

m. King
Ghazi of
IRAQ

TALAL

(*b.* 1910; King
of JORDAN,
1951; deposed
for health
reasons, 1952)

GHAZI

(*b.* 1912; King
of IRAQ,
1933; killed in
car crash, 1939)

HUSSEIN

(*b.* 1936; King
of JORDAN,
1952; died,
1999)

FAISAL II

(*b.* 1935; King
of IRAQ, 1939;
minority ended,
1953; assassin-
ated, 1958)

NOTES

1 Introductory

1. Seeley, *The Expansion of England*, p. 17.
2. Kimche, *The Unromantics*, p. 74.
3. Ledger and Luckhurst, 'Introduction: Reading the "Fin de Siècle"', in *The Fin de Siècle: A Reader in Cultural History c.1880–1920*, p. xvi.
4. Brantlinger, *Rule of Darkness*, pp. 227, 230, 253.

2 The Ottoman Empire

1. Cumming, *Franco-British Rivalry in the Post-War Near East*, p. 10.
2. For a fascinating account of Germany's policy towards the Ottoman Empire, and of the different strands of thought in both Berlin and Constantinople, see a gripping and most readable book which does much more than its title suggests: McMeekin, *The Berlin-Baghdad Express*.
3. Hopkirk, *The Great Game*, pbk edn, p. 5.
4. Robinson and Gallagher, *Africa and the Victorians*, p. 12.
5. Piers Brendon, *The Decline and Fall of the British Empire*, 1781–1997, pbk edn, p. 55.
6. First Report of the Committee of Imperial Defence.
7. Margaret Fitzherbert, *The Man who was Greenmantle*, pbk edn, pp. 47–8.
8. *Oxford Dictionary of National Biography*.
9. Fromkin, *A Peace to End All Peace*, pbk edn, pp. 42, 43.

3 Turkey and the War

1. Fromkin, *A Peace to End All Peace*, pbk edn, pp. 60–1.
2. Barbara Tuchman, *The Guns of August*, p. 183.
3. Fromkin, *A Peace to End All Peace*, p. 63.
4. Fromkin, *A Peace to End All Peace*, p. 70.
5. Churchill to Lloyd George, 25 January 1921, Churchill papers 2/114, Gilbert, *Winston S. Churchill*, Companion Vol. 2 to Vol. IV, pp. 1322–3.

4 India in the War

1. Busch, *Britain, India and the Arabs 1914–1921*, p. 6.
2. Busch, *Britain, India and the Arabs 1914–1921*, p. 18.
3. Satia, *Spies in Arabia*, pbk edn, pp. 25–7.
4. Winstone, *Captain Shakespear*, p. 211.
5. Busch, *Britain, India and the Arabs 1914–1921*, p. 37.

5 Making Policy in the War

1. Busch, *Britain and the Persian Gulf*, p. 338.
2. Klieman, *Foundations of British Policy in the Arab World*, p. 28.
3. Fisher, *Curzon and British Imperialism in the Middle East*, p. 4.

4. Fisher, *Curzon and British Imperialism in the Middle East*, p. 6.
5. Fromkin, *A Peace to End All Peace*, pbk edn, p. 401.
6. MacMillan, *Peacemakers*, pbk edn, p. 394.
7. Nicolson, *Peacemaking 1919*, 2001 pbk edn, p. 263.
8. Busch, *Britain, India and the Arabs, 1914–1921*, p. 69.
9. Crewe to Curzon 7 January 1916, quoted Fisher, *Curzon and British Imperialism in the Middle East*, p. 21.
10. This quotation, like most of the detail of this passage, is taken from an interesting and helpful article by Martin Sugarman, 'When the spirit of Judah Maccabee Hovered over the Whitechapel Road: The March of the 38th Royal Fusiliers', *Stand To! The Journal of the Western Front Association*, No. 87 (December 2009/January 2010), p. 46 *et seq.*

6 Making Policy: The Arab Dimension

1. Clayton, *British and the Eastern Question: Missolonghi to Gallipoli*, p. 231.
2. Fromkin, *A Peace to End All Peace*, pbk edn, p. 106.
3. Antonius, *The Arab Awakening*, p. 132.
4. Antonius, *The Arab Awakening*, p. 193.

7 The McMahon–Hussein Correspondence

1. Antonius, *The Arab Awakening*, p. 139.
2. Mark Sykes Papers, quoted Fromkin, *A Peace to End All Peace*, pbk edn, p. 223.
3. Sanders, *High Walls*, p. 221.
4. Lawrence, *Seven Pillars of Wisdom*, p. 57.
5. Townshend, *When God made Hell*, p. 446.
6. Fromkin, *A Peace to End All Peace*, pbk edn, p. 92.
7. For a fascinating investigation of this topic, see Satia, *Spies in Arabia*.
8. Quoted Winstone, *Illicit Adventure*, p. 59.
9. See Fieldhouse, *Western Imperialism in the Middle East 1914–1958*, pbk edn, p. 54.
10. Fromkin, *A Peace to End All Peace*, p. 85.
11. Kedourie, *The Chatham House Version*, 2004, pbk edn, pp. 15, 16.
12. Busch, *Britain, India and the Arabs, 1914–1921*, pp. 40–2.
13. Asquith, *Letters*, pp. 510, 469.
14. Kedourie, *The Chatham House Version*, p. 31.
15. Kedourie, *The Chatham House Version*, p. 17.
16. Kedourie, *The Chatham House Version*, p. 14.
17. Sykes Papers, quoted Fromkin, *A Peace to End All Peace*, p. 326.
18. Clayton Papers, quoted Fromkin, *A Peace to End All Peace*, p. 185.
19. Kedourie, *Anglo-Arab Labyrinth*, p. 108.
20. Kedourie, *Anglo-Arab Labyrinth*, p. 189.
21. Amery MS Diary, 17 March 1917 quoted Louis, *In the Name of God, Go!*, p. 71.
22. Busch, *Britain, India and the Arabs 1914–1921*, pp. 65–6.
23. Morris, *Farewell the Trumpets*, p. 252.
24. MacMillan, *Peacemakers*, pbk edn, p. 398.
25. Monroe, *Britain's Moment in the Middle East, 1914–1956*, p. 36.
26. McMahon to Hussein 30 August 1915, CAB24/89.
27. Cumming, *Franco-British Rivalry in the Post-War Near East*, p. 34.
28. Antonius, *The Arab Awakening*, p. 166.
29. Hussein to McMahon 9 September 1915, CAB/24/89.
30. Busch, *Britain, India and the Arabs 1914–1921*, p. 76.
31. Gaston Gaillard, *The Turks and Europe*, p. 312.
32. The Correspondence is most conveniently available on the website of the United Nations Information System on the Question of Palestine (UNISPAL): http://unispal.un.org.

33. Curzon to Cornwallis, 29 September 1919, CAB/24/89.
34. Leclerc, 'The French Soldiers in the Arab Revolt. Some Aspects of their Contribution', *Journal of the T.E. Lawrence Society*, Vol. 9, No 1 (Autumn 1999).
35. CAB/24/68.
36. Antonius, *The Arab Awakening*, p. 167.
37. Busch, *Britain, India and the Arabs 1914–1921*, p. 79.
38. Clayton to Wingate, 6 January 1916 quoted Busch, *Britain, India and the Arabs 1914–1921*, p. 91.
39. Nicholson to Hardinge, 16 December 1915 and 16 February 1916, quoted Busch, *Britain, India and the Arabs 1914–1921*, p. 91.
40. Hirtzel Minute, 23 February 1916, quoted Busch, *Britain, India and the Arabs 1914–1921*, p. 92.
41. Nicolson, *Peacemaking 1919*, 2001 pbk edn, pp. 140–1.
42. *Arab Bulletin* No. 5, 18 June 1916.
43. Fromkin, *A Peace to End All Peace*, p. 184.
44. *Report of a Committee Set Up to Consider Certain Correspondence between Sir Henry McMahon and the Sharif of Mecca in 1915 and 1916*, UNISPAL, Annex H.
45. See, for interpretations, e.g., Friedman, *Palestine, A Twice-Promised Land*, and Kedourie, *Anglo-Arab Labyrinth*.
46. PRO.CAB 27/24.
47. Biger, *The Boundaries of Modern Palestine, 1840–1947*, p. 48.
48. White Paper of June, 1922.
49. UNISPAL.
50. Cmd 5974, Report of the Committee set up to consider certain Correspondence between Sir Henry McMahon and the Sharif of Mecca in 1915 and 1916, p. 8.
51. *Parliamentary Debates*, House of Commons, 19 July 1920.
52. Kedourie, *The Chatham House Version*, p. 22.
53. Hogarth 'Wahabism and British Interests', *Journal of the British Institute of International Affairs*, IV (1925), pp. 72, 73.
54. *Parliamentary Debates*, House of Commons, 11 July 1922.
55. Lawrence, *Seven Pillars of Wisdom*, p. 275.
56. Lawrence, *Seven Pillars of Wisdom*, p. 275.
57. Kedourie, *Anglo-Arab Labyrinth*, 2nd edn, p. 18.
58. Cumming, *Franco-British Rivalry in the Post-War Near East*, p. 39.
59. CAB/24/68.

8 The Arab Revolt

1. Satia, *Spies in Arabia*, pbk edn, p. 47.
2. Fitzherbert, *The Man who was Greenmantle*, pbk edn, p. 173.
3. Fitzherbert, *The Man who was Greenmantle*, p. 143.
4. Fitzherbert, *The Man who was Greenmantle*, p. 72.
5. Fitzherbert, *The Man who was Greenmantle*, p. 144.
6. Fitzherbert, *The Man who was Greenmantle*, p173.
7. Monroe, *Britain's Moment in the Middle East, 1914–1956*, pp. 36–7.
8. Fitzherbert, *The Man who was Greenmantle*, p. 39.
9. Wallach, *Desert Queen*, pbk edn, p. 160.
10. Wallach, *Desert Queen*, p. 65.
11. Letters of Gertrude Bell, 11, 18 May 1917.
12. Lady Bell, ed., *The Letters of Gertrude Bell*, pbk edn, p. 555.
13. Lady Bell, ed., *The Letters of Gertrude Bell*, p. 336.
14. Lady Bell, ed., *The Letters of Gertrude Bell,* p. 564.
15. Lady Bell, ed., *The Letters of Gertrude Bell*, p. 626.
16. Anthony Bruce, in *The Last Crusade: The Palestine Campaign in the First World War*, deals with the revolt in the context of the whole military campaign in Palestine.

17. Shlaim, *Lion of Jordan*, pbk edn, p. 5.
18. Shlaim, *Lion of Jordan*, p. 2.
19. Weizmann Archives, quoted Fromkin, *A Peace to End All Peace*, pbk edn, p. 287.
20. Wallach, *Desert Queen*, p. 182.
21. Grant to Hardinge 1 July 1916, quoted Busch, *Britain, India and the Arabs*, p. 167.
22. Busch, *Britain, India and the Arabs*, p. 177.
23. G.D. Clayton, *British and the Eastern Question: Missolonghi to Gallipoli*, p. 232.
24. See, for instance, Antonius, *The Arab Awakening*.
25. Antonius, *The Arab Awakening*, p. 231.
26. Fromkin, *A Peace to End All Peace*, p. 328.
27. Kedourie, *The Chatham House Version*, 2004 pbk edn, p. 318.
28. Fieldhouse, *Western Imperialism in the Middle East 1914–1958*, pbk edn, pp. 20–9.
29. Catherwood, *A Brief History of the Middle East*, pbk edn, p. 163.
30. Catherwood, *A Brief History of the Middle East*, p. 154.

9 Kut and Beyond

1. Lady Bell, ed., *The Letters of Gertrude Bell*, pbk edn, p. 305.
2. Lady Bell, ed., *The Letters of Gertrude Bell*, p. 375.
3. Sherson, *Townshend of Chitral and Kut*, p. 81, and see Townshend, *When God made Hell, The British Invasion of Mesopotamia and the Creation of Iraq, 1914–1921*, p. 95.
4. Neave, *Remembering Kut*, p. 158.
5. Brendon, *The Decline and Fall of the British Empire*, 1781–1997, pbk edn, p. 259.
6. Townshend, *When God made Hell*, p. 368.
7. An excellent account of the military campaign is given by Roger Ford in *Eden to Armageddon*.

10 Sykes–Picot

1. Cumming, *Franco-British Rivalry in the Post-War Near East*, p. 19.
2. Antonius, *The Arab Awakening*, p. 248.
3. Antonius, *The Arab Awakening*, p. 248.
4. Wallach, *Desert Queen*, pbk edn, p. 72.
5. See Fieldhouse, *Western Imperialism in the Middle East 1914–1958*, pbk edn, pp. 20–9.
6. See Fisher, *Curzon and British Imperialism in the Middle East*, p. 24.
7. Sykes to Drummond 20 July 1917; Sykes Papers, quoted Fisher, *Curzon and British Imperialism in the Middle East*, p. 84.
8. Sykes Papers, quoted Fromkin, *A Peace to End All Peace*, pbk edn, p. 190.
9. Kedourie, *England and the Middle East*, pp. 65–6.
10. Fieldhouse, *Western Imperialism in the Middle East 1914–1958*, p. 52.
11. Antonius, *The Arab Awakening*, p. 255.
12. Antonius, *The Arab Awakening*, p. 257.
13. Busch, *Britain, India and the Arabs 1914–1921*, p. 88.
14. Kedourie, *The Chatham House Version*, 2004 pbk edn, pp. 29, 30.
15. MacMillan, *Peacemakers*, pbk edn, p. 405.
16. Bell to Hirtzel, 16 January 1919, Cox MSS, file 4, St Antony's College, Oxford, quoted Townshend, *When God made Hell*, p. 440.
17. Quoted Townshend, *When God made Hell*, p. 440.
18. MacMillan, *Peacemakers*, p. 395.
19. Minutes of the War Cabinet, 3 October 1918.
20. Fromkin, *A Peace to End All Peace*, p. 365.
21. Fisher, *Curzon and British Imperialism in the Middle East*, p. 195.
22. Cumming, *Franco-British Rivalry in the Post-War Near East*, p. 29.
23. Hans Cohn, *Western Civilization in the Near East*, p. 201.

11 The Background to the Balfour Declaration

1. Monroe, *Britain's Moment in the Middle East, 1914–1956*, p. 43.
2. Shlaim, *Lion of Jordan*, pbk edn, p. 8.
3. Lloyd George, *War Memoirs*, Part 2, p. 585.
4. Hyam, *Britain's Declining Empire*, pbk edn, p. 51.
5. Lloyd George, *War Memoirs*, Part 2, p. 586.
6. Weizmann, *Trial and Error*, pp. 192–3.
7. Dugdale, *Arthur James Balfour*, p. 226. See also Elizabeth Balmer, 'Acetone, Cordite and the Balfour Declaration' in the Western Front Association, *Stand To!*, No.83, p. 56.
8. Dugdale, *Arthur James Balfour*, Vol. 1, p. 435.
9. L.S. Amery, *My Political Life*, Vol. 2, p. 1.
10. Egremont, *Balfour*, pbk edn, p. 264.
11. MacMillan, *Peacemakers*, pbk edn, p. 424.
12. MacMillan, *Peacemakers*, p. 424.
13. Cohen, ed., *A.J. Balfour, Speeches on Zionism*, p. 28.
14. Tomes, *Balfour and Foreign Policy*, p. 199.
15. Tomes, *Balfour and Foreign Policy*, p. 201.
16. 10 July 1905, *Parliamentary Debates,* vol. 149, col. 155.
17. *The Times*, 11 May 1904, 'Mr. Balfour and the Aliens Bill'.
18. For an intelligent and interesting analysis of the micro-dissection of the public records, see Levene, 'A Case of Mistaken Identity', *English Historical Review* (January 1992), p. 54 *et seq.*
19. Introduction by Balfour to Nahum Sokolov, *History of Zionism*, pp. xxix–xxx.
20. Tomes, *Balfour and Foreign Policy*, p. 207.
21. Johnson, *A History of the Jews.*
22. Kenneth N. Newton, 'Second Sight: Is Edward Said right about Daniel Deronda?' *The Times Literary Supplement*, 9 May 2008.
23. Tomes, *Balfour and Foreign Policy*, p. 208.
24. Amery, *My Political Life*, Vol. 2, pp. 160–1.
25. Amery, *My Political Life*, Vol. 2, p. 163.
26. Amery, *My Political Life*, Vol. 2, p. 197.
27. Barnes & Nicholson, eds, *Amery Diaries*, p. 189.
28. Amery, *My Political Life*, Vol. 1, p. 253.
29. Louis, *In the Name of God, Go!*, p. 20.
30. Amery Diary, 26 July 1928, Barnes and Nicholson, eds, *The Leo Amery Diaries, 1896–1929*, Vol. 1, p. 559.
31. Amery Papers, quoted Louis, *In the Name of God, Go!*, p. 65.
32. *Amery Diaries*, Vol. 1, p. 206.
33. Amery to Lloyd George, 16 August 1918, quoted Louis, *In the Name of God, Go!*, p. 72.
34. Renton, *The Zionist Masquerade*, p. 153.
35. See Louis, *Ends of British Imperialism*, pbk edn, p. 383.
36. Amery, *My Political Life*, Vol. 2, p. 115.
37. L.S. Amery, *My Political Life*, Vol. II, pp. 115, 116.
38. Fieldhouse, *Western Imperialism in the Middle East 1914–1958*, pbk edn, p. 134.

12 Gestation of the Declaration

1. Monroe, *Britain's Moment in the Middle East, 1914–1956*, p. 26.
2. Kitchener Papers, quoted Fromkin, *A Peace to End All Peace*, pbk edn, p. 413.
3. Lloyd George, *War Memoirs*, Vol. 4, p. 68.
4. See Stein, *The Balfour Declaration*, p. 223 and Monroe, *Britain's Moment in the Middle East, 1914–1956*, Chapter 14.
5. Quoted Egremont, *Balfour*, pbk edn, p. 293.
6. See Renton, *The Zionist Masquerade*, pp. 63–4.

7. Ronaldshay, *The Life of Lord Curzon*, Vol. 3, p. 159.
8. Stein, *The Balfour Declaration*, p. 309.
9. Basheer, *Montagu and the Balfour Declaration*.
10. Stein, *Balfour*, p. 552.
11. M. Vereté, 'The Balfour Declaration and its Makers', *Middle Eastern Studies*, Vol. 6, No. 1 (January 1970), reprinted in Rose, ed., *From Palmerston to Balfour, Collected Essays of Mayir Vereté*, Chapter 1. See also Fieldhouse, *Western Imperialism in the Middle East 1914–1958*, pbk edn, p. 138.
12. For example, in Fieldhouse, *Western Imperialism in the Middle East, 1914–1958*, p. 149.
13. MacMillan, *Peacemakers*, pbk edn, p. 433.
14. Stein, *Balfour Declaration*, p. 529.

13 The Birth of the Declaration

1. Tomes, *Balfour and Foreign Policy*, p. 210.
2. See Renton, *The Zionist Masquerade*, pp. 13–14.
3. See Renton, *The Zionist Masquerade*, p. 72.
4. Egremont, *Balfour*, pbk edn, pp. 313–14.
5. Balfour to Curzon, 11 August 1919.
6. Tomes, *Balfour and Foreign Policy*, p. 212.
7. Dugdale, *The Balfour Declaration*, p. 5.
8. Campbell, *F.E. Smith, First Earl of Birkenhead*, p. 251.
9. Mosley, *Curzon*, p. 157.
10. Arnold-Foster, Diary 17 June 1908, quoted Tomes, *Balfour and Foreign Policy*, p. 17.
11. Renton, *The Zionist Masquerade*, pp. 2–3.
12. PRO, FO 800/74 (Grey Papers) Buchanan to Grey, 10 March 1915, quoted Levene, 'A Case of Mistaken Identity', *English Historical Review*, January 1992, p. 61 *et seq.*
13. PRO, FO 371/2767/938, Sykes to Nicolson, 18 March 1916, quoted Levene, 'A Case of Mistaken Identity', *English Historical Review*, January 1992, p. 62 *et seq.*
14. Renton, *The Zionist Masquerade*, p. 24.
15. See Johnpoll, *The Politics of Futility. The General Jewish Works Bund of Poland, 1917–1943*, p. 61.
16. Tuchman, *Bible and Sword*, p. 216.
17. Lloyd George, *War Memoirs*, Vol. 2, p. 721.
18. *Punch*, 19 December 1917, p. 415.
19. PRO, Notice D.607, 15 December 1917.
20. Lloyd George, *War Memoirs*, Vol. 2, pp. 1090–1.
21. CAB/23/2, 2 April 1917.
22. FO/395/139, 10 April 1917.
23. Beevor, *D-Day: The Battle for Normandy*, pbk edn, p. 78.
24. Eitan Bar-Yosef, 'The Last Crusade, British Propaganda and the Palestine Campaign. 1917–18', *Journal of Contemporary History*, Vol. 36, No. 1 (January 2001), pp. 87–109.
25. WO to GHQ Egypt, 21 November 1917.
26. Quoted Renton, *The Zionist Masquerade*, p. 92.
27. Sykes to Clayton, 15 January 1918, FO/371/3383.
28. The different strands of British policy are described very well by Bar-Yosef in 'The Last Crusade, British Propaganda and the Palestine Campaign, 1917–18'. I have also to record the profit and pleasure with which I heard Eitan Bar-Yosef read a paper on the same subject during a conference, 'Palestine, Britain & Empire: 1841–1948', at King's College, London, on 14–15 May 2008.
29. Renton, *The Zionist Masquerade*, p. 93.
30. Allenby to YMCA 1933, quoted Eitan Bar-Yosef, 'Re-visiting Last Crusade' at King's College London, 'Palestine, Britain and Empire, 1841–1948', 14–15 May 2008.
31. Quoted, *Report of a Committee Set Up to Consider Certain Correspondence between Sir Henry McMahon and the Sharif of Mecca in 1915 and 1916*, UNISPAL, Annex H.

32. Antonius, *The Arab Awakening*, pp. 270–3.
33. Wallach, *Desert Queen*, pbk edn, pp. 225–6.
34. Gertrude Bell to her parents, quoted Wallach, *Desert Queen*, pp. 202–3.

14 Personalities

1. Fitzherbert, *The Man who was Greenmantle*, pbk edn, p. 64.
2. Thesiger, *A Life of my Choice*, p. 171.
3. Pearce, *Sir Bernard Bourdillon*, p. 69.
4. Townshend, *When God made Hell*, p. 281.
5. Wallach, *Desert Queen*, p. 206.
6. Lady Bell, ed., *The Letters of Gertrude Bell*, pbk edn, p. 375.
7. Lady Bell, ed., *The Letters of Gertrude Bell*, p. 378.
8. Lady Bell, ed., *The Letters of Gertrude Bell*, p. 396.

15 The Entente under Pressure

1. Monroe, *Britain's Moment in the Middle East, 1914–1956*, p. 62.
2. Meinertzhagen, *Middle East Diary*, pp. 30, 32.
3. Nicolson, *The Great Silence*, pbk edn, p. 143.
4. Fromkin, *A Peace to End All Peace*, pbk edn, p. 498.
5. Wallach, *Desert Queen*, pbk edn, p. 229.
6. MacMillan, *Peacemakers*, pbk edn, p. 400.
7. Amery, *My Political Life*, Vol. 2, p. 249.
8. Diary, and see Louis, *In the Name of God, Go!*, p. 83.
9. Monroe, *Philby of Arabia*, p. 116.
10. Antonius, *The Arab Awakening*, pp. 321–2.
11. Lawrence, *Seven Pillars of Wisdom*.
12. Satia, *Spies in Arabia*, pbk edn, p. 64.
13. Garnett, ed., *The Letters of T.E. Lawrence*, p. 196.
14. Allenby Papers quoted Fromkin, *A Peace to End All Peace*, p. 338.
15. Fromkin, *A Peace to End All Peace*, pp. 339–40.
16. Wallach, *Desert Queen*, p. 198.
17. T.E. Lawrence to Robert Graves, quoted Fromkin, *A Peace to End All Peace*, p. 342.
18. PRO, Eastern Committee. CAB 27/24.
19. Fromkin, *A Peace to End All Peace*, pp. 375, 376.
20. Lloyd George, *Memoirs of the Peace Conference*, Vol. 2, pp. 665–8.
21. Antonius, *The Arab Awakening*, pp. 310–11.
22. Storrs, *Orientations*, pp. 505–6.
23. Townshend, *When God Made Hell*, p. 444.
24. Fromkin, *A Peace to End All Peace*, p. 29.
25. Lloyd George, *Peace Conference*, Vol. 2, p. 673.
26. MacMillan, *Peacemakers*, p. 392.
27. *Documents on British Foreign Policy 1919–1939*. London: HMSO Series I: Vol. IV Document 242 of 11 August 1919, pp. 340–1. See Monroe, *Britain's Moment in the Middle East, 1914–1956*, pp. 50–1.
28. Harry N. Howard, *The Partition of Turkey*, p. 197.
29. MacMillan, *Peacemakers*, p. 401.
30. Cumming, *Franco-British Rivalry in the Post-War Near East*, p. 96.

16 The End of Turkey's War

1. MacMillan, *Peacemakers*, pbk edn, p. 378.
2. Lloyd George, *War Memoirs*, Vol. 6, pp. 3309–10.
3. Lloyd George, *War Memoirs*, Vol. 6, pp. 3311–12.
4. Lloyd George, *War Memoirs*, Vol. 6, pp. 3313–14.
5. Lloyd George, *War Memoirs*, Vol. 2, p. 238.

17 Versailles

1. Quoted Manela, *The Wilsonian Moment*, p. 20.
2. Keynes, *The Economic Consequences of the Peace*, pp. 34–5.
3. See Manela, *The Wilsonian Moment*, p. 47 *et seq.*
4. Taylor, ed., *Lloyd George: A Diary by Frances Stevenson*, p. 171.
5. Wilson, June 1917.
6. See Manela, *The Wilsonian Moment*.
7. Quoted Egremont, *Balfour*, pbk edn, p. 304.
8. Egremont, *Balfour*, pp. 304–5.
9. Egremont, *Balfour*, p. 305.
10. Nicolson, *Peacemaking 1919*, pbk edn, p. 24.
11. Nicolson, *Peacemaking 1919*, p. 329.
12. W.K. Hancock and J. van der Poch, eds, *Selections from the Smuts Papers*, Vol. 4, Nos 985, 986.
13. Nicolson, *Peacemaking 1919*, p. 269.
14. Tomes, *Balfour and Foreign Policy*, p. 163.
15. Nicolson, *Peacemaking 1919*, 2001 pbk edn, p. 153.
16. Nicolson, *Peacemaking 1919*, pp. 207–8.
17. Nicolson, *Peacemaking 1919*, pp. 137–8.
18. MacMillan, *Peacemakers*, pbk edn, p. 470.
19. Nicolson, *Peacemaking 1919*, p. 15
20. Nicolson, *Peacemaking 1919*, pp. 15–16.

18 The Balkans at Paris

1. MacMillan, *Peacemakers*, pbk edn, p. 364.
2. Nicolson, *Peacemaking 1919*, 2001 pbk edn, p. 251.
3. MacMillan, *Peacemakers*, p. 389.
4. MacMillan, *Peacemakers*, p. 390.

19 Britain and France Again

1. David Hunter Miller, *The Drafting of the Covenant*, Vol. 2, p. 40 *et seq.* and pp. 65–93.
2. Miller, *My Diary at the Conference of Paris*, 30 January 1919.
3. MacMillan, *Peacemakers*, pbk edn, p. 392.
4. MacMillan, *Peacemakers*, p. 406.

20 The Meeting at the Rue Nitot

1. Nicolson, *Peacemaking 1919*, pbk edn, pp. 332–3
2. Nicolson, *Peacemaking 1919*, p. 337.
3. Nicolson, *Peacemaking 1919*, p. 339.
4. 19 March 1919, Taylor, ed., *Lloyd George: A Diary by Frances Stevenson*.
5. The Council of Four, Minutes of Meetings 20–24 March 1919.

6. Nicolson, *Peacemaking 1919*, p. 143.
7. Churchill to Balfour, 12 October 1921, FO 371/7053. See Louis, *Ends of British Imperialism*, pbk edn, p. 271.
8. Memorandum by Balfour, 'Respecting Syria, Palestine and Mesopotamia', 11 August 1919, FO 406/41.

21 Faisal at Versailles

1. MacMillan, *Peacemakers*, pbk edn, p. 400.
2. MacMillan, *Peacemakers*, p. 398.
3. Quoted Wallach, *Desert Queen*, pbk edn, p. 227.
4. Wallach, *Desert Queen*, pp. 229–30.
5. Cumming, *Franco-British Rivalry in the Post-War Near East*, p. 105.

22 The Middle East Defeats Paris

1. Busch, *Britain, India and the Arabs*, p. 277.
2. Busch, *Britain, India and the Arabs*, p. 298.
3. India Office to Foreign Office, 17 February 1919, quoted Busch, *Britain, India and the Arabs*, pp. 298–9.
4. Lawrence Minute, 28 January 1919; Hirtzel Minute, 29 January 1919. See Busch, *Britain, India and the Arabs*, pp. 299–300.
5. Nicolson, *Peacemaking 1919*, pbk edn, p. 142.
6. Hirtzel Minute, 6 January 1919. See *Busch, Britain, India and the Arabs*, p. 293.
7. Wallach, *Desert Queen*, pbk edn, p. 230.

23 Mandates

1. Louis, *Ends of British Imperialism*, pbk edn, p. 267.
2. *The Oxford History of the British Empire*, Vol. 4, p. 11.
3. Morris, *Farewell the Trumpets*, p. 208.
4. Brendon, *The Decline and Fall of the British Empire, 1781–1997*, pbk edn, p. 317.
5. Vincent, ed., *The Crawford Papers*.
6. Eastern Committee, 9 and 16 December 1918, quoted Tomes, *Balfour and Foreign Policy*, p. 47.
7. Antonius, *The Arab Awakening*, p. 351.
8. I am indebted to Susan Pedersen for her paper on 'The Powers and uses of the Mandates system', which she gave at the conference 'Palestine, Britain and Empire: 1841–1948' at King's College, London, 14–15 May 2008, and for her subsequent assistance, including supplying me with a copy of her essay 'The Meaning of the Mandate System: An Argument', *Geschichte und Gesellschaft*, Vol. 32, No. 4 (October–December 2006), pp. 560–82.
9. Monroe, *Britain's Moment in the Middle East, 1914–1956*, p. 141.
10. The *Empire Review*, July 1923.
11. Susan Pedersen, 'The Meaning of the Mandates System: An Argument'.

24 Palestine and Zionism

1. MacMillan, *Peacemakers*, pbk edn, p. 429.
2. MacMillan, *Peacemakers*, p. 421.
3. The Letters and Papers of Chaim Weizmann, quoted Fromkin, *A Peace to End All Peace*, pbk edn, p. 324.

25 Resort Diplomacy: San Remo, Sèvres, Lausanne and Cairo. Introduction

1. Cumming, *Franco-British Rivalry in the Post-War Near East*, p. 96.
2. Nicolson, *Peacemaking 1919*, pbk edn, p. 35.
3. Nicolson, *Peacemaking 1919*, p. 364.
4. Nicolson, *Peacemaking 1919*, p. 343.

26 San Remo and Sèvres

1. MacMillan, *Peacemakers*, pbk edn, p. 453.
2. Ronaldshay, *The Life of Lord Curzon*, Vol. 3, p. 231.
3. Antonius, *The Arab Awakening*, p. 306.

27 Lausanne

1. MacMillan, *Peacemakers*, pbk edn, p. 463.
2. Cmd 1814, p. 212.
3. Cumming, *Franco-British Rivalry in the Post-War Near East*, pp. 194, 195.
4. MacMillan, *Peacemakers*, p. 464.
5. Ronaldshay, *Life of Lord Curzon*, p. 322.
6. Hansard, *Parliamentary Debates, House of Commons,* 21 July 1920.
7. Kohn, *Western Civilisation in the Near East*, p. 205.
8. Gilbert, *Winston S. Churchill*, Companion Volume 4, Part 3, pp. 165–6.
9. Churchill, *The Aftermath*, p. 429.
10. Sforza, *Makers of Modern Europe*, pp. 94–5.
11. Ronaldshay, *Life of Lord Curzon*, pp. 304–5.
12. Marcello de Cecco, quoted in Skidelsky, ed., *The End of the Keynesian Era*, p. 24.
13. Turkey, No.1 (1922), Cmd1570. Correspondence between H.M. Government and the French Government, respecting the Angora Agreement, 20 October 1921.
14. Turkey, No.1 (1922), Cmd1570. Correspondence between H.M. Government and the French Government, respecting the Angora Agreement, 20 October 1921.
15. *The Morning Post,* 5 November 1921.
16. *The Times*, 7 November 1921.
17. Ronaldshay, *The Life of Lord Curzon*, Vol. 3, p. 240.
18. Ronaldshay, *The Life of Lord Curzon*, Vol. 3, pp. 286–7.
19. Ronaldshay, *The Life of Lord Curzon*, Vol. 3, p. 290.
20. Nicolson, *Curzon, The Last Phase*, pp. 324–5.
21. Note in pencil describing Curzon's interview with Lord Stamfordham, quoted Ronaldshay, *The Life of Lord Curzon*, Vol. 3, p. 352.
22. Ronaldshay, *The Life of Lord Curzon*, Vol. 3, p. 341.

28 Preparing for Cairo: Churchill Takes the Reins

1. Churchill, *Memorandum for Cabinet* 1 May 1920, quoted Busch, *Britain, India, and the Arabs, 1914–1921*, p. 398.
2. Busch, *Britain, India, and the Arabs, 1914–1921*, p. 409.
3. *The Observer*, 8 August 1920.
4. Hirtzel to Wilson, 16 July, 17 September 1919, 3 February 1920, Wilson MSS, British Library Add.Ms 52455, quoted Townshend, *When God made Hell*, pp. 450, 451.
5. Wilson to Cox, 29 July 1920, quoted Busch, *Britain, India, and the Arabs, 1914–1921*, p. 412.
6. Busch, *Britain, India, and the Arabs, 1914–1921*, p. 419.
7. Busch, *Britain, India, and the Arabs, 1914–1921*, p. 450.
8. Churchill to Lloyd George, 4 January 1921, quoted Busch, *Britain, India, and the Arabs, 1914–1921*, p. 456.

9. Churchill to Cox, Churchill Papers 17/16, Gilbert, *Winston S. Churchill*, Companion Vol. 4, Part 2, p. 1297.
10. Cox to Churchill 13 January 1921, Churchill Papers, 17/16, Gilbert, *Winston S. Churchill*, Companion Vol. 4, Part 2, pp. 1308–9.
11. Hirtzel to Churchill, 14 January 1921, Churchill papers 17/2, Gilbert, *Winston S. Churchill*, Companion Vol. 4, part 2, pp. 1309, 1310.
12. Churchill to Shuckburgh, Colonial Office Papers: 730/3, quoted in Gilbert, *Winston S. Churchill*, Companion Vol. 4, Part 3, p. 1547.
13. Churchill to Cox, Churchill Papers: 17/16, quoted Gilbert, *Winston S. Churchill*, Vol. 4, Part 3, p. 1548.
14. Cox to Churchill, Churchill Papers: 17/7 quoted Gilbert, *Winston S. Churchill*, Companion Vol. 4, Part 3, pp. 1566–7.
15. Churchill to Lloyd George, 8 January 1921, quoted Busch, *Britain, India, and the Arabs, 1914–1921*, p. 458.
16. CAB/24/119, Memorandum by the Secretary of State for War, 10 February 1921; from Secretary of State to High Commissioner, Mesopotamia, 23 January 1921.
17. Gilbert, *Winston S. Churchill*, Companion Vol. 4, Part 2, p. 638.
18. Sir Henry Wilson, Diary, 28 January 1921.
19. Gilbert, *Winston S. Churchill*, Companion Vol. 4, Part 2, p. 938.

29 Churchill's Durbar: The Cairo Conference

1. Morris, *Farewell the Trumpets*, p. 260.
2. Wallach, *Desert Queen*, pbk edn, p. 295.
3. CAB/24/126.
4. Catherwood, *Churchill's Folly*, pbk edn, p. 111.
5. Lawrence, *Seven Pillars of Wisdom*, p. 276.
6. Kedourie, *The Chatham House Version*, 2004 pbk edn, p. 33.
7. Churchill, *Great Contemporaries*, 1941 edn, p. 136.
8. Catherwood, *Churchill's Folly*, pp. 195–6.
9. Catherwood, *Churchill's Folly*, p. 128.
10. Catherwood, *Churchill's Folly*, p. 162.
11. Catherwood, *Churchill's Folly*, p. 151.
12. Draft telegram, Churchill to Cox, Churchill papers: 17/16, quoted Gilbert, *Winston S. Churchill*, Companion Vol. 4, p. 1601.
13. Churchill Minute, 24 November 1921, Colonial Office papers 730/16.
14. Catherwood, *Churchill's Folly*, pp. 164–5.
15. Churchill to Cox, telegram 12 January 1921, Churchill papers: 17/16, quoted, Gilbert, *Winston S. Churchill*, Companion Vol. 4, p. 1300.
16. Churchill to Curzon, 12 January 1921, Colonial Office papers: 17/12, quoted, Gilbert, *Winston S. Churchill*, Companion Vol. 4, p. 1301.
17. CAB/24/126, p. 40.
18. Catherwood, *Churchill's Folly*, p. 159.
19. Kirkbride, *A Crackle of Thorns*, p. 27, quoted Shlaim, *Lion of Jordan*, pbk edn, pp. 11–12.
20. CAB/24/126, appendix 2.
21. CAB/24/126, pp. 97–8.
22. See, for example, Catherwood, *Winston's Folly*, and Catherwood, *A Brief History of the Middle East*, pbk edn, p. 179.

30 Egypt

1. Monroe, *Britain's Moment in the Middle East, 1914–1956*, p. 118.
2. 17 November 1919, *House of Commons Debates,* Vol. 121, Col. 771.
3. Darwin, *Middle East*, p. 87.

4. Gollin, *Proconsul*, p. 593.
5. Wavell, *Allenby in Egypt*, p. 77.
6. Brendon, *The Decline and Fall of the British*, pbk edn, p. 326.

31 Persia

1. Monroe, *Britain's Moment in the Middle East, 1914–1956*, p. 95.
2. Erik J. Dahl, 'From Coal to Oil', *Joint Forces Quarterly*, winter 2000–2001 edn, p. 50 *et seq.*
3. Monroe, *Britain's Moment in the Middle East, 1914–1956*, p. 102.
4. Nicolson, *Curzon: The Last Phase 1919–1925*, p. 122.
5. Ronaldshay, *The Life of Lord Curzon*, Vol. 3, p. 216.
6. Nicolson, *Curzon: The Last Phase*, p. 136.
7. Cleveland, *History of the Modern Middle East*, 3rd edn, pbk edn, p. 188.
8. William Cleveland, *History of the Modern Middle East*, pp. 294–5.

32 Syria

1. Stark, *The Valleys of the Assassins*.
2. Woodward, *British Foreign Policy in the Second World War*, Vol. 3, p. 86.

33 Jordan

1. Shlaim, *War and Peace in the Middle East*, pbk edn, p. 14.
2. Aruri, *Jordan*, p. 3, quoted Cleveland, *History of the Modern Middle East*, 3rd edn, pbk edn, p. 213.
3. Monroe, *Philby of Arabia*, p. 54.
4. Quoted Monroe, *Philby of Arabia*, p. 60.
5. *Arab Bulletin*, Cairo. No. 74, quoted Monroe, *Philby of Arabia*, p. 78.
6. Monroe, *Philby of Arabia*, p. 79.
7. Monroe, *Philby of Arabia*, p. 80.
8. Monroe, *Philby of Arabia*, p. 101.
9. Monroe, *Philby of Arabia*, p. 134.
10. Busch, *Britain, India and the Arabs 1914–1921*, p. 322.
11. Wilson to Cox, 15 August 1919, Busch, *Britain, India and the Arabs 1914–1921*, p. 333.
12. Cleveland, *History of the Modern Middle East*, p. 213.
13. Gilbert, *Winston S. Churchill*, Vol. 4, p. 576.
14. Gilbert, *Winston S. Churchill*, Vol. 4, pp. 583–4.
15. Monroe, *Philby of Arabia*, p. 119.
16. Wilson, *King Abdullah*, p. 74.

34 Strategy

1. Quoted Townshend, *When God made Hell*, p. 374. Townshend gives a very useful account of events surrounding the capture of Baghdad.
2. Wilson to Colonel Yate, MP, 28 November 1914, quoted Fisher, *Curzon and British Imperialism in the Middle East*, p. 113.
3. Gilbert, *Winston S. Churchill*, Vol. 4, p. 615.
4. Gilbert, *Winston S. Churchill*, Vol. 3, p. 1499.
5. Fisher, *Curzon and British Imperialism in the Middle East*, p. 45.
6. Fisher, *Curzon and British Imperialism in the Middle East*, p. 57.
7. Fisher, *Curzon and British Imperialism in the Middle East*, pp. 51, 52.
8. Fisher, *Curzon and British Imperialism in the Middle East*, p. 59.
9. Bell to Hirtzel, 15 June 1917, St Antony's College, Oxford, Cox MSS File 4, quoted Townshend, *When God made Hell*, p. 380.

10. CAB/24/72.
11. Shlaim, *War and Peace in the Middle East*, pbk edn, p. 14.
12. Clayton, *Britain and the Eastern Question: Missolonghi to Gallipoli*, pp. 244–5.
13. Fisher, *Curzon and British Imperialism in the Middle East*, p. 111.
14. Cecil to Balfour 8 January 1918, quoted Fisher, *Curzon and British Imperialism in the Middle East*, p. 116–17.
15. Lloyd George, *War Memoirs*, Vol. 5, pp. 63–73.
16. Sykes Memorandum, quoted Busch, *Britain, India and the Arabs*, p. 154.
17. Shuckburgh to Sykes, 29 January 1918, quoted Busch, *Britain, India and the Arabs*, p. 154.

35 Establishment

1. Wallach, *Desert Queen*, pbk edn, p. 221.
2. Wallach, *Desert Queen*, pbk edn, p. 239.
3. Wallach, *Desert Queen*, p. 268.
4. Wallach, *Desert Queen*, pbk edn, p271, 273, 274.
5. Wallach, *Desert Queen*, pbk edn, p. 257.
6. Fieldhouse, *Western Imperialism in the Middle East 1914–1958*, pbk edn, p. 85.
7. Quoted Catherwood, *Churchill's Folly*, pbk edn, p. 82.
8. Brendon, *The Decline and Fall of the British Empire, 1781–1997*, pbk edn, p. 318.
9. Fieldhouse, *Western Imperialism in the Middle East 1914–1958*, pbk edn, p. 87.
10. Townshend, *When God made Hell*, p. 59.
11. Sluglett, *Oxford Dictionary of National Biography*, and see Bray, *A Paladin of Arabia*.

36 Churchill and Mesopotamia

1. Tuohy, *The Crater of Mars*.
2. Gilbert, *Winston S. Churchill*, Companion Vol. 4, Part 2, p. 1260.
3. Churchill to Lloyd George, 4 December 1920, Churchill Papers: 2/111, Gilbert, *Winston S. Churchill*, Companion Vol. 4, Part 2, pp. 1260–1.
4. Catherwood, *Churchill's Folly*, pbk edn, pp. 90, 91, 95.
5. Catherwood, *Churchill's Folly*, p. 94.
6. Departmental minute 24 November 1921. Colonial Office papers: 733/17A, quoted Gilbert, *Winston S. Churchill*, Companion Vol. 4, part 3, p. 1675.
7. Royle, *Glubb Pasha*, p. 98.
8. Townshend 'Civilisation and "Frightfulness": Air Control in the Middle East between the wars', in Wrigley, ed., *Warfare, Diplomacy and Politics*, p. 150.
9. Sluglett, *Britain in Iraq*, p. 264.

37 Nation-Building

1. Lady Bell, ed., *The Letters of Gertrude Bell*, pbk edn, p. 454.
2. Lady Bell, ed., *The Letters of Gertrude Bell*, p. 455.
3. *Historical Summary by Sir Percy Cox* in Lady Bell, ed., *The Letters of Gertrude Bell*, p. 427.
4. Catherwood, *Churchill's Folly*, pbk edn, p. 70.
5. CAB/24/118, High Commissioner, Mesopotamia, to Secretary of State for India, 26 December 1920.
6. CAB/24/118, High Commissioner, Mesopotamia, to Secretary of State for India, 2 January 1921.
7. Wallach, *Desert Queen*, pbk edn, pp. 303, p4.
8. CAB/24/119, High Commissioner, Baghdad, to Secretary of State for War, 24 January 1921.
9. CAB/24/126.
10. Wallach, *Desert Queen*, p. 304.

11. CAB/24/126 pp. 41–2.
12. Fieldhouse, *Western Imperialism in the Middle East 1914–1958*, pbk edn, p. 91.
13. Shlaim, *War and Peace in the Middle East*, pbk edn, p. 13.
14. Wallach, *Desert Queen*, p. 321.
15. Churchill to Cox, telegram 28 November 1921, Colonial Office papers: 730/16, quoted Gilbert, *Winston S. Churchill*, Companion Vol. 4, part 3, pp. 1677–8.
16. Wallach, *Desert Queen*, p. 331.
17. Wallach, *Desert Queen*, p. 331.

38 British Iraq

1. Kedourie, *The Chatham House Version*, 2004 pbk edn, p. 258.
2. Catherwood, *A Brief History of the Middle East*, pbk edn, p. 20.
3. See, e.g., Mira and Tona Rocc, eds, Violett Shamash, *Memoirs of Eden: A Journey through Jewish Baghdad*.
4. Quoted Kedourie, *The Chatham House Version*, p. 302.
5. Quoted Wallach, *Desert Queen*, pbk edn, p. 330.
6. Fromkin, *A Peace to End All Peace*, pbk edn, p. 451.
7. Wallach, *Desert Queen*, p. 347.
8. Kedourie, *The Chatham House Version*, p. ix.
9. Kedourie, *The Chatham House Version*, p. x.
10. Kedourie, *The Chatham House Version*, p. xv–xvi.
11. Kedourie, *The Chatham House Version*, p. 262.
12. Kedourie, *The Chatham House Version*, 2004 pbk edn, p. 239.

39 Moving Forward

1. Robert de Caix, *Histoire des colonies françaises: Syrie*, p. 523, quoted Cumming, *Franco-British Rivalry in the Post-War Near East*, p. 119.
2. CAB/24/126.
3. CAB/24/166.
4. CAB/24/175.
5. See, for instance, Bashkin, *The Other Iraq*, and Luizard, *La Question Irakienne*.
6. Antonius, *The Arab Awakening*, p. 363.

40 'Mandatory of the World'

1. CAB/24/72.
2. Roger Owen at conference, 'Palestine, Britain and Empire: 1841–1948' at King's College, London, 14–15 May 2008.
3. Antonius, *The Arab Awakening*, p. 396.
4. Shlaim, *War and Peace in the Middle East*, pbk edn, p. 15.

41 Administration in Practice

1. Kedourie, *The Chatham House Version*, 2004 pbk edn, pp. 54, 55.
2. Cmd 1499. An Interim Report on the Civil Administration of Palestine during the period 1 July 1920 to 30 June 1921, p. 8.
3. See, for instance, Wasserstein, *The British in Palestine*; Wasserstein, *Herbert Samuel*; and Huneidi, *A Broken Trust*.
4. Rose, *Harold Nicolson*, p. 20.
5. Wasserstein, *The British in Palestine*, p. 79.
6. Sykes, *Crossroads to Israel*, p. 39.
7. Pimlott, ed., *The Political Diary of Hugh Dalton*, p. 207.

8. Fieldhouse, *Western Imperialism in the Middle East 1914–1958*, pbk edn, p. 153.
9. Egremont, *Balfour*, pbk edn, pp. 331–2.
10. Cmd 1540 Reports of the Committee of Enquiry into Disturbances in May 1921, pp. 22, 23.
11. Cmd 1540 Reports of the Committee of Enquiry into Disturbances in May 1921, p. 59.
12. Cmd 1989. Correspondence between the High Commissioner for Palestine (*sic*) regarding the Proposed Formation of an Arab Agency.
13. Brendon, *The Decline and Fall of the British Empire, 1781–1997*, p. 465.
14. Fieldhouse, *Western Imperialism in the Middle East 1914–1958*, pbk edn, p. 163.
15. Glubb, *Britain and the Arabs*, p. 145.
16. Fieldhouse, *Western Imperialism in the Middle East 1914–1958*, pbk edn, p. 164.
17. Glubb, *Britain and the Arabs*, p. 149.
18. Barbour, *Nisi Dominus*, quoted Glubb, *Britain and the Arabs*, p. 149.

42 Churchill's Work

1. CAB/24/126, pp. 142–50.
2. CAB/24/126, pp. 153–5.
3. CAB/24/26, pp. 150–3.
4. CAB/24/126, pp. 156–7.
5. Gilbert, *Winston S. Churchill*, Vol. 4, p. 571.
6. Gilbert, *Winston S. Churchill*, Vol. 4, p. 484.
7. Gilbert, *Winston S. Churchill*, Vol. 4, p. 630.
8. See Stein, *The Land Question in Palestine, 1917–1939*.
9. Gilbert, *Winston S. Churchill*, Vol. 4, pp. 594–5.
10. Gilbert, *Winston S. Churchill*, Vol. 4, p. 599.
11. Central Zionist Archive, quoted Gilbert, *Winston S. Churchill*, Companion Vol. 3 to Vol. 4, p. 1610, 1611.
12. Correspondence with the Palestine Arab Delegation and the Zionist Organisation Cmd 1700, p. 5 *et seq.*
13. Correspondence with the Palestine Arab Delegation and the Zionist Organisation Cmd 1700, p. 19 *et seq.*
14. Correspondence with the Palestine Arab Delegation and the Zionist Organisation, Cmd 1700, see p. 21 *et seq.*

43 Disturbances and Commissions

1. Cmd 3530. Report on the Palestine Disturbances of August 1929, pp. 150–1.
2. Cmd 3530. Report on the Palestine Disturbances of August 1929, p. 151.
3. Cmd 3582, Statement with regard to British Policy.
4. Brendon, *The Decline and Fall of the British Empire, 1781–1997*, p. 467.
5. Antonius, *The Arab Awakening*, p. 401.
6. I am very grateful to Penny Sinanoglou for supplying me with a copy of a fascinating paper, 'Half a Loaf? Re-evaluating the Peel Commission's Enquiry and Partition Proposal, 1936–1938' which she gave at the conference 'Palestine, Britain and Empire: 1841–1948' at King's College, London, 14–15 May 2008.
7. Litvinoff, ed., *The Letters and Papers of Chaim Weizmann*, Vol. 17, Series A, p. 268.

44 Arab Reaction and the British Response

1. Sherman, *Mandate Days*, p. 109, quoted Brendon, *The Decline and Fall of the British Empire, 1781–1997*, p. 469.
2. Curry, *Tegart of the Indian Police*, p. 7.
3. I must record my gratitude to Simon Anglim for his help in connection with Wingate,

particularly his kindness in allowing me to read in draft his chapter on Wingate in Palestine from his book *Orde Wingate and the British Army, 1922–1944*, Pickering and Chatto, London, 2010. I also benefited from hearing his paper, 'Orde Wingate and Anglo-Jewish Military Co-operation in the Arab Revolt of 1936–1939' at the conference 'Palestine, Britain and Empire: 1841–1948', held at Kings College, London, 14–15 May 2008.

4. Weizmann, *Trial and Error*, p. 335.
5. Bierman and Smith, *Fire in the Night*, p. 115–16, quoted Anglim, *op. cit.*
6. O'Connor to his wife, 2/3 November 1938, Liddell Hart Centre for Military Archives, O'Connor Papers 3/1/18, quoted Anglim, *op. cit.*
7. Montgomery to Adam, 4 December 1938, p. 5, quoted Anglim, *op. cit.*
8. Matthew Hughes, paper on 'British Armed Forces and Brutality during the Arab Revolt 1936–39' conference 'Palestine, Britain and Empire: 1841–1948' held at Kings College, London, 14–15 May 2008. Some of these punishments and reprisals (such as packing a bus with Arab villagers and forcing them to drive over a landmine) were barbarous and indefensible.

45 More Commissions and the Approach of War

1. Cmd 5634.
2. Glubb, *Britain and the Arabs*, p. 155.
3. Cmd 5893, Statement on Policy in Palestine, p. 3.
4. Cmd 5893, Statement on Policy in Palestine, p. 10.
5. Brendon, *The Decline and Fall of the British Empire*, 1781–1997, pp. 470, 471.
6. Fieldhouse, *Western Imperialism in the Middle East 1914–1958*, pbk edn, p. 180.
7. Monroe, *Britain's Moment in the Middle East, 1914–1956*, p. 88.

46 War

1. Sykes, *Crossroads to Israel*, p. 246.
2. See Colin Shindler reviewing Benny Morris, *1948: The First Arab-Israeli War*, in *The Times Literary Supplement*, 20 June 2008, p. 25.
3. Sykes, *Cross Roads to Israel*, p. 88.
4. Hyam, *Britain's Declining Empire*, pbk edn, p. 56.
5. Brendon, *The Decline and Fall of the British Empire*, 1781–1997, p. 472.
6. Fieldhouse, *Western Imperialism in the Middle East 1914–1958*, pbk edn, p. 205.

47 The End of British Palestine

1. Monroe, *Britain's Moment in the Middle East, 1914–1956*, p. 164.
2. Hyam, *Britain's Declining Empire*, pbk edn, pp. 123, 124.
3. Louis, *Ends of British Imperialism*, pbk edn, pp. 435–6.
4. Weiler, *Ernest Bevin*, p. 171.
5. *Oxford Dictionary of National Biography*.
6. Harris, *Attlee*, p. 390.
7. Weiler, *Ernest Bevin*, p. 171.
8. Louis, *Ends of British Imperialism*, pbk edn, p. 444.
9. Glubb, *A Soldier with the Arabs*, pp. 63–6.
10. Bullock, *Ernest Bevin*, p. 165.
11. Bullock, *Ernest Bevin*, p. 166.
12. Pimlott, *Hugh Dalton*, p. 596.
13. Mayhew, *War*, p. 24.
14. Bullock, *Ernest Bevin*, pp. 88–9.

48 Bevin Starts Work

1. Bullock, *Ernest Bevin*, p. 178.
2. Fieldhouse, *Western Imperialism in the Middle East 1914–1958*, pbk edn, p. 205.
3. Foreign Office Minutes, 6 September 1945, FO 371/45379.
4. PREM 8/627/5, 4 October 1946, quoted Louis, *Ends of British Imperialism*, pbk edn, p. 430.

49 Events

1. Bullock, *Ernest Bevin*, p. 299.
2. CAB 129/16, 6 February 1947, quoted Hyam, *Britain's Declining Empire*, pbk edn, p. 126.
3. Memorandum by Bevin and Creech Jones, 13 February 1947, CP (47) 59.
4. Parliamentary Debates, 25 February 1947, Col. 2007.

50 Surrendering the Mandate

1. See Weiler, *Ernest Bevin*, p. 172.
2. Weiler, *Ernest Bevin*, p. 171.
3. Weiler, *Ernest Bevin*, p. 174, and see Louis, *The Ends of the British Empire*, pp. 567–8.
4. Bethell, *Palestine Triangle*, p. 358.
5. Cohen, *Palestine and the Great Powers, 1945–1948*, p. 268.
6. Louis, *Ends of British Imperialism*, pbk edn, p. 439.
7. *Daily Mail*, 1 August 1947.

51 After the Announcement

1. Bullock, *Ernest Bevin*, p. 448.
2. Louis, *Ends of British Imperialism*, pbk edn, p. 439.
3. Brendon, *The Decline and Fall of the British Empire, 1781–1997*, p. 476.
4. *Parliamentary Debate, Commons*, Vol. 445, 12 December 1947.
5. Cabinet Minutes 93(47), 4 December 1947.
6. Marlowe, *The Seat of Pilate*, p. 252.
7. Cleveland, *History of the Modern Middle East,* 3rd edn, pbk edn, p. 266.

52 Tentative Judgements

1. Fieldhouse, *Western Imperialism in the Middle East 1914–1958*, pbk edn, p. 151.
2. Khalidi, *Palestine Reborn*, p. 76.
3. Shlaim, *Collusion across the Jordan*, p. 219.
4. Louis, *The British Empire in the Middle East 1945–1951*, p. 530.

SELECT BIBLIOGRAPHY

There is a huge number of books about the history of the Middle East, some of them extremely partisan. What follows is only an eclectic and personal selection.

Ahmad, Feroz, *The Young Turks: The Committee of Union and Progress in Turkish Politics, 1908–1914* (Oxford: Clarendon Press, 1969).

Aldington, Richard, *Lawrence of Arabia: A Biographical Enquiry* (London: Collins, 1955).

Allenby, Edmund H.H., *A Brief Record of the Advance of the Egyptian Expeditionary Force under the Command of General Sir Edmund H.H. Allenby. July 1917 to October 1918,* compiled from official sources (London: HMSO, 1919).

Amery, L.S., *My Political Life* (London: Hutchinson, 1953).

Anderson, M.S., *The Eastern Question, The Great Powers and the Near East, 1774–1923* (London: Edward Arnold, 1970).

Andrew, Christopher M., *The Climax of French Imperial Expansion, 1914–1924* (Palo Alto, CA: Stanford University Press, 1981).

Anglim, Simon, *Orde Wingate and the British Army, 1922–1944* (Aberystwyth: University of Wales, 2007).

Antonius, George, *The Arab Awakening: The Story of the Arab National Movement* (London: Hamish Hamilton, 1938, and several subsequent editions).

Aruri, Naseer H., *Jordan: A Study in Political Development (1921–1965)* (The Hague: Martinus Nijhoff, 1972).

Asquith, H.H., *Letters of the Earl of Oxford and Asquith to a friend, 1915–1922* (London: Geoffrey Bles, 1933).

Avineri, Shlomo, *The Making of Modern Zionism: Intellectual Origins of the Jewish State* (New York: Basic Books, 1981).

Banani, Amin, *The Modernization of Iran, 1921–1941* (Palo Alto, CA: Stanford University Press, 1961).

Barbour, Nevill, *Nisi Dominus: A survey of the Palestine Controversy* (London: George Harrap & Co., 1946).

Barker, A.J., *The Neglected War – the Mesopotamia Campaign of 1914–18* (London: Faber & Faber/New York: The Dial Press, 1967).

Barnes, J. and Nicholson, D. (eds), *The Leo Amery Diaries, 1896–1929* (London: Hutchison, 1980).

Basheer, Edwin, *Montagu and the Balfour Declaration* (New York: Arab Information Center, 1967).

Bashkin, Orit, *The Other Iraq: Pluralism & Culture in Hashemite Iraq* (Palo Alto, CA: Stanford University Press, 2009).

Batatu, Hanna, *The Old Social Classes and the Revolutionary Movement of Iraq: A study of Iraq's Old Landed and Commercial Classes and of Its Communists, Ba'thists, and Free Officers,* (Princeton: Princeton University Press, 1982).

Beevor, Antony, *D-Day: The Battle for Normandy* (London: Viking, 2009).

Bell, Gertrude, *The Arab War. Confidential Information for GHQ Cairo from Gertrude L. Bell. Despatches from the Arab Bulletin* (London: Golden Cockerel Press, 1940).

Bell, Gertrude, *Gertrude Bell: The Arabian Diaries, 1913–1914.* Edited by Rosemary O'Brien (Syracuse: Syracuse University Press, 2000).

Bell, Lady, *The Letters of Gertrude Bell* (London: Ernest Benn, 1927).

Bethell, Nicholas, *Palestine Triangle: The Struggle between the British, the Jews and the Arabs, 1935–1948* (London: Deutsch, 1979).

Betts, Ernest, *The Bagging of Baghdad* (London: John Lane, 1920).

Bevan, Edwyn, *The Land of the Two Rivers* (London: E. Arnold, 1917).

Bierman, John and Smith, Colin, *Fire in the Night: Wingate of Burma, Ethiopia and Zion* (London: Macmillan, 1999).

Biger, Gideon, *The Boundaries of Modern Palestine, 1840–1947* (London: Routledge Curzon, 2004).

Bluett, Antony, *With our Army in Palestine* (London: Alexander Melrose, 1919).

Brantlinger, Patrick, *Rule of Darkness: British Literature and Imperialism, 1830–1914* (London: Cornell University Press, 1988).

Bray, Norman, *A Paladin of Arabia: The Biography of Brevet Lieutenant-Colonel G.E. Leachman, CIE, DSO, of the Royal Sussex Regiment* (London: John Heritage, 1936).

Brendon, Piers, *The Decline & Fall of the British Empire, 1781–1997* (London: Jonathan Cape, 2007).

Bruce, Anthony, *The Last Crusade: The Palestinian Campaign in the First World War* (London: John Murray, 2002).

Buchan, John, *Greenmantle* (1916; reprint: Oxford: Oxford University Press, 1993).

Bullock, Alan, *The Life and Times of Ernest Bevin, Foreign Secretary, 1945–1951* (London: Heinemann, 1983).

Busch, Cooper, *Britain and the Persian Gulf, 1894–1914* (Berkeley: University of California Press, 1967).

Busch, Cooper, *Britain, India and the Arabs, 1914–1921* (Berkeley & London: University of California Press, 1971).

Campbell, John, *F.E. Smith, First Earl of Birkenhead* (London: Jonathan Cape, 1983).

Cannadine, David, *Ornamentalism: How the British Saw Their Empire* (London: Allen Lane, 2001).

Catherwood, Christopher, *Winston's Folly: Imperialism and the Creation of Modern Iraq* (London: Constable, 2004); also available as *Churchill's Folly: How Winston Churchill created Modern Iraq* (New York: Carroll & Graf Publishers, 2005).

Catherwood, Christopher, *A Brief History of the Middle East* (London: Robinson, 2006).

Churchill, Winston S., *Great Contemporaries* (London: Thornton Butterworth, 1937).

Churchill, Winston S., *The World Crisis*, 5 vols (London: Thornton Butterworth, 1923–1931).

Clayton, Sir Gilbert, *An Arabian Diary*, ed. Robert D. Collins (Berkeley and Los Angeles: University of California Press, 1969).

Clayton, G.D., *Britain and the Eastern Question: Missolonghi to Gallipoli* (London: University of London Press, 1971).

Cleveland, William L., *A History of the Modern Middle East* (Boulder, CO and Oxford: Westview Press, 1994).

Cohen, Israel (ed.), *A.J. Balfour, Speeches on Zionism* (London: Arrowsmith, 1928).

Cohen, Michael, *Palestine, Retreat from the Mandate: The Making of British Policy, 1936–1945* (London: Elek, 1978).

Cohen, Michael, *Palestine and the Great Powers, 1945–1948* (Princeton and Guildford: Princeton University Press, 1982).

Crawford, David Lindsay, Earl of, *The Crawford Papers: Journals 1892–1940*, ed. John Vincent (Manchester: Manchester University Press, 1984).

Cumming, Henry, *Franco-British Rivalry in the Post-War Near East. The Decline of French Influence* (London: Oxford University Press, 1938).

Curry, John, *Tegart of the Indian Police* (Tunbridge Wells: Courier Co., 1960).

Daly, M.W. (ed.), *The Cambridge History of Egypt*: vol. 2, *Modern Egypt, from 1517 to the End of the Twentieth Century* (Cambridge: Cambridge University Press, 1998).

Dann, Uriel (ed.), *The Great Powers in the Middle East, 1919–1939* (New York: Holmes & Meier, 1988).

Darwin, John, *Britain, Egypt and the Middle East: Imperial Policy in the Aftermath of War, 1918–1922* (London: Macmillan, 1981).

Dawisha, Adeed, *Arab Nationalism in the Twentieth Century: From Triumph to Despair* (Princeton and Oxford: Princeton University Press, 2003).

Deeb, Marius, *Party Politics in Egypt: The Wafd and Its Rivals* (Oxford: Ithaca Press for the Middle East Centre, 1979).

Dugdale, Blanche, *Arthur James Balfour* (London: Hutchinson and Co., 1936).

Egremont, Max, *Balfour: A Life of Arthur James Balfour* (London: Collins, 1980).

Falls, Cyril and MacMunn, Sir George, *Military Operations – Egypt & Palestine,* vols. I and II (London: HMSO, 1928, 1930).

Farouk-Sluglett, Marion and Sluglett, Peter, *Iraq Since 1958: From Revolution to Dictatorship* (London: KPC, 1987).

Fieldhouse, D.K., *Western Imperialism in the Middle East 1914–1958* (Oxford: Oxford University Press, 2006).

Fisher, John, *Curzon and British Imperialism in the Middle East, 1916–1919* (London: Cass, 1999).

Fisher, John, *Gentleman Spies: Intelligence Agents in the British Empire and Beyond* (Stroud: Sutton, 2002).

Fitzherbert, Margaret, *The Man who was Greenmantle: A Biography of Aubrey Herbert* (London: Murray, 1983).

Ford, Roger, *Eden to Armageddon: The First World War in the Middle East* (London: Weidenfeld & Nicolson, 2009).

Friedman, Isaiah, *Palestine, A Twice-Promised Land? The British, the Arabs and Zionism 1915–1920* (New Brunswick, NJ: Transaction Publishers, 2000).

Fromkin, David, *A Peace to End All Peace: Creating the Modern Middle East 1914–1922* (London: Deutsch, 1989).

Gaillard, Gaston, *The Turks and Europe* (London: Murby & Co, 1921).

Garnett, David (ed.), *The Letters of T.E. Lawrence* (reissue of 1938 edition; London: Spring Books, 1964).

Gilbert, Martin, *Winston S. Churchill*, Vols 3–6 and relative companion volumes (London: Heinemann, 1972–82).

Glubb, John Bagot, *Arabian Adventures: Ten Years of Joyful Service* (London: Cassell, 1978).

Glubb, John Bagot, *Britain and the Arabs* (London: Hodder & Stoughton, 1959).

Glubb, John Bagot, *A Soldier with the Arabs* (London: Hodder & Stoughton, 1957).

Gollin, Alfred M., *Proconsul in Politics. A study of Lord Milner in Opposition and in Power* (London: Anthony Blond, 1964).

Graves, Philip, *Life of Sir Percy Cox* (London: Hutchinson, 1941).

Haldane, Sir James Aylmer, *The Insurrection in Mesopotamia* (London: Blackwood, 1922).

Harris, Kenneth, *Attlee* (London: Weidenfeld & Nicolson, 1982).

Hill, A.J., *Chauvel of the Light Horse: A Biography of General Sir Harry Chauvel* (Melbourne: Melbourne University Press, 1978).

Hopkirk, Peter, *The Great Game: Secret Service in High Asia* (London: John Murray, 1990).

Hopkirk, Peter, *On Secret Service East of Constantinople: The Plot to Bring Down the British Empire* (London: John Murray, 1994).

Hourani, Albert, *Arabic Thought in the Liberal Age, 1798–1939* (Oxford: Oxford University Press, 1962).

Hourani, Albert, *Syria and Lebanon: A Political Essay* (London: Oxford University Press, 1946).

Howard, Harry, *The Partition of Turkey: a diplomatic history 1913–1923* (New York: H. Fertig, 1966).

Huneidi, Sahar, *A Broken Trust: Herbert Samuel, Zionism & the Palestinians, 1920–1925* (London: Tauris, 2001).

Hyam, Ronald, *Britain's Declining Empire: The Road to Decolonisation, 1918–1968* (Cambridge: Cambridge University Press, 2006).

Inalcik, Halil and Quataert, Donald (eds), *An Economic and Social History of the Ottoman Empire, 1600–1914* (Cambridge: Cambridge University Press, 1994).

Jankowski, James, *Egypt: A Short History* (Oxford: Oneworld, 2000).

Johnpoll, B.K. *The Politics of Futility. The General Jewish Workers Bund of Poland, 1917–1943* (Ithaca, NY: Cornell University Press, 1967).

Johnson, Paul, *A History of the Jews* (London: Weidenfeld, 1987).

Johnson, Paul, *A History of the Modern World: From 1917 to the 1980s* (London: Weidenfeld & Nicolson, 1983).

Karsh, Efraim, *Palestine Betrayed* (New Haven, CT and London: Yale University Press, 2010).

Kattan, Victor, *From Coexistence to Conquest: International Law and the origins of the Arab-Israeli Conflict, 1891–1949* (London: Pluto, 2009).

Kayali, Hasan, *Arabs and Young Turks: Ottomanism, Arabism, and Islamism in the Ottoman Empire, 1908–1918* (Berkeley and London: University of California Press, 1997).

Kedourie, Elie, *England and the Middle East: The Destruction of the Ottoman Empire, 1914–1921* (Hassocks: Harvester Press, 1978. Originally published Bowes and Bowes, 1956).

Kedourie, Elie, *Chatham House Version and Other Middle Eastern Studies* (London: Weidenfeld & Nicolson, 1970).

Kedourie, Elie, *In the Anglo-Arab Labyrinth: The McMahon–Hussayn Correspondence and its Interpretations, 1914–1939* (Cambridge: Cambridge University Press, 1976).

Keynes, Maynard J., *The Economic Consequences of the Peace* (London: Macmillan & Co., 1919).

Khadduri, Majid, *Independent Iraq: A Study in Iraqi Politics, since 1932*, 2nd edition (London: Oxford University Press, 1960).

Khalidi, Rashid, *British Policy towards Syria and Palestine, 1906–1914: A Study of the Antecedents of the Hussein–McMahon Correspondence, the Sykes–Picot Agreement, and the Balfour Declaration* (London: Ithaca Press, 1980).

Khalidi, Rashid et al. (eds), *The Origins of Arab Nationalism* (Oxford and New York: Columbia University Press, 1991).

Khalidi, Walid, *Palestine Reborn* (London: I. B. Tauris, 1992).

Khoury, Philip S., *Syria and the French Mandate: The Politics of Arab Nationalism, 1920–1945* (Princeton: Princeton University Press, 1987).

Kimche, Jon, *The Unromantics: the Great Powers and the Balfour Declaration* (London: Weidenfeld & Nicolson, 1968).

Kinross, Lord, *The Ottoman Centuries: The Rise and Fall of the Turkish Empire, 1288–1918* (London: Cape, 1977).

Kirkbride, Sir Alec, *A Crackle of Thorns: Experiences in the Middle East* (London: John Murray, 1956).

Klieman, Aaron, *Foundations of British Policy in the Arab World: The Cairo Conference of 1921* (Baltimore and London: John Hopkins Press, 1970).

Knightley, Phillip, *The Secret Lives of Lawrence of Arabia* (London: Nelson, 1969).

Kohn, Hans, *Western Civilisation in the Near East* (London: Routledge, 1936).

Lawrence, T.E., *Seven Pillars of Wisdom* (London: Jonathan Cape, 1926).

Ledger, S. and Luckhurst, R. (eds), *The* Fin de Siècle: *A Reader in Cultural History c.1880–1900* (Oxford: Oxford University Press, 2000).

Leslie, Shane, *Mark Sykes: His Life and Letters* (London: Cassell & Co., 1923).

Litvinoff, Barnet and Weiner, Hanna (eds), *The Letters and Papers of Chaim Weizmann* (Oxford: Oxford University Press, 1974).

Lloyd George, David, *War Memoirs* (London Weidenfeld and Watson, 1933–36).

Lloyd George, David, *Memoirs of the Peace Conference* (New Haven, CT: Yale University Press, 1939).

Louis, William Roger, *The British Empire in the Middle East, 1945–1951: Arab Nationalism, the United States, and Postwar Imperialism* (Oxford: Clarendon, 1984).

Louis, William Roger (ed.), *The Oxford History of the British Empire.* 5 vols (Oxford: Oxford University Press, 1998–1999).

Louis, William Roger, *In the Name of God, Go! Leo Amery & the British Empire in the age of Churchill* (New York and London: W.W. Norton, 1922).

Louis, William Roger, *Ends of British Imperialism, The Scramble for Empire, Suez and Decolonization* (London: I.B. Tauris, 2006).

Luizard, Pierre-Jean, *La Question Irakienne* (Paris: Fayard, 2004).

Manela, Erez, *The Wilsonian Moment: Self-Determination and the International Origins of Anti-Colonial Nationalism* (Oxford: Oxford University Press, 2007).

Mango, Andrew, *Atatürk: The Biography of the Founder of Modern Turkey* (London: John Murray, 1999).

Marlowe, John, *The Seat of Pilate: An account of the Palestine Mandate* (London: Cresset Press, 1959).

MacMillan, Margaret, *Peacemakers: the Paris Peace Conference of 1919 and its attempt to end war* (London: John Murray, 2001).

McMahon, Sir Henry, *Correspondence between Sir Henry McMahon and the Sherif Hussein of Mecca* (London: HMSO, 1939).

McMeekin, Sean, *The Berlin–Baghdad Express: the Ottoman Empire and Germany's bid for world power, 1898–1918* (London: Allen Lane, 2010).

Meinertzhagen, Richard, *Army Diary, 1899–1926* (Edinburgh: Oliver and Boyd, 1960).

Meinertzhagen, Richard, *Middle East Diary, 1917–1956* (London: Cresset Press, 1959).

Miller, David Hunter, *The Drafting of the Covenant* (New York: Johnson Reprint Corp, 1969).

Miller, David Hunter, *My Diary at the Conference of Paris, 1918–19* (New York, 1924).

Monroe, Elizabeth, *Britain's Moment in the Middle East, 1914–1971*, 2nd edition (London: Chatto & Windus, 1981).

Monroe, Elizabeth, *Britain's Movement in the Middle East, 1914–1956* (London: Methuen, 1963).

Monroe, Elizabeth, *Philby of Arabia* (London: Faber, 1973).

Morris, Jan, *Farewell the Trumpets: An Imperial Retreat* (London: Faber, 1978).

Mosley, Leonard, *Curzon: The End of an Epoch* (London: Longmans Green, 1960).

Neave, Lady Dorina, *Remembering Kut* (London: Arthur Barker, 1937).

Nicolson, Harold, *Curzon: The Last Phase, 1919–1925. A Study in Post-War Diplomacy* (London: Constable, 1934).

Nicolson, Harold, *Peacemaking 1919* (London: Constable, 1933).

Nicolson, Juliet, *The Great Silence: 1918–1920: Living in the Shadow of the Great War* (London: John Murray, 2009).

Owen, Roger, *The Middle East in the World Economy, 1800–1914* (London: Methuen, 1981).

Owen, Roger, *State, Power and Politics in the Making of the Modern Middle East* (London: Routledge, 1992).

Pearce, Robert D., *Sir Bernard Bourdillon: the Biography of a Twentieth-century Colonialist* (Oxford: Kensal, 1987).

Picard, Elizabeth, *Lebanon: A Shattered Country, Myths and Realities of the Wars in Lebanon,* trans. Franklin Philip (New York: Holmes & Meier, 1996).

Pimlott, Ben, *Hugh Dalton* (London: Cape, 1985).

Pimlott, Ben (ed.), *The Political Diary of Hugh Dalton, 1918–1940, 1945–1960* (London: Cape, 1986).

Polk, William R. and Chambers, Richard L. (eds), *Beginnings of Modernization in the Middle East: The Nineteenth Century* (London and Chicago: University of Chicago Press, 1968).

Reinharz, Jehuda, *Chaim Weizmann: The Making of a Zionist Leader* (Oxford and New York: Oxford University Press, 1985)

Reinharz, Jehuda, *Chaim Weizmann: The Making of a Statesmen* (New York: Brandeis University Press, 1985).

Renton, James, *The Zionist Masquerade: The Birth of the Anglo-Zionist Alliance, 1914–1918* (Basingstoke: Palgrave Macmillan, 2007).

Robinson, Ronald and Gallagher, John (eds), *Africa and The Victorians* (London: Macmillan, 1965).

Ronaldshay, Earl of, *The Life of Lord Curzon* (London: Ernest Benn, 1928).

Rose, Norman (ed.), *From Palmerston to Balfour, Collected Essays of Mayir Vereté* (London: F. Cass, 1922).

Royle, Trevor, *Glubb Pasha* (London: Little, Brown and Company, 1992).

Said, Edward, *Orientalism* (London: Routledge and Kegan Paul, 1978).

Salibi, Kamal S., *The Modern History of Lebanon* (London: Weidenfeld & Nicolson, 1965).

Sanders, Ronald, *The High Walls of Jerusalem: a History of the Balfour Declaration and the Birth of the British Mandate for Palestine* (New York: Holt, Rinehart & Winston, 1984).

Satia, Priya, *Spies in Arabia: The Great War and the Cultural Foundations of Britain's Covert Empire in the Middle East* (Oxford: Oxford University Press, 2008).

Seeley, Sir John Robert, *The Expansion of England* (London: Macmillan, 1885).

Sforza, Count Carlo, *Makers of Modern Europe* (London: Elkin Mathews, 1930).

Shamash, Violette, *Memories of Eden: A Journey through Jewish Baghdad,* ed. Mira and Tona Rocc (London: Forum, 2008).

Shaw, Stanford J. *History of the Ottoman Empire and Modern Turkey,* 2 vols (Cambridge: Cambridge University Press, 1976, 1977).

Shepherd, Naomi, *Ploughing Sand: British Rule in Palestine, 1917–1948* (London: John Murray, 1999).

Sherman, A.J., *Mandate Days: British Lives in Palestine, 1918–1948* (London: Thames and Hudson, 1997).

Sherson, Errol, *Townshend of Chitral and Kut* (London: Heinemann, 1928).

Shlaim, Avi, *Collusion across the Jordan: King Abdullah, The Zionist Movement and the Partition of Palestine* (Oxford: Clarendon, 1988).

Shlaim, Avi, *The Iron Wall: Israel and the Arab World* (London: Allen Lane, 2000).

Shlaim, Avi, *Lion of Jordan: The Life of King Hussein in War and Peace* (London: Penguin, 2008).

Shlaim, Avi, *War and Peace in the Middle East: A Concise History* (London: Penguin, 1995).

Simon, Reeva S., Mattar, Philip and Bulliet, Richard W. (eds), *The Encyclopedia of the Modern Middle East*, 4 vols (New York: Macmillan reference USA, 1996).

Skidelsky, R. (ed.), *The End of the Keynesian Era* (London: Macmillan, 1977).

Sluglett, Peter, *Britain in Iraq, 1914–1932* (London: Ithaca Press for the Middle East Centre, Oxford, 1976).

Smith, Charles D., *Palestine and the Arab–Israeli Conflict*, (New York: St. Martins Press, 1988).

Smuts, Jan Christian, *Selections from the Smuts Papers*, ed. W.K. Hancock and J. van der Paul, Vol. 4 (Cambridge: Cambridge University Press, 1996).

Sokolov, Nahum, *History of Zionism, 1600–1918* (London: Longmans & Co., 1919).

Stark, Freya, *The Valleys of the Assassins: other Persian travels* (London: John Murray, 1934).

Stein, Kenneth, *The Land Question in Palestine, 1917–1939* (London: Chapel Hill, 1984).

Stein, L., *The Balfour Declaration* (London: Vallentine Mitchell, 1961).

Storrs, Sir Ronald, *Orientations* (London: I. Nicholson & Watson, 1937).

Sykes, Christopher, *Cross Roads to Israel* (London: New English Library, 1967).

Taylor, A.J.P. (ed.), *Lloyd George: A Diary by Frances Stevenson* (London: Hutchinson and Co., 1971).

Thesiger, Wilfred, *The Life of my Choice* (London: Collins, 1987).

Tignor, Robert L., *Modernization and British Colonial Role in Egypt, 1882–1914* (Princeton: Princeton University Press, 1966).

Tomes, Jason, *Balfour & Foreign Policy: The International Thought of a Conservative Statesman* (Cambridge: Cambridge University Press, 1977).

Townshend, Sir Charles, *My Campaign in Mesopotamia* (London: Thorton Butterworth, 1920).

Townshend, Charles, *When God made Hell: The British Invasion of Mesopotamia and the Creation of Iraq* (London: Faber & Faber, 2010).

Tripp, Charles, *A History of Iraq* (Cambridge: Cambridge University Press, 2000).

Tuchman, Barbara W., *Bible and Sword: England and Palestine from the Bronze Age to Balfour* (London, 1956).

Tuchman, Barbara W., *The Guns of August: August 1914* (London: New English Library, 1964).

Tuohy, Ferdinand, *The Battle of Brains* (London: W. Heinemann, 1930).

Tuohy, Ferdinand, *The Crater of Mars: Reminiscence of the European War* (London: William Heinemann, 1929).

Wallach, Janet, *Desert Queen: The Extraordinary Life of Gertrude Bell* (New York and London: Nan A. Talese, 1996).

Wasserstein, Bernard, *The British in Palestine: The Mandatory Government and the Arab–Jewish Conflict, 1917–1929* (London: Royal Historical Society, 1978).

Wasserstein, Bernard, *Herbert Samuel: A Political Life* (Oxford: Clarendon, 1992).

Wavell, Archibald, *Allenby in Egypt (Vol II of Allenby, a Study in Greatness)* (London: George G. Harrap and Co., 1943).

Wavell, Archibald, *Allenby: Soldier and Statesman* (London: George G. Harrap, 1944).

Weiler, Peter, *Ernest Bevin* (Manchester: Manchester University Press, 1993).

Weizmann, Chaim, *Trial & Error: The Autobiography of Chaim Weizmann* (Philadelphia: Jewish Publication Society of America, 1949).

Wilson, Sir Henry, *Life and Diaries, Major-General Sir C.E. Callwell (ed.)* (London: Cassell, 1927).

Wilson, Mary, *King Abdullah, Britain and the Making of Jordan* (Cambridge: Cambridge University Press, 1987).

Wingate, Ronald, *Wingate of the Sudan* (London: John Murray, 1955).

Winstone, Harry, *Captain Shakespear: A Portrait* (London: Cape, 1976).

Winstone, Harry, *The Illicit Adventure: the story of political and military intelligence in the Middle East from 1898 to 1926* (London: Cape, 1982).

Woodward, Ernest, *British Foreign Policy in the Second World War* (London: HMSO, 1962).

Wrigley, Chris (ed.), *Warfare, Diplomacy and Politics* (London: Hamilton, 1986).

INDEX

Index